PURSUING PLAY

REBECCA BEAUSAERT

PURSUING PLAY

Women's Leisure in
Small-Town Ontario,
1870–1914

UNIVERSITY OF MANITOBA PRESS

Pursuing Play: Women's Leisure in Small-Town Ontario, 1870–1914
© Rebecca Beausaert 2024

28   27   26   25   24   1   2   3   4   5

University of Manitoba Press
Winnipeg, Manitoba, Canada
Treaty 1 Territory
uofmpress.ca

Cataloguing data available from Library and Archives Canada
ISBN 978-177284-077-3 (PAPER)
ISBN 978-177284-079-7 (PDF)
ISBN 978-177284-080-3 (EPUB)
ISBN 978-177284-078-0 (BOUND)

Cover photo of young Tillsonburg women posing with tennis racquets,
c. 1890s, Annandale National Historic Site (ANHS) Photograph
Collection.
Cover and Interior Design by Galley Creative Co.

This book has been published with the help of a grant from the
Federation for the Humanities and Social Sciences, through the Awards
to Scholarly Publications Program, using funds provided by the
Social Sciences and Humanities Research Council of Canada.

The University of Manitoba Press acknowledges the financial support for
its publication program provided by the Government of Canada through
the Canada Book Fund, the Canada Council for the Arts, the Manitoba
Department of Sport, Culture, and Heritage, the Manitoba Arts Council,
and the Manitoba Book Publishing Tax Credit.

Funded by the Government of Canada   Canadä

CONTENTS

LIST OF TABLES AND FIGURES

Tables

Figures

INTRODUCTION

Life's so thrilling in a city, there's
So much to hear and see;
Fine churches, plays and operas,
Bright lights and gaiety.
But passing faces all are strange,
You feel an alien guest.
Ah, if you're sad or lonely, then
A little town is best.

For in the little country towns
Your friends are everywhere,
And high and low, and young and old
The common interests share;
And if you are in trouble they
Come flocking to your door,
Kind hands outstretched to bring you aid,—
Their kind hearts, too, are sore.

In little towns the people say
"Good morning" when you meet,
And smiling children stop their play
To greet you in the street.
It may be little towns are slow,
But they are quick to see
That what is needed most in life,
Are friends, and sympathy.[1]

N 1900, TWENTY-NINE-YEAR-OLD Olive Anderson Snyder of Elora, Ontario, published a collection of poems titled *Little Towns*. The piece above was the first in the collection and inspired the book's title. Born and raised in Elora, Olive remained in the town until her death in 1952 at the age of eighty-one. The Snyder family was of German descent, Methodist, and comfortably middle class in rank and stature. Patriarch William Snyder was a well-known Grand Trunk Railway agent and station master. Between 1913 and 1914, Olive maintained a daily diary where she recorded details of her very active social life in the community. She never married or had children, so she was able to devote her spare time to pleasurable activities such as playing music (she was an accomplished organist and violinist), gardening, spending time with friends and family, and writing. She especially enjoyed composing poetry. Several of Snyder's pieces appeared in the local newspaper and were regular features in the *Toronto Star*'s "Little of Everything" column. When the *Little Towns* compilation was published, one reporter remarked that "Miss Snyder's little book should find a welcome among the people of big towns as well as little ones."[2]

In the later Victorian and Edwardian years, many women and girls like Olive Snyder "lived through the written word," spending countless "hours at writing desks producing pages of letters, composing poetry, copying passages from literature, [and] keeping all manner of diaries and journals."[3] From these pieces of material culture, we are provided glimpses of how literate, middle- and upper-class women and girls viewed themselves and the worlds they inhabited. We are privy to what was important to them, what they fantasized about, and what caused them angst. With its traces of romanticism, the opening poem of *Little Towns* seems somewhat allegorical—both a rosy recollection of Snyder's childhood in Elora *and* a defence of small-town values. Though the community and other "little country towns" she champions were somewhat idealized depictions of small-town Ontario, the poem correctly acknowledges that smaller communities were often labelled "slow" and discounted for lacking the "bright lights and gaiety" of larger cities.[4] Little did Olive Snyder know that for more than a century, her contention would endure in the ways that small-town culture has been portrayed in the fields of Canadian history, women's and gender studies, and histories of sport and leisure.

This book explores women's leisure activities in three small towns in southern Ontario—Dresden, Tillsonburg, and Elora—and their surrounding rural areas between the years 1870 and 1914. The rapid movement of goods, people, and "new cultural ideas"[5] characteristic of this era resulted in a greater variety of recreational opportunities in smaller communities and influenced the ways that women pursued leisure in public and private spaces. In this period, women noticeably asserted more agency and autonomy in their choice of leisure activities, spearheading both formal and informal women-specific and mixed-sex clubs and other social events. By examining leisure activities in these three small towns, we access important insights on the social, cultural, economic, political, and religious transformations occurring beyond the borders of Canada's cities.

Broadly, this study addresses the activities available to women (and, to a lesser extent, girls) and explores the importance of leisure when creating social networks, strengthening long-standing ties of kinship and friendship, and creating more opportunities for community involvement. One of the primary objectives of this work is to move away from the conventional practice of examining leisure's appeal through the lenses of urbanization, industrialization, and masculinity. In doing so, this book challenges some late nineteenth- and early twentieth-century assumptions (and those of many historians thereafter) that rural and small-town Ontario generally, and women especially, lacked or had limited access to popular forms of cultural enlightenment and systems through which to spend leisure time.

This study also considers the forces of modernity, continuity, and change. As historians often note, modernity is a complicated and difficult term to define, especially at the turn of the twentieth century, when "becoming modern, as a deliberate goal, was not something most people considered consciously with any consistency."[6] An even more complex question is how to define modernity in regions that were supposedly reluctant to modernize. In the American context, historians such as David B. Danbom, Janet Galligani Casey, Ronald R. Kline, and Thomas J. Schlereth have problematized the "rural as antithetical to modern" archetype,[7] and this study is influenced by their findings. Kline, for example, argues that rural and farm families willingly adopted facets of urban, middle-class consumer culture (albeit selectively), resulting in "new rural cultures, new forms of rural modernity—many of which were individual modernities."[8] The extent to which women in Dresden, Tillsonburg, and Elora incorporated the new trends and advancements in leisure activities bombarding them in the print media also points to a willingness (whether conscious or not) to display and embody "modern" (or novel) modes of dress, living, and entertainment. As Kline similarly found, this occurred selectively, with women often revamping older and more traditional social practices. The sedate tea social and fundraising garden party, for example, became the trendier "crazy tea" and the around-the-world-themed garden party. Modernity, at its core, was about transformation, flux, and "becoming rather than being,"[9] and such broad definitions have been adopted throughout this book.

Methodology

While completing my master's degree at Western University in 2006, I read Lynne Marks's *Revivals and Roller Rinks: Religion, Leisure, and Identity in Late-Nineteenth-Century Small-Town Ontario*. I found the book's focus on the communities of Thorold, Campbellford, and Ingersoll a refreshing addition to the historiography of Canadian leisure. Marks emphasizes the importance of examining small-town Ontario, leisure, and religion together, which are "subjects that have largely been studied in isolation."[10] Gender is another important category of analysis in Marks's book and contributes to ongoing discussions about how much leisure was contentious ground between the sexes. My examination builds on the important work done by Marks and others to incorporate small-town histories into broader analyses of how Canadians were affected by and contributed to the growth of a new leisure culture around the turn of the century. Arguably, my book's most important contribution to the extant literature is the emphasis on women's experiences to show the various roles they played as opportunities for leisure expanded, and the reactions of local citizens to women's more visible presence in this regard.

Dresden, Tillsonburg, and Elora have been chosen as case studies because of their class structures, economic systems, and natural landscapes. Together, they also highlight some of the geographical, environmental, historical, economic, and socio-cultural differences present in smaller communities at the time. In terms of their citizens, the three towns are quite demonstrative of the ethnic and religious homogeneity that defined much of rural and small-town Ontario around the turn of the century. These White settler societies were mostly composed of Christian people with roots in the United Kingdom and Western Europe, apart from Dresden, where a small population of Black Canadians resided. All three towns are situated in southern Ontario, Dresden in the municipality of Chatham-Kent,[11] Tillsonburg in Oxford County, and Elora in Wellington County.[12] The choice to focus on southern Ontario was determined by the large number of towns that existed in the region by 1870. Industrialization (to varying degrees) was underway, and many towns contained distinct class groupings determined by income, lineage, and status. I selected Dresden, Tillsonburg, and Elora after consulting the *1888–89 Ontario Gazetteer and Business Directory*, which provides basic statistics for incorporated communities, such as their location, amenities, industries, and transportation networks. Inspired by other micro-historical studies, my choice of towns was restricted to those with populations larger than 1,000 but smaller than 5,000.[13] At least one weekly newspaper had to be in circulation and the community established by 1871 to be included in the decennial censuses beginning that year. The number of towns in the late nineteenth century that adhered to such criteria was substantial but my contacting several community museums and county archives assisted in narrowing the options. Eventually I determined that the range of diverse information available about women's leisure activities in Dresden, Tillsonburg, and Elora was comprehensive enough to present a sound analysis of how women initiated and/or pursued leisure. The sources also speak to the social and cultural transformations and continuities that occurred in these locations over a period of forty-plus years.

The Growth of Leisure and Its Justifiers

The years between 1870 and 1914 were formative ones in Ontario's history, marked by settler colonialism, industrialization, urbanization, immigration, agricultural expansion, and the cultural practices of the Victorian and Edwardian eras. Across the Western world, "a new phase in the history of leisure" was occurring.[14] Specifically, there were vast changes in the meaning and construction of leisure activities for men, women, and children. Previous studies of leisure in rural and small-town Canada have largely focused on the pre-industrial era, examining spaces and places like taverns, work bees, and men's sporting contests,[15] or the growth of sports, community life, and teen culture in the interwar and postwar years.[16] But by the latter part of the nineteenth century, greater emphasis was being placed on appropriate and respectable leisure activities, thanks to the social reform impulse gripping Ontario. This study examines how these discourses also influenced the countryside, especially their concerns about new leisure offerings and participants' conduct. During this period most Canadians still lived, worked, and played outside of large cities, so small towns and their surrounding rural areas must also be considered important sites of analysis when examining how leisure was evolving.

In the nineteenth century, the concept of leisure time was being redefined for the middle and working classes especially, thanks to the Industrial Revolution and new labour legislation that regulated working hours and conditions. Alterations to the daily regimen provided Canadians with the opportunity to consider how they wanted to spend their "free" time. Many middle-class reformers feared that idleness provoked moral depravity, so greater effort was devoted to creating purposeful and "rational" leisure activities for all classes. The emerging realm of leisure, however, was as contested a space as any other in Canadian society. Indeed, as Donald G. Wetherell and Irene Kmet note in their study of Alberta, "leisure, both for the dominant culture and for those who stood outside it, thus posed a number of problems and opportunities, raised fears and optimism, and represented resistance and acceptance."[17] In the 1970s and 1980s, when Western social historians began studying the "private sides of history, family, community, and work that had been so long neglected," they realized how much these "social spheres" were connected to "popular culture, much of which is leisure."[18] As a category of historical analysis, leisure can offer a more complete understanding of class identities, gender roles, social reform, colonialism, respectability, the separate spheres doctrine, and sexual relations around the turn of the century.

The Scope of the Study

To understand leisure, a broad framework is employed here which refuses the notion of rigid divisions between public and private spaces to determine what sorts of activities small-town women were participating in and how they constructed and utilized these spaces. The types of activities examined include religious, charitable, and self-improvement organizations (such as the Woman's Christian Temperance Union and the Ladies' Travel Club); amateur sports and physical recreation (like lawn tennis and ice skating); informal groupings of women (like "at homes" and tea parties); public events (including dances and holidays); church socials (like religious concerts and fundraising fairs); shopping and fashion; theatre and cinema; gardening and outdoor recreation that included cottaging, picnicking, boating, and swimming; dining; reading; courting; and what were considered disreputable vices, such as drinking, gambling, and vagrancy. This is not an exhaustive examination of all the activities that small-town women enjoyed around the turn of the century, but they are the ones most visible in available sources. Collectively, they illuminate the sheer variety of leisure pursuits available and, I hope, will prompt future scholars to explore the meanings behind these and other activities on a more individual and contextually diverse basis.

Though it is necessary to recognize men's, children's, and family-centred leisure when analyzing women's preferences, this book places women's lives and experiences at the forefront. While the writing of women's, gender, and feminist history has flourished since the 1970s, many examinations of women's public and private lives have focused on the formal roles they occupied in late nineteenth- and early twentieth-century society: daughter, wife, mother, or worker. My work contributes to a growing body of literature that addresses women's lives both within and outside these formal contexts to determine how women were spending their time when the duties of home and work could be temporarily put aside or, if necessary, integrated into their leisure. Especially, women who were managing large families or living on farms are often assumed to have been too overburdened and overworked to make time for leisure. But as this study shows, middle- and working-class women without agricultural or domestic help frequently mixed their labour and leisure to maximize the little "free" time available.

Histories of women's leisure in Canada still largely frame participation around formal activities like organizations, sports teams, and private clubs that required a proper commitment to membership.[19] While these studies include some of the more ubiquitous activities women engaged with in small-town Ontario, informal yet highly important activities, such as afternoon tea and "disreputable" hobbies like card playing, deserve more attention. Generally, formal and informal leisure are studied separately. In the small towns examined here, domestic spaces were important sites for casual and sporadic modes of leisure. What occurred behind closed doors also provides insights into how women interacted privately with their friends and family, brief glimpses of female sexuality, and the pressure placed on mothers to construct healthful modes of recreation for all family members.

This study also calls attention to the significance of age and the female life cycle. The different seasons and trajectories of women's lives—as daughter, adolescent, wife, mother, widow, worker, or single woman—determined uniquely overlapping sets of leisure activities. For example, many of the activities available to teenage girls incorporated courtship rituals so that a suitable match might be made in a reputable setting. Once women were married and caring for a family, their leisure was often centred in the home so that chores and childcare could still be managed. At this stage in life, many of the leisure activities in public settings provided opportunities for women to discuss shared commonalities such as home improvement, the latest styles and trends in dining and entertainment, and child-rearing techniques. In their advancing years, most women continued to engage in leisure activities within the confines of the home, spending time with family and enjoying activities like music or handicrafts that accommodated health or mobility limitations. For each stage of a woman's life, particular sets of circumstances shaped how and where women were spending their leisure time.

A dilemma that historians often encounter is that many women's lives were not dependent on a time clock that determined when they began and ended their daily labour. Without such strict parameters, it is difficult to establish which parts of the day were considered available for leisure. Because of this complexity, historians must search for those moments during the day when women put their work aside and devoted a small chunk of time to some sort of pleasurable activity. Along with time of day, the structure of the workweek and the creation of the "weekend" are also significant factors that must be considered. In this context, issues such as Sabbatarianism are important, particularly as reformers struggled with secular leisure on Sundays. Additionally, many women scheduled household chores such as washing, mending, and baking to take place on certain days of the week. These structural shifts in the meaning of time can be understood through modernity discourses that explained how time itself became altered,[20] along with notions of privacy and respectability, and ultimately how leisure became associated with new ideas about consumption, consumerism, and secularization.

Defining "leisure" is challenging: the term is problematic, and no single, widely accepted definition exists. Leisure has been defined and redefined based on the circumstances individual historians encounter in their research. In earlier studies, leisure was associated with industrialization and the workforce and constituted formal activities deemed recreational outside of work. This approach, however, ignored many informal activities and often women's experiences altogether. Also problematic is what functioned as leisure for some was considered work by others and vice versa.[21] This study borrows historian James Walvin's broad but effective definition of leisure as "the ways in which people voluntarily chose to spend their non-working hours of rest."[22] Throughout this book, "work" refers to waged employment and the unpaid domestic labour that was traditionally under women's purview and responsibility.

The assorted meanings of other terms for recreation, such as "sport," are equally tricky to define. In Dresden, Tillsonburg, and Elora, it does not appear that there were any professional sports teams for women prior to the First World War. The sports they played most often, like lawn tennis, are considered amateur here because they were "played for [their] own sake rather than for pecuniary gain."[23] In this book, "sport" consists of both informal and organized play, the latter defined as a codified set of rules that members of "clubs, schools, provincial and national sport organizations" agreed to abide by to "regulate the competitions."[24] Professional sports, on the other hand, typically involved larger numbers of players (usually men) who competed in matches against teams from other towns and earned some sort of compensation for their efforts. The level of physicality required to engage in an activity is used as a measurement when referring to an activity as a sport or game. I consider croquet, for example, a game because though played in teams, it requires only moderate mobility and range of movement.

The concept of "rural" is also rather difficult to classify. As historian Ruth Sandwell poses, are the boundaries geographical or cultural?[25] Arguably, both apply so both are considered throughout this study. While small towns and rural areas were (mostly) distinct spaces, they worked in tandem because the town was the nucleus and service centre for rural inhabitants, and rural farms and businesses offered important goods and services to town dwellers. Residents of larger cities and urban historians often collapse small towns and rural areas into one characterization of "rural" or "country." In this study, Dresden, Tillsonburg, and Elora are considered "urban" to an extent because they were incorporated, had concentrated groupings of people, and provided essential services like banks, schools, and shops. These characteristics distinguished them from rural areas—the surrounding countryside that contained small villages, homes, and farms. The extent to which rural residents and townsfolk interacted was determined by distance and modes of travel; generally, people walked, rode horses, navigated buggies and wagons, and eventually, cycled and drove motorcars to move within a few kilometres of town and country.

I wish to note that the closest reserves to Dresden (Walpole Island First Nation, or Bkejwanong; and Delaware Nation at Moraviantown, or Eelünaapéewi Lahkéewiit), and Tillsonburg and Elora (Six Nations of the Grand River; and Mississaugas of the Credit First Nation, or Mazina'iga-ziibing Misi-zaagiwininiwag) have not been included in this examination. Within the sources consulted, which were largely created by White, Euro-North American people, it is unclear how much sustained contact women in Dresden, Tillsonburg, and Elora had with Indigenous people for the purposes of leisure, apart from instances when Indigenous people were employed by entertainment companies, engaged in the commodification of their culture, or played sports against White teams. Some of the circuses and Wild West shows that visited small-town Ontario, for example, featured Indigenous performers. As Chapter 6 discusses, citizens from Dresden enjoyed excursions to the unceded territory of Walpole Island First Nation, where they frolicked on beaches and purchased Indigenous women's craftwork. In Elora, lacrosse matches between White members of the Elora Rocks and their rivals from Six Nations of the Grand River were a popular community activity throughout the 1860s to 1880s.[26] In other regions of Ontario, some scholars have explored how clubs and organizations were a way that Indigenous and non-Indigenous women encountered one another, especially when Indigenous women desired to join a branch of a specific organization that did not exist on their reserve.[27] Possibilities for future researchers include a more thorough examination of social relations between Indigenous and settler women or a study of Indigenous peoples' labour in settlers' homes, on farms, or for the purposes of leisure. Using Indigenous-authored sources and perspectives, these topics would be a welcome addition to historiographies of colonialism, community, gender, and leisure in Ontario's past.

The dynamics of movement and space are integral to studying where leisure took place, so it is necessary to study towns and, to a degree, rural areas together. In the context of the leisure offerings in Dresden, Tillsonburg, and Elora, proprietors of entertainment halls and members of women's organizations, for example, needed and relied on the patronage of farmers and rural people when a concert or fundraiser was being held. It should also be clarified that unlike some of the earlier scholarship on rural Ontario, this study does not use "farming" and "farm women" interchangeably with "rural" and "rural women." Though farmers generally resided in rural areas, it is necessary to distinguish between the two because not all rural inhabitants earned a living through agriculture, and not all farms were located outside town borders. "Farmers" refers specifically to those who "earned their living by agricultural pursuits or a portion of the population who lived on farms."[28]

Just as the study of formal and informal leisure activities can benefit from a joint analysis, both "public" and "private" leisure pursuits are examined here. Often, the two spheres are studied in isolation. As many scholars have shown, the separate realms doctrine was largely a discursive construct, and movement between home and public was more common and fluid than previously understood. As Chapter 4 details, the home served as an important setting for many types of leisure activities, but that fact does not eclipse how much small-town women also socialized and pursued hobbies in public. Outside of occupying spaces like churches, workplaces, or retail shops, however, their presence in public was downplayed in earlier community studies. In his work on the town of Greenbank, Ontario, for example, W.H. Graham claims that a woman was "absorbed into the family of the man she married, took his name and disappeared (in public terms) as an individual. In newspapers and legal documents, she appears only through her connection with a man."[29] Recent scholarship has debunked the antiquated notion that women were passive homebodies, but more scholarly work needs to recognize how intricately tied women's public and private lives were. Piety, for example, was widely considered to be a cardinal virtue of "true" womanhood and integral to the construction of a happy home, but women's involvement in the religious life of their communities meant traversing the "public locus of the church," where "private concerns" like "intemperance, poverty, and family relations" could be addressed.[30]

Weather, the environment, and seasonal differences also shaped leisure and recreational opportunities. In this study, both local *and* distant land-scapes are examined. While some small-town men and women had the privilege of escaping to a cottage or embarking on a "grand tour" of Europe, many stayed near home, taking advantage of the waterways and wooded areas in their region. Though day trips, excursions, picnicking, and amateur sports became increasingly accessible for people across socio-economic strata in Dresden, Tillsonburg, and Elora, their enjoyment depended on weather conditions, the seasons, and the existence of safe spaces for play. Recent work by environmental historians has acknowledged the importance of gender and class when examining how White Euro-Canadians occupied and interacted with green spaces and waterways,[31] and this book, and Chapter 6 especially, complements and expands on these findings. Certainly, the natural environment was also navigated by rural and small-town women, though this was often dependent on the reformation or feminization of outdoor spaces.

A key issue emerging from Canadian studies of gender, sexuality, and the law is the notion of leisure as a problem, and the ways in which it was controlled and legislated by lawmakers. When examined in a more rural context, this approach prompts questions about how prominent the "rough versus respectable" paradigm was in communities that contained smaller populations and fewer recreational spaces. Though the policing of leisure activities was initially the job of the church, by the end of the nineteenth century religious bodies had lost much of this power. As Chapter 7 explores, curtailing instances of crime and deviancy among women was often tied to desires to maintain the image of rural and small-town women as paragons of virtuous femininity. In the face of waning religious authority, families, community members, town/municipal councils, and the legal system exercised various modes of censure that controlled and shaped leisure offerings for women, and the behaviours considered appropriate when engaging in such activities.

The question of inclusivity is considered throughout this study. At times, options for leisure appear to have been more inclusive (though not exclusively so) on account of population size. For example, in the 1870s and 1880s, when opportunities for community-wide recreation were more limited, church functions were interdenominational gatherings. The two dominant sects—Protestants and Catholics—appear to have coexisted amicably. In

Dresden, there were instances when newspapers referenced the Black hosts and organizers of clubs and events, but these were often patronized by White residents and vice versa. Some local historians and descendants, however, believe that uncodified rules dictated how the Black and White populations were supposed to coexist. In nineteenth-century Kent County, historian Deirdre McCorkindale explains, "there was an entrenched belief in the inherent inferiority of Black people,"[32] as demonstrated by Dresden's segregated churches and school system.[33] When Rev. Thomas Hughes, a White, English missionary, served as the first rector for Dresden's Black Anglican congregation between 1859 and 1876, he noted in his diary that "the unchristian prejudice against color seems to be ineradicable."[34] In the context of leisure, there would have been instances when non-White participants *were* treated unjustly by the White, Euro-Canadian majority in Dresden and other communities. In the surviving sources, there is limited evidence of these incidents, but their absence does not mean they did not occur; more conceivably, victims of prejudice were unwilling or unable to recall and record such events. Examples of overt discrimination in the towns under study are certainly most discernible in Dresden's public records: in 1888, for example, an article in the *Dresden Times* noted that during a match between the men's baseball teams from Dresden and nearby Wallaceburg (a predominantly White and British town), an umpire made discriminatory remarks about Dresden's players.[35] The entrenched racism that McCorkindale identifies in Kent County continued well into the twentieth century. Though the Ku Klux Klan did not have much of a presence in Ontario until the 1920s, some Confederate sympathizers relocated to Canada after the American Civil War, a handful of which settled in London, Ontario (just over 100 kilometres northeast of Dresden), and terrorized Black citizens in that city.[36] In Chatham-Kent, White-owned businesses were known to refuse services to members of the Black community, and voters in Dresden disallowed a local bylaw that intended to ban racial discrimination in 1949.[37]

While race certainly acted as a barrier to inclusion, arguably more so than any other social practice in these towns, leisure could bring people of differing socio-economic positions together. Though discernible class structures were present and selective socializing occurred, groupings of elites were so small (and the middle class so large) that social circles often contained both middle- and upper-class men and women. In cities where larger groups of people were clustered in neighbourhoods, they had the capacity to construct their own sites for play and attract participants. In Dresden, Tillsonburg, and Elora with their smaller populations, opportunities to construct separate spaces and modes of leisure were more limited. Though not necessarily at the same time, most residents tended to occupy the same halls, sports fields, fairgrounds, and theatres, but, occasionally, barriers like admission fees assisted in keeping the "roughs" away from the "respectable."

Through the lens of leisure, we also see the dominance of a hegemonic middle-class culture in these towns and the extent to which middle-class and elite women aspired to project refinement, respectability, and success through their activities. Indeed, leisure became an important marker of socio-economic status and allowed some women to cultivate class exclusivity. We also see attempts by elites and the middle class to use leisure to impart cultural norms and values among working-class and marginalized residents. Resultingly, though not purposely, this study is a history of women who enjoyed varying levels of privilege in their towns. Available sources contain considerably less information about working-class and other marginalized women, so little about their social lives has been gleaned for this book beyond barriers related to finances and their alleged participation in "disreputable" social practices as described in gossipy newspaper articles, jail registers, and court records.

Sources

Most of the research conducted for this book occurred in smaller community museums, libraries, and county archives located throughout southern Ontario. As other rural historians can confirm, conducting primary research can be a tricky and time-consuming feat. Compared to holdings in larger provincial and national archives, where digitized cataloguing systems are used, the primary sources contained in smaller institutions are often unlabelled, unorganized, and uncatalogued because of insufficient staff and funding. After reaching out to local bloggers and newspaper columnists, I was fortunate that they willingly advertised this project and urged community members to come forward if they had pertinent family memorabilia (none did, unfortunately). Communicating with local writers, former residents, curators, archivists, and town historians over phone, email, and in person, however, provided helpful insights into community dynamics that published sources cannot capture.

Local newspapers, principally the *Tillsonburg Observer*, the short-lived *Tillsonburg Liberal*, the *Dresden Times*, the *Elora Express*, and the *Elora Lightning Express*, compose the bulk of the primary sources used throughout this book. These small-town "weeklies" were a hodgepodge of local, provincial, national, and world news, advertisements, serialized fiction, prescriptive literature, and advice columns. They typically numbered somewhere in the range of three to four pages in the 1870s, increasing to seven or eight pages by the 1910s as small towns and their literate readership grew. According to Wetherell and Kmet, "like city newspapers, they served important and unique functions in promoting the town and in providing news, commentary, and entertainments."[38] My focus was largely restricted to the local news columns that reported the majority of each town's events, gatherings, fundraisers, and sports matches.[39] I was cognizant, though, of the fact that what was published in the newspaper was not representative of the town or its populace. Editors strove to appeal to their largely middle- and upper-class readers, so most stories concerned the activities of their respective social circles. The exception was reports from the local courts that provided details of the "crimes" being committed locally and emphasized the gender, ethnicity, and/or class of the victim(s) and the accused. Over time, the amount of space devoted to social columns expanded to the point where, in the 1910s, virtually the entire first and/or second page of the newspaper was composed of local happenings. Not only does this point to the prevalence of leisure in these towns, but the ways that reporters boasted about offerings for leisure demonstrates a conscious effort on their part to promote "social cohesion"[40] and advertise these towns as progressive, modern, and suitable for prospective investors, businesses, and residents.

The prescriptive literature contained within rural and agrarian periodicals like the *Farmer's Advocate and Home Magazine*,[41] the *Rural Canadian*, and the *Canada Farmer* provides a sense of the pressure placed on both men and women (though more so the former) living outside of Canada's major urban centres to seek out "healthful" and "rational" modes of recreation. As did the weeklies, over time these periodicals devoted more space and effort to advice, instructions, and recommendations for their rural and small-town readers regarding everything from constructing the perfect tea table to the importance of amateur sports and outdoor play for boys and girls.

Government documents like the Canadian censuses conducted between 1871 and 1911 have been used here for the statistical data they contain about each town, including population, geographic size, and citizens' vital statistics. One of the problems of studying smaller communities and rural areas is that, depending on the year consulted, some of the statistics may not be divided by village or town but rather are presented as totals for an entire county or district. Major industries, employers, and professionals in each town, for instance, were presented this way. Late nineteenth-century gazetteers, business directories, and local histories were consulted to complement the census and resolve some of its data. At the individual level, the nominal census was useful in recreating a more complete profile of some of the women described in this study. Details pertaining to employment, wages, and household composition helped to better define class groupings. Though as Marks rightly notes, "quantitative records take us only so far,"[42] surviving membership lists from various clubs, auxiliaries, and associations were consulted in conjunction with the census to gauge how often and to what extent socio-economic circumstances may have determined participation in leisure activities. Sources mediated by county and municipal governments, such as jail registers and bylaws, as well as case files and judge's bench books located at the Archives of Ontario, were helpful in reconstructing instances of crime and "deviance" that occurred in the context of leisure.

Women's diaries, scrapbooks, personal reminiscences, and letters hold an important place in this book. Indeed, as historian Catharine Anne Wilson argues, "no source is more intimate and everyday than the diary."[43] They can help scholars "gain a fuller understanding of rural life in general," notes historian J.I. Little, by complementing the quantitative sources prominent in rural histories.[44] In the nineteenth century, thanks in part to developments in print technology and rising literacy rates, North Americans became avid record keepers. In smaller, more isolated communities, as American historian Gayle R. Davis explains, diaries could be a substitute "for personal contact with women friends or relatives, mediating between isolation and communication."[45] The diaries kept by women living in small towns and rural areas were often terse accounts of their daily activities, diverging from the introspective confessionals characteristic of some city women.[46] As will be discussed more thoroughly in Chapter 4, many diaries suggest how much women's labour and leisure occurred simultaneously. Notations about female friends and family members socializing are often followed by descriptions of the domestic work they accomplished together. Such personal records, however, can take us only so far. Working-class women, for instance, owing to a lack of time, ability, or inclination, were less likely to write down the details of their lives. When they did, collection and preservation practices impacted their survival and accessibility. Before second-wave feminism pushed women's history to the fore in the 1970s, local historical societies, museums, and archives may not have considered marginalized women's papers and personal effects sources worth saving.

Structure of the Study

Chapter 1 begins by positioning Dresden, Tillsonburg, and Elora in the broader history of settlement in late eighteenth- and nineteenth-century Ontario. It presents a truncated history of each town, including the treaties that redistributed Indigenous-occupied land, the arrival of the first non-Indigenous settlers, the establishment of capitalist economic systems, and the geographic layout. The major ethnic groups and religious affiliations in each community are classified and compared, as well as total populations calculated by censuses conducted between 1871 and 1911. Class groupings are identified and defined, arguing against the oft-cited notion that smaller, less industrialized populations lacked distinguishable differences. Indeed, local citizens clearly understood where they ranked in relation to others when interacting or socializing together. It also describes major employers in each town and how the elite families who owned these businesses acquired their wealth. Finally, the chapter briefly examines some of the more notable alterations to each town's physical landscape in the late nineteenth and early twentieth centuries, especially the building of public entertainment halls and theatres, which communicated that the citizens desired to pursue leisure and that the towns considered themselves progressive, modern, and permanent.

Chapter 2 re-examines the separate spheres construct by paying much-needed attention to the ways that small-town women increasingly came to occupy the public spaces of their communities. In this context, some of the activities that historians traditionally dwell on are identified (such as church auxiliary work and social reform organizations), but I argue that women's presence in public, particularly when pursuing leisure, was not confined to civic or self-improvement initiatives. New secular entertainments, such as circuses and public concerts, at times divided citizens for reasons of cost and timing. The ability to pursue leisure certainly illuminated class differences among women, but working-class residents found ways around financial constraints. Finally, investigating the extent to which women became involved in the club movement and the variety of single- and mixed-sex clubs available before the First World War demonstrates that participation was increasingly considered a way for women to better themselves; this was dependent, however, on a prospective member's ability to meet the criteria outlined in the club's constitution. Church and charity work remained important, but these traditional pursuits were balanced by membership in social and self-improvement clubs where the interests of the individual were supported.

Popular sports and modes of physical recreation for women and girls are explored in Chapter 3. In the period under examination, organized sport for females was still in its infancy. Though small-town women, and especially those who lived on farms, were physically active out of necessity, it was only in the 1870s and 1880s that ideas and opinions concerning physical fitness and its purpose began to change. When it pertained to women, however, the new rhetoric was accompanied by concerns about virtue, maternal well-being, and modesty. Cycling, skating, sledding, and lawn tennis were much enjoyed by women living in Dresden, Tillsonburg, and Elora, indicating that women's desires to be outdoors and active superseded concerns like weather, cost, availability, or gender appropriateness. The women in these communities pursued sports and physical recreations individually, in pairs, in small groups, and as families. In doing so, they strengthened bonds of kinship and friendship, attended to their physical and mental wellness, and created a niche for themselves in public.

Chapter 4 analyzes the venue most often used for women's leisure activities: the home. For women in Dresden, Tillsonburg, and Elora, the home was the site of both labour and leisure and of family and friendship. Alterations to the physical layouts of homes in the late nineteenth century, particularly the separation of spaces for work and play, helped women to pursue leisure more readily than ever before. In some homes, though, the boundaries between these spaces were less discernible when women mixed their labour and leisure. This chapter grapples with the forces of consumerism and consumption as home-based entertainments were increasingly influenced by new trends in dining, decorating, and hosting. Examining the home as a significant site of leisure also highlights class distinctions in these towns. While middle- and working-class women without the help of domestic servants combined socializing with the accomplishment of household chores, upper-class women with help were freer to host a variety of elaborate and expensive teas, dinners, and soirées that were divorced from their own domestic labour and cemented their positions in the local social hierarchy.

The late nineteenth- and early twentieth-century phenomenon of "armchair travelling," a new trend in leisure activities whereby individuals imaginarily travelled by incorporating ethnic food, dress, activities, and mannerisms into their dinner parties, social clubs, and fundraisers, is examined in Chapter 5. Bolstered by a fascination with "exotic" peoples and cultures, local citizens played with the idea of momentarily becoming a "foreigner." The chapter largely focuses on residents in the town of Tillsonburg and their desires to appear worldly in the 1890s and early 1900s, as evidenced by prominent social gatherings that incorporated markers of foreignness. Two of the more notable leisure activities where participants acted out racialized identities—the Garden Party of the Nations and the Ladies' Travel Club—showcased women's desires to consume markers of foreignness, while at the same time asserting their beliefs about the supremacy of White, Euro-North American, Christian people. For the female participants and organizers of these activities, engaging with "the foreign" in their patterns of leisure and consumption was a way to convey an air of cosmopolitanism and problematize popular perceptions of small towns being insular and unsophisticated.

Chapter 6 explores how natural environments, both near and far, were increasingly navigated by women and used for recreational purposes. The importance of transportation innovations is highlighted, along with the seasonality of leisure, greater free time after work and on weekends, and efforts to clean up both natural and human-made landscapes. While upper-class men and women could afford the privilege of escaping to summer homes in Muskoka or health spas in western Europe, increasingly the desires of middle- and working-class residents to travel were addressed by tourism companies at home and abroad. Specially designed train and steamer excursions, for example, accommodated those with less time and money to spend.

Finally, Chapter 7 argues how women and girls in small towns and rural areas also engaged in "disreputable pleasures," though on a different scale than their city counterparts, who have been the focus of historians' studies of female delinquency. Analyzing local bylaws and newspapers, where concerned community members and law enforcement officials publicly shamed those who flouted authority, confirms that leisure was often targeted as the motive behind what was deemed misbehaviour among women and girls, from vagrancy and petty theft to public intoxication. This chapter assesses the impact of regulatory structures in these towns to keep women and girls "good"—mainly parental, community, and legal authorities—and how interconnected they were. While most females who allegedly acted out were from the working class, it is unclear if their behaviours were simply being scrutinized and reported more closely than the activities of others.

While Canadian historians have accomplished much in terms of reconstructing women's public and private lives, there remains some work to be done in terms of balancing urban studies with more rural ones. Building on previous work about rural and small-town culture, this study adds a new dimension whereby women and their leisure are examined through the prisms of both private and public engagement and formal and informal participation. Resultingly, we see the variety of ways women pursued leisure, either in their "free" time or amid their daily responsibilities, no matter how minuscule or limited their participation was. Investigating a period in Canadian history that was integral to the formation and growth of leisure activities and a region that deserves more attention from historians illuminates how gender, class, and place factored in the new emphasis on leisure pursuits. Finally, this book contributes new understandings about the social dynamics of turn-of-the-century small-town Ontario by showcasing how three communities that lacked sizable populations and the trappings of large cities managed to cultivate a range of social, educational, and cultural offerings for citizens. Between 1870 and 1914, alongside the clubs, organizations, and sports leagues that allowed men to socialize, the women living in and around Dresden, Tillsonburg, and Elora carved spaces for themselves and their leisure. A variety of physical, intellectual, reformist, religious, and secular recreations offered women occasions when they could be part of their communities in a more meaningful and engaging way, nurture and develop networks of kinship and friendship, improve or sustain their physical health, enhance their education and desires to appear modern, and assist with charitable causes.

ONE

Situating the Small Town:
Dresden, Tillsonburg, and Elora
from Foundations to 1914

I N THE EARLY nineteenth century, the towns of Dresden, Tillsonburg, and Elora were established by White, European men and their families, who built on the dispossessed lands of the Anishinaabeg, Attawandaron, and Haudenosaunee peoples. Prior to 1784, only 6,000 non-Indigenous inhabitants resided in Upper Canada. This number would more than double by 1792 and jump to 70,000 by 1812,[1] thanks in part to British sympathizers and displaced Loyalists who moved north after the American Revolutionary War and the War of 1812. Some estimates put the Indigenous population of what is now southwestern Ontario, alone, at 65,000 in the mid-sixteenth century;[2] by 1835, there were only 9,300 Indigenous people living in Upper Canada.[3] Land grants available through the Canada Company, particularly in the western portion of the province, enticed White settlers seeking economic opportunities. They felled the region's forests and built roads (often using established Indigenous routes) to facilitate trade and the expeditious movement of goods and people. Many settlers earned their living from agriculture; about three-fifths of Canadians were farming by 1867,[4] most of whom resided in Ontario, which had grown to a remarkable 1,620,851 residents (including Indigenous people) by 1871.[5] Around that time there were two larger "towns" with populations over 25,000 (Toronto and Hamilton), ten towns that had between 5,000 and 25,000 inhabitants, and sixty-nine small towns that were home to between 1,000 and 5,000 citizens each.[6] Most of Ontario's population was concentrated in these smaller communities and rural areas. Urban centres of varying sizes serviced much of the rural population, which in 1870 was four times as large as that of towns and cities.

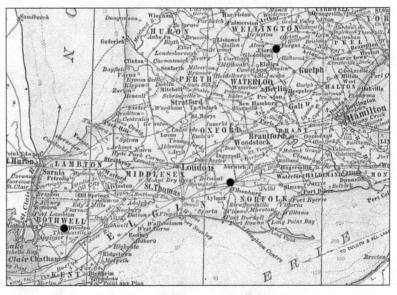

Figure 1. Close-up of a map of southern Ontario, showing (left to right) Dresden, Tillsonburg, and Elora, 1902. Source: Historic Canadian Maps Viewer, The Century Co., Ontario (Century Co., 1902), https://www.lib.uwo.ca/madgic/projects/canadianoriginals/007.jpg.

As Ontario historians such as Peter Baskerville have noted, the years between 1815 and 1865 were foundational for Upper Canada/Canada West, thanks to an unprecedented immigration boom. During this period, more than one million immigrants from the British Isles relocated to the colony,[7] leaving behind lagging economic growth, poor agricultural prospects, crowded cities, and dilapidated urban housing. Promotions featuring the rich agricultural lands of rural Ontario and job opportunities for unskilled workers in the emerging industrial centres of York (Toronto) and Hamilton enticed settlers. In the 1820s, while conditions aboard immigrant ships remained abhorrent, the cost of travelling to Canada became more affordable.[8] A sizable number of Germans, Dutch, French, and Scandinavians migrated to Ontario in the mid-nineteenth century, but the largest proportion of Ontario's million-plus population came from the British Isles. Most of Tillsonburg's citizens were English or from elsewhere in Great Britain, though there was also a considerable concentration of Germans. Elora was part of a cluster of towns in Wellington County where Scots settled, while Dresden, as a recognized terminus on the Underground Railroad, was home to a sizable number of Black Americans and Canadians until the mid-nineteenth century, when their numbers began declining.

Beyond immigration, as David Gagan notes in his study of mid-Victorian Peel County in Canada West, a "series of events" with socio-economic importance occurred in the middle of the nineteenth century, marking a revolution of sorts in central Canada. Gagan stresses that "the Irish famine emigrations of 1847–8, the advent of responsible self-government in 1849, the completion of the St. Lawrence canal system, a reciprocal trading agreement with the United States of America, and an expanding imperial market for Canadian wheat all contributed, in less than a decade (1846 to 1854), to the definition of a new era in Canadian history."[9]

These transformations, coupled with the British Crown's seizure of Indigenous territories and the creation of the reserve system, helped Euro-Canadian farmers to prosper and scores of towns that served the local farming and rural populations to be established. By 1891 Ontario was home to seventy-eight towns that, like Tillsonburg and Dresden, had populations between 1,500 and 5,000 inhabitants.[10] The installation of communication and transportation networks, an immigrant population eager to settle and plant roots, and the need to service a growing agricultural sector were some of the major catalysts for this town-building craze. Railroads, of course, significantly contributed to this process. As Nancy B. Bouchier notes in her study of sport in small-town Ontario, new transportation networks, and rail especially, "signaled the beginnings of [a] new era of growth, development, and social change," because "access to rail lines made or broke many nineteenth century communities and stimulated rapid and profound changes everywhere in the province."[11] Across Upper Canada/Canada West, the construction of towns can be summarized as "uneven"[12] because while some steadily expanded, others fluctuated or shrank in size. Writing about the towns of Galt and Goderich in southern Ontario, Andrew C. Holman describes their development as a gradual maturation from "pioneer settlements to bustling, 'go-ahead' locales."[13] This explanation also captures the evolution of Dresden, Tillsonburg, and Elora, and similar towns. Most communities were "preconceived" in that they were "consciously planned and located with specific functions in mind." Others were more "spontaneous" settlements that "evolved around a mill, a crossroads, a store, or a church."[14] The European and Euro–North American "founders" and early settlers of Dresden, Tillsonburg, and Elora all envisioned the accumulation of great wealth from their purchase of what was considered unoccupied and uncultivated wilderness. They established commercial enterprises (mostly agricultural and resource extraction mills and factories), social hubs (taverns and hotels), churches, and schools to attract prospective settlers.[15] Especially, their proximity to navigable bodies of water, abundant tracts of timber, and cultivable land helps explain how, when, and why Dresden, Tillsonburg, and Elora were settled and, more broadly, how they fit into the bigger socio-economic history of rural and small-town Ontario.

To understand the evolution of leisure offerings for citizens in these three towns, this chapter introduces each community's unique history, including its founding, settlement, and subsequent political, economic, religious, and cultural development. The chapter also explores the social relations determined by class and status in these communities, identifying where relevant their founding families or prominent members of the local elite, along with their manufacturers, industrialists, businesspeople, wage earners, and farming populations. The primary sites for leisure that emerged in these towns are noted, which assists in constructing a broader picture of what sorts of leisure activities were available, how they changed over time, and their impact on women's lives.

Dresden

Located in the far southwesterly region of Ontario in the municipality of Chatham-Kent, approximately thirty kilometres north of the county seat of Chatham, the town of Dresden contains a population of 2,451 citizens according to 2016 census figures.[16] While many small towns that were incorporated in the nineteenth century have grown to become larger towns (like Tillsonburg) and some into small cities, Dresden's population remains comparatively small. Like Tillsonburg and Elora, the town is located on a waterway—the Sydenham River—which played an integral role in its settlement and consequential growth. The town's current website invites visitors to "Explore Dresden";[17] today the community is known for its surrounding agricultural lands and food processing plants, as well as being home to attractions such as the Dresden Raceway and the Josiah Henson Museum of African-Canadian History (formerly Uncle Tom's Cabin Historic Site).

Early reminiscences of Dresden and its surrounding villages recall that the land was heavily forested and abundant with game. The region where present-day Dresden and Chatham-Kent are located is the traditional territory of the Anishinaabeg and Attawandaron people. On 19 May 1790, McKee's Treaty (Treaty 2) was signed by representatives of the British Crown and several Indigenous chiefs living in the area.[18] As was the case with many of the treaties brokered with Indigenous people, the British believed they were receiving 5,440 square kilometres of land, while Indigenous signatories interpreted the terms much differently. Ultimately, land dispossession, coupled with outbreaks of infectious disease, have been noted as important factors in the sharp decline of the Indigenous population in the Dresden area by the mid-nineteenth century.[19]

Local historians have long disagreed over the designation of an "official" founder in Dresden, as they have for Elora. The more popular account identifies Jared Lindsley as founder,[20] on account of his 1825 purchase of a parcel of land "from a speculator named Larkin," according to town historian Helen Burns.[21] This parcel was eventually developed and became the townsite. Around the same time as Lindsley's purchase, Black American migrants

Levi Willoughby and Weldon Harris also purchased land and settled in the district. Though Dresden historians Jeffrey Carter and Marie Carter recognize Willoughby and Harris as "founders"[22] alongside Lindsley, most others attribute the town's origins to Lindsley or Daniel R. Van Allen, who obtained seventy acres from Lindsley and completed the first land survey on the present townsite in 1845. Local historian Robert Brandon deems Van Allen the town's founder because of the permanence of this settlement. Van Allen himself viewed his contributions as worthy of "founder" status. When the *Chatham Daily Planet* newspaper published an article in 1901 insinuating that much-famed Black American preacher Josiah Henson founded Dresden, Van Allen wrote to the paper asking that the error be corrected as it was he, not Henson, who had purchased the land and "laid out the place" that became the town.[23]

As a settler, Josiah Henson has received much recognition from local history enthusiasts. Born enslaved in Maryland, Henson escaped to Upper Canada, settling in the Dresden area in 1830 (then known as Dawn Township).[24] Henson went on to become renowned (and Dresden's claim to fame) for allegedly inspiring the title character in Harriet Beecher Stowe's acclaimed antebellum novel, *Uncle Tom's Cabin*.[25] While scholars and literary critics still debate whether Henson was the enslaved Uncle Tom, Brandon writes that at one time Stowe and Henson were acquaintances, and many of Uncle Tom's mannerisms and experiences in the book parallel those recorded by Henson in his memoirs.[26] A more recent explanation contends that during the course of researching her book, Stowe came across Henson's memoirs and used them to craft the character.[27] Similar to the ways Elora embraced Indigenous lore to enhance its attraction as a tourist site, Dresden has tried to capitalize on the association between Henson and Stowe. In 1940, Henson's original cabin was converted into a museum, which the Ontario Heritage Trust gained ownership of in 2005. "Uncle Tom's Cabin," renamed the Josiah Henson Museum of African-Canadian History in 2022, still operates as a cultural and heritage centre, honouring the efforts of Henson and other abolitionists who assisted Black refugees along the Underground Railroad. Waves of tourists have flocked to the town (especially during the Civil Rights

Movement of the 1950s and 1960s) to see Dresden and "Uncle Tom's Cabin," bringing money and recognition of its important place in the history of Black settlement in southwestern Ontario. Some townsfolk and historians, however, believe that Henson's fame has overshadowed the successes of other Black settlers in the region, many of whom used the Underground Railroad to flee involuntary servitude and became noteworthy "conductors" and abolitionists themselves.[28]

Arguably, Henson's greatest offering to the town of Dresden was his work with the British-American Institute (BAI), a manual training school and "institution where escaped slaves could be assisted and taught to maintain themselves."[29] Here, at what became the Dawn Settlement and currently occupies the southwest portion of the town, it was long believed that Henson and abolitionists James Fuller and Hiram Wilson purchased 200 acres of land in 1841 for the BAI to build a school. Recently, based on data found in surviving land records, some scholars have questioned whether Henson made the purchase, so the validity of this claim is under investigation.[30] The establishment of the BAI coincided with a large northward exodus in the mid-nineteenth century of Black men and women from the United States (both free and enslaved) who were seeking refuge after the Fugitive Slave Act was passed in 1850. Communicating and travelling via the Underground Railroad, thousands sought freedom and opportunity in some of the "terminals" north of the border. It has been estimated that by 1850 there were 3,000 Black refugees residing in Canada West alone.[31]

According to Brandon, Black men and women had begun migrating to Dawn Township as early as 1828. Communities in southwestern Ontario such as Buxton, Chatham, Sandwich (later Windsor), and Dresden became logical sites for settlement because of their locations on or near river systems, which were relatively close to the United States border and aided the transportation of refugees inland. Dresden's small population and lack of a recognizable infrastructure provided a semblance of safety and seclusion from bounty hunters and slave catchers.[32] Part of the mandate of the BAI was to provide a social safety net of sorts to newly arrived Black migrants by offering jobs, shelter, education, and other means of support. Proceeds from the sale of goods manufactured by BAI students helped to finance its endeavours. The efforts of the Institute drew several free Black men and women to Dresden, particularly those already involved in the abolitionist movement in the northeastern United States, who desired to live in a free community north of the border.

According to Michael Wayne, the Black population of the area referred to as Dawn or the Dawn Settlement (which included Dresden) "rose as high as 500 for a brief time in the early 1850s, but was never stable."[33] Throughout the latter part of the nineteenth century, residents made their living primarily as farmers and labourers, though the Carters note that a "good proportion" were also employed as business and tradespeople.[34] Families of colour, like the Whippers and Hollensworths, for instance, flourished in Dresden by building lumber mills, purchasing real estate, and establishing stores.[35] By the early 1870s, however, eager White settlers were avidly acquiring commercial and residential land previously occupied and owned by the town's first Black settlers. The Emancipation Proclamation of 1863 and the end of the American Civil War in 1865 prompted many Black men and women living in southern Ontario to leave for the United States in hopes of reuniting with loved ones; others moved on to investigate better employment opportunities in Ontario's rapidly growing cities. After years of controversy and debate surrounding its management, the land occupied by the BAI was sold in 1871. While slavery had been abolished, it was abundantly clear that being a free person did not guarantee social or legal equality in Ontario: many Black men, women, and their families realized that freedom did not change racist perceptions related to their skin colour and ancestry.

White, Euro-Canadian settlers eventually took the place of most of Dresden's founding Black families. The town continued to prosper financially and socially until the economic depression of the 1890s. Timber, an abundant resource in and around Dresden, had become increasingly profitable in the mid-nineteenth century, when wood for shipbuilding and fuel was in demand. Dresden's proximity to a river system facilitated the export of logs and timber. Several sawmills were established in the west end of town around the Sydenham River by enterprising men, including Alexander

McVean, Alexander Trerice, and John French. These mills provided, at least briefly, reliable income for unskilled workers. Dresden became a port of call for several ships importing and exporting goods. The timber-based industries that developed in the town and the subsequent shipping boom stimulated the local economy by providing jobs and enticing new settlers. Within a period of forty years, the population of the town jumped from a handful of residents in the early 1830s to more than 1,000 people by 1871.

At that time, a group of "leading citizens" applied for Dresden to be officially incorporated as a village.[36] Until then, the town had been part of a cluster of rural communities managed by the municipal government of Dawn Township. When a community sought incorporation, it was not only seeking independence but also demonstrating a desire to be considered modern and urban. More importantly, incorporation provided towns with "greater borrowing power" and civic services that signified progress; water and sewage systems, for example, could now be installed through debenture debt.[37]

Various explanations have been proposed for the origins of the name "Dresden." One suggestion is that the town was named for the Moravian missionaries stationed on the Sydenham River who had German roots. Another explanation attributes the name's origins to the well-known Shadd family, who owned land in Dresden and were descendants of a German mercenary soldier who married his Black nurse. A third theory argues that since the region was once known as the District of Hesse, Dresden was chosen to maintain the German connection, particularly during the reign of Queen Victoria, whose husband, Albert, was German nobility.[38] Some communities in Dawn Township, like Dawn Mills, retained the "Dawn" eponym, but the choice of "Dresden" at a time when White settlers were increasingly outnumbering Black settlers may have been a conscious attempt to discount the town's Black American roots.

After incorporation in 1872, a burst of municipal improvements occurred, including the establishment of new schools and a small police force, and the installation of streetlamps. By 1881, the town's population had doubled, which the Carters argue was a result of the many lumber, planing, and stave mills that provided jobs to skilled and unskilled labourers.[39] In the wake of the 1890s depression, when the lumber industry lost much of its profitability, mill owners like the McVeans took advantage of the rich cultivable land surrounding the town and delved into agro-industrial milling. Their grist, woollen, and food processing mills provided much-needed employment to local labourers who had struggled since the downturn in the lumber trade.

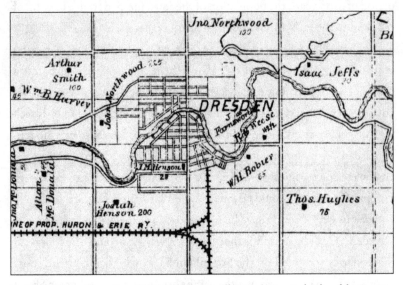

Figure 2. Town of Dresden, c. 1880–81. Source: *Illustrated Historical Atlas of the Counties of Essex and Kent* (Toronto: H. Belden and Co., 1880–81), 81.

By 1895, other major municipal improvements, including the establishment of two public schools, two private banks, and a weekly newspaper—the *Dresden Times*—provided town dwellers and settlers on the periphery with most of their necessities. A small population of professionals offered medical, dental, and legal services. Most businesses were in the centre of town, around St. George and Main Streets on the south side of the Sydenham. The Erie and Huron (E&H) Railway system and daily stagecoaches enabled transportation to and from the town, while steamboats ran "twice a week to all points."[40] The Great North Western (GNW) and Canadian Pacific Railway (CPR) telegraph offices, a telephone connection, and daily mail service facilitated relatively fast and reliable communication within and beyond the town.[41] As of 1911, the town occupied 642 acres (1.00 square miles), or 2.59 square kilometres.[42]

Dresden's early history of Black settlement distinguishes it from the predominantly White, Anglo-Celtic, and Protestant communities of Tillsonburg and Elora. In 1881, while descendants of immigrants from the British Isles (primarily English and Scots) and Germany accounted for most of Dresden's 1,979 citizens, 174 Black residents also lived in the town. Most citizens, both Black and White, had been born in Ontario. By 1901, however, the Black population had shrunk even further while the White population had grown. Ten years later, only 109 Black men and women lived in Dresden, and this number continued to fall throughout the early twentieth century. The 1911 census notes two other people of colour resided in the town, one of Chinese origin and one listed as "Indian."[43] In terms of religious affiliation, Methodists made up the largest group throughout the entire period under study, followed closely by Presbyterian, Baptist, and Roman Catholic adherents. Initially, the Anglican church served Dresden's Black population; what came to be known as Christ Church was constructed in 1867 on land donated by a Black woman named Nancy Thomas.[44] Brandon writes that most of the parishioners eventually left to attend services at other Black churches, and newly arrived White English settlers took their place in the later nineteenth century.[45] There was also a significant Black congregation at the Queen Street Baptist church, built in 1857, though Baptist services were being held as early as 1850 near the land once occupied by the BAI.[46]

Tillsonburg

According to the 2016 census, Tillsonburg's population was 15,594 residents.[47] The town is located roughly 175 kilometres southwest of Toronto in the county of Oxford, where it is near major highways, the city of London, and the north shore of Lake Erie. Arguably, it is best known for being immortalized in the 1971 song "Tillsonburg," by Canadian country-folk artist Charles Thomas "Stompin' Tom" Connors, which describes Connors's experience picking tobacco as a youth.[48] The people and

TABLE 1. ORIGINS OF THE PEOPLE, 1881 AND 1901						
	Dresden		Tillsonburg		Elora	
	1881	1901	1881	1901	1881	1901
African*	174	147	10	—	—	—
Chinese and Japanese	—	—	—	3	—	1
Dutch	75	16	—	31	—	2
English	641	546	817	1,148	400	362
French	36	23	14	49	1	7
German	310	162	85	214	81	92
Irish	426	399	309	374	307	210
Scandinavian	1	1	2	2	—	5
Scotch	281	290	293	410	507	489
Swiss	2	—	—	1	—	—
Welsh	29	—	—	—	34	—
Others (British)**	N/A	10	N/A	5	N/A	19
Various other origins	—	1	4	2	2	—
Not given/ unspecified	4	18	405	2	12	—

* In the 1881 census, "African" is used to describe Black citizens, while "Negro" is used in 1901.
** This category appears only in the 1901 census.
Source: *Census of Canada, 1880–81*, Vol. I (Ottawa: Maclean, Roger, and Co., 1882); *Fourth Census of Canada, 1901*, Vol. I (Ottawa: S.E. Dawson, 1902).

cultures of small-town Canada were prominent themes in Connors's music, and "Tillsonburg" cemented the image of the tobacco leaf as an expression of the town's collective identity. The tobacco industry undoubtedly played a formidable role in the growth and expansion of the region's agricultural sector in the middle and later years of the twentieth century, but Tillsonburg was initially a mill town. Timber, oat, flour, and split pea milling brought wealth and recognition to local manufacturers and provided a steady and reliable stream of labour for unskilled workers. While great care has been taken by local historians and the town's museum to preserve this rich history, Tillsonburg's story prior to the "green gold rush"[49] of tobacco production has received little academic attention.

Like much of southern and central Ontario, the land around Tillsonburg is that of the Anishinaabeg, Attawandaron, and Haudenosaunee peoples, who were largely displaced in the late eighteenth and early nineteenth centuries as a result of perfidious land negotiations with the British Crown. Looking to relocate Loyalist refugees, in 1784 British representatives engaged in treaty negotiations with the Mississaugas of the Credit First Nation, who stewarded approximately 3,000,000 acres of land between Lakes Erie and Ontario. On 7 December 1792 an amendment was made to the 1784 agreement because the large tract had been inaccurately described. While the Between the Lakes Treaty (Treaty 3) was supposed to clarify the extent of British ownership, ambiguities remained around Indigenous rights to the land and its water resources.[50] On this land, the town of Tillsonburg was constructed. The first recorded White, Euro-North American settler, George Tillson (from whom Tillsonburg derives its name), emigrated from the United States to Upper Canada in 1822, settling along the north shore of Lake Erie in the village of Normandale. In 1824 Tillson, along with his son-in-law, Benjamin Van Norman, and nephew, Harvey Tillson, ventured inland, heading northwest toward present-day Oxford County. In his travels, Tillson found plentiful bog iron and ore, considered ideal for establishing an iron forge, near the Talbot Settlement in Houghton and Middleton Townships. The heavily forested region also contained abundant pine and hardwood, while Big Otter Creek promised a power source for future logging operations. Tillson purchased 600 acres from the estate of Maria Willcocks, the unmarried daughter of prominent landowner William Willcocks, and in 1825 began to establish permanent roots in the new settlement initially called Dereham and then renamed Tillsonburg in 1836. When the town was incorporated in 1872, it was spelled with only one l—a mistake only officially corrected in 1902.[51]

Between the late 1820s and early 1830s, Tillson oversaw the construction of a dam, blast furnace, forge, lock, axe factory, sawmill, and tannery near Big Otter Creek.[52] Word spread among the scattering of settlers in the region of the economic opportunities in the new settlement. To improve movement and communication, Tillson oversaw the surveying and construction of roads that connected the settlement with shipping and business opportunities near London to the north and Lake Erie and the Talbot Settlement to the south.[53]

Tillsonburg's population began to expand in the late 1850s and early 1860s, thanks to the presence of natural resources, such as the abundance of waterpower provided by Big Otter Creek. By this time, Tillson's son Edwin Delevan (E.D.), born in 1825, had assumed control over most of his father's enterprises and built upon the family's early successes. In 1861 he was running saw, grist, and planing mills, a door and sash factory, and a dry goods store under the auspices of the newly formed Tillson Company. After venturing into food manufacturing, some of their products, such as Tillson Pan-Dried Oats, became household staples across North America and were exported internationally.[54] For this reason, Tillsonburg was once known as the "Pan-Dried Town." Despite the "inflation, depression, falling commodity prices, blight, and market dislocation"[55] that marked the 1860s, Tillsonburg and its namesake family prospered. E.D. was elected Tillsonburg's first mayor after the town was incorporated in 1872, also serving as Reeve of Dereham Township, postmaster, and orchestrator of the town's first secondary school and waterworks system. Most of the municipal improvements installed in the town's early years were at least partly financed and/or championed by the Tillson family.

In the late 1880s, the recently established *Tillsonburg Liberal* newspaper, acting as a town promoter of sorts, reported that Tillsonburg "[was] meeting with a substantial development of various business interests and is enjoying a status of business equalled by very few towns of its size in Western Ontario. There is no doubt Tilsonburg [*sic*] possesses real advantages that doubtless will acquire for the town still greater progress in the future."[56] In addition to the economic enterprises of the Tillson Company, the "flourishing" town was home in the mid-1880s to a cigar factory, woollen mill, agricultural implements company, liveries, foundries, a brewery, tannery, and a stoneware manufacturer.[57] These businesses, and the Tillson mills especially, provided employment to local men and allowed farmers living on the town's periphery the ability to process and sell their fall and spring wheat, barley, oats, rye, corn, peas, and other grains.

Several professionals practised in Tillsonburg, including veterinary surgeons, barristers and solicitors, dentists, and physicians whose offices dotted primarily the main thoroughfare, Broadway Street. Scattered among them were hotels, drug and stationery stores, carriage manufacturers, millinery shops, and dry goods stores. In most small towns, "main street was highly mixed, with service, professional, mercantile, commercial, and residential uses interspersed."[58] These professionals and successful businessmen occupied seats on the local town council, were elected as mayors or reeves, orchestrated and joined fraternal societies, and sat on various municipal and civic improvement organizations.

Two newspapers, the above-mentioned *Liberal* and the *Tillsonburg Observer*, enjoyed a wide circulation. Noted in the 1895 *Ontario Gazetteer and Directory* was the presence of "good" public schools, two banks, electric power, an "excellent" system of waterworks, daily mail service, a telegraph office, and a telephone connection. Stagecoaches and several railways, including the Grand Trunk (GTR), Michigan Central (MCR), and Brantford and Tillsonburg (B&T), provided daily transportation to and from the town.[59]

According to the first federal enumeration after Tillsonburg received incorporation status in 1872, the town contained a population of 1,873 residents. Ten years later it had grown slightly, but the greatest increase occurred between 1901 and 1911, when a population of 2,758 residents was listed. The town then covered 2,000 acres (809.4 hectares), or 8.1 square kilometres (3.13 square miles).[60] Socially, Tillsonburg's ethnic and religious groups were comparable to other towns similar in size and population around the turn of the century. Protestants with English ancestry overwhelmingly represented most of the citizenry, followed by Irish, Scots, Germans, and the

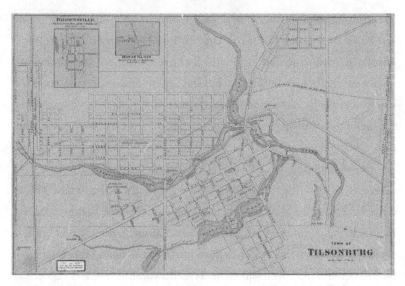

Figure 3. Town of Tillsonburg, c. 1876. Source: County of Oxford Archives, Wadsworth, Unwin and Brown, *Topographical and Historical Atlas of the County of Oxford, Ontario* (Toronto: Walker and Miles, 1876), 72–73.

French. A small group of Chinese and Japanese immigrants were enumerated in the census (three in 1901 and four in 1911), but prior to the First World War, Tillsonburg was a predominantly White, Anglo-Celtic town. The presence of Methodist, Presbyterian, Anglican, Baptist, and Roman Catholic churches reinforced the *Liberal*'s claim that Tillsonburg was "animated by a truly religious zeal."[61]

Elora

The small town of Elora is approximately 120 kilometres northeast of Tillsonburg and twenty kilometres northwest of the city of Guelph. Situated in the centre of Wellington County, one of the richest agricultural districts in Canada, Elora stands at the confluence of the Grand and Irvine Rivers. Within Wellington, all major settlements were established on a stream, lake, creek, or river, but the role of the Grand and Irvine Rivers in the development of Elora and its surrounding communities occupies a unique place in small-town Ontario's history. If popular culture identifies Tillsonburg with rows of tobacco plants, Elora remains well-known for its gorge and surrounding vistas, at one time dubbed "some of the grandest and most thoroughly enjoyable scenery on the North American continent."[62] Today, day-trippers still visit the town and its population of roughly 7,000 people,[63] hoping to catch a spectacular view of the Elora Gorge Falls or to camp in one of the local conservation areas.

Local histories of Elora differ over the official date of European settlement. Peter R. Sinclair and Kenneth Westhues claim that "the first settler [. . .] took his family there around 1816 because of the waterpower available. His venture was not successful but later settlers came for the same purpose and succeeded."[64] Other histories, particularly the well-known but dated history of Elora by John R. Connon, trace Elora's founding to 1817, when "the earliest white settler," Roswell Matthews, arrived with his family and lived there for nine years before moving to Guelph.[65] Naval Captain William Gilkison, however, is generally recognized as Elora's "official" founder for his 1832 purchase of almost 14,000 acres of land from businessman and politician Thomas Clark, land the town currently stands on. His many travels inspired Gilkison to name the town Elora after the Ellora Caves in India.[66] The success of his friend and Canada Company agent John Galt provided Gilkison with a "'system' of settlement" on which to build his "fairly clear ambitions for the land," which included the little town becoming *the* milling destination for farmers in the region.[67]

Elora's first White settlers steadily arrived throughout the 1830s and into the middle decades of the nineteenth century, primarily emigrating from rural Scotland. Nina Perkins Chapple explains that they "purchas[ed] vast areas of unbroken forest in Upper Canada and establish[ed] new communities at the best water-power sites available, a movement modelled after the eighteenth-century Scottish 'new towns.'"[68] According to Elizabeth Waterston and Douglas Hoffman, these settlers were not "destitute like the clansmen who had been swept out of the glens," nor were they "as wealthy as the genteel settlers who established country estates around Woodstock or London." Rather, the Scots who immigrated to Wellington County were "middle-of-the-road workers."[69] They typically lived around their compatriots in the neighbouring communities of Elora, Fergus, and Bon Accord. Over time, a (mostly) friendly rivalry developed between Fergus and Elora as the growing towns competed for settlers, the business of the adjacent rural population, and bragging rights on sports fields.

The Indigenous history of the Elora area has been deeply romanticized in the pages of local history books. The compilers of the Elora Women's Institute Tweedsmuir History book write that after a great battle between the Haudenosaunee and Wendat near the present site of Hamilton in 1651, a number of Haudenosaunee people sought shelter in the deep ravines and caves of Elora Gorge, where artifacts such as wampum beads were recovered.[70] Allegedly, in the early nineteenth century when Indigenous groups skirted Elora during their annual trip to Niagara for provisions, their interactions with local citizens were cordial and friendly. In the mid-nineteenth century, former Elora resident Mrs. Charles Allan Sr. recalled that from their farm west of Elora, she and her family could hear the "sweet singing of the Indians, at camp, across from the old stone barn in the new park."[71] Reminders of Indigenous peoples' presence were deployed in Elora throughout the nineteenth and twentieth centuries, embodied in stories told by locals and town boosters to drum up tourism. In the 1870s, the principal of the Elora Public School, David Boyle, established a makeshift museum in the town for his collection of "historical and Indian relics."[72] The story of a rock formation in the gorge known as "Lover's Leap" was a much-favoured anecdote. White townsfolk alleged it was named after an "Indian maiden, whose lover had been killed in battle [...] leaped from the rock to the swirling waters below [in the gorge] to join her lover."[73]

As these stories and lore were harnessed to attract tourists, Indigenous people were being pushed off the land to make way for White settlement. In her poem "A Saga of Elora," Olive Snyder describes this process. She writes, "Where the waters of the Irvine / Rush to meet the Grand's swift flow / Once the Indians went roving / Long and long and long ago / Paddled through the falls and rapids / Hid their wampum beads in caves— / Till the white man claimed the rivers / Harnessed up their turbulent waves."[74] In 1784, the Haldimand Proclamation transferred six miles of land along each side of the Grand River from its source to Lake Erie to the Haudenosaunee people for their loyalty to the British Crown during the American Revolutionary War. The Simcoe Patent (Treaty 4) of 1793 redefined the boundaries of the Haldimand Grant (or Tract), denying the Haudenosaunee thousands of acres promised to them and prompting ongoing disputes between the Six Nations of the Grand River and the Crown over land title.[75] A small portion of the original 950,000-acre (or 385,000-hectare) tract includes land that Elora currently stands on.

Deemed a "nontransferable village asset, one that has had a vital integrating effect on the residents of the village," Elora Gorge was, and remains, the town's most definitive attribute. Between the Grand and Irvine Rivers rests the deep gorge with its waterfalls, cliffs, and rocky embankments. Elora's topography starkly contrasts with what Sinclair and Westhues describe as the "mainly flat terrain of Southern Ontario."[76] Indeed, in *Lovell's Province of Ontario Directory for 1871*, adjectives such as "romantic" and "very beautiful" were invoked to describe Elora's natural environs.[77] In the entry for Dresden, *Lovell's* simply noted that "lumber and country produce afford the principal trade."[78] Though Tillsonburg was dubbed "an important village," little mention was made of its natural environment beyond the town's "excellent water privilege."[79] The striking qualities of Elora, the gorge, and the Grand River were highlighted in several late nineteenth-century magazines and books and became the inspiration for dozens of works by writers, artists, photographers, and poets. In its 1895 profile of Elora, the *Guelph Herald* newspaper stated, "In no portion of our Dominion has nature been more lavish in her gifts than here, and to the lover of the beautiful, in what way you turn, there is an ever varying scene of liveliness, of which one never tires."[80]

Sinclair and Westhues argue that it was the lumber and grain milling operations established in Elora's early years that drove the economic prosperity of the town well into the twentieth century. Such ventures were successful because mill owners utilized the rapid waterpower produced by the Grand and Irvine Rivers.[81] For a time, thanks to its location and amenities, Elora operated as an important service centre for farmers from the surrounding countryside who needed an adjacent town where they could buy or sell

Figure 4. Town of Elora, c. 1906. Source: Frank P. Lloyd, *Historical Atlas of the County of Wellington, Ontario* (Toronto: Historical Atlas Pub. Company, 1906), VIII.

goods.[82] The village was renowned for its livestock fairs, where thousands of cattle were sold each year. Along with large dairy operations, local farmers grew hay, wheat, barley, oats, potatoes, turnips, peas, and beans.[83] The majority of Elora's labour force, however, consisted of craftsmen employed in locally owned small-scale industries.[84] Successful entrepreneurs in the later nineteenth century ran a variety of mills, factories, foundries, and shops. Though Elora's downtown "core" straddles the Grand River, many of the town's businesses were located on its northern banks in the "newer" business section, near the hotels that provided housing to seasonal labourers.

By the 1890s, GTR and CPR lines ran through Elora, transporting goods and offering daily travel to and from a variety of locales, including Toronto. Public elementary and secondary schools and a separate Catholic school had been erected. A bank, a weekly newspaper (the *Elora Express*),[85] and the GNW Telegraph Co. office could be found in the small yet bustling downtown in and around Metcalfe, Mill, and Geddes Streets. A "good" fire department, telephone connection, electric power, and daily mail service were also products of late nineteenth-century municipal improvements.[86] Such services were key signifiers of "community progress" in small towns, part of a carefully constructed image created by local boosters that exemplified "the respectability that could be found in their town and its people."[87]

Despite a wide variety of employment opportunities and town amenities, population growth in Elora was stagnant throughout the late nineteenth and early twentieth centuries. According to the federal census, 1,387 citizens called Elora home in 1881.[88] Ten years later, the population had dropped slightly to 1,304, and even further to 1,187 in 1901. Over the next ten years, the population increased slightly but remained below 1,200 citizens. Though it had always been higher than Elora's, the population of Fergus, Elora's rival town, also dropped during this period. Elora's population in 1881 was the highest recorded for at least forty years, unlike that of Tillsonburg and Dresden (and many other small Ontario towns), which witnessed steady albeit limited growth in the decades leading up to the First World War.[89]

Such demographic decline was not uncommon in Ontario's small towns and rural areas at the time.[90] In the cases of Fergus and Elora, their shrinking populations were likely caused by the growth of nearby Guelph as an important service centre in Wellington County. As transportation networks expanded, rural farmers could more ably travel to Guelph, where the breadth of services and amenities available (including opportunities for leisure) surpassed those found in Elora and other smaller towns. At this time, larger

TABLE 2. LOCATION, DATE OF INCORPORATION, POPULATION			
	Dresden	Tillsonburg	Elora
County/ municipality (2024)	Chatham-Kent	Oxford	Wellington
Historic census district/ sub-district	Bothwell (1871–1901); Kent East (1911)	Oxford South/ Norfolk North (1871–81); Norfolk North (1891–1901); Oxford South (1911)	Wellington (1871); Wellington Centre (1881–1901); Wellington South (1911)
Date of incorporation	1872	1872	1858
Population, 1871	about 1,000*	about 1,000*	1,498
Population, 1881	1,979	1,939	1,387
Population, 1891	2,058	2,163	1,304
Population, 1901	1,613	2,241	1,187
Population, 1911	1,551	2,758	1,197

* In the 1871 census, Dresden and Tillsonburg were not enumerated separately from other towns and villages. The figure of "about 1000" was found in *Lovell's Province of Ontario Directory for 1871* (Montreal: John Lovell, 1871), 344, 806.
Source: *Census of Canada, 1870–71*, Vol. I (Ottawa: I.B. Taylor, 1873); *Census of Canada, 1880–81*, Vol. I (Ottawa: Maclean, Roger, and Co., 1882); *Census of Canada, 1890–91*, Vol. I (Ottawa: S.E. Dawson, 1893); *Fourth Census of Canada, 1901*, Vol. I (Ottawa: S.E. Dawson, 1902); *Fifth Census of Canada, 1911*, Vol. I (Ottawa: C.H. Parmelee, 1913).

cities like Toronto also began to absorb small-town manufacturers because they offered better opportunities for trade and investment, marketing, and a larger labour pool. An "ingrain carpet factory near Elora," for instance, "was removed to Toronto about 1874."[91] In 1900, the Ontario Bureau of Labor reported that in Elora, there was an "opening for almost any industry" because of "several vacant premises."[92] Other factors such as changing economic environments, costs associated with using water power, reduced incentives for new industries, and the exhaustion of local raw materials account for changes in manufacturing, which greatly affected the ebb and flow of town populations, particularly after the turn of the century.

Geographically, Elora was small, only comprising 750 acres (303.5 hectares), or 1.17 square miles (3 square kilometres).[93] Most Elorans indicated that they were of Scottish origin in the census, followed by English, Irish, and Germans. Apart from two people of Chinese origin listed in the 1911 census, the townspeople were predominantly of White, Western European descent. This homogenous culture, which also defined Tillsonburg, "was and is the most orthodox variety of Ontario culture" according to Sinclair and Westhues.[94] Like Dresden and Tillsonburg, most of the population was Protestant, though the preponderance of Scots meant that Presbyterians outnumbered Methodists and Anglicans. These were closely followed by Roman Catholic adherents.

Class and Social Stratification

Beyond their ancestry and religious affiliations, who were the people of these towns and how did they relate to each other? How did they distinguish themselves financially, spatially, socially, and culturally? Many historians have underlined the difficulties of describing class relations and groupings in small towns and have cautioned against using the frameworks often applied to larger cities. Traditional Marxist class theory, for example, identified two main historical groupings: capitalists who owned the means of production and the proletariat who sold their labour, supplemented by a smaller group of petite bourgeoisie who owned their means of production and typically did not purchase labour power. In the late nineteenth century, unlike Toronto and Hamilton, which were already industrialized, smaller towns like Dresden, Tillsonburg, and Elora were in the process of industrializing to varying degrees, so gaping economic distinctions between the classes were less extreme. There is also less evidence of public demonstrations of working-class consciousness in these towns, potentially due to the fact

TABLE 3. RELIGIONS OF THE PEOPLE, 1881 AND 1901

	Dresden		Tillsonburg		Elora	
	1881	1901	1881	1901	1881	1901
Anglican/ Church of England	221	157	243	337	267	202
Baptist*	235	223	339	379	28	6
Jew	—	—	—	31	1	—
Lutheran	—	2	2	14	—	4
Methodist**	1283	743	949	914	286	319
Presbyterian	194	306	299	449	568	491
Roman Catholic	39	62	74	84	193	148
Salvation Army	—	87	—	—	—	—
No religion	—	—	—	—	5	—
Unspecified/ not given	—	13	25	4	4	—
Others***	7	17	8	1	35	12

* "Baptist" also includes Free Will Baptists.
** "Methodist" includes Episcopal Methodists, Bible Christian Methodists, Primitive Methodists, and "Other" Methodists.
*** "Others" includes Tunkers, Mennonites, Brethren, Congregationalists, Disciples, Unitarians, Adventists, Universalists, Pagans, Quakers, Protestants, and Mormons.
Source: *Census of Canada, 1880–81*, Vol. I (Ottawa: Maclean, Roger, and Co., 1882); *Fourth Census of Canada, 1901*, Vol. I (Ottawa: S.E. Dawson, 1902).

that only a few unions appear to have existed between 1870 and 1914.[95] However, as historian Linda Ambrose has argued, areas located outside cities were "most definitely [...] stratified place[s]."[96] How to quantify such social distinctions was a subject debated in an 1881 article in the periodical *Rural Canadian*, where the author explains the difficulties of applying industrial-based ideas about class to more agrarian locales. This suggests that nineteenth-century understandings of class structure were neither static nor dependent on the presence of an extensive industrial sector. While the article notes that "the labouring man and woman, the farmer, the mechanic, the artisan, the inventor, [and] the producer" are ranked as the "low" or "middling classes" by "fashionable" society, in reality they "are nature's nobility." This rural critique discounts the notion "that [the] class who spend without earning, who consume without producing, who dissipate on the earnings of their relatives" be regarded as the "highest." Instead, individual merit and hard work should be the markers of "high" society.[97]

Previous analyses of class cleavages in small towns and rural areas have concluded that rigid and predetermined perceptions of social stratification must be modified to consider a community's unique set of circumstances, including its establishment and settlement, dominant ethnic groups, major businesses and industries, and levels of agricultural production. In her work on female labour in Upper Canada, for instance, Jane Errington argues that "an individual's place in society rested on a combination of factors, including relative wealth, occupation, skills, education, land holding, and self-expectation."[98] Paul Voisey points out that the evolution of Vulcan, Alberta, from an agricultural outpost to a bustling prairie town makes it difficult to slot citizens into distinct class groupings based on net worth alone, because the "rapid social mobility continually altered class memberships" in that community.[99] And in Andrew C. Holman's analysis of the formation and pervasiveness of a distinct middle-class culture in the Ontario towns of Galt and Goderich, he notes that class consciousness was based on local circumstances, and that placement in the towns' social hierarchies resulted from individuals' own recognition of their place within it.[100]

In thinking through social inequalities, class structures and consciousness, and social relations in Dresden, Tillsonburg, and Elora, organizing around similarly broad frameworks is a prudent choice. Certainly, each town contained a distinguishable elite. In Tillsonburg this stratum was dominated by the Tillson family and their relatives who owned land, businesses, and factories. The McVean family played a similar role in Dresden. Compared

with the other two towns, Elora's prominent families were less observable
in the community's social scene, though citizens like John McGowan
and Charles Clarke were well-known local politicians and, in the case of
McGowan, amassed considerable wealth. The elites in these towns were
primarily industrialists and businessmen who hired significant numbers of
waged labourers or service workers. Most citizens were the "middling sort,"
or Marx's petite bourgeoisie, a largely heterogeneous collection of professionals, small-scale businessmen, artisans, and others who provided services,
produced goods, and sold commodities on their own accounts, sometimes
with the help of an apprentice. When they employed office or store clerks,
occasionally these workers were male or female relatives. In 1901, for instance,
the nominal census noted that forty-seven-year-old Mary Smith worked
as a "saleswoman" in her husband's Elora grocery store, earning an annual
wage of $300. That same year, Elora "Merchant grocer" Mary Griffin, aged
seventy, employed her son as a "salesman."[101] Monetary compensation was
not always listed for those employed by family members, perhaps because
the business was understood to be a family enterprise where earnings were
shared, or because of how census enumerators interpreted guidelines around
occupational status.[102]

Each town also included farmers within and outside its boundaries.
Agricultural enterprises can be difficult to classify and track because of the
huge discrepancies in estimations of net worth,[103] as well as the variability
of financial success year to year, so I have categorized farmers separately
from other class groupings. Despite the prestige attached to owning large
tracts of land, proprietorship was not always profitable, nor did it guarantee
wealth. Measuring the amount of help farmers employed (if any) is challenging because of the seasonal nature of agricultural work. Many farmers
depended on the unpaid labour of family members to survive.[104] In Dresden,
Tillsonburg, and Elora, occupational pluralism was common.[105] Some farmers and their family members sought waged labour in factories and shops
while establishing their farm or to complement their farm's income,[106] so
wage earning and farming could overlap. For some industrialists, agriculture
was a pastime. The farm surrounding E.D. Tillson's grandiose residence, for

example, was a hobby farm used primarily for research and experimentation. Though the family largely subsisted off the farm's bounty, their income was not dependent on selling foodstuffs.

Situating females in social categories based on occupation or wealth alone is an even more complex undertaking because most women who appear in this book were not gainfully employed. Some helped husbands or fathers with agricultural duties or performed domestic labour for friends and family, but generally this sort of work was not considered "employment" in the eyes of census enumerators. As historian Kenneth M. Sylvester notes, women's agricultural labour was "often informal or unpaid," so their participation in the local workforce was "dramatically understated" in the census.[107] Some historians have argued that women's "unpaid community labour" in the way of voluntary society membership should also be recognized as legitimate forms of work, though it rarely was.[108] According to late nineteenth- and early twentieth-century censuses, most women in Dresden, Tillsonburg, and Elora who earned wages were employed as domestics, seamstresses, dressmakers, tailoresses, hotel workers, laundresses, and saleswomen. A small number of educated women worked as nurses, schoolteachers, and music instructors. Some older and/or widowed women refashioned their homes into boarding houses. Illegal activities, such as owning a brothel, were also sources of income. Compared to Tillsonburg and Dresden, Elora had more women (married and single, middle and working class) who worked. Though their father was a well-known railway agent and station master in Elora, Olive Snyder and her sisters all worked in some capacity while residing at home. In 1895, Olive offered music lessons in town;[109] she later worked as a domestic servant, making a modest income of $200.[110] Most historians link women's placement in the social hierarchy with that of their husband or father, and here I mostly consider women as similarly linked to their husbands or fathers in the hierarchies of their communities. Historian Leo Johnson notes that "although women did occasionally cross class lines, their movement invariably came about either because their husbands or fathers had crossed those lines, or the woman had married into a different class from that of her father."[111]

Of course, this does not mean that they were considered men's equals, or that they expressed their status and identity in the same way men did.

Generally, individuals and families demonstrated their class identities in combination with other aspects of their lives, such as social relations, housing, clothing, and a wide range of cultural practices, including their choice of leisure activities. Though categorized separately, the farm wives and daughters who are cited in this study were largely middle class in the sense that they joined voluntary societies, performed unpaid labour for their churches, and displayed other qualities that fit within definitions of middle-class respectability. Broader and more qualitative indicators of socio-economic standing, such as moral character, community involvement, achievement in the arts (such as musical education), devotion to home and family, and ancestry (particularly when descended from a founding family) are also employed in this study to better understand economic distinctions and identify women's social groupings.

In terms of the presence of a distinguishable assemblage of elite families or individuals, there are variances between the towns under study. In Tillsonburg, and to a lesser extent Dresden, the vast wealth of a few families was derived mostly from natural resource extraction and agro-industrial milling enterprises. Deep roots and links to early community settlement also bestowed on this group an enhanced level of prestige. The number of streets named in honour of these families, for instance, demonstrates the reverence with which they were held in their respective communities. In Tillsonburg, the two families who arguably occupied the highest social echelon—the Tillsons and, to a lesser extent, the Sinclairs—were related through marriage.

In July 1850, twenty-year-old Mary Ann Van Norman married twenty-five-year-old E.D. Tillson in Tillsonburg. The couple had seven children: Nancy Margaret, Catherine Marilla ("Lillie"), Frederick Bloomfield, Benjamin DeWitt, Harriet Adele ("Hattie"), George Whiting, and Edwin Van Norman (E.V.).[112] When E.D. died in February 1902, the *Tillsonburg Liberal* referred to him as not only "our first citizen" but also the town's "most honored citizen."[113] Though the financial success of E.D.'s many businesses provided the family with opportunities to live a far more lavish lifestyle than

Figure 5. E.D. and Mary Ann Tillson, later nineteenth century. Source: ANHS, Photograph Collection.

any other in town, Mary Ann was well-respected in her own right because of her Van Norman lineage.

In 1876, daughter Lillie married Lachlin Sinclair, a widower and well-known physician, politician, and Worshipful Master of the Masonic lodge. The marriage established Lillie as one of the town's pre-eminent hostesses. The Sinclairs' two daughters—Lillian Mary, born in 1879, and Marguerite Van Norman, born in 1883—had countless social advantages, including world travel, summers spent in Muskoka, and time to pal around with their Tillson cousins in town. The Sinclair girls were also part of larger social circles beyond Tillsonburg, often being invited to social functions in nearby towns and cities.

The grandiose houses that the Tillsons and Sinclairs began constructing in the late 1870s and early 1880s became tangible and public symbols of their positions atop the social hierarchy. Named Annandale House for Mary Ann's maternal Scottish roots, the Tillson home was located on Cranberry Avenue (now Tillson Avenue), which was considered the town's easterly limits at the time. Dubbed one of the "finest in Canada,"[114] the house took several years to build and was completed in 1887. It was constructed of yellow brick from

Figure 6. Annandale House at the time its exterior construction was completed, c. 1883.
Source: ANHS, Photograph Collection.

the Tillson brickyard and contained three floors of elaborately decorated
rooms. The painted motifs on the ceilings of the first- and second-floor rooms
marked the home as one of the most distinctive in the country. Just before
the Tillsons began constructing their home, an article in the *Observer* noted
that the estimated cost was $8,000, though the final tally was around $30,000.
Clearly disapproving of the Tillsons' very public display of wealth, the author
remarked that "many other citizens are erecting less pretentious homes."[115]

Figure 7. Marguerite and Lillian Sinclair, with the Sinclair mansion in the background, early 1890s. Source: ANHS, Photograph Collection.

The Sinclairs' mansion, located just northwest of Annandale House on Lisgar Avenue, was renowned for its grand walnut staircase and ballroom.[116] When construction began, the *Observer* noted that the "fine mansion" was to be built of "stone and brick" and would cost "$8,000 or $10,000." Upon completion, the *Observer* believed, it would be "one of the finest and most commodious dwellings in Ontario."[117]

In Dresden, the distinguishable (yet small) upper class was largely composed of McVean family members. Catherine McVean, whose name is now synonymous with the establishment of Dresden's branch of the Imperial Order Daughters of the Empire (IODE) in 1914, married hub and spoke factory owner Osgoode McVean in 1883, and the marriage produced eight children. Jeffrey Carter and Marie Carter write that it was Osgoode and his brother William who "made the McVean name synonymous with affluence and luxury."[118] In their later years, the two brothers "had an affinity for fine things," including having their lunch shipped to them via train from Toronto's Royal York Hotel.[119] Osgoode and Catherine lived in one of the finest houses in Dresden, a large brick residence called Georgia Place that was built in 1907 and located in the affluent "Quality Hill" neighbourhood on Hughes Street. Other McVean family members also resided in that part of town and their factories were located just west of the homes, adjacent to the Sydenham River. Despite their propensity to display affluence, the McVeans were well-respected in the community and Catherine was seen as "a public-spirited individual."[120] With her material wealth, a widely recognized name, and a domestic servant to oversee home matters, Catherine was afforded the privilege of becoming deeply involved in community affairs. By the time she was involved with organizing the IODE, her youngest child was fourteen years old, allowing Catherine more time to devote to club membership and other hobbies.

The small population densities of Dresden, Tillsonburg, and Elora meant that local elites might reach out to people of similar socio-economic status elsewhere in the province, but in town they could not maintain social circles that were exclusively composed of similarly endowed individuals. The broad social category of "middle class" citizens whom elites often socialized with is the most difficult to define in Dresden, Tillsonburg, and Elora because this "new" social grouping was "the most novel product of late nineteenth-century economic change."[121] Holman argues that mostly, the middle class of the late nineteenth century was "transitory, incohesive, and amorphous."[122] In Dresden, Tillsonburg, and Elora, where notices of businesses opening and closing were common and professionals experienced varied levels of financial success, the middle class contained the largest group of citizens who moved up and down the social ladder with regularity.

As noted by E.P. Thompson in his seminal work, *The Making of the English Working Class*,[123] beyond occupational and economic distinctions were the shared culture and experiences that gave middle-class men, women, and families a communal sense of identity. Like the towns of Ingersoll, Thorold, and Campbellford studied by Lynne Marks, middle-class residents in Dresden, Tillsonburg, and Elora had parallel "values, beliefs, and lifestyles" that helped them to distinguish themselves and one another from the local elite or the working class.[124] Historians have identified some of the more pervasive commonalities among middle-class men and women, including a strong work ethic, philanthropy, and being family- or child-centred.[125] Women's diaries, letters, and reminiscences attest to the prevalence of such middle-class cultural practices in these towns. The importance of religion in their lives also bonded middle-class individuals. Churches in Dresden, Tillsonburg, and Elora were largely located in middle-class residential areas that were a block or two away from the main street. Aside from worship, churches served as social centres in neighbourhoods, particularly for women, and involvement in church-sponsored leisure activities was an important marker of middle-class respectability. Membership in educational or self-improvement societies, reciprocal visiting with friends and family, hosting and attending teas and dinners, and participating in amateur sports were also ingrained in the lives of the middle class.

No matter how fluid or flexible the class structures of Dresden, Tillsonburg, and Elora were, individual citizens (and particularly working-class ones) understood where they ranked in relation to others in the local social hierarchy. Born in 1880,[126] one of three children whose father was a farmer, Agnes Waller remembered how she and her family often encountered E.D. and Mary Ann Tillson in public. Waller's brother was employed at one of E.D.'s mill offices and because of this, Waller recalls, the Tillsons would stop and talk to Agnes and her family. She says Mary Ann referred to her as "little darling" and would allow Agnes and her brother to play and skate on their trout pond. Waller remembered Mary Ann as not especially friendly though she grew to become so "as she got older and sicker." Her opinion was that "the Tillsons esp. E.D. & M.A. [were] reserved due to class structure."[127] Even in her youth, Waller was aware of the Tillsons' socio-economic rank in town and understood that her brother's position in the mill office facilitated this connection between two families of disparate status.

Other less privileged residents also understood their position in the local social order. In the memoirs of long-time Tillsonburg resident Bert Newman, there are frequent mentions of how his working-class background shaped the social and work opportunities available to him. At times he revels in his modest upbringing, boasting how he often "made his own fun" or found ways around financial constraints when it came to enjoying leisure.[128] His acute awareness of who composed the local elite intensified when he was tasked with delivering groceries to hostesses he likened to the American "Four Hundred,"[129] a moniker for prominent Gilded Age New Yorkers. Any confusion or lingering questions about where citizens sat in the town's socio-economic hierarchy could be clarified after perusing the local newspaper. Because of smaller population densities, small-town weeklies were able to report in detail on the dinner parties, soirées, theatricals, and fundraisers being hosted by upper- and middle-class men and women. Lists of guests and attendees often accompanied these stories, signifying that some events were invitation-only affairs dominated by the elite and their affluent middle-class friends.

Another indication of the fluidity of class structures in these towns was that changes in economic circumstances and/or family dynamics did not always alter how citizens viewed themselves or were viewed by others in local society. Elora politician Charles Clarke, for instance, was an "educated immigrant" from England who evolved from "modest beginnings to a position of substance and respectability," in keeping with the tenets of nineteenth-century liberalism.[130] Biographer Kenneth C. Dewar describes the family as middle class in rank and status while Clarke was married to his first wife, Emma, who refused to associate herself and the family with "anything that smacked of aristocratic pretension," like employing full-time servants. She believed that "servants hindered intimacy within a household, encouraged 'tattle' without, and generally made one feel slightly insecure."[131] Though suffering from a debilitating illness, she allowed only "day help" in the Clarke home.

Three years after Emma succumbed to tuberculosis in 1878, fifty-four-year-old Charles married eighteen-year-old Rose Halley. Though age-gap relationships were common in the nineteenth century (and especially when the groom was a widower), the union still sparked controversy in and around Elora. Clarke's children, all older than his new bride, disapproved of the marriage, resulting in strained relations among family members for several years. Outside of the family, Rose's Irish Catholic heritage and Clarke's English Protestant roots provoked "strong reactions" from Elorans who disapproved of interfaith unions.[132] Despite this, Clarke went on to serve as the Member of Provincial Parliament for the ridings of Wellington Centre and then Wellington East, as well as Speaker of the House and Chairman of the Public Accounts Committee in the Liberal government of Premier Oliver Mowat. During that time, Charles and Rose hobnobbed with Toronto high society, including Mowat and his wife, Jane, who were charmed by Rose's youth and vibrancy.[133] Outside of town, the couple's differences appear to have mattered very little to their new-found friends and acquaintances.

Charles and Rose had three children together and shared a love of literature. Rose became a writer and worked as a reporter for the *Elora Express*. Data from the 1891 census demonstrate the changing socio-economic dynamics within the Clarke family. Though Charles had initially agreed with first wife Emma's disapproval of employing full-time help, by 1891, when three young children had joined the Clarke household, Charles and Rose employed three live-in domestics, one of whom was a nurse.[134] Though he had the privilege and ability to afford household help, only two years earlier Clarke had written in his diary that he did not believe that "Providence" had "blessed [him] monetarily." He revelled, instead, in a different kind of richness, that of his "loving wife, three attractive and loving children, and an unruffled family circle."[135]

When discussing the leisure patterns of elite and middle-class women living in small-town Ontario, it is imperative that the assistance of domestic servants be acknowledged. In the late nineteenth and early twentieth centuries, employing domestics was considered "crucial to the creation and elaboration of a respectable bourgeois home and lifestyle" in both large cities and small towns. According to historian Magda Fahrni, "the hallmark of a middle-class household was the financial ability to maintain at least one servant; the servant, then, was a status symbol."[136] As the disposable wealth of the late Victorian middle and upper classes rose and greater pressure was placed on women to maintain high standards of cleanliness and tidiness, paid help alleviated the incessant burden of household chores. Some, like Emma Clarke, preferred "dailies" who arrived in the morning and left in the evening, often hired for a specific task such as housekeeping or laundry. Others employed full-time help who resided with the family and oversaw all manner of domestic labour. Historians note that the job was a very transient one; the drudgery, loneliness, physical labour, and oftentimes abuse that accompanied domestic service forced many women to seek other employment. Wages also varied considerably, depending on the employer's generosity and the domestic's breadth of responsibilities. According to Fahrni, in 1901 the average wage for domestics in Canada was $120 per year.[137] She further notes that servants in rural areas typically made less than their urban counterparts. However, in Dresden, Tillsonburg, and Elora, most domestics made somewhere between $150 and $275 annually, according to the census. In 1901, wealthy Eloran John McGowan paid his twenty-three-year-old domestic $300, while the twenty-one-year-old domestic in William McVean's home in Dresden earned $200.[138] Notices for help appeared regularly in small-town newspapers because of the job's high turnover rate, so it is difficult to track how many women in Dresden, Tillsonburg, and Elora employed domestics unless one was residing with the family when the census was enumerated.

Based on available data, it appears that most women in these communities who employed live-in domestics were the wives of local manufacturers and more successful merchants, politicians, and professionals. Data from the 1891 census indicate that both Lillie Sinclair and Mary Ann Tillson employed full-time help. Mary Ann appears to have constantly been in search of what she considered "trustworthy" domestics, based on the number of advertisements she posted in the *Observer*.[139] According to the 1901 census, in Dresden Catherine McVean employed a twenty-year-old Black woman named Louisa.[140] A small handful of households earning more modest incomes from trades like tailoring or photography, for example, also employed domestics. Hiring "dailies" was a more common practice among the middle class, particularly at certain times of the year or when hosting larger and more involved social events. At other times women relied on the help and labour of friends, family, and neighbours when organizing gatherings or other social activities.

Farm women rarely hired domestic help; mothers and their older daughters usually performed most of the household work, thereby saving the expense of a hired girl.[141] In both farming and non-farming families in Elora, several young women were listed as "house keepers" in the 1901 census. Unlike domestics who lived away from home and were not related to their employers, housekeepers tended to be older, unmarried daughters residing with their aging parents or elder siblings. Census data indicate that some earned a wage. In 1901 thirty-five-year-old Ellen Dalton, for example, lived with her brother Henry (a barber) and his family in Elora and made eighty-four dollars a year in her role as "house keeper."[142] Though employing full-time domestics allowed women like Mary Ann Tillson, Lillie Sinclair, and Catherine McVean a greater degree of freedom to pursue leisure activities and other social obligations outside the home, less privileged women still maintained active social lives, though they often had to manoeuvre their socializing into the rhythms of daily life, which meant visiting with or helping one another while completing domestic chores such as sewing, quilting, or cooking.

Setting the Stage for Leisure: Later Nineteenth-Century Developments

Though they somewhat differed socially, geographically, economically, and to a lesser extent ethnically, Dresden, Tillsonburg, and Elora all experienced similar developments and changes to the ways that citizens interacted with one another, occupied public and private spaces, and enjoyed leisure activities between 1870 and 1914. Such transformations are often associated with communities that experienced rapid population and economic growth in the late nineteenth century,[143] but Dresden and Tillsonburg's limited growth and even Elora's slight population decline did not prevent an expansion in opportunities for leisure and recreation for all citizens, and women especially. In these towns, as elsewhere in the province, local governments altered the physical landscape by installing modern lighting and sewer systems, laying sidewalks, smoothing roads, and tending to green spaces as they embraced progressive ideas about infrastructure that enhanced day-to-day life. In small towns, failure to devote time and effort to beautifying and refurbishing vacant fields and town land, as Bouchier notes, "increasingly became a social embarrassment—a sign of backwardness."[144] Reconfiguring the natural spaces of these communities was also part of a larger colonial project; the expansion of White settlement was dependent on various transformations that made the land "civilized" and thus capable of attracting White settlers and economic opportunities.

The men of these communities had long found opportunities for socializing in a variety of public spaces, such as fraternal halls, hotels, and barrooms, but until the 1880s few spaces were constructed with both men and women in mind, or women specifically. In Dresden, Tillsonburg, Elora, and scores of other small towns, the period between the 1880s and 1914 witnessed a massive growth in the establishment of town halls, opera houses, theatres, dance platforms and halls, sports fields and facilities, parks, picnic grounds, fairgrounds, and driving parks. In their respective newspapers' "progress edition," reporters exulted over their town's new recreational offerings, boasting that they were the best and most spacious available anywhere. This would not have been possible, however, without the efforts of local municipal councils, religious organizations, and civic improvement associations to construct or restore venues that housed a variety of religious, secular, associational, and commercial entertainments. Aside from catering to citizens' needs, recreational facilities were also "designed to show off their town's progressivism"[145] and signified a collective respectability. Concurrently, expanded transportation networks in the way of rail lines, stagecoach services, and steamer excursions facilitated the movement of more goods and people at a faster rate. These networks also tied small towns and rural areas more closely to larger cities and expanded opportunities to draw a wider variety of shows, entertainers, and audiences.

Constructing new sites for leisure or feminizing ones already standing was a conscious act. Largely, it was town councils and local (male) elites who decided what should be built or refurbished and the purpose it would serve. Women do not appear to have had any agency in this regard, apart from organizing and hosting fundraisers that helped finance the construction or maintenance of these buildings, or through some behind-the-scenes lobbying. Most venues were meant to cater to mixed-sex audiences, but middle-class women in particular came to be regarded as an untapped financial resource; filling a seat at a public entertainment meant money being reinvested in the local economy. At the same time, it is worth considering how much these public halls and the desire to attract female patrons were a reaction to some of the more pressing social concerns of the time—especially the loss of "good" young women to larger urban areas and what seemed to be an increase in subversive leisure activities occurring both publicly and privately. These new venues acted as another moral regulator by drawing women in and offering them reputable entertainment in a public setting.

As will be discussed more thoroughly in Chapter 2, town halls and opera houses were arguably the most important social centres in Dresden, Tillsonburg, and Elora, and instrumental in facilitating options for a greater number of women to pursue leisure activities, both as spectators and as organizers. Prior to the late nineteenth century, most communal leisure activities took place in schools, churches, or hotels. The building of civic halls, however, represents not only "a shift away from reliance upon schools and churches"[146] but also a recognition of the need to accommodate larger numbers of women, children, and entire families. According to scholar Charlotte M. Canning, "it was the rare small town that did not have an opera house or academy of music."[147] These large brick or stone structures and their surrounding green spaces not only gave the town a facelift of sorts, they also served as symbols of civic pride that local politicians hoped would "translate into economic growth and investment."[148] Not just the buildings themselves but the materials they were constructed of were emblems of progress. According to Wetherell and Kmet, "brick and stone were permanent, non-combustible, high-status materials. Their expense confirmed that the town's future was secure and warranted investment."[149]

Located in Elora at Metcalfe and Clyde Streets on the south side of the Grand River is the Drill Shed/Armoury Hall, which currently houses an LCBO (Liquor Control Board of Ontario) franchise. The building was constructed for the Elora Rifle Company to use during the Fenian Raids in 1865. Though a considerable population of Irish residents lived in Elora at the time, the town's citizens, like many others in Upper Canada, feared the repercussions of an Irish invasion, so the Elora Rifle Company was sent to Chatham for six weeks in 1866 to help protect the border.[150] Only a year later, the building was hosting public entertainments,[151] and eventually the "handsome stone structure"[152] became the primary setting for the town's social functions and entertainments after a stage, furnace, and lighting fixtures were installed. Soon after, an elliptical front and footlights were installed on the stage to accommodate a wider variety of performances.[153] In 1886, a dancing platform and picnic grounds were constructed in the grove at the rear of the hall, used primarily in the summertime by locals and day-trippers.[154] In 1905, the federal government acquired the building after it fell into disrepair, and soon after it received a makeover, when it was renamed Armoury Hall and improved with electric lighting and hardwood flooring.[155] The building is unique in that most small-town entertainment halls were constructed in and around the market square, town square, or "main street," where important services like post offices, courthouses, banks, hotels, and retail shops were clustered in a central location. This commercial hub was a town's focal point and usually the first section to be electrified and paved. Because of its original purpose, Armoury Hall was considered beyond the town's "core" by the late nineteenth century, when Elora's downtown was principally located north of the Grand River around Mill and Geddes Streets. At the time the Drill

Shed was constructed, however, most business was conducted south of the river, where the town's initial settlement had been located.

In Dresden, a two-storey town hall was built in 1864 on the town's Market Square, located two blocks west of bustling St. George Street. The upper floor contained a stage and served as a concert hall, while the lower floor was used as a marketplace and the town's jail.[156] Common throughout small-town Ontario, town halls were often multi-functional, bringing local authorities, trade, commerce, and entertainment together under one roof. Another venue, Shaw's Opera House, was built later in Dresden at the corner of Lindsley and St. George Streets.[157] References to a privately owned Wright's Hall also appear in the *Dresden Times*. Especially during the 1870s and 1880s, when town halls were just beginning to be built, some enterprising local entrepreneurs established private concert halls on the upper floors of their businesses, which "were meant to make money or at least to break even."[158] In Tillsonburg, a few local businessmen owned entire blocks on Broadway Street, and many contained their own upper-level concert hall.[159]

Tillsonburg's first full-fledged community hall appears to have been the Sons of Temperance Hall on Broadway Street, which housed the earliest comedic and theatrical troupes to arrive in the 1870s along with the conventional religious lectures and fundraising socials. By 1880, it was known as the more generic Sons Music Hall.[160] Though the town considered itself progressive, local historian Laurel Beechey explains that an official town hall was not constructed in Tillsonburg until 1898 because citizens feared its construction and ongoing maintenance would be a burden on taxpayers.[161] The finished hall, a large and imposing red brick structure located just off Broadway Street in the Market Square, consisted of three floors. As with Dresden's town hall, the basement was used as a marketplace. The main floor housed the municipal council chambers and fire hall while the opera house was located on the upper floor. Beneficial to both government officials and the citizenry, the building of the town hall brought important political, economic, and social services together in one commodious and centrally located dwelling.

Figure 8. Tillsonburg's town hall/opera house, c. 1910. Source: ANHS, Photograph Collection.

In April 1898, the *Observer* toured readers through the newly constructed opera house, calling attention to the high ceiling, from which hung electric lights, and the plethora of windows that dotted the white walls on each side. There was ample seating for 650 spectators, with raised terraces on the floor to ensure all spectators had an "equally advantageous view." Electric footlights illuminated the stage, with its "gracefully overarched [...] concave ceiling adorned with ornamental tracery by the painter's brush." A variety of painted scenes had been prepared in anticipation of the entertainments to come. The inaugural play at the opera house was *All the Comforts of Home*, performed by the Wesley Stock Co. The proceeds from ticket sales were directed toward the completion of reading rooms on the hall's second floor.[162] Beechey says "reserved seating" for the event cost fifty cents, which some citizens complained was exorbitant.[163]

Such efforts to modernize and revolutionize the ways that citizens socialized with one another and pursued leisure contradicts some of the critiques from turn-of-the-century reformers and social commentators, who argued that the lack of healthful leisure was responsible for stagnant population growth in some areas of rural and small-town Ontario.[164] In Dresden, Tillsonburg, and Elora, however, options for "respectable" recreation were plentiful. By the First World War, several social clubs, charitable societies, amateur sports teams, public and commercial entertainments, socials and dinners, parties, and games were available to townsfolk and residents of the surrounding areas. Indeed, as historian and educator David Mizener explains, "rural and urban people came to share the same pleasure preferences because of exposure to 'modern systems of transportation and communication.'"[165] Weekly newspapers in these towns kept locals up-to-date on global, national, provincial, and regional developments, provided advice on a variety of household and agricultural concerns, and served as a sort of social barometer by announcing the various activities occurring in and around the community.

Rarely isolated from one another, rural and town dwellers came into frequent contact with visitors (and with each other) through the exchange of services, goods, leisure, and news. In these service centres, many merchants needed and relied on the business of the adjacent rural population. It became important for towns to offer amusement and education to rural and farming families, because leisure helped draw business. When rural men and women came to town to shop, post letters, or do their banking, they used the opportunity to visit with friends and family, support a local fundraiser, or attend a club meeting. They might spend the morning shopping in the marketplace in the basement of the town hall and then see a matinee performance in the upper-level theatre. Kate Aitken, a prominent figure in Canadian media in the first half of the twentieth century, was keenly aware of the social interactions that occurred in her small town of Beeton in Simcoe County (located approximately eighty kilometres northeast of Elora). Born in 1891, Aitken was the daughter of a shopkeeper, and in 1956 published a memoir titled *Never a Day So Bright*. She recalls that while growing up, she felt envious of the farm children "who were allowed to come to town every Saturday night, roam up and down the streets enjoying all the festivities." She also recalls the courting couples that came to town. After securing their buggy, the couple often "parted, the lad to meet his friends, his lady-love to do her own shopping. Then later on they would rendezvous at Stewarts' Ice-cream Parlour, enjoy a huge heaping dish of the frozen custard and then he would drive her home."[166]

As much as these towns appeared to be embracing modern and progressive modes of living, they also upheld and defended symbols of agrarianism and country living, including a sense of moral superiority, piety, hard work, neighbourliness, reverence for their settler pasts, and the maintenance of kin networks. "Modernity did not precipitate a wholesale alteration of social practices and recreational preferences in the countryside," Mizener argues. Rather, "men and women used these technologies to reinforce and expand upon their existing customs."[167] As subsequent chapters will detail, many popular leisure activities from this period offer a window into populations grappling with ways to reconcile their deep-seated traditional values and practices while they selectively embraced modernity. In these communities, we increasingly see a "blending of new urban traits and traditional rural values."[168] Especially after the 1890s, popular and long-standing modes of leisure like garden parties and charitable fundraisers began to take on more sophisticated and cosmopolitan characteristics that were borrowed from advertisements and columns in city dailies and North American women's magazines. By implementing trendy themes, decorations, and motifs, locals conveyed their own sense of the wider popular culture of the time as well as a practical awareness that novel forms of entertainment generally garnered more interest and enthusiasm from participants.

Conclusion

Though Dresden, Tillsonburg, and Elora were settled and populated by somewhat different ethnic, cultural, and religious groups who derived their economic livelihoods from various kinds of agricultural and industrial production, their subsequent growth is indicative of some of the more fundamental changes occurring across small-town Ontario in the late nineteenth and early twentieth centuries. To varying degrees, by the start of the First World War many townscapes had received or were in the process of undergoing dramatic renovations. New modes of transportation, a modern public works system, the construction of municipal buildings, widespread efforts to beautify green spaces and waterways, formalized schooling, and a breadth of professional and commercial services represent just some of the ways that these communities matured from rustic outposts in the mid-nineteenth century to bustling country towns by 1914.

Despite their moderate size, Dresden, Tillsonburg, and Elora were undoubtedly socially stratified places. Disparate levels of wealth and prestige resulted in groupings of identifiable elites responsible for employing large numbers of skilled and unskilled workers at their profitable mills and factories. By far, the largest category of citizens in Dresden, Tillsonburg, and Elora was the White, Anglo-Celtic, Christian middle class, a group composed of small business owners, professionals, politicians, and other service providers who were connected by their commitment to hard work, religious devotion, and upholding family values. Concurrent with the growth in religious, commercial, and social services was the expansion of cultural offerings for these middle-class citizens who were eager to demonstrate their own respectability and that of their towns.

Even in their earliest days, Dresden, Tillsonburg, and Elora were not devoid of religious lectures, political debates, and temperance oratories, but audiences were almost wholly composed of men. Where schools and churches once housed most communal social events, by the later nineteenth century opera houses, town halls, and concert halls were increasingly being built with entertainment (and larger, mixed-sex audiences) in mind. Not only did these institutions provide more in the way of recreational offerings, but the proliferation of halls and churches was also a conscious effort on the part of local municipal officials to convince surrounding towns and cities that they, too, were modern, progressive, and permanent. Here we see the strength of settler colonialism and Euro-Canadian ideas about land ownership and occupation at the time; altering the physical landscape of these towns and erecting permanent structures contributed to the removal of Indigenous people from these regions and reinforced the belief that the land stewarded by them was now available for White settlement and profit. As the following chapter reveals, churches and their ancillary activities remained important social institutions well into the twentieth century, but the changing physical and cultural landscapes of Dresden, Tillsonburg, and Elora offered upper- and middle-class women more options for leisure outside of church and charity and resulted in the reconfiguration and feminization of traditionally male-dominated public spaces.

TWO

A Reconnaissance of Recreation:
Leisure in Public Spaces

N THE 21 December 1871 issue of the *Tillsonburg Observer*, a letter to
the editor was published under the heading "How Very Lady-Like." Using
the pseudonym "JUNIUS Jun.," the author informed readers that five
young women had recently snuck into a local church with the intention of
spying on a group of men meeting as a newly organized literary association.
The (presumably) male author identified the women's "inquisitiveness" as a
"distinguishing trait of female character" and further likened their actions
to that of "some Biddy or Molly of Stanley street notoriety," suggesting they
were brazen and low class. Condescendingly labelling them "dear little pets,"
the author reasoned that their "over-stepp[ing] the bounds of prudence" was
either a crippling fear that the association was corrupting the men's morals
or that the women just happened to be "strong admirers of eloquence."
Instead of worrying about such nonsense, the author declared, the women
should stay home and "nurs[e] some of their recently castaway dolls." The
infantilizing and misogynistic rant concluded by stating that the women
ought to have recognized the error of their ways, since "forbidden fruit is
ever bitter, and forbidden joys though they may give a momentary pleasure,
leave a bitter sting behind."[1]

Various motives may explain the reasons behind the women's decision to
leave their so-called private sphere to spy on the men's literary association.

As JUNIUS Jun. states, perhaps they were fearful that the meeting did not have benevolent intentions. The women also could have just been curious about the association and its objectives. Or by infiltrating a male-dominated gathering where they were clearly unwelcome, were these women demonstrating a similar desire to have an intellectual retreat away from home and family? While the author's allusion to "forbidden fruit" and "forbidden joys" is a reminder of the consequences of Eve's folly in the Garden of Eden, it also seems to reference the imagined boundaries that marked where men's and women's leisure activities ought to and often did take place at the time, and what might happen if women stepped beyond their prescribed sphere.

Though this incident demonstrates that men "viewed 'clubland' as a male terrain and were wary of women's incursions into the public cultural sphere,"[2] by the later nineteenth century the ideological construct of gendered spheres was increasingly being challenged and negotiated by women. As work by Canadian women's historians has shown, these discursive prescriptions were neither fixed nor static, nor did the separate spheres doctrine explain the trajectory of many women's lives. Indeed, as religious scholar Jeanne Halgren Kilde has argued, "women frequently entered supposedly off-limits public space."[3] Between 1870 and 1914, Dresden, Tillsonburg, and Elora experienced marked socio-economic changes, greater opportunities for mobility, more modern communication methods, the erection of public buildings, the novelty of commercialized entertainment, and the blossoming of a mainstream consumer culture, resulting in a reordering of the ways that public spaces were utilized and occupied in these communities. Though women still faced barriers when it came to engaging in the spheres of governance, law-making, and commerce, the built space of "the public," including its streets, sidewalks, and structures, was becoming a more mixed-sex territory. An important manifestation of these changes was the myriad ways that women, both those living within town and individuals from the surrounding rural areas, began enjoying leisure and recreational activities in public.

Some earlier studies of leisure in the Western world created a problematic juxtaposition in characterizing "public" leisure activities as coarse and masculine, and "private" recreation as refined and woman-appropriate. The exception has been the study of public leisure under the aegis of the church and charitable organizations, along with Canadian studies of self- and civic-improvement clubs with local and provincial branches.[4] Such stark distinctions between the meanings of public and private leisure meant that the presence and visibility of Canadian women in public prior to the First World War, whether urban or rural, has not received adequate attention. But as women's and gender historians continue to demonstrate, there were countless other ways that women engaged with personal pleasures and hobbies outside of home and work.

This chapter adds another dimension to those studies by providing a reconnaissance of the continuities and changes in small-town women's involvement in leisure activities outside the home, examining their participation in traditional church- and charity-related activities but also going beyond to assess how different forces at play contributed to increasing numbers of women gaining a more public presence through their leisure. In the American context, cultural historian David Nasaw contends that though women around the turn of the century remained "the emblems and guarantors of middle- and working-class respectability," they were also "challenging the notion that the only proper amusements for the 'gentler sex' were those that were sponsored by church or confined to the home."[5] As this chapter shows, such a shift meant that the proprietors and organizers of public amusements had to adjust the tone of their offerings by domesticating and feminizing those pastimes once deemed "raw" or "rough,"[6] such as theatre and musicales, in order to attract female spectators and participants. Women also exerted agency in this regard by spearheading the organization of groups or planning events with their own interests in mind.

The distinctive class structures of Dresden, Tillsonburg, and Elora unquestionably shaped the leisure activities that women sought beyond the home. Socio-economic status dictated how much time and money women could devote to leisure, though it should be noted that "not all distractions required cash outlays."[7] Some women and girls living in rural areas, for example, mention going to town despite the fact that there was "nothing doing" that day.[8] The hustle and bustle of a Saturday morning or the simple sights and sounds of a Monday afternoon were enough to draw women out to the streets and into public buildings. For rural youth in particular, a nearby town was an "important location for social life."[9] Watching parades and processions or listening to the town band perform on a Saturday night were much enjoyed and cost nothing. The Dresden Concert Band, for instance, was a well-known brass ensemble first organized in 1876 that provided entertainment in the town bandshell, at picnics and other public entertainments, and on steamer excursions to nearby Walpole Island and other points of interest.[10]

Figure 9. Members of the Citizens' Band of Dresden, 1895. Source: DA, Jim Coyle Collection.

While working-class residents in Dresden, Tillsonburg, and Elora were more likely than the middle and upper classes to attend these free events, diaries and letters that would provide evidence of their activities have been difficult to locate or were never composed because of time and literacy constraints. Though local newspapers published details about most events happening in town, what appeared in print tended to reflect the social habits of the upper and middle classes. Consequently, little has been gleaned from available sources about the ways less privileged women in these towns enjoyed leisure outside the home. But just as upper- and middle-class women sought out various amusements, we can assume the working class did as well, when possible and affordable.

Though the homes of middle- and upper-class women remained choice venues in which to host and attend a variety of leisure activities (as Chapter 4 will demonstrate), women increasingly strove to balance their domestic recreations with those taking place outside the home; for some, this was necessary to "preserve their mental health."[11] In small-town Ontario, the period between 1870 and 1914 saw a massive growth in the number of leisure activities that women not only participated in but also planned, shaped, and promoted in public. By the First World War, secular amusements were rivalling the traditional (though still enormously popular) church and charity work. As British historian Amanda Vickery rightly notes, committee work signalled "an expansion of the female role, not a diminution,"[12] but as will be shown, church activities began to be integrated with other forms of leisure and thus will be discussed here as part of a much broader framework of women's culture.

This chapter focuses on three important ways that women engaged in leisure in public spaces: through activities linked to or initiated by churches; in public and commercial entertainments; and as part of local, provincial, and national women's associations. Sources indicate that such activities were the most popular among middle- and upper-class women and helped to equalize the gender balance in public. These activities also demonstrate how the notion of personal fulfillment, rather than the good of the collective, was becoming more important as women used leisure to nurture their social, physical, emotional, and intellectual well-being. These activities also represent some of the more recognizable ways women embraced greater opportunities to participate in civic improvement initiatives and were instrumental in providing important niches for females of different ages, class groupings, marital statuses, and ethnic backgrounds outside of the domestic sphere.

Religion

Throughout the later nineteenth century, despite a boom in the building of secular recreation halls in Dresden, Tillsonburg, and Elora, religious institutions remained the locus of countless leisure activities and a vital component of each town's social life. For many late nineteenth-century Canadians, regardless of their class or ethnic background, piety was entrenched in social and cultural norms and acted as an important signifier of respectability and refinement. Ideologically, though the churches "did not exist to entertain their members or to serve their social needs," growing concerns over decreasing congregation sizes and congregants' morals meant that church officials had no choice but to acknowledge leisure and integrate its purpose into religious teachings. "In doing so," however, "they attempted to 'elevate its objectives' to improve character and morality."[13] Efforts to curtail the growing number of "immoral" and "disreputable" leisure practices resulted in churches offering more "wholesome" and "proper" amusements under their auspices, broadly dubbed "rational recreation." The definition of reputable leisure, however, varied from region to region and town to town. In Elora, for instance, two religious zealots who enjoyed preaching near the local baseball field became involved in a "brawl" with players after they criticized the much-beloved game as "belonging to the devil."[14]

The increasingly close relationship that developed between religion and leisure was also affected by a church-building boom that transpired in many communities across southern Ontario in the latter third of the nineteenth century. Parallel to town halls and arenas, newly built churches symbolized for their respective communities "urban maturity, prosperity, and vitality," as well as confirming that the townsfolk were "solidly Christian."[15] In smaller congregations, especially, the cost of building new churches (or repairing older ones) was difficult to support through donation alone,[16] so churches looked to "rational recreation" to fulfill their financial goals. Though religious officials were wary of leisure's growing appeal and steadfastly disapproved of any sort of pleasurable activity that contradicted Christian principles, many began to embrace new recreational offerings, cloaking their worth in the rhetoric of the Social Gospel and moral reform movements.[17] Instrumental music during services, for example, was once cause for debate among Presbyterian clergymen, some of whom referred to organs specifically as the "carnal instrument."[18] By 1900, however, all kinds of music had become a fundamental component of Presbyterian services, prayer meetings, and Sunday school programs.

At the same time, both Protestant and Catholic evangelicals were fighting a losing battle against religious apathy. In that melee, women were lauded as the embodiment of wholesomeness and a formidable force that could bring society back from the brink of ungodliness. Piety had long been associated with feminine virtue; in all aspects of their daily routines, from domestic chores to children's education and their choice of leisure activities, women were to abide by, promote, and represent the Christian doctrine.[19] This notion that women had an innate fondness and proclivity for religious adherence was a pervasive one. In 1895, when a Tillsonburg man was asked whether he supported the idea of women's enfranchisement, he responded that women had no place in politics because "church work would suffer." Typecasting all women as "more spiritual-minded than men," he stated that he liked to "see them so."[20]

The depth of female religiosity during this period only partly accounts for women's higher rate of attendance at church functions when compared to men's.[21] The ways that middle- and upper-class women exercised their piety, such as attending services and becoming involved in auxiliary work, was also a concerted effort to be visible in their communities and to demonstrate respectability. For many, going to church was an important social outing as it was an opportunity to mingle with friends and neighbours. After the service, many continued their socializing into the afternoon by enjoying the midday meal or a cup of tea together. Between 1912 and 1914, the diary entries from Annie Hill of Fergus demonstrate how interwoven church and socializing were. After attending morning services, the married mother of four regularly joined or hosted friends and/or family for lunch and then travelled to Elora for afternoon tea with her grandmother.[22] The evening service offered by many churches also promised social opportunities. Kate Aitken recalls how her mother "got all dressed up and went down to the Methodist church service—whether for religion or for social life, or for a quiet hour uncomplicated by a boisterous family was always a moot question."[23]

The diaries of women who lived in and around Elora communicate how frequently Sundays were characterized by the blending of religious activities and secular socializing. On Sunday, 25 May 1913, Olive Snyder wrote: "Stayed up at Junes & K & I took a walk this PM. All went to Libs after church." On another Sunday one month later, she remarks: "Hot again. Girls over at Libs for tea. Do up to spend the night. Mrs. Godfrey and Lizzie in for a while." Though Snyder went to church most Sundays, her attendance in the summer was more sporadic; ebbs and flows in church attendance were common in smaller communities, especially among the farming population when the demands of the growing season took precedence over church services. In Snyder's diary, other activities occurring on Sundays tended to receive more attention. On Sunday, 22 July 1913, she wrote: "No rain yet. Had a nice tea on lawn at Carters. Went to Library after."[24] Snyder also had no qualms with discussing the times she was less than impressed with the minister, his sermon, or the musical entertainment. On a stormy Sunday in February 1914, she writes that she went to hear "Rev. Kerruish of Fergus preaching." Afterward, she recorded "Me no likee," but does not elaborate on why the sermon and/ or Rev. Kerruish displeased her so.[25] In December 1878, Ann Amelia Day of Eramosa Township mentions attending an evening sermon given by a travelling preacher. She appears to have been looking forward to the event because she says that though "the church was full [...] I was rather disappointed."[26]

Many women did take pleasure in and looked forward to attending church and its ancillary activities, but the "spiritual entertainment"[27] they received on Sundays was often supplemented by other forms of secular recreation. As options for leisure expanded, groups like the Lord's Day Alliance (LDA), first established in Canada in 1888, organized crusades against the increasing number of congregants eschewing church pews for new modes of recreation. Before the LDA was established, local bylaws, such as that passed by Oxford County in 1859, sought to control citizens' choices by criminalizing games and activities like skittles, football, and foot races if they occurred on Sunday.[28] Not all types of leisure were condemned, however; Olive Snyder's tea parties and trips to the library do not seem to have caused angst among Elora's citizens. With little evidence to the contrary, we can assume that most small-town women's Sunday socializing was considered appropriate, even by local Sabbatarians who opposed the use of the Lord's day for anything other than religious reflection.

What concerned devout Sabbatarians the most was that some of the recreations being pursued were considered rough or disreputable in nature. Historian Neil Semple explains that Methodists generally recognized "the advantages of healthy recreation and sports"[29] but disapproved of activities like drinking, gambling, fighting, and smoking, which were thought to promote idleness and threatened the moral order.[30] Such "raucous" behaviour was usually associated with the working class (and men especially). According to Lynne Marks, in small-town Ontario "leisure pursuits that were unacceptable during the week were particularly so on Sunday."[31] Citizens of rural and small-town Ontario were generally characterized as pious, churchgoing people,[32] and local elites were presented as exemplars of such behaviour. When the *Elora Observer* reported in July 1870 that a game of croquet had occurred on a Sunday "within a few feet of the house of one of our magnates," the incident shocked the "moral sense" of neighbours.[33] In 1895, the *Tillsonburg Observer* remarked that a "party of Sunday gamblers" was admonished for their activities in the nearby town of Ingersoll, but according to the local police force, "the same evil exists in Tilsonburg."[34] When needed, local branches of national organizations like the Woman's Christian Temperance Union (WCTU) acted as proxies for the LDA, enforcing and supporting Sunday observance in small towns.[35] Within these groups and among Sabbatarians generally, some women "had a relaxed attitude toward what was permissible on that day," while others strictly abided by the notion that "even the most innocent of games and light reading were forbidden."[36]

In addition to attending services, women in Dresden, Tillsonburg, and Elora were involved in their churches in other ways. In all three towns, the Sunday and Sabbath schools of the Protestant and Catholic churches were popular social and educational institutions for the youth (and sometimes adults) who attended them, as well as for the women who taught them. After marrying a prominent Tillsonburg druggist Charles Thomson in 1881, Jessie McLean gave up her career as a schoolteacher but found an outlet for her passion for education in the Sunday school of Avondale Presbyterian church, where she taught its male congregants for fifty years.[37] In 1900, it was estimated that two-thirds of all Sunday and Sabbath school instructors in Canada were women, the total number amounting to around 22,000.[38] Sunday school teaching was considered a natural vocation for women because of its maternal connotations, as well as satisfying the prescribed womanly duty of spreading the gospel (though not from the pulpit).[39] Sunday school teaching also became "a public space for social interaction and perhaps even for the exercise of some power."[40] In Tillsonburg, Mary Ann Tillson was on the managing committee for the Methodist Sunday school and was often involved in the planning of field trips. Picnicking was one of the children's favourite pastimes. Later in his life Tillson's son E.V. reminisced about his mother's role in organizing one of the more memorable outings for the children: "Mother, at her own expense chartered a train to give the Sunday school children a picnic at Fredericksburg. It was a huge success from the youngsters standpoint and I recall that on the journey home in going through the train, mother found some of the children minus their hats, cap or coats and she promptly replaced them upon arriving in town."[41]

The class distinctions that pervaded late nineteenth-century church participation, such as pew renting and the ordering of pews based on class,[42] resonate in the extravagance with which Mary Ann planned the Sunday school outing. Outside of belonging to the Salvation Army and attending services, working-class women in these towns participated in far fewer religious activities than did their middle- and upper-class counterparts. Surviving auxiliary membership lists, for example, demonstrate how much working-class women were underrepresented in these groups. Reasons for this vary, but "the social gulf may have been too large or the values and interests too different,"[43] even among the most devout Christian women. Moreover, a hotel chambermaid whose meagre income amounted to about $120 annually had little money left over to devote to auxiliary membership

Figure 10. Mount Pleasant Methodist Church (from Nichol Township) Sunday school picnic, Elora Rocks, c. 1892. Source: WCMA, A2005.33, ph 18789.

dues, in addition to the other donations, pecuniary or otherwise, required of group members.[44] Age, dress, appearance, and level of education may also have deterred working-class women from joining groups whose membership was dominated by older and more affluent women. Class did not necessarily define or explain the strength of religious observance in these towns, but the sizable contributions of time, money, effort, and skill that were required to sit on fundraising committees or engage in auxiliary work left working-class women with fewer options for involvement.[45] They certainly would not have been able to manage the personal expense that Mary Ann Tillson undertook when she coordinated the Sunday school picnic to Fredericksburg. Though she took her duties as teacher and mother very seriously and felt an obligation to provide the children of the town with memorable outings, chartering a private train was an opportunity for Tillson to assert her class privilege and display wealth. The more typical Sunday school outings, like sleigh rides or the occasional day trip to a local lake, were far humbler in their cost and scale.

Performing the musical selections offered during church services was another popular and much-enjoyed form of recreation for elite and middle-class women and girls. Proficiency in playing a musical instrument required training, education, and access to an instrument, and most working-class parents could not afford private lessons for their daughters. Since musical talent was a signifier of feminine gentility and respectability, women were urged to use their skills to enhance religious services and social get-togethers.[46] When long-time Tillsonburg resident Ada Thomson died, her obituary paid homage to "her hands and her musical talents," which "never tired through long hours at the piano and gay private parties or church or social events while others danced to her music or sang with her."[47] In small communities, it was common for residents to provide some sort of vocal or instrumental music to accompany both secular and religious gatherings. Specific details of these events, including the names of performers and the pieces they played, regularly appeared in the local newspaper in the days following an event. The glowing reviews suggest that both men and women thoroughly enjoyed a good church concert. Some groups, like the Elora Choral Society, were composed of both male and female participants and their meetings provided a reputable social environment where the sexes could mingle outside of church. Olive Snyder was a member of a choir that met on an almost weekly basis in Elora. When she mentions going to practice in her diary, the entries are often followed by details of the socializing that occurred afterward. In January 1914, she wrote that one evening choir practice ended with "coffee and delicious sandwiches and much conversation."[48] For Snyder, choir practice blended her love of singing *and* socializing.

The large numbers of women who not only faithfully attended choir practice but also joined the more religiously oriented voluntary societies did so because these activities provided some "with their first opportunity to move beyond the home and work together with other women in organized groups."[49] In Dresden, Black and White women were part of Ladies' Aids and guilds that were affiliated with the Methodist church, the Anglican Christ church, and St. Andrew's Presbyterian church. In Tillsonburg, Avondale Presbyterian, St. John's Anglican, and the Methodist church established women's auxiliaries. And Knox Presbyterian and the Wesleyan Methodist church in Elora provided organizations for women, young and old, to join.

In that town, according to historian Stephen Thorning, the social activities arranged by religious organizations "provided women with a public venue to socialize, show off their skills, and give back to their church and community." Indeed, they "began to fulfill a social role in Elora, beyond that of simple religious observation."[50] Auxiliaries were the most popular way for women to engage in leisure activities sponsored by churches, and often they were the first organizations established exclusively for women in small towns and rural areas.[51] Prior to the 1890s, they were arguably the most popular and acceptable places for women to congregate, socialize, and become involved in civic improvement projects outside the home. Even well into the twentieth century when a myriad of social clubs existed in these communities, religious auxiliaries remained a cornerstone of many women's lives.

The ability of auxiliaries to continually attract sizable memberships is evident in the number of references made to their fundraising work in local newspapers. Town and church histories also confirm the worth bestowed on these groups by their communities. Writing many years after the zenith of women's auxiliary work, the authors of the Molly Creek Women's Institute Tweedsmuir History book recognized the local Methodist Ladies' Aid as a "very valuable organization" in Dresden.[52] In many ways, the work that auxiliaries performed mimicked that accomplished by middle-class women in their homes. This transference of domestic skills made auxiliary membership a logical choice for many women. The diligent multi-tasking, for example, that was required to run a home was also valuable in the auxiliary. The activities of Dresden's Christ Church Ladies' Guild provide sufficient evidence of this fact. Initially, Christ Church served a Black Anglican congregation but as the Black community shrank, the church began to fulfill the spiritual needs of White citizens. The very full agenda for one meeting in 1913 contained business related to designating a church cleaning day, followed by a discussion of future socials, and then deciding that the next meeting would be a "sewing meeting."[53] Much like women's home lives, here we see the impossibility of separating the public from the private and religious labour from leisure.

Some historians have argued that the enduring patriarchal structure of churches accounts for auxiliaries' reliance on women's domestic skills for their fundraising efforts. American historian Nancy Grey Osterud, for example, notes that as in the wider gender hierarchy, women in auxiliaries tended to hold subservient positions, donating their labour to clergymen and male church officials.[54] However, the amount of power auxiliaries wielded within their communities and the sorts of activities they oversaw varied greatly. Furthermore, many auxiliaries were meant to be temporary, often existing only until a specific fundraising goal had been achieved. Others were "provid[ed] [with] unique opportunities for community and voice."[55] The Christ Church Ladies' Guild, for example, was responsible for most expenses incurred by the parsonage, including its mortgage, taxes, utilities, and janitorial services.[56] The trust bestowed on the guild and its ability to adeptly manage finances undoubtedly contributed to the church's ability to maintain its parsonage.

The breadth of tasks and responsibilities undertaken by groups such as the Christ Church Ladies' Guild speaks to the efficient and multi-faceted character of women's auxiliaries. These qualities are most apparent when perusing the organizations' surviving minute books. In contrast to the auxiliaries whose "power was very limited,"[57] the Christ Church Ladies' Guild appears to have largely made its own decisions regarding how, when, and why money needed to be raised. The few surviving minute books from the 1910s suggest the guild maintained a regular schedule of meetings and events, typically gathering monthly in the church's rectory or at the home of a member.[58] Meetings were highly structured, overseen by an executive, and any propositions were subject to a group vote. Members paid dues to maintain continuous membership, in addition to donating extra time, money, or fancywork when needed. One of the guild's chief responsibilities was to organize fundraisers, where fastidiousness and frugality were paramount. In 1913, when the idea of holding a fish supper was suggested, members carefully researched the best ways to maximize profits. The details of these bazaars, suppers, and socials, down to every dish served or item sold, were planned, arranged, and conducted by the guild. In advance of an event, "work meetings" were held where members cleaned, decorated, cooked, baked, and sewed.[59] All monies collected were carefully tracked, and final tallies often published in local newspapers. Fundraising ventures could make anywhere from ten dollars to $150, depending on the size and scale of the event and the number of patrons.

While guilds may have faced the burden of incessantly fundraising to ensure the parish's survival, members "undoubtedly [...] found satisfaction and took pride in their work, and it served an important social function, especially for those smaller settlements."[60] In a diary entry from 4 August 1893, twenty-three-year-old Minnie Smith of Norwich, Ontario, mentions travelling to the nearby village of Springford for a Ladies' Aid meeting "with Mrs. Woodward."[61] For women like Smith, whose town lacked a group, travelling to meetings in other communities provided important social interaction. When the ladies of Knox Presbyterian church in Elora arranged a strawberry festival to raise funds for the "beautifying" of their new parish, the *Lightning Express* described the undertaking as a "way that will combine pleasure with profit" for the ladies involved.[62] Occasional conflicts likely erupted between auxiliaries of different denominations who competed for citizens' patronage, but generally the time spent together working toward a common goal helped to form, nurture, and strengthen bonds of friendship among women. Just as household chores were often accomplished in the company of others, auxiliaries facilitated female bonding. By working together to achieve fundraising goals, female sociability was forged.[63]

The most popular fundraising ventures that religious auxiliaries in Dresden, Tillsonburg, and Elora organized were musical concerts, lectures, themed suppers, arts and crafts bazaars, seasonal fruit socials, picnics and garden parties, tea socials, and tea meetings. Like private parties, fundraisers allowed hosts to showcase their respectability and social aspirations by indulging in some of the new dining trends. In Tillsonburg, for instance, the ladies of the Methodist church hosted a "C Supper" in 1898, where participants were offered dishes beginning with the letter "C," such as "chosen cheese concealing no crawling creatures [...] choice churned cream not colored with carrots, corned beef and cold cabbage, crushed crabs clarified and capped, cakes cookies and [a] comfortable collection of cuisine conquests by contemporary cooks."[64] Notices in the social columns of Dresden's,

Tillsonburg's, and Elora's newspapers suggest that fundraisers structured around one notable (and fashionable) ingredient, like oysters or ice cream, also garnered large crowds.[65]

Fundraisers took place in a variety of venues, with the nature and scope of the event usually dictating the setting. Concerts, lectures, bazaars, and fairs were conventionally held in the town hall, opera house, or the respective church's auditorium or basement. In the warmer months, green spaces like public parks were used. Smaller-scale events such as teas and recitations often occurred in more intimate settings like congregants' homes. In their descriptions of the events, reporters never failed to mention which local politician, entrepreneur, or affluent family had offered up their home, business, or garden. When Dresden's Presbyterian Ladies' Aid Society hosted a lawn social in July 1891, the residence of well-known lumberman Edward Huston was used for the occasion. The lawn, replete with glowing Chinese lanterns, "presented a brilliant appearance," according to the *Times*.[66] Hosting church fundraisers allowed more affluent citizens to not only demonstrate benevolence and religious devotion but also reassert their enviable position within the socio-economic hierarchy of the town.

Other fundraisers were humbler in their offerings. According to Tillsonburg's Bert Newman, each autumn, much to the delight of congregants, churches in and around Tillsonburg hosted chicken pie suppers. Newman and his sweetheart sometimes provided the after-dinner entertainment, a gig he remembered fondly because the church ladies gave them "all the chicken pie you could eat, all the coffee you could drink, and all kinds of cookies."[67] Grander events might offer a range of musical entertainments, such as the garden party hosted by the Ladies' Aid of Elora's Knox Presbyterian church in July 1905, which featured musical selections from a pianola, a male quartet of singers, and a female soloist. The *Express* declared that "the ladies deserve great credit for the excellent supper they provided and the arrangements generally in connection with the event."[68] Despite cool temperatures the event was well-attended, producing a profit of forty dollars for church improvements. Working-class residents were less visible at events like lawn socials and garden parties, where location, theme, and ticket price dictated one's ability to attend. In contrast, the simplicity, affordability, and unpretentiousness of a chicken pie supper permitted less affluent residents to participate.

An important (and often overlooked) aspect of auxiliary work is how frequently socials drew men, women, and children together who normally would not interact because of prescriptions regarding age, class, gender, and, to an extent, religious appropriateness. In a pamphlet published in 1972 to mark the centenary of Dresden's St. Andrew's Presbyterian church, the authors remarked that "newspaper accounts of church activities in the 1880s reflect a cheerfully busy congregation for whom the church was very much the centre of social life, as well as spiritual guidance."[69] When a concert was held in Elora in 1872 to raise funds for the building of a new Catholic church, it was estimated that the attendees consisted of "crowds of people, great and small, old and young" amounting to somewhere in the range of 1,000 persons.[70] At the time, Elora contained a population of roughly 100 Catholics,[71] and though residents of Guelph and the surrounding communities of Fergus and Salem were also present, likely not all of the event's patrons were Catholic. For the most part, as Marks has shown, in late nineteenth-century small-town Ontario, "Catholics and Protestants lived together fairly peacefully" and further, "many Protestants were willing to make gestures towards toleration."[72] At the time of the Catholic concert, there were only a few community-wide leisure offerings in Elora, so church socials often garnered large and interdenominational groups of participants. Compared to secular recreations, leisure activities organized by church women more easily broke down barriers related to religious difference, gender, and generation. But as towns grew, most socials were able to attract enough support from their respective congregants that they no longer had to rely on interdenominational assistance.

Not all entertainments, socials, or dinners sponsored by churches were widely praised or patronized by the laity. A few fell under intense scrutiny for their so-called moral ambiguity.[73] In 1910, layperson Amenzo J. Herrick contributed an opinion piece to the *Tillsonburg Liberal*, arguing that entertainments hosted or sponsored by a religious body were in direct violation of the Bible's teachings and the tenets of Methodism. Herrick argued that church was solely meant to be a place for "public worship and for public and other meetings and services of a religious or spiritual character, held according to the rules, discipline and general usages of the Methodist church." He clarified that "other meetings and services" meant "religious meetings and religious services, not entertainments." So-called illicit events like tea meetings, musical programs, recitations, and auctions were concerns for Herrick and others who believed such leisure desecrated churches, which should be "places of worship only."[74]

Seven months later, in July 1910, another letter criticizing activities sponsored by local churches appeared in the *Liberal*. Nevill L. Ward of Tillsonburg's St. John's Anglican church wrote to the editor, explaining that he was bothered by the fact that town officials levied fees for all sponsors of entertainments and events taking place in the local opera house. He felt the town council should allow the churches to use the building at least once a year, free of the usual rental charge of fifteen dollars. He also suggested that all entertainments taking place in the local opera house require a designation such as "church entertainment" or "purely secular" to clarify the nature and objectives of the event. This, Ward seemed to believe, would suppress any rumblings about the inappropriateness of amusements masquerading as church fundraisers.[75] Though it is unclear whether the publication of Herrick's and Ward's pieces elicited any reaction from readers, later notices in the *Liberal* show that the laity and church auxiliaries alike continued to invoke religious pretexts when hosting fundraisers, whether within the sacred space of the church or out in the rougher, public spaces of the town.

Though not cited for inappropriateness by either Herrick or Ward, in 1903 and 1905 moving picture entertainments, the precursor to modern-day films, were hosted by Methodist women's auxiliaries in Tillsonburg and Elora, exemplifying one of the more notable ways that modes of popular leisure were being integrated into auxiliary work. Ironically, clergymen had once been some of the loudest and most vocal critics of moving pictures and their theatres.[76] In the turn-of-the-century hierarchy of culture, "legitimate" art, opera, and theatre were deemed high culture while moving pictures, vaudeville, and burlesque were considered lowbrow entertainment.[77] In large cities, the earliest movie theatres (called nickelodeons) were often located in rundown, working-class neighbourhoods, marked by their gaudy posters and dirty, unventilated interiors. The images, content, and messages of these shows were considered by reformers to be too risqué for the "respectable" crowd. After the turn of the century, however, the more genteel sounding "movie palace" began to replace the nickelodeon and strove to appeal to more middle-class tastes and standards. Moving pictures were being shown in Dresden as early as 1910, but only in halls licensed for that purpose.[78] In Elora, Chalmer's church (the town's Church of Scotland) was used as a moving picture theatre,[79] providing a "familiar environment in which to experience movies" that had been approved by the minister.[80] In the early years of film, popular genres included comedies, farces, romances, historical epics, and westerns, many of which demonstrated the racism, chauvinism, misogyny, and antisemitism characteristic of the era. By the 1910s, movie theatres (sometimes called "bijous") could be found throughout small-town Ontario.[81] Supporters of moving pictures believed that they "would bring cosmopolitan attitudes to social backwaters, would reduce the isolation of rural communities and would fill a cultural void."[82] According to historian Kathryn Helgesen Fuller, in small-town America, watching films was an important cultural link between city and country because participating created a "common movie-going experience" and was part of a larger set of urban social customs increasingly being adopted by small-town and rural, middle-class men and women.[83]

The inclusion of this novel and somewhat controversial form of media for the purposes of fundraising reveals the Methodist women's desires to break from tradition, as well as their awareness of being part of a wider popular culture. More logically, the ladies recognized that the uniqueness of the moving picture show might draw a sizable crowd and produce handsome profits from ticket sales. Though moving picture entertainments were the sort of fundraiser that raised the ire of detractors like Amenzo Herrick, the Methodist church of the early twentieth century was decidedly more liberal, progressive, and enlightened in its stance toward certain types of leisure. Shrinking congregation sizes and diminishing donations meant that the Methodist church, despite its predominance in rural and small-town Ontario, had to show greater effort and a willingness to accept leisure as an integral part of its congregants' lives.[84] The softening of attitudes toward some of the new and popular leisure activities likely explains why moving picture entertainments were integrated into the Methodist women's auxiliary fundraisers.[85] At least in the case of Elora, however, measures were still taken to ensure that the show was not only appropriate but also highly spiritual.[86] The subject of the Tillsonburg show is unknown, but following its debut the *Observer* reported that it was "the best ever seen in Tillsonburg" despite only an "average audience" attending.[87] It is unclear why, but six years after the Tillsonburg Methodist women hosted their moving picture entertainment, a bylaw was passed banning the showing of moving pictures in any public venue unless a licence or permit at the exorbitant cost of thirty-five dollars was secured.[88]

Public and Commercial Entertainments

While public events like moving picture shows, dances, and fancy-dress balls served an important civic function as fundraisers, they and other occasions became increasingly important spaces for courting, particularly among the local elite. In Tillsonburg in the 1870s and early 1880s, fraternal organizations like the Masonic lodge (Freemasons) and the Independent Order of Odd Fellows (IOOF) sponsored a multitude of social events constructed for groups of mixed-sex participants. The Masonic lodge first appeared in Upper Canada in the late eighteenth century and was well-known for its secretive, androcentric, and exclusive approach to activities and membership. Ontario's first chapter of the IOOF, commonly known as the Oddfellows, was established in Belleville in 1845. Another group composed entirely of male members, the IOOF's purpose was to have a positive and reforming influence on members and their respective communities. While women were barred from joining such groups, enjoying the socials that they sponsored was a way to breach the exclusivity of their "masculine ramparts."[89] Another men's organization, the Tillsonburg Bachelors' Club, was renowned for its chic social gatherings. In the early 1870s, the club was the town's pre-eminent host and organizer of communal social functions. As the name suggests, it was likely composed of Tillsonburg's unmarried men. Not only were their dances and entertainments meant to "enliven the general dullness of [the] village" at the time, but some were held specifically for matchmaking. At one social in 1872, the town's "unmarried sisterhood" was expressly invited to a supper and ball at a local hotel. The guests included several married couples along with their single daughters, some of whom had travelled in from the nearby towns of Woodstock, Ingersoll, and Simcoe for the event.[90] By the 1890s, the elaborate themes and motifs of the Bachelors' Club's balls were attracting guests from as far away as Guelph, Hamilton, and Peterborough. Tillsonburg's most affluent citizens became the preferred guests, and their proclivity for dressing in elaborate costumes demonstrates these women's desires to flaunt their wealth and finery.[91] Such entertainments, once meant to bring a variety of citizens together, had become occasions when class exclusivity could be cultivated.

Not all dances were so formal or private. While growing up in the early 1900s just outside of Dresden, Inez B. (Eagleson) Perrin, the daughter of an Irish farmer, fondly remembered "dancing the night away" with friends at the home of a "highly-respected family" whose Black patriarch had been enslaved.[92] In town, there were "quadrille parties" every two weeks in the Dresden town hall and the "old Joe Shaw block." Courting couples paid $1.50 to attend and music was provided by an orchestra from London, Ontario. It was noted that a meal was not served during the dancing, which began at 8:00 p.m. and ended at midnight, so that there would be "no time lost between dances."[93] Dancing was often the concluding event at both public and private functions like fundraisers, holiday and house parties, and associational celebrations. While evangelical clergymen considered dancing to be indecent and licentious, many churchgoing and "respectable" small-town Ontarians enjoyed it nonetheless.[94] Before early twentieth-century dancers began engaging in "close body contact, a fast pace, and various shakes and shimmies that hinted strongly at sexual intercourse,"[95] the more sedate waltz and quadrille were standard. In larger towns and cities, the relative anonymity of dance socials and dance halls allowed men and women a considerable degree of freedom, but in a small town, the usual mix of married couples and the unwedded who were familiar with one another meant single men and women were never far from the watchful gaze of community monitors.

Like their city counterparts, many rural and small-town Ontarians in the latter decades of the nineteenth century displayed a fondness for carnivalesque attractions like circuses and menageries, both new features on the cultural scene. In smaller communities such as Dresden, Tillsonburg, and Elora, the arrival of the circus with its feral animals and striking human performers piqued citizens' interest because the shows provided an escape from everyday life; momentarily, one could revel in a topsy-turvy, exotic, and unconventional world. According to historian Jane Nicholas, the audience's desire to gaze at performers "was an important part of modern culture as it allowed people to study, attempt to organize, and make sense of the shifting world around them."[96] Ontario's inefficient transportation infrastructure meant that only a few of the American shows could ably make their way to more secluded locales prior to the 1870s. Once railroad services expanded, even the smallest communities were included in the circuits of the big-ticket shows.[97]

In the late spring and early summer of 1872, the world-famous Van Amburgh Menagerie visited Tillsonburg and Elora as part of a tour across Ontario. Menageries were known for their collections of captive animals, while early circuses typically consisted of human performers. Considered at the time to be the largest of the American travelling shows, what distinguished Van Amburgh's from the dozens of others was its ability to combine the most attractive features of the menagerie and the circus into one grand spectacle.[98] The show included an "instructive museum" or "freak show," complete with an albino family, an "infant giantess," and a bearded lady. When the menagerie arrived in Tillsonburg in May of 1872, the *Observer* reported that despite "disagreeable" weather, the show was well-attended. Speaking for the community, the *Observer* declared that "we can say of it, what cannot be said of many of these travelling shows, that [the menagerie] deserved the patronage it received."[99] Responses to the menagerie were mixed, however, demonstrating that its entertainment value was not necessarily appreciated by small-town folk. In Elora, the *Express* reported that the show "caused less stir and excitement than a dog fight on the streets would have done." Citizens were so unimpressed by the shabby and outdated appearance of the troupe's wagons that only a small assembly of citizens attended the performance.[100]

As a young girl, Tillsonburg's Jessie McLean rejoiced at the arrival of "Barnum's circus," calling it "a red letter day in our year."[101] When Bailey's Circus visited Elora in 1871, "an unofficial public holiday" was declared as thousands attended the two performances.[102] By the turn of the century, several other well-known circus troupes like Lemen Bros., Sells & Downs, Sells-Floto, and Sanger were making stops in smaller communities.[103] Improved transportation networks, enhanced methods of communication (such as the telegraph), and mass production of advertising materials helped circuses and other travelling entertainers garner the attention of rural and small-town Ontarians. Promoters ensured that word got around about their impending arrival by plastering large posters on barns and in storefronts. Smaller and more amateur spectacles, like the "Indian Circus" with its "fancy rifle shooting, Indian dances, trapeze work, and tumbling" that visited Dresden,[104] were also well-attended. In 1876, Elora's Irvine Park was the setting for a performance of "showmanship and skill" by members of the Six Nations of the Grand River.[105] Both events seem to have been in the vein of the famous American Wild West show, popularized by showmen like William "Buffalo Bill" Cody who romanticized "the West" as conquered territory during and after the American Frontier Wars. A cornerstone of these shows was the Indigenous people hired to perform various "Indian" stereotypes. Such circuses and Wild West shows "attempted to affirm the superiority of whiteness" and communicated a narrative of White progress and conquest of Indigenous peoples.[106] Generally, however, it was the larger and more famous circus companies that drew the biggest crowds. Small-town weeklies often wrote about the notable acts and attractions visiting cities like

New York and Philadelphia, so local readers were familiar with the travelling show circuit.

When the circus arrived in a small town, daily life was momentarily disrupted because "the mere presence of circus folk [. . .] symbolically ruptured town life, then [the circus] moved on quickly, leaving the rupture a tangy memory."[107] Bert Newman remembers the children of Tillsonburg gathering at the train station in the early morning hours to catch a glimpse of the performers as they arrived. Excited boys and girls then ran home to beg their parents to take them to the show. It was common to see captive animals like elephants paraded down a town's main thoroughfare to drum up interest. The arrival of the circus prompted great excitement in the streets, compounded by the wagonloads of visitors from the countryside who came to take in the show. When the Lemen Bros. circus visited Tillsonburg in May 1900, an estimated 5,000 people attended the show, a remarkable number considering the population of the town itself was only around 2,000 at the time.[108]

When a circus troupe visited the community of Norwich (located roughly twenty-four kilometres northeast of Tillsonburg) in 1904, twenty-six-year-old Francis Poole remarked in her diary that a single admission was one dollar,[109] a rather large sum at the time for a few hours of entertainment. On average, shows charged the more manageable price of twenty-five cents per person, though age and gender, as well as the scope of the show, could influence admission fees. The inclusion of more commercialized entertainments in these towns meant that at times, higher admission fees were necessary to cover the costs of bringing the entertainer(s) to town. Working-class men and women could not afford to see every show that appeared, so their attendance was sporadic at best. Fees also kept local ruffians away from the "more respectable" audience members, but resourceful pleasure-seekers found ways around financial constraints. When in June 1895 Tillsonburg hosted a production of the ever-popular *Uncle Tom's Cabin*, a show that typically featured White actors in blackface, "a curious feminine group on the sidewalk opposite the music hall balanced themselves on their weary tip-toe [*sic*] to see the curtain rise." The doorkeeper, however, blocked their view, earning himself the title of "meanest man in Canada" by the *Observer*.[110] Bert Newman, who referred to himself as a "poor, barefoot boy," concocted schemes that allowed him and his family to attend shows at the opera house. In one scenario, Newman's father paid the twenty-five-cent fee for himself, shoving young Bert ahead into the crowd, unbeknownst to the ticket takers.[111] Young William Harcourt Popham and his friends also regularly snuck into Tillsonburg's opera house and other events with admission fees. One member of the posse would purchase a ticket and then go up to the gallery at the top of the building, open a window, and let in the rest of the group who were waiting on the fire escape.[112] Just because "high-class" acts were being shown did not mean that working-class folk were totally excluded from their viewing.

Conversely, as the daughter of a wealthy physician and the great-granddaughter of the town's founder, Marguerite Sinclair enjoyed the social position and privilege that allowed her to be an avid patron of the many entertainments that graced Tillsonburg's stages. Between the late 1890s and early 1900s, the teen kept a scrapbook containing handbills of the various shows she attended, such as the farcical comedy *A Cheerful Liar*, along with her handwritten musings about the quality of the performances. Sinclair, along with her immediate family, the various social clubs she was part of, and her mixed-sex groups of friends, were fixtures at the town's opera house. For local elites, attending entertainments was part of their "social duty to see and be seen."[113] In her reviews, with their undertones of boredom and cattiness, Sinclair's class consciousness and youthfulness are perceptible. In May 1899, for instance, she attended the annual Empire Day Concert with her "S.S."[114] and remarked that "it was hotter than blazes in the Opera House & a baby behind us took sick. Ah it was awful. We thought the speeches would never be over."[115]

During the short time that she maintained the scrapbook, Sinclair attended musical concerts, minstrel shows, plays, theatricals, elocution recitals, and historical pageants. Before such a breadth of options was available to small-town theatregoers, the provisioning of public entertainments was contingent on the construction or refashioning of halls capable of holding large audiences. By the turn of the century Dresden, Tillsonburg, and Elora all had town halls, concert halls, and/or opera houses that operated as both community centres and auditoriums. According to art historian Russell Lynes, the number of entertainment halls constructed in the late nineteenth century speaks to how much they served as "monuments [. . .] to civic pride and urban rivalry as to the arts they were intended to foster."[116] In cities and small towns especially, the construction of entertainment halls and their ensuing ability to attract travelling shows was "evidence of material progress."[117] Immense pressure was placed on managers of publicly owned halls to secure the most popular and trendy theatrical offerings, as portions of ticket sales were often deposited into the town's coffer.

Both amateur and professional entertainments were shown in halls in Dresden, Tillsonburg, and Elora. What theatre historian D. Layne Ehlers refers to as "home talent" always garnered great interest in these communities. Shows directed, performed, and arranged by local citizens allowed men, women, and children to "strut their stuff" and, in many cases, raise money for religious or charitable causes.[118] When a Methodist Sunday school in Dresden hosted a Christmas entertainment at Shaw's in 1888, the *Times* called it "one of the most enjoyable held for years" based on the packed seats and lack of standing room.[119] Inez Perrin recalls that the audiences at Dresden's Christmas concerts typically consisted of "excited children, anxious and tired parents, grandparents and friends coming to watch the young people display their talents with Christmas songs, Tableaux, drills and a 3 act play."[120] Though visits to Elora by songstress Annie Louise White or the Baird Dramatic Company were well-patronized, the shows that women attended and appeared to enjoy the most were those that showcased local talent because of possible personal connections to the players on stage.

Over time, the offerings at public halls underwent considerable changes. In Elora in the 1870s, for instance, church concerts and socials, educational lectures, temperance meetings, and horticultural and art exhibitions were highlighted on the playbills at the Drill Shed, but by the 1890s and early 1900s, more secular concerts and plays by recently organized choral and dramatic societies had almost completely replaced the earlier religious offerings.[121] Historians often associate the supply of such a wide variety of shows with larger towns and cities because greater numbers of people were needed to fill seats, but as American historian Mary Neth argues, "this does not make them urban by nature."[122] Notices in newspapers suggest that although Dresden, Tillsonburg, and Elora each had only one main hall alongside the smaller private ones, entertainments were just as able to draw large and enthusiastic crowds as they did in other towns and cities. A range of genres, including the works of Shakespeare, costume dramas, modern life dramas, melodramas, temperance plays, comedies, variety shows, farces, lectures, political debates, and minstrel shows regularly packed halls.[123] Though named so, opera houses were seldom visited by opera companies. According to theatre historian William F. Condee, the moniker "Opera House" was actually "a euphemism to accommodate small-town morality and to evade anti-theatrical prejudice."[124] Because these publicly owned halls were "a nexus of entertainment, politics, and community,"[125] town councils and facility managers ensured that the entertainments shown did not threaten religious values or moral codes. In these towns, the preponderance of entertainments with didactic or religious undertones, rather than more risqué offerings like vaudeville or burlesque, demonstrates the importance placed on bringing the respectable crowd into public halls. Indeed, local jurisdictions often had the legal authority to ban an entertainment troupe if the content of their show was considered too coarse for local audiences. In Tillsonburg, for example, an 1894 bylaw barred any "folly or gaiety troupe or any entertainment, show or performance" that had an "immoral or indecent character."[126] In this context, "immoral or indecent" can be read as irreligious content or sexual behaviour and imagery.

Unlike larger towns and cities, where a variety of concert halls, theatres, and auditoriums catered to customers of different religions, ethnicities, and classes, Dresden, Tillsonburg, and Elora lacked variety in this regard. Owners and operators, as a result, pandered to a range of interests and incomes, though largely it was White Anglo-Celtic and Christian people whose interests were considered. When it advertised a spelling match held in the Drill Shed in 1875, the *Elora Lightning Express* remarked that "the charge—ten cents—is so low that nobody will be left out in the cold."[127] In small towns, entertainment halls were instrumental in creating a collective identity among the large crowds of community members attending shows. Whether doing so with their families or in groups of friends, gathering for a similar purpose and revelling in some much-needed social interaction outside the home was important for women especially. According to Ehlers, in small towns, "stage entertainments meant a time for people to get together, to forget troubles with money, with weather, with the railroad, with keeping food on the table." At the town hall or opera house, "for fifty cents each—sometimes less—the whole family could watch their neighbors put on a play for a good cause, thrill to the exploits of Eliza and Uncle Tom as they fled the horrors of Simon Legree, see a favourite novel brought to life, laugh at a minstrel show, or enjoy a lyceum course event."[128] Sources from Dresden, Tillsonburg, and Elora confirm that among the female population, middle- and upper-class teens and single women frequented public entertainments the most. Though it is unclear how often married women and mothers were in the audience, the timing of shows undoubtedly posed barriers for some, particularly when the rise of the curtain conflicted with work hours, mealtime, children's bedtimes, or other household and family obligations.

As with attending church services, going to see a play or musical could prompt sociability beyond the actual show. When Tillsonburg's Young Ladies' Sewing Club reserved a section of the opera house in December 1903 to see Elmer Buffham's production of the antisemitic play *The Merchant of Venice*, a handful of club members (including Marguerite Sinclair) had a "dandy" time after the performance when a fellow member invited them over for an onion supper.[129] For these middle- and upper-class women and girls, attending commercial entertainments included "ancillary activities" such as dining, conversation, and dressing up.[130] A trip to the theatre meant donning one's best attire, especially a hat adorned with fanciful ribbons, flowers, feathers, or stuffed birds. Some hats were so large and elaborate that they obstructed the view of fellow audience members. At the short-lived Pastime Theatre in Tillsonburg, ladies who refused to remove their hats during performances were forced to sit in the rear seats.[131]

One commercial entertainment that had little trouble attracting both male and female audience members in Dresden, Tillsonburg, and Elora was minstrelsy. White minstrel shows (featuring White performers in blackface) first appeared in the early nineteenth century and were born out of the backlash against the growing American abolitionist movement. Pro-slavery advocates hired White actors to perform "Blackness," using bumbling comedic and musical routines to portray Black men and women as child-like, ignorant, and subservient. According to scholar Cheryl Thompson, to "stress their authenticity," Black minstrel shows (Black actors in blackface) became popular during and after the American Civil War. Black actors were hired, many of whom had been enslaved, to darken their skin and play up popular stereotypes of people in bondage.[132] Eventually, only White actors continued to use blackface as they performed the clichés about Black culture and plantation life that had become integral to the shows. Like the circus, minstrelsy also made its way to Canada, where White audiences revelled in the "all in fun" racism that pervaded the shows.[133] Few notices about minstrel shows visiting Elora have been uncovered apart from one that was sponsored by the Elora Rocks Lacrosse Club in March 1905.[134] In Dresden, where a significant population of formerly enslaved people and their Canadian-born children once resided (and a small population of Black men and women remained), minstrels and other shows featuring actors in blackface still performed. In 1893, under the auspices of Dresden's Presbyterian Ladies' Aid Society (an organization composed of White women), a notice appeared in the local newspaper about the impending Sunny South minstrel show. The *Times* stated that "a grand musical treat is in store for our music-loving citizens," consisting of a program of "plantation melodies, splendid solos, grand choruses and comic songs."[135] It is unclear, however, if any members of Dresden's Black population attended this event.

In Tillsonburg, the Guy Brothers Minstrels were always a popular ticket when they came to town. This entertainment was dubbed "first class" by the *Tillsonburg Liberal* because its "orchestra is fine, the singing elegant the dancing great; the acrobats wonderful, the scenery superb, the costumes pretty, [and] the electrical effects beautiful."[136] Bert Newman remembered how the Guy Brothers troupe used their costumes, props, and scenery to transform the opera house for their productions. Other minstrel companies, such as George Southwell, the Sunny South, and Beyond the Bonnie Briar Bush, also visited the town.[137] William Harcourt Popham recalled that you could always count on minstrels to attract a "full house."[138]

Minstrel shows allowed the White audiences of rural and small-town Ontario to indulge their fascination of the blackened "other" and celebrate their "own 'whiteness.'"[139] As historians Afua Cooper, Barrington Walker, Constance Backhouse, Cheryl Thompson, and others have shown, though geographically distant, socially and culturally Canada was not that far removed from the antebellum South or the Jim Crow years.[140] Thompson notes that White Canadians were drawn to minstrel shows because of their "Negrophobia" *and* "Negrophilia."[141] Even in Dresden, where some citizens and their ancestors had been born in bondage, the popularity of minstrelsy among the White population points to how much local audiences took for granted popular imagery and racist depictions of Black history and culture. In their study of Niagara Falls, Joan Nicks and Jeannette Sloniowski have shown that the racism inherent in these productions was virtually absent from any public discourse about minstrels' appropriateness.[142]

According to the *Tillsonburg Liberal*, the Guy Brothers productions were superb because you could take "your family to see [them] and not be offended with anything rough."[143] The fact that minstrel shows were considered family-friendly outings in Tillsonburg contrasts with the typical audience member at the American shows. Historian David R. Roediger describes how American "minstrelsy was a way for men to carouse after work in largely sexually segregated audiences. The theater's 'pits' were especially male preserves."[144] In antebellum urban America, "women were usually not even on the sidelines" at minstrel shows, and in the postbellum years they were even less visible because so many productions were known for their lewdness, sexuality, and homoeroticism.[145] After minstrel sheet music became available for private use, however, the entrance of the "rollicking minstrel show into the intimate confines of the American home" permitted women and children the opportunity to "'blacken up' and step into the limelight." In this way, "the potentially threatening atmosphere of the minstrel theatre was neutralized."[146]

The minstrel shows that appeared on stage at Tillsonburg's opera house were also "domesticated" in the sense that shows centred on theatrics, music, and acrobatic feats that were more suited to feminine and middle-class tastes. Due to its so-called gentler and more entertaining nature, this genre of minstrelsy was considered an acceptable social outing for men, women, children, couples, and families. The smaller population densities of Dresden, Tillsonburg, and Elora meant that minstrel shows (and commercial entertainments generally) had to appeal to the interests and tastes of the town's predominantly White, middle-class citizenry. But the shows also found favour among local elites. When Marguerite Sinclair attended the McKinney Brothers' minstrel show in 1902, she remarked that "there was a crowded house as usual,"[147] demonstrating her and others' frequent attendance at these productions. Recurring appearances from minstrel troupes, productions of plays like *The Merchant of Venice*, and choreographed circus routines from Indigenous people reveal the extent to which racist rhetoric and imagery were commonplace in public entertainments patronized by rural and small-town Ontarians; in some cases, the more misrepresented a group of people was, the more attractive the show. Though some communities attempted to ban shows containing lewd or inappropriate content, glimpses of sexuality or critiques of religion seem to have provoked more concern than prejudicial depictions of Black, Jewish, and Indigenous peoples.

Socio-political satire was another popular genre for concerts and variety shows. In Elora in 1903, one particularly memorable feat of mockery was put on as a fundraiser for the town's library. In late November of that year, handbills were distributed advertising an upcoming "Spinsters' Convention" on the night of the 20th at Armoury Hall. A fictional social club, the "Young Ladies' Single-Blessedness Debating Society" (YLSBDS), was listed as the evening's hosts. YLSBDS members Misses "Patience Desire Mann," "Sophia Stuckup," and "Frances Touchmenot" were included in the handbill as some of the evening's notable speakers.[148] The show began with Elora's own "spinsters" on stage, who were soon joined by their counterparts from nearby towns, including Fergus. In her assessment of the entertainment, *Elora Express* reporter Rose Clarke remarked how the women donned various items of clothing believed to be over half a century old. As part of their "convention," the gathered spinsters sang songs, read poetry, discussed women's rights, debated dress reform, and lamented the pitiful state of matrimonial options in the town. Near the conclusion of the entertainment, the troupe announced that they would be travelling to the Klondike after hearing that the region contained a surplus of eligible men. Prior to leaving, they attempted to undergo physical transformations, courtesy of "Prof. Makeover" and his "Remodeloscope" machine. As part of the fun, when the "gorgeous" professor arrived, he was virtually "besieged by [the] eager females." The amount of work required to remodel the spinsters, however, caused the machine to explode. Clarke writes that the two-hour show was thoroughly enjoyed by the packed audience, as evidenced by the many peals of laughter and hearty clapping heard throughout. In the end, the event garnered a profit of $100 for the library.[149]

It was not uncommon around the turn of the century for public spectacles like the Spinsters' Convention to invoke feminine imagery and popular stereotypes. Though women were not always physically part of these public displays, historians Craig Heron and Steve Penfold note that some organizers did employ them "as mythical figures or as symbols of such abstract concepts as liberty or justice." Furthermore, in a less flattering manner, some women were "used as parody" and in these guises were habitually admonished for "transcend[ing] their proper sphere."[150] In the case of the Spinsters' Convention, however, instead of male civic officials constructing the façade for them, the women performing the farce seem to have been actively involved in the construction of their individual identities. Not all their true selves were revealed, but as the photograph of "Mary Ann Fraddler" and "Cleopatra Belle Brown" indicates, most (and likely all) were married and simply masquerading as single girls.

Through this sort of farcical leisure, the costumes and alter egos adopted by the YLSBDS allowed participants to publicly address women's issues that might otherwise have been taboo or provoked strong disagreement among

Figure 11. "Mary Ann Fraddler" (Mrs. Margaret McGowan) and "Cleopatra Belle Brown" (Mrs. Moore) wearing costumes at the Spinsters' Convention at Armoury Hall, Elora, 1903. Source: WCMA, A1952.311.96, ph 503.

Figure 12. Cast of the Spinsters' Convention at Armoury Hall, Elora, 1903. Source: UGASC, Connon Collection, XR1 MS A114_B4.

townsfolk. The way the parody was constructed suggests it may have been a response to some emerging feminist actions and ideals. Women's rights, or the lack thereof at the time, especially regarding suffrage, property laws, and labour legislation, were very real concerns. Some propertied women in Tillsonburg, for example, wished for the franchise, but as a group of them explained to a local reporter in 1895, they did not understand politics, nor had they faith in unscrupulous politicians, so they relied on their husbands' political views.[151] Few small-town women appear to have had an opportunity, let alone felt comfortable, to voice their opinions about such matters. As Monda Halpern and other Canadian women's historians have shown, feminism certainly existed in rural areas and small towns, but overt examples of feminist actions in these regions can be difficult to locate.[152] The mockery embedded in the Spinsters' Convention infers that a strong sense of conservatism existed in Elora, especially among married women, regarding "unconventional" lifestyles and behaviours. Indeed, a prominent message in the show was that single women with feminist leanings should be pitied.

During the mock debate on dress reform, for instance, all but one of the participants declared their desire to keep "things as they are."[153]

It is doubtful that the purpose of the entertainment was to lament inadequacies in the town's marriage market, as data from the 1901 census indicate virtually equal numbers of unmarried men and women resided in Elora.[154] Rather, the specific "difficulties consequent upon a state of single blessedness,"[155] though woven into the satirical fabric of the Spinsters' Convention, stand out as a contentious point. In smaller communities, many single women owned property and businesses and played important roles within their families, particularly when they acted as caregivers for aging parents.[156] However, single women continued to be pitied and belittled in novels and poetry despite a recasting of the roles of "spinster" and "old maid" in the later nineteenth and early twentieth centuries. When Rose Clarke lightheartedly remarked that "to discuss local matrimonial indications is to tread on very delicate ice indeed," it is doubtful that she was wholly joking.[157] Even rural publications like the *Farmer's Advocate* weighed in on the marriage debate. In 1883, the following passage was printed: "A clever maiden lady once said that it was far better to be laughed at because you were not married than not to be able to laugh because you were. There is sound logic in that. It is well for woman to marry if she meets a good, true man, who loves her, and whom she loves; if not, she had better remain single."[158]

Though the *Farmer's Advocate* proclaimed that singlehood was better than an unhappy marriage, it was still positioned as subordinate to a "good" marriage. When it came to engaging in feminist, legal, or socio-political debates in public, historian Bonnie Huskins explains, "gender ideology limited the range of performative roles open to women." However, there were still "a few very respectable and visible roles for a minority of female participants."[159] Like street parades and demonstrations, the Spinsters' Convention was a "medium for potent collective expression" in a public space.[160] While there is no evidence that small-town women were explicitly barred from attending or even participating in public debates, when vocalizing their views on social or political affairs, they often faced resistance from men who were reluctant to take their concerns seriously. In the absence of the franchise and other forms of political expression, donning old-fashioned garb in a joking atmosphere was one way that some Elora women negotiated a space for themselves and their opinions on marriage and feminism in a public space.

Clubs and Societies

Whereas the YLSBDS was a fictional group, the women of Dresden, Tillsonburg, and Elora eagerly joined the growing number of bona fide social clubs increasingly appearing around the turn of the century. Like church auxiliaries, social clubs used members' homes as meeting places or found space in schools and civic buildings for their fundraisers and socials. The membership, composition, and objectives of clubs, however, varied from town to town. Some organizations, particularly those that were branches of national ones, could be found in almost every community. Others were unique to local circumstances and culture. Some required a formalized commitment to membership (including paying club dues and meeting on a regularly scheduled day), while others consisted of informal and infrequent gatherings. While there was no shortage of women's groups in these towns, after the turn of the century an increasing number were marked by their mixed-sex memberships. The breadth of options available to women in Dresden, Tillsonburg, and Elora speaks to the appeal of the club movement and, especially, desires to gather with like-minded women (and occasionally men) for a few hours of social intercourse.[161]

By the early twentieth century, many organizations with broader societal, reformist, or imperialist concerns, like the WCTU and the IODE, had established chapters across small-town Ontario. Founded in 1884, Tillsonburg's WCTU branch was largely composed of White, middle-class women whom one *Observer* reporter characterized as "intelligent and devoted."[162] The executive elected in 1895 consisted of women whose husbands were merchants, skilled artisans, clergymen, photographers, and conveyancers. Most members were married, over the age of fifty, and active in other philanthropic groups such as the King's Daughters.[163] In their role as the "unofficial moral arbiters of small communities,"[164] clubs like the WCTU used Christian teachings to justify and moralize a variety of initiatives and concerns, including home economics, poor relief, and teetotalism. In February 1900, the *Observer* mentioned that during the previous year, the local WCTU had "assisted a number of deserving enterprises." As many organizations did, their meetings often blended labour and leisure. One gathering, for instance, "combined a business meeting and a quilting" where "a nice quilt was finished up, which will be sent to the Girls' Shelter in Toronto." The *Observer* mentioned that "those who assisted in the quilting were entertained at an enjoyable tea shortly after six o'clock, after which work was resumed again."[165]

According to scholars Jody Baltessen and Shelagh J. Squire, "Canada has a rich history of women organizing and forming groups,"[166] and within them, members hoped to encourage personal, social, or political change. The first mainstream groups of this sort, as mentioned, were religious auxiliaries. Though they continued to attract large memberships, as Linda Ambrose found, for some women "involvement in church activities [. . .] did not provide enough stimulation."[167] By the later years of the nineteenth century, several secular and issue-specific organizations had been established for participants who shared common interests outside of the church, including labour reform, political equality, and a variety of social issues. Here, women met and socialized with like-minded women and in the process "formalized pre-existing informal groups," which also included a "large social component."[168]

Most reformist organizations were populated by middle- and upper-class women, because they had "spare time and a penchant for involvement in social causes."[169] The goal of these social causes, however, was to "improve" the lives of the less fortunate by imparting elitist standards and ideas about education, morality, respectability, and domesticity. More informal and regionally specific groups, such as study and leisure clubs, often attracted a greater cross-section of the population because of their emphasis on pedagogy and self-improvement. Across North America, the home study club movement of the late nineteenth and early twentieth centuries was part of a massive growth in men's, women's, and mixed-sex social organizations that were purely educational in nature. Unlike groups who desired to improve society, study clubs centred on artistic or cultural pursuits like travel, literature, or theatre, which acknowledged a growing awareness of the interests of the individual and their need for personal fulfillment and education. The meetings of Tillsonburg's Shakespeare Club, for instance, "afforded to the members great social and intellectual pleasure,"[170] as well as the opportunity to celebrate the transference of British heritage and culture.

According to the *Farmer's Advocate*, rural areas and small towns needed organized clubs for men and women because within every person lay a desire to explore "knowledge, culture, self-improvement, [and] broader views of life and life's problems." Allegedly, the way to fully harness such ambitions was to join a club, because it was the best way to "exert an elevating influence in the community." Though location and distance hindered options, rural and small-town women also desired the bonding and educational initiatives that clubs offered. More practically, clubs afforded both men and women the opportunity to develop their social lives and expand personal horizons by mingling with a variety of people and personalities. In doing so, they could avoid becoming "narrow, one-sided [...] 'cranks.'" Clubs that explored literature, art, nature study, physical culture, or community beautification were just a few of the options proposed by the *Farmer's Advocate*. Inculcating a "distinctly uplifting influence" in the community was paramount, though including much-enjoyed social components like skating, tobogganing, or sleighing helped promote unity among members.[171] Evidence from Dresden, Tillsonburg, and Elora suggests the work clubwomen did to help build and solidify community ties was highly valued in their respective towns, based on the number of references made to their activities in local newspapers.

Literary and dramatic societies were just some of the "ideal" clubs established around the turn of the century. Earlier offerings, particularly in the 1870s and 1880s, were almost entirely composed of male members. By the 1900s and 1910s, though, the *Farmer's Advocate* was encouraging rural women to also pursue such leisure because "preparing papers and addresses [...] compels research and study that might otherwise, perhaps, never be taken."[172] If a woman had only received the most basic of educations (or nothing at all), clubs could at least partly fill that intellectual gap. Whether acting out literary pieces or verbally discussing their merits, women and girls were advised that clubs should ideally contain about ten members who abided by a written constitution and elected officials.[173] The extent to which study clubs figured in women's social lives is evident in one Wellington County girl's diary. On 10 February 1899, she wrote that though the temperature was so frigid she was unable to attend school that day, she still "went down to Tompson's in the evening to see if the Dramatic Club met tonight but they did not."[174]

Some groups were spearheaded by private citizens while others were formed within the school system. In Dresden, a literary program conducted by the "Old Folks (Colored)" of the town was advertised in the *Times* in November 1888.[175] That same year, the pupils of the Dresden Public School formed themselves into a literary society and provided public entertainments every Friday at 3:00 p.m.[176] Local newspaper reporters often pressured community members to mimic neighbouring towns that had more plentiful and diverse offerings for social and study clubs. When the *Times* mentioned that four separate literary societies would be meeting throughout the winter in nearby Ridgetown, the reporter pointedly asked what Dresden would be doing in this regard.[177]

For some women, joining a club and the many opportunities it afforded them was a way to circumvent the more limiting social and economic circumstances inherent in rural and small-town life. Baltessen and Squire argue that in Winnipeg, for example, several factors determined club participation and that "social class, ethnicity, education, leisure time, and external circumstances" acted as divisive forces.[178] Similar barriers affected women living outside larger urban centres, though in the cases of Tillsonburg and Elora, ethnicity does not appear to have played as significant a role owing to the hegemonic influence of White, Anglo-Celtic people. Smaller populations also meant that usually there was only one iteration of a club available. Typically, there were not enough women of colour or non-Christian women to establish and maintain their own branches of clubs. This was also largely the case in Dresden, though its Black population was still sizable enough around the turn of the century that some of the town's clubs, entertainments, and religious activities, such as the one hosted by the "Old Folks (Colored)," were distinguished by the participants' and organizers' skin colour. This underscores the fact that though the Black population was shrinking, it was still visible enough to stand out against the predominantly White backdrop of the community. The White citizens calling attention to their difference, notably newspaper editors and reporters, clearly considered the Black community to be a separate social group.

Some forms of club work, such as giving papers at meetings and overseeing the treasury, could help women "overcome deficiencies in their education" by providing them an outlet with which to hone skills such as writing, reading, and arithmetic.[179] Other benefits, such as access to informative political discussions and a much-needed break from household chores, were also important, but as many rural historians have shown, clubs were crucial to bridging the distance between town and country. For farm women, distance and agricultural duties limited opportunities for socializing, but diaries indicate that when they were able to do so, travelling to nearby towns to attend club meetings and other public activities was considered time well-spent. In March 1879, for example, Ann Amelia Day mentions travelling to the village of Eden Mills for a "tea-meeting" where she saw friends Janet and Louisa McKersie, and the three "had a good time."[180] At such meetings, the sociability that occurred around the consumption of food and beverages, as Ambrose astutely notes, "was an important antidote to the isolation they experienced in their work routines at home or on the farm. Indeed, the opportunity to gather in an all-female setting was something they looked forward to and valued very much."[181]

In small-town Ontario, some organizations were dominated by elite women whose affluence and pre-existing social ties determined membership. Indeed, class must be considered an important factor when assessing the pervasiveness of the club movement anywhere in North America at the time.[182] One such example is the IODE, or Imperial Order Daughters of the Empire, which was established in Canada in 1900 due to the imperialist fervour generated by the Boer War. Paralleling the renewed zeal in British affairs after the First World War began in August 1914, a local IODE chapter was established in Dresden in October of that year with the help of Catherine McVean. Tillsonburg did not initiate an IODE chapter until after the First World War, and it appears that one never existed in Elora. The first official meeting of Dresden's chapter was held in November, when 104 women enrolled as members, a significant number considering Dresden was home to only about 1,500 citizens at the time.[183] This original group was composed of White women, as was the norm at the time, many of whom were the wives of the town's professionals and entrepreneurs. The first woman of colour, Uma Arya, was "invited to join" in 1969. The first Black member, Sandra Thompson, was invited in the 1970s and installed as regent (a position of prestige) between 1990 and 1992.[184]

In the group's early days, McVean was named first regent, and the organization became known as the Sydenham Chapter after Lord Sydenham, governor general of British North America between 1838 and 1841, and his namesake river that flowed through town. After her death in 1935 and in honour of her devotion to the organization, Dresden's IODE was renamed

Figure 13. Charter members of Dresden's IODE chapter, 1914. Founder and first regent, Catherine McVean, is on the far left. Source: DA, Photograph Collection.

the Catherine McVean chapter. Primarily, the club engaged in charitable work. During both world wars, IODE members raised money and sent care packages overseas to members of the armed forces, along with providing aid to their families at home. Local histories note that Dresden's chapter also supported welfare initiatives, including fighting the spread of tuberculosis, delivering food to the sick during the 1918 to 1920 influenza pandemic, and improving access to health care.[185]

The organization's motto, "one flag, one throne, one empire,"[186] summarizes the IODE's desire to be an umbrella organization of sorts for female subjects of the British Empire. At the turn of the century, when non-British immigration to Canada was increasing, the IODE sought to solidify ties with the empire and instill British values in Canada through charitable work and fundraising socials. Membership afforded White, female imperialists the opportunity to meet and work together to achieve their broad, patriotic goals. Compared to other women's organizations, membership in the IODE was far more restrictive and associated with British lineage; for example, many IODE members could trace their ancestry to White United Empire Loyalists. Though allegedly open to any female member of the British Empire who held a "true allegiance" to the Crown,[187] participation was often more dependent on family ties, blood lines, class alliances, and region of origin than passion for the cause. Historian Katie Pickles and others who have studied the IODE have shown that the early history of the organization is a complicated one; while it accomplished many charitable deeds, it also supported British hegemony in Canada and beyond. Dubbed "forgotten colonizers"[188] by Pickles, the IODE habitually discriminated against people of colour and non-British immigrants, groups who did not fit within their interpretation of an ideal Canada. Indeed, a newspaper article found in the Molly Creek Tweedsmuir History book notes that one of the "chief interests" of Catherine McVean was the "welcoming and Canadianization of the foreign-born."[189]

Described by Margaret Kechnie as "uniquely Canadian,"[190] the Women's Institute (WI) is the only one of the larger women's groups that was born in Canada and then spread across the globe. The WI was also one of the few (if not only) clubs formed with rural interests in mind. Prior to its establishment, many women attended Farmers' Institute meetings with their husbands, where they were relegated to spectator status. Those living outside large cities lacked a group where woman-specific rural and agricultural issues could be discussed. In February 1897 Erland Lee, a prosperous farmer from Stoney Creek, Ontario, invited domestic science crusader Adelaide Hoodless to speak at his local Farmers' Institute's "ladies' night." Here, Hoodless discussed the importance of elevating and improving women's homemaking capabilities, but more importantly stressed the necessity of a new organization where rural women could meet and discuss their unique personal, familial, social, and cultural concerns. The female audience was receptive to the notion, and that night the first WI was assembled. Initially called the Women's Department of the Farmers' Institutes of South Wentworth, it was later changed to the Women's Institute of Saltfleet, and finally to the Stoney Creek Women's Institute.[191]

Despite the considerable spread and growth of this new organization, WI branches were not formed in every Ontario town or village, nor was there an overwhelmingly positive response to its objectives.[192] Spokespeople embarked on tours of the province to convince local women of the benefits of forming branches.[193] In February 1903, WI advocate Ida Hunter visited Tillsonburg with the intention of overseeing the formation of a local branch. A group gathered at the home of Mrs. Jane Smith to listen to Hunter's proposal, agreeing to establish the first Women's Institute in Tillsonburg, with Smith and Mrs. Frances Livingstone elected co-presidents. At this initial meeting, twenty-two women pledged to join immediately while ten others promised to join later.[194]

In Elora, a WI branch was not formed until 1931, though a junior group briefly existed from 1921 to 1922. In contrast, the nearby villages of Ennotville, Speedside, and Cumnock all had WIs by the early 1900s,[195] an indication that the organization was more appealing to women residing outside the service centres of Elora and Fergus. In February 1913, Annie Hill of Fergus remarked that she had to travel to Cumnock to attend a WI meeting (roughly nine kilometres away), as a branch was not established in her community until 1921.[196] The first WI was initiated in Dresden in 1926, though, as in Elora, it was just a short-lived junior branch. An adult equivalent, the Molly Creek Women's Institute, was not formed until 1947,[197] though Dresden women may have joined the branches of the smaller surrounding communities or larger township-wide ones.

The lack of interest in establishing full-fledged WIs in Dresden and Elora is perhaps indicative of the elitism that dominated some WI executives in the early years.[198] The first presidents of Tillsonburg's WI are good examples. Jane Smith's husband was a well-known mill owner, contractor, and former mayor, while Frances Livingstone was a lawyer's wife. In those situations, less affluent rural and farm women living on the town's outskirts may have been reticent to join, uncomfortable with the socio-economic differences between themselves and the executive. However, on at least one occasion, the Tillsonburg WI reached out to rural women, hoping they might consider joining. In 1908, the *Observer* advertised a forthcoming meeting and noted that "ladies from the country are especially invited to attend."[199] Hesitations to join the WI may also reflect the fact that Hoodless and other domestic science advocates strove to impart notions of urban, middle-class respectability and domesticity as the WI's objectives. Meetings typically consisted of lectures given by members regarding the "proper" way to cook a meal, raise children, or maintain the home, and some women likely perceived this instruction as a criticism of their knowledge, practices, and abilities. Historian Donica Belisle argues that in the early twentieth century, WIs actively participated in the new culture of consumption and consumerism by urging rural women to purchase domestic goods and labour-saving devices that would lighten their workloads. For many, this was financially impossible and created tension between the haves and the have-nots within the organization.[200] Though the work and efforts of WIs were highly praised by civic officials and members took great pride in their endeavours, in Dresden, Elora, and to a lesser extent Tillsonburg, the WI was not considered the foremost organization for local women.

Because the WI focused so much on improving agrarian lifestyles, middle-class and elite women in Dresden, Tillsonburg, and Elora likely found that other clubs better met their needs and interests. The members of

Tillsonburg's WI, however, seem to have appreciated how the organization offered instruction on domestic science, especially in striving "to introduce better methods of work in the home."[201] At the institute's first meeting, for instance, papers were presented on "Cuts of Meat and How to Prepare Them," "Kitchen Work," and "The Proper Way to Cook Beefsteak."[202] In addition to homemaking, Tillsonburg's WI was heavily involved in civic improvement projects. At its sixtieth anniversary celebration in 1963, past members were congratulated on some of their more notable achievements, including purchasing park benches and a drinking fountain, financing bathing houses at Lake Lisgar, and providing prizes at Tillsonburg's fall fair.[203]

Small towns may have functioned as important service centres for families living in the surrounding rural areas, but some town women (especially those who were farm wives, like Annie Hill of Fergus) did not have access to clubs that catered to their interests, so they travelled out to the country to attend WI meetings and socialize with like-minded farm women. Though townsfolk frequently attended parties and socials that were held in rural areas, outside of the WI there are scant references to women pursuing club work in the countryside. The WIs around Dresden, Tillsonburg, and Elora seem to have flourished not only because they provided leisure and sociability to women unable or unwilling to travel to town, but also because they drew town women to their meetings. Clubs like the WI, then, acted as a bridge between town and country. As a resident of a bustling community like Fergus, opportunities to join various secular and religious groups were at Hill's disposal. According to her diary, she was a devoted member of the town's WCTU,[204] but she still desired to join the Cumnock WI because she needed to converse with other farm women who shared similar circumstances and concerns. When it came to club membership, movement between town and country was a regular occurrence as women travelled across townships and county lines to pursue leisure with self-improvement and educational purposes.

Conclusion

While in the earlier part of the nineteenth century, men and women had largely pursued leisure in separate spaces and places, by the end of the century, fewer activities were marked by gender-based participation as more women sought recreational offerings outside the home. The reaction to the group of Tillsonburg women caught spying on the men's literary association in 1871, for instance, suggests that the women had violated an unwritten code of acceptable behaviour and were attempting to step beyond their prescribed sphere without invitation. Throughout the next three decades, however, this spatial separation of the sexes narrowed considerably. Partly thanks to women's own initiatives, sites and options for single- and mixed-sex leisure were increasingly extended into public spaces.

By the First World War, though more traditional endeavours such as church auxiliary work remained important, women also engaged in a grow-ing variety of activities and amusements that they were instrumental in initiating, organizing, and managing. The period between the late 1880s and early 1900s saw a burst in the number of female-run organizations that offered middle- and upper-class women the chance to engage in civic improvement projects, social reform initiatives, and poor relief. Other groups were more educational in nature, offering learning opportunities for the purposes of personal development. Public amusements that were once the preserve of men, such as minstrelsy, began to be advertised as family-friendly entertainments, resulting in the fostering of a collective identity among women and townsfolk generally. The establishment of public buildings that catered to female customers (and the entertainments shown within them) showcases the importance of bringing women (and their money) out into these public spaces.

Though some clubs and activities remained the preserve of the elite, as this chapter has shown, enjoying leisure in public spaces did not always have a price. When it did, some working-class residents found savvy ways around financial constraints. The expansion of options for public leisure activities was also instrumental in bringing more rural women into towns.

Rural areas were not devoid of options for entertainment, but when the circus or a theatrical troupe arrived, the novelty of these new commercial entertainments drew women and their families into town. Rural women also travelled to town to attend various club meetings, while some town women found their needs were better met by rural clubs where agrarian matters were more prominent. Though towns had always been centres of trade and commerce for rural people, the growing number of leisure activities available also solidified the small town as a locus for recreation, socializing, and fun. By the late nineteenth century, along with the newly built music halls and opera houses, spaces for physical activity, like bicycle tracks and tennis courts, began to appear. As the following chapter discusses, the expanding leisure opportunities for women also included a variety of sports, physical recreations, and modes of outdoor play. Just as movie theatres and opera houses did, these activities also provoked debate and discussion among citizens about gender, leisure, and appropriate behaviour in public.

THREE

Safeties, Skates, and Sleds:
Sports and Physical Recreation for Women

N ITS MAY 1892 edition, the *Farmer's Advocate* published a short piece titled "Physical Exercise" that outlined the benefits of sport and recreation for both young men and women. The author noted:

> Care should be taken not to discourage the young in their natural fondness for physical exercise. Many boys and girls have relinquished sports eminently fitted to invigorate and strengthen them, and which they thoroughly enjoyed, because of slighting remarks of their elders, and from fear of being thought childish. We cannot estimate the evil consequences that may follow when we persuade a young girl that good hard play is unladylike, or a boy that it is unmanly. On the contrary, such sports should receive our most thorough respect and most cordial sympathy. Not to shorten, but to prolong the time during which they may be suffered to promote health and happiness should be our aim; and when the taste for them declines, our effort should be to replace them by more congenial exercise.[1]

Pieces such as this from the *Farmer's Advocate* and other periodicals of the day were important disseminators of information regarding new trends in sport, leisure, and recreation. Increasingly, alongside the articles offering tips for setting the perfect tea table and ways to enliven winter evenings, columnists began providing advice and support for constructing healthful modes of physical recreation. The first articles privileged men's and then boys' needs, and by the later 1880s and 1890s, some attention was being given to women's and girls' physical fitness. This is not to say, of course, that prior to the later nineteenth century women were not engaging in formal and informal modes of physical recreation, but those who did, whether for pleasure or profit, were often scolded by their respective societies for "challeng[ing] Victorian notions of female propriety by engaging in unusual activities, more vigorous than most."[2]

Rather than shunning women's and girls' interests, the *Farmer's Advocate* piece with its encouraging tone reveals that attitudes toward physical recreation and gender appropriateness were shifting in late nineteenth-century Canada. Before the 1880s, White, Euro-Canadian women had few sports or other means of physical recreation at their disposal, minus unorganized and informal activities like walking or horseback riding, which they did as individuals or as families. In larger cities, the growth of organized sports clubs in the 1860s and 1870s offered White, middle- and upper-class men opportunities for membership, fraternization, and healthful exercise, but women were largely barred from joining these exclusive organizations. Occasionally, women's divisions were formed tangentially, but these "lady associates" tended to be family members of male participants.[3] In rural areas and small towns, geographic and population constraints meant that such organizations for women were few and far between. The recognized settings where women and girls pursued sports and physical recreation in larger towns and cities, like the gymnasiums at settlement houses and the Young Women's Christian Association (YWCA), did not exist in most small towns. Resultingly, within smaller communities, opportunities for physical recreation and sports prior to 1900 were limited and opportunities to play tended to be informal and sporadic.

While there may not have been plentiful options for female-specific and mixed-sex sports clubs and teams, this chapter details how women in Dresden,

Tillsonburg, and Elora still found ways to engage with various forms of physical activity and took an active role in creating such opportunities. When small increments of time could be carved out of the day, playing a game of lawn tennis or going for a quick skate on a pond were activities important to women for their healthful properties, their ability to prompt socialization, their accessibility, and their affordability. Though initially participating in activities like cycling required a substantial amount of money, by the turn of the twentieth century, mass production and lower prices meant game sets, membership in a sports club, and even bicycles were within most people's financial reach. While physical activity could be a "strategy for separating themselves by class,"[4] as this chapter demonstrates, women in small-town Ontario favoured sports and outdoor pastimes, particularly cycling, lawn tennis, ice skating, and sledding, that were enjoyed by many, especially the middle class, despite costing little or nothing. Women also had the choice to pursue many of these activities independently, though often they were enjoyed in groups, to maximize the free time allotted to leisure. Some of their preferred sports and games, like croquet and lawn tennis, also reveal the extent to which British social traditions were exported to small-town Ontario throughout the later nineteenth and early twentieth centuries.

The eventual recognition that women and girls, like their male counterparts, also needed fresh air and exercise, though for specific feminine purposes, was a gradual process. In the early years of organized sports in Ontario, women's presence at makeshift baseball diamonds, skating rinks, and horseracing tracks was infrequent and restricted to the role of spectator. Initially, women were advised not to spectate over concerns that violent sports and male bodies in motion might affront women's genteel natures. However, as sports historian Colin D. Howell notes, "luring women to the park became an important objective" for the "astute businessman." The "idealized image of the 'lady' spectator" was soon constructed, defined as a middle-class woman whose presence at men's sporting events helped "purify the moral atmosphere."[5] In this role, women acted as arbiters of respectability, gathering with other like-minded women, often at a reduced cost, to watch and support their local sportsmen.

It was a combination of social, religious, medical, and cultural changes in the late nineteenth century that prompted physicians, social reformers, clergymen, and journalists to admit that the healthful properties to be gained from sports and physical recreation also benefited females. Particularly, new feminist activities and thought, the growth of the industrial labour force, urbanization, environmental activism, the emergence of physical education, and a new consumer culture resulted in greater opportunities for women that challenged traditional gender roles and ideals. Over time, the antiquated idea that intense physical activity disrupted women's reproductive abilities was replaced by a new belief that moderate (yet respectable) exercise enhanced maternal instincts, resulting in happier, healthier, and stronger mothers and offspring. This was also the era when the "New Woman" emerged, someone who desired a more fulfilling life beyond the home and greater equality in education, employment, and leisure. However, a fine line existed between healthy, gender-appropriate recreation and activities that produced "mannish" bodies and qualities. Rougher and more violent team sports like lacrosse and hockey were thought to deprive women of their femininity, while cycling (to an extent), lawn tennis, croquet, ice skating, and canoeing were generally promoted for their physical and emotional benefits.

Cycling

The history of the bicycle is unique for how much it contributed to ongoing discussions and concerns about new modes of sport and the continuance of traditional gendered behaviours in small-town Ontario. By the 1890s, great strides had been made in terms of viewing cycling from the standpoint of health and wellness, but some citizens continued to condemn bicycles because of fears that they damaged the reproductive system and prompted sexual immorality.[6] The polarity that developed between supporters and opponents of female cyclists was not unique to that activity; across rural and small-town Ontario, as the previous chapter noted, when women began participating in more leisure activities in public, local citizens became privy to and heartily participated in both sides of the debate about gender appropriateness outside the home. Women who ran foot races (also known as pedestrianism), for instance, struggled to be regarded as "respectable" because it was traditionally a male-dominated sport.[7] In Dresden, Tillsonburg, and Elora, men's foot races were customary at the celebration of holidays like Victoria Day and Dominion Day in the latter part of the nineteenth century, but women's races were not added to the bill until about the turn of the century. A precursor to the modern track and field day, some local schools held children's races, but as Nancy B. Bouchier points out, the sexes never competed against one another because "biologically based physical attributes" like size and strength became determinants of one's abilities.[8]

Perhaps more so than any other mode of leisure to emerge in Western society in the late nineteenth century, cycling became a divisive issue among riders, local lawmakers, pedestrians, and police forces. Both male and female cyclists were criticized for competitive behaviour, lack of decorum, endangering pedestrians, and flaunting conspicuous consumption. From a practical standpoint, bicycles provided women a relatively affordable option for mobility and helped them to move about at a quicker pace. Elites like Mary Ann Tillson could get around town quite easily thanks to the privilege of having their own buggies, while less affluent women were forced to walk long distances or rely on their husbands or fathers for transportation. The introduction of the bicycle, however, revolutionized travel. Though many women enjoyed walking for its healthful properties and navigated buggies and wagons independently, the novelty of the bicycle made it a more exciting option.

The cycling craze that captured Canadians in the later nineteenth century began in the 1860s when the first contraptions, called velocipedes, appeared in cities like Toronto, Montreal, and Halifax. These aptly nicknamed "bone-shakers" were replaced by the "ordinary" bicycle a decade later. Also called high wheelers and penny farthings, ordinaries would be found on many public thoroughfares,[9] but their high cost (around $100)[10] relegated use to those in the upper echelons of society. In addition, their heavy, solid iron frames and high-wheeled fronts made them difficult for women to mount and navigate on uneven streets and sidewalks. Most bicycles[11] built prior to the 1890s were androcentric modes of recreation that provided riders with a "unique status signaling both economic stature and a manly physical competence."[12]

Residents of Tillsonburg displayed a distinctive fondness for cycling, likely a consequence of the town's location. Approximately forty kilometres west of Tillsonburg in the small town of St. Thomas, a national organization representing cyclists' interests, the Canadian Wheelman's Association (CWA), was established in 1882. North and east of Tillsonburg, the towns of Ingersoll and Woodstock regularly held large bicycle parades and Woodstock even hosted the CWA's annual meet in 1885, attracting dozens of cyclists from across the province.[13] Bicycle manufacturers could be found across southwestern Ontario, their factories a visible reminder of how prominent and popular the activity had become. By the mid-1890s, businessman Charles Burkholder, a dealer in bicycles and other metal implements, had refurnished a vacant factory on Broadway Street in Tillsonburg that became Burkholder's Bicycle Works. When the initial idea for the venture was broached in 1895, the *Observer* declared that "a bicycle works for Tilsonburg would suit everybody all around."[14]

The invention of the safety bicycle in 1885 marked a pivotal moment in bicycle manufacturing, which many sports historians identify as the reason why so many women in Western Europe and North America became cycling enthusiasts.[15] Often described as a saviour for middle-class women, the safety bicycle was one of the most highly coveted consumer technologies and novel forms of transportation to emerge in the late nineteenth century. Cycling historian Clare S. Simpson writes that for women, "the bicycle offered unique opportunities to move spontaneously and independently beyond accepted geographic and social boundaries."[16] The safety's frame was constructed of thin-walled tubes of metal that made the contraption lighter, stronger, and more durable than that of its predecessors. Two wheels of roughly equal size replaced the large front wheel characteristic of the ordinary bicycle, and recently invented rubber tires softened the ride considerably. The first safety bicycles contained a high crossbar fitted between the seat and handlebars, but eventually the drop frame was introduced to provide women with greater ease, comfort, and modesty when mounting and riding.[17] Mass production of the widely popular safety brought the cost down to the point where a brand new machine could be purchased at the turn of the century for around thirty dollars, a significant decrease from the price of bicycles a decade earlier.[18] In Tillsonburg in 1892, merchants Wood and Co. advertised a brand new boys' safety bicycle for twelve dollars.[19] Though the cost of purchasing a new bicycle remained high and out of reach for most working-class Canadians, it was no longer the preserve of the *haute bourgeoisie*. The growing middle class, with their disposable incomes and desires to showcase modernity and prosperity, eagerly embraced bicycles for both leisure and professional use. Over time, the bicycle became instrumental in "domesticating" and "anes-thetiz[ing]" public spaces,[20] altering traditional social and geographic orders and, to an extent, reshaping barriers between the sexes and classes. By the late 1890s, male and female cyclists were riding together as friends, couples, and members of clubs, and for those able to afford it, cycling provided families with a mode of recreation that could be enjoyed as a group outside the home. Professional bicycle races were also a popular event to attend, though small-town women generally did not compete.[21]

As someone who grew up in Tillsonburg in the 1910s, Bert Newman reminisced that "bicycles weren't for everybody in those days—certainly not for the working man who made a dollar a day. By the time he raised his family and paid the rent he wouldn't have enough money left over to buy a bicycle. Very few boys—only rich kids—had bicycles."[22] Newman came of age well after the bicycle craze captured the town, but as he notes, interest in cycling largely remained the privilege of the middle and upper classes. During the bicycle's 1890s heyday, however, interest was so pervasive that the *Observer* reported that not only was Tillsonburg's oldest citizen suffering from the "fever" but that men from the "mercantile, iron road and clerical callings" had all been seen of late riding at the local race track.[23] If the cost of a new bicycle was too high, used bicycles could be acquired if one perused advertisements in the local newspaper.[24]

A decisive moment in Tillsonburg's cycling history occurred in the summer of 1891, when the first "ladies' safety bicycle" arrived in town. The

Observer reported that two of the "handsome" machines had been acquired by local agents connected with the Goold Bicycle Co. of Brantford, Ontario. One quickly sold, while the other remained in store for public viewing. The *Observer* dubbed the machine "ahead of anything that has come to town yet."[25] Undoubtedly, the new bicycle's appearance enhanced the public's (and particularly women's) interest in the phenomenon, as evidenced by increasing numbers of references to female cyclists in the social columns of the *Observer* and *Liberal*. In 1895, the *Observer* remarked that "a wheel that is cutting a dash in town just now is made of aluminum, fitted with the latest improvements, and hand painted in a rose design."[26] Women's recollections also substantiate cycling's growing appeal. In her unpublished autobiography, Tillsonburg's Agnes McGregor devotes considerable space to retelling stories from her childhood, including those involving bicycles. McGregor, born in 1882, was the daughter of Presbyterian minister Malcolm McGregor and his wife, Jane. The McGregors lived a comfortably middle-class existence, as demonstrated in Agnes's recollections. When the family hosted visitors in the summer of 1894, the group greatly enjoyed cycling together (because it was the "latest fashion") though some bicycles had to be borrowed to ensure everyone was outfitted.[27]

After the ladies' safety bicycle debuted, law enforcement officials and the local press began paying increasing attention to riders' etiquette. In September 1891, the *Observer* reported that "quite a number" of residents were displeased with cyclists who frequented sidewalks instead of using road beds.[28] Cyclists were encouraged to make use of a driving park that had been built, but the yearly charge of fifty cents per rider likely deterred many, and women do not appear to have used the facility.[29] Even in Elora and Dresden, where cycling was popular but on a more modest scale, bylaws passed in 1902 and 1903, respectively, sought to maintain pedestrian safety by barring bicycles on sidewalks.[30] Frustrated that riders unashamedly continued to disobey orders, Tillsonburg's police chief Archie Pow used the local newspaper as a platform to chastise errant behaviour. In April 1894, the following appeared on the front page of the *Observer*: "Chief Pow requests THE OBSERVER to state in plain English so that it cannot be misunderstood that after this notice has been published he will summon before the magistrate all parties, either gentlemen or ladies, boys or girls, who persist in riding bicycles on the sidewalks in town contrary to the town bylaws. He means business this time, and says that riding on any of the walks in town must cease at once. A word to the wise is sufficient."[31]

In June of that year, again prompted by complaints from citizens, Pow singled out the town's female population, "who still indulge in riding bicycles on the walks in town." He warned that if they continued to disregard bylaws he would "summon them before the magistrate."[32] Despite the passage of local bylaws that sought to control riders' behaviour, accidents inevitably occurred. In September 1894, a seven-year-old Tillsonburg boy was struck by a cyclist while crossing a street with an armful of groceries. Luckily no severe damage was sustained beyond a large gash on the boy's forehead.[33] Over time, the sidewalk bylaws became less stringent to provide cyclists with more freedom, but riders' behaviour was still closely monitored.[34]

As early as 1884, residents were expressing interest in forming a bicycle club in Tillsonburg.[35] Six years later, in May 1890, an information session was held for potential members and a large audience gathered, eager to join the town's first club of this kind. The Rover Bicycle Club,[36] as it came to be known, met on Monday mornings at 5:30 a.m. and Friday evenings at 7:30 p.m. for their "runs," when they travelled as a group out into the surrounding countryside. In the club's early years, Rev. McGregor "commanded" the runs, which likely influenced daughter Agnes's interest in cycling. Despite the growing number of female riders appearing in public, women were not invited to contribute to the establishment of the Rover Bicycle Club.[37] Most clubs organized around this time were populated by wealthy bachelors who cultivated hero worship by demonstrating manly chivalry atop their machines. Club members usually donned military-style uniforms and paraded down busy streets to much fanfare before heading out for their runs. Joining a bicycle club became a way for men to see and be seen, to protect oneself from critiques of riders' behaviour, and to buttress popular representations of masculinity.

Bicycle clubs, and bicycle culture generally, were also present in Elora and Dresden, though their activities received considerably less coverage in local newspapers compared to Tillsonburg's Rovers. According to club statistics published in Canada's pre-eminent cycling magazine, the *Canadian Wheelman*, in 1896 the Dresden Stars Bicycle Club consisted of an impressive thirty-eight members (compared to the Rovers' thirty-one), while the Elora Irvine club had only sixteen members.[38] As with most bicycle clubs, Dresden's executive was wholly composed of White men. In terms of growth, the *Wheelman* noted that the club was "making rapid strides" in the 1896 season and that membership was expected to "far exceed that of last year."[39]

In May 1895, five years after the founding of the Tillsonburg Rovers, local women were invited to join when a "special run" was organized to attract new members. It was advertised in the *Observer* that the pace would be slower than normal to allow less agile riders to keep up. Women were "particularly urged to be present" to lend the "good influence of their society to this occasion."[40] This invitation (though sexist) suggests that traditional and conservative ideas about gender and social appropriateness in public were being re-evaluated (albeit slowly and selectively) as options for leisure expanded. Bicycle clubs were one of the few organizations in turn-of-the-century small towns that allowed women to join, but the sort of membership offered was disproportionate, as women were sought to fill seats and abstain from sitting on the executive. Examples of women's marginalization within bicycle clubs can be found in magazines like the *Canadian Wheelman*, where misogynistic articles and cartoons were published, criticizing female cyclists' looks and demeanour.

The oldest surviving photograph of the first generation of female Rovers showcases the gender disparity in the club's early years. Taken in 1895, the Rovers were posed in front of the ornate home of businessman S.B.W. Carpenter. When the *Observer* mentioned the photograph was being taken, it noted that extra copies would be made for sale.[41] The picture shows more than the twenty-six Rovers who belonged to the club at the time, and only nine of the subjects are women. By 1896, the club had grown to forty-eight members, though none of the new applicants for membership were female.[42]

Figure 14. The Rover Bicycle Club of Tillsonburg, 1895. Source: ANHS, Pollard Photo, Photograph Collection.

In the photo, the dress and stance of the women standing directly beside bicycles suggests they were members of the club, while those who are less visible and hovering in the background were likely the friends, relatives, or sweethearts of the male riders. Scholar Fiona Kinsey argues that portraits of mixed-sex bicycle clubs like the Rovers tended to emphasize the social and romantic prospects of club membership. By choosing to "privilege the group over the individual woman" cyclist, the "cooperative nature of excursionist recreational cycling" was accentuated.[43]

Unlike bicycle clubs in larger towns and cities, the Rovers do not appear to have adopted any sort of uniform or dress code. In the 1895 photograph, the men's attire ranges from three-piece suits to simpler ensembles of jackets and trousers. The women, on the other hand, are dressed rather formally and similarly in flat-topped caps, wide-lapelled and puffy-sleeved jackets, loose white blouses, and long, slim, belted skirts that may have been "split skirts." The female Rovers look as if they have abandoned corsets, but their riding attire was not altogether different from women's everyday wear. The ensemble was certainly far from the scandalous bloomers worn by some female cyclists in cities like Toronto, New York, and London. The Tillsonburg women's formal attire was likely pieced together purposefully to avoid claims that women cycled to achieve sexual gratification or to catch a husband. Donning more traditional modes of dress was also about convincing male members (who outnumbered the women considerably) that they, too, were serious and skilled riders. At the same time, the modestly cut high-necked blouses and lengthy skirts maintained the women's femininity and down-played fears about masculinized bodies. The "social sensibilities" of bicycle clubs, Bouchier argues, "compelled women to wear respectable, appropriate clothing to avoid charges of immorality."[44]

It is important to acknowledge how much dress reform in the late nine-teenth century contributed to women's ability to engage in a wider array of physical activities, such as cycling. In many respects, popular fashion mimicked women's position in nineteenth-century society. Accessories like bustles and corsets and long, cumbersome skirts constrained women by limit-ing their range of motion and diaphragmatic activity; consequently, their dress "projected the ideal of the fragile, feminine, delicate woman."[45] Well into the early twentieth century, women's fashions were not only restrictive but also dangerous. The dyes and treatments used in fabric production prompted a host of health concerns, such as mercury and arsenic poisoning. The garments themselves could augment the female shape so much that disfiguration occurred. Though stylish, voluminous skirts and puffy blouses posed hazards around open fires and in the workplace.[46]

Dress reform came to Canada later than it did to the United States and Britain and was not politicized to the same degree. Early supporters of dress reform had a reputation for being radicals and extremists, which may have deterred Canadian women from publicly supporting the cause.[47] Social status is also an important issue to consider in the history of dress reform: working-class women arguably needed more practical clothing the most, but because of their socio-economic position in society, such desires for social change were either silenced or ignored. However, once Western medical journals began paying more attention to the obvious connections between fashion, health, and hygiene, the style and function of women's clothing began to change. Over the course of the later nineteenth and early twentieth centuries, alterations to skirt lengths, fabric types, and garment construction occurred; lighter textiles, slimmer silhouettes, and looser-fitting dresses improved women's health and allowed them to move their bodies with greater ease while working, doing chores, or playing sports.

Within the pages of cycling magazines and local newspapers, bicycles and heterosexual companionship were habitually linked, especially after increasing numbers of women began taking up the activity and joining bicycle clubs. Alongside the gallantry and male camaraderie that defined bicycle clubs, the admission of female members became an opportunity to establish romantic connections. Like the Rovers, in May 1896 the Membership Committee of the Ingersoll Meteors Bicycle Club encouraged female cyclists to join the group and participate in its next run. To entice women, only a "nominal membership fee of 50c." was requested, which allegedly still entitled female riders to "full membership" in the CWA, along with semi-monthly copies of the *Canadian Wheelman*.[48] Though several women were already part of the club by this point, executives clearly wished to expand the membership.

The week after women were invited to join the Tillsonburg Rovers in 1895, a piece appeared in the *Observer* about a scandalous incident that occurred while the club was out for a run. On a warm May evening, the Rovers headed a few miles north of Tillsonburg to the village of Mount Elgin, where they rendezvoused with twenty male and eleven female members of the Meteors.[49] The details of their Mount Elgin meeting suggest much of the Rovers' and Meteors' contact was social in nature. After assembling, the cyclists enjoyed ice cream, lemonade, and "very pleasant social intercourse" with some of Mount Elgin's residents. On the ride home, however, one of the male Rovers, dubbed the "Adonis" of the group, was reported missing from the procession until located by fellow riders a short time later. Evidently, he had stayed behind to indulge in some "leave-taking ceremonies" with the "fairest Meteor of them all." After a stern rebuke from the Rovers' captain, "Adonis" promised not to repeat such an "offence."[50] It is unclear if this salacious encounter resulted in any sort of disciplinary action, but two months later an article in the *Canadian Wheelman* reminded the Meteors that they "must look sharp, and not fly away from the club, even if the Captain's substitute is 'out-of-sight.'"[51] Romantic scandals such as this buttressed the sexual and moral anxieties around women's right to cycle. The impropriety committed by the Rovers' Adonis and the female Meteor undoubtedly raised the ire of community members still concerned with the consequences of women's more observable presence in public spaces. Though cycling was enjoyed as both a homo- and heterosocial form of recreation, as well as a recommended means by which young people could meet and form attachments (particularly with persons from other towns), many continued to argue that the balance between proper decorum and danger required monitoring and regulation.[52]

Arguably, what concerned critics the most was that bicycles had the potential to transport couples away from town and therefore away from the scrutiny of parents, church officials, and neighbours. The traditional courting opportunities, such as supervised visits to a girl's home or attendance at a church-sponsored social, were supplemented by a host of new leisure activities that were not only secular but also took place in public. Bert Newman recalled that tandem bicycles were quite popular among courting couples in Tillsonburg. The fact that Burkholder's factory produced tandems right in town only added to the contraption's availability and popularity. By incorporating cycling into their courting rituals, couples could better establish more fulfilling relationships with one another and share intimacies (both sexual and non-sexual) in a private manner.[53] The tandem's unique construction, however, reinforced gendered, heterosexual, and patriarchal behaviours.[54] Newman says, "If a gentleman and a lady went riding together, the lady would ride behind, and she could pedal along with the man in front or, if he didn't want her to tire, he could pedal it alone."[55] In contrast to the freedom provided by the safety bicycle, women were placed in a subordinate position on tandems, with the man controlling the speed and direction of the machine.

Sleighing, Sledding, and Skating

Women's ability to pursue activities like cycling outdoors was greatly dependent on the weather and the recreational possibilities that lay in the local landscape. Though rural and small-town women were more likely to be prompted

Figure 15. Men and women snowshoeing in Elora, c. 1909. Source: WCMA, A2006.112, ph 20829.

outdoors by the warmer temperatures of later spring, summer, and early autumn, increasingly they also found opportunities for recreation during the colder winter months. Historians argue that the "northern character theme," or the notion that the "bracing climate" made Canadians more robust,[56] partly explains why so many reformers and social commentators began urging men and women in the later nineteenth century to head outdoors and counter the sedentary tendencies of winter. Encouraging enjoyment of the outdoors brought women's interests to the fore, particularly in rural areas and small towns, where open spaces and local waterways could host a range of seasonal pastimes such as snowshoeing, sledding, sleighing, and skating.

Heterosocial activities such as sleighing and sledding parties served a variety of purposes. Aside from providing transportation during the winter months, sleds and sleighs also became mediums for simple and informal gatherings of friends, neighbours, and families. Sleighs were large, horse-drawn vehicles with skis that could carry several people at a time. Sleds (or toboggans), on the other hand, were smaller and used by a single person or pair of people to ride down a hill.

In 1869, Emma Clarke of Elora wrote to her sister Florence that "it is winter in earnest now, the snow is very deep here & it is splendid sleighing."[57]

Figure 16. Two women with a sled in Tillsonburg, early 1900s. Source: ANHS, Photograph Collection.

In February 1890, the *Tillsonburg Observer* commented on the lively appearance of sleighs throughout town, with "everybody owning or able to obtain a vehicle being out enjoying the sleighing."[58] Some religious organizations used sleighing for fundraising purposes: when the Ladies' Aid Society of Tillsonburg's Methodist church organized a sleighing party fundraiser in 1895, an estimated twenty-five sleighs containing approximately 150 participants took part, from which "the financial proceeds were very satisfactory."[59]

Sleighing was also a favoured pastime among courting couples.[60] Like bicycles and "moonlight specials" by rail, sleighs had the ability to transport couples away from town and the prying eyes of community monitors. Periodicals like the *Farmer's Advocate* advised rural women on proper sleighing etiquette, arguing that though it was not wholly improper for a young lady to accept an invitation for a sleigh ride, she must remember that "to be respected is a greater compliment than to be loved, and enduring love can only follow after respect." Women who found themselves in a compromising position were reminded to make sure they "check all ungentlemanly advances."[61] It is unclear if men were similarly warned to curtail such unseemly behaviour.

Like sleighing, sledding also brought young people together and was a popular activity among courting couples. William Harcourt Popham recalled that "bob-sledding" was popular with the "young fellows" of Tillsonburg because "it gave them a chance to hug the girls all the way down the hill."[62] Sledding could also be enjoyed as an individual activity. Similar to snowshoeing and other winter pastimes, in the later nineteenth century sledding/tobogganing was considered a quintessential Canadian leisure pursuit, "an Indigenous activity that had been tamed, organized, and made more scientific"[63] through the mass production of sleds, the grooming of local hills, and widely understood rules about riders' behaviour. The ability to capably fly down a hill on a sled and withstand the bracing temperatures of winter signified one's hardiness and fortitude, and contributed to the growth of a distinctly White Canadian identity that was shaped by climate and geography. Recalling her childhood, Jessie McLean, then Mrs. Charles Thomson, described how "all the children piled out of the front doors of the school to what is now the Lancaster house hill, for a glorious long toboggan slide right down to Oxford street."[64] Tillsonburg was so "hilly" that "tobogganing was literally 'at the door' for [the] young fry."[65] Agnes McGregor also recalled sledding on Tillsonburg's "many steep hills" during her youth.[66] Echoing the changes occurring in the ways that public spaces were occupied and utilized, in 1880 the *Farmer's Advocate* proclaimed that "as a winter sport, the use of the sled" should also be "encouraged for girls, not less than for boys."[67] Julia McNair Wright's nineteenth-century etiquette guide affirmed that "in winter, sleds should not be denied: they are good for both boys and girls."[68] Though sledding was typically enjoyed by children and teens, alterations to women's dress in the late nineteenth century allowed greater numbers of "lady tobogganists" to take to the hills. By ditching onerous hoops and crinolines and wrapping themselves in sheets, women could more ably careen down snow-topped embankments.[69]

Though residents of Dresden, Tillsonburg, and Elora enjoyed all sorts of winter activities, arguably ice skating stood above the rest in terms of its popularity and ability to draw female participants.[70] Inconsistent weather patterns and the lack of assurance that "good" ice would appear every winter only added to its allure. In small towns, ice skating was so appealing that rinks were often the first sports facility to be constructed.[71] Once the preserve of upper-class males, by the early twentieth century class and gender segregation were less "central to the organization of the activity."[72] Particularly after the 1870s and 1880s, when the activity had become a regular fixture in the winter social calendar, newspaper articles from Dresden, Tillsonburg, and Elora indicate that seemingly equal numbers of men and women, adolescents, and children from across socio-economic strata had become avid participants. Because ice skating was classified as a hybrid of walking and classical dance,[73] it was generally considered to be a positive and socially appropriate activity for women, and an enjoyable way to exercise the body. Compared to male-dominated team sports that were defined by players' speed and strength, the artistry and agility required for skating meant it was considered more suitable for females. The activity, however, also required a great deal of stamina and physical strength. In 1892, the *Farmer's Advocate* remarked that girls should not be persuaded away from this sort of physical activity and "good hard play" because it was allegedly "unladylike." Doing so, the author argues, would inevitably result in "evil consequences."[74] Female readers of the *Elora Express* were advised that during the "crisp, bracing weather" of winter, they should "play out in the open air, in God's sunshine, until your lungs breathe deeply of the invigorating atmosphere," because "every breath taken will be an inspiration of joy and health to you."[75]

As the middle class, especially, embraced ice skating, manufacturers began marketing equipment specifically to female consumers, including wooden supports for stability and more functional outerwear. "Hand-in-hand" skating, where men or more experienced women guided novice skaters around the ice, also encouraged greater numbers of women to try the activity.[76] This heterosocial mixing, though carefully monitored by nearby skaters and community members, allowed men and women an opportunity to spend time together in a recognized public setting. As with comparable forms of mixed-sex leisure, bodies often came into close contact while skating, allowing some couples the opportunity to flirt and form romantic attachments. In 1882, one "pulpit orator" from southwestern Ontario protested

Figure 17. Man and woman ice skating in Tillsonburg, 1913. Source: ANHS, Photograph Collection.

this sort of heterosexual interaction, dubbing the skating rink the "gate of hell" where "the better the skater the bigger the devil."[77]

According to Inez B. (Eagleson) Perrin, Dresden's first skating rink was located on the "bleak, cold Sydenham river," and when she ventured out onto its frozen landscape, she used her mother's "old-fashioned spring skate," which had once been the "latest thing."[78] Invented in 1861 in Dartmouth, Nova Scotia, by industrialist John Forbes, the spring skate was the first removable, adjustable, and mass-produced skate to be patented.[79] It remained popular until the more modern invention of the tall skating boot with an attached blade. Because spring skates accommodated various foot widths and sizes, Perrin writes, one pair could be shared by several members of a family, thus making skating a reasonably affordable activity. The 1897 T. Eaton Co. Christmas catalogue, popular among rural and small-town Ontario consumers, advertised pairs of skates ranging in price from fifty cents to $2.75.[80] Perrin remembers that "they were sold as small, medium and large. A spring lever spread the front clips, and when closed clamped the skate to the sole of the boot. A strap tightly buckled over the toe and another from the heel secured the skate more firmly to the boot."[81]

Having a vast body of water like the Grand River running through Elora undoubtedly heightened the appeal of skating for its citizens. In Tillsonburg, Big Otter Creek and various mill ponds served skaters' needs. In 1879, plans were drawn up by a group of local businessmen for Elora's first properly enclosed skating facility, which became the Elora Rink Co. (later renamed the Elora Curling and Skating Rink Co.). The ice surface measured 156 by 70 feet and the surrounding structure was outfitted with space for spectators and dressing rooms for skaters. At the time of its construction, season passes to the rink were two dollars for men, $1.50 for women, and $1.00 for children. A family pass was four dollars and a single admission cost ten cents.[82] In her diary, Olive Snyder mentions another "rink" in town that she frequented with "the kids" but does not elaborate on its size, amenities, or location.[83]

The original Elora rink was primarily used for recreational skating, and to a lesser degree for hockey games, ice-skating carnivals, and travelling performers. According to newspaper reports, local hockey games were always well-attended. A single admission was relatively affordable at fifteen cents for men and ten cents for women and children. Often this included a "free skate" for the spectators after the game finished.[84] Beginning in 1898, touring companies of professional speed skaters began visiting the area, and these events became quite popular, with spectators packing the arena whenever a race was scheduled.[85] Gamblers even made money off the favoured skaters.

Tillsonburg's first skating rink was "in full blast" by December 1880 and named the Victoria Skating Rink. "Though an open air rink," the *Observer* reported after its grand opening, "it is well kept, and owing to its greater size and keener ice, is far ahead of any covered rink."[86] Over the course of the 1880s and 1890s, several open air rinks were constructed as owners competed for the business of skating enthusiasts. Town councils tended to remain detached from these rinks, leaving their supervision and maintenance to private investors hoping to turn a profit. To entice skaters (and draw them away from competing rinks), owners provided various amenities, including stoves for warmth and even cigars and coffee. As small-town rinks were outfitted with middle-class comforts in mind, skating began to attract even more converts, many of whom were women. Enclosed rinks that offered protection from the elements partially account for the enhanced interest.[87] Some of the prescriptive literature, however, discouraged women from using these facilities for health reasons. One late nineteenth-century discourse on physical culture advised women that "skating is good exercise; but is best practiced out-of-doors. Rinks are too often damp and not well ventilated."[88]

Some towns, like Elora and Tillsonburg, began constructing enclosed rinks in the late nineteenth century because similar facilities had been erected in nearby communities. It was commonplace for small towns to compete with one another to see who had the latest and greatest advancements in recreational offerings, technology, and social services. Like in cities, local officials used these qualities to promote their town as "a place worth living in, worth working in, and worth investing in."[89] It was always considered a boon for a community when it could boast that it was following the trends of larger towns and cities in building modern and novel sports facilities. The revenue produced by these venues, such as ticket sales to hockey games and ice-skating shows, stimulated the local economy. The establishment of more modern public buildings and sports facilities also cemented links with the surrounding countryside by establishing the town as a centre for economic, commercial, social, and leisure services, fostering a sense of civic pride among residents.[90]

Ice skating was the sort of sport that did not necessarily have to cost a lot of money, but elements of it were certainly distinguished by class lines. Because local rivers were public spaces, skaters could use them free of charge. However, there was significant work involved in clearing snow from the ice and ensuring that it was safe. Some, like Kate Aitken's family, constructed their own rinks in backyards. She says: "We had our own rink in our back yard, flooded with pails of water that froze as fast as we threw it on. Father allowed us to make a bonfire at the far end of the yard, using old boxes. Sitting on logs from the woodpile, with chilled hands we would buckle on our skates, then dash round and round that little enclosure until there was absolutely no feeling in the feet, and cheeks and nose were frostbitten. Then we would clump into the kitchen for warmth and hot food."[91]

While some preferred constructing their own rinks, those who chose to casually use public waterways increased the likelihood of hurting themselves, or worse, falling through the ice; at a privately owned rink, however, all this work and worry was taken care of by the owner(s). This reason alone prompted many to pay a single or seasonal fee to skate at local rinks and join skating clubs. By the 1870s, skating clubs had been established in many of Canada's larger cities, though like other sports organizations, they limited membership to male applicants. Some early skating clubs do list women on their rosters, but often membership was obtained through family connections. At the Lorne skating and curling rink on the Waterhouse millpond in Tillsonburg, season tickets for the winter of 1882 cost $2.50 for families, two dollars for doubles, and $1.50 for singles. A single admission cost ten cents.[92] The fees were comparable to those of the Elora skating rink, though both facilities charged much less than those cited by Marks in *Revivals and Roller Rinks*, where she estimates that season tickets, on average, ranged between four dollars and $2.50 in the later nineteenth century.[93] The range of costs likely reflects how much care and maintenance a rink needed and how much profit the private owner hoped to make. Season ticket owners were almost entirely middle- and upper-class men and women. Most working-class women and girls would not have been able to afford a season pass, so spending time at skating rinks was relegated to the occasional purchase of a single admission or a ticket to a special show.[94] The rest of the time, they used ungroomed and unsupervised waterways. In Tillsonburg, Agnes Waller recalled that she was allowed to skate on E.D. Tillson's trout pond because her brother worked at one of the Tillson mill offices.[95]

Skating rinks (and sports venues generally) became sites where class differences and, to a lesser extent, religious and ethnic tensions played out in small towns.[96] When the annual skating club carnivals were held, the social exclusivity attached to club membership was on display as the middle and upper classes performed their class privilege. Here, local high society moved "from the ballroom onto the ice."[97] Though these spectacles involved both male and female participants, women performed triple duty as performers, set designers, and seamstresses. Considerable time and effort were necessary to transform the rink and construct the elaborate costumes. Carnivals could be held as frequently as once a month or even once a week if there was enough interest. Though the numbers of participants varied from town to town, one carnival in Elora in 1914 featured thirty-five to forty people performing in the show.[98] At skating carnivals in the town of Beeton, Kate Aitken was amazed by the "many hours [that] went into manufacturing those costumes." She recalls that most were made of "crepe paper, tacked together and decorated with feathers, veiling, paper hearts, [or] just anything," despite concerns that the costumes were too flimsy and cold for children.[99] Popular turn-of-the-century carnival themes included historical pageants, fairytale motifs, and ethnographic displays of Indigenous and foreign peoples. At one Elora skating carnival in 1905, the rink's members competed in front of a mixed-sex panel of judges to determine whose costume was the "Best." This carnival's categories speak to prominent and racist representations of religious and ethnic difference at the time: participants, for example, competed for "Best Indian Chief," "Best Three of Kind (Irishman, Dutchman and Jew)," and the best representation of a person of African ancestry. Admission was "Gents 15c; Ladies and Children 10c."[100] In Tillsonburg in January 1903, approximately 500 spectators and performers attended a skating carnival that featured local citizens in "fancy" costume, such as the "Japanese lady," impersonated by Rosalind Harrison, Marguerite Sinclair's "Pocahontas," and Minnie Andrews, the "colored lady."[101] Akin to the way travel clubs and garden parties allowed small-town men and women to act in ways they considered more worldly and refined, as Chapter 5 discusses, the attire donned by carnival performers permitted them a measure of freedom in which to "engage in 'disorderly' conduct" or "mockery."[102] Resultingly, the competitions and racialized garb reinforced and reproduced popular and discriminatory stereotypes for both audiences and participants.

Despite its popularity and reputation for providing healthful amusement, skating was not always a safe or accessible means of outdoor recreation. In a letter to her sister Muriel in 1914, thirty-one-year-old Euphie Clark wrote there was a "dandy rink" in Elora that year where she hoped to go for a skate "at least once a week."[103] Unfortunately, that winter's extremely poor road conditions deterred her from travelling to town as often as she would have liked. In January 1920, Margaret Templin of Fergus wrote in her diary that during one recent skate, "it was so cold we nearly froze but we had a good time. I had to stop a little ahead of time, because I had an awful cramp in my foot."[104] Enclosed rinks required regular maintenance and were often criticized for the poor state of their amenities. Before the invention of artificial ice, the condition of natural ice in arenas was at the whim of temperature variations, so uneven, soft, and bumpy surfaces were common. In addition to upgrades to the lighting system and the expansion of spectator seating, other "necessary improvements" were made to Elora's rink in 1899 so that every "convenience" was available to women. Especially, safety measures such as the construction of lockers and the hanging of wire screens to protect spectators from flying hockey pucks enhanced the experience for all users.[105]

For reasons of preference and affordability, many Elora skaters continued to use open-air and unmonitored waterways despite the dangers they posed. In December 1903, it was reported that a young skater out on the Grand

River was "treated to an involuntary cold bath" one evening, though no serious harm was done.[106] In 1891, while skating on the Sydenham River near Dresden, young Stella Ripley fell through the ice. The *Dresden Times* reported that the girl's screams attracted a nearby man, who was able to come to her rescue and save her from a "watery grave."[107] Tillsonburg resident William Harcourt Popham recalled that during his youth in the early 1900s, "many skating parties—all, lots of fun—were held on the pond which was quite deep—but I only recall one drowning!"[108] During one winter in Tillsonburg, it was reported that the "horrible pullback" would prevent women from skating that season, which may have been a reference to receding ice.[109] Even skating equipment posed difficulties. Popham remembered that hitting an exposed tuft of grass could easily cause a spring skate to separate from a boot. The time required to properly re-fasten the skates, Popham remembered, was a frustration shared among skaters.[110]

Ladies and Lawns

When the weather cooperated, rural and small-town women enjoyed spending time outdoors on the lawns surrounding their homes. After the snow had melted and temperatures moderated, women left their cozy parlours and sitting rooms behind and used their grass, porches, and verandas for various formal and informal leisure activities. The lawn served as an extension of the home's interior, a pseudo-domestic space with its well-kept greenery, shrubbery, and outdoor furniture.[111] In the summer months, gardens of various size and composition took up a great deal of women's time. In 1881, the *Rural Canadian* strongly recommended that "every country woman have a garden that she keep and dress with her own hands, or that she supervise and manage," because if "any employment is feminine, it would seem that this is. If any is healthy, this must be. If any be pleasurable, none can be more so than this."[112] Promised feelings of usefulness, happiness, and health, women were advised to grow a mixture of fruits and vegetables, sprinkled with a few flowers for decorative effect. Even children were told to take up gardening for the healthful properties of outdoor time. Diaries from rural and small-town

Figure 18. Girls from Dresden holding flowers and leaves. The girls were likely attending a science or botany class at the nearby town hall. Photo taken in front of the Huston house, c. 1910. Source: DA, Photograph Collection.

Figure 19. Man and two women playing croquet in Tillsonburg, c. 1890s. Source: ANHS, Pollard Photo, Photograph Collection.

Figure 20. Women playing croquet in Tillsonburg, early 1900s. Source: ANHS, Photograph Collection.

women often detail the particulars of garden maintenance and, for some, the necessity of growing their own produce.

Though gardening straddles the line between labour and leisure because it can be physically demanding and tied to the preparation of food, many women gardened in the company of female friends and neighbours and took great pride in their efforts, which suggests it was considered a pleasurable pastime. The fact that many agricultural exhibitions welcomed women's submissions of cut flower displays and window box arrangements shows that gardening was not always about sustenance. The establishment of horticultural societies throughout Ontario in the mid-nineteenth century also speaks to the widespread interest in the activity. Formed in 1850, Elora's horticultural society was initially an androcentric organization that eventually offered women the opportunity to submit entries in its shows.[113] Ornamental horticulture was a hobby men and women shared, and entering competitions and shows provided a sense of fulfillment as they placed their efforts on display.[114]

For many women, the lawn served as the backdrop for some of the new sporting and game crazes imported from Europe, such as croquet. On the lawn adjoining Avondale Presbyterian church and its manse, for example, Agnes McGregor's family set aside a small tract of grass explicitly for croquet matches. In their diaries, Minnie Smith and Olive Snyder both mention playing croquet at home and at their friends' homes.

Just as popular as (and perhaps more so than) croquet was lawn tennis. In Dresden, Tillsonburg, and Elora, tennis was played quite regularly in the summer months among small groups of friends or sisters. Evidence of women playing lawn tennis began appearing in local newspapers around 1900.[115] Women's tennis championships were held in Canada as early as 1883, but the sport really took off in the 1890s as more women played the game at a competitive level. In Tillsonburg, women's matches and tournaments were originally held on the grounds of the public high school until a tennis court was constructed at the Sinclair residence. In 1902, Lillian and Marguerite Sinclair were instrumental in forming one of the first female-centred sports organizations in town, the Grasshopper Tennis Club. Along with playing tennis, the Grasshoppers also hosted popular fortnightly teas.[116] A women's tennis club was formed in Elora in 1905. At the initial meeting, a small group of "officers" was appointed, consisting of both married and single women. The club primarily used the facilities at Irvine Park, though many private courts were also at its disposal.[117] While members of Tillsonburg's elite were drawn to the formal qualities of the Grasshopper Tennis Club, middle-class women like Olive Snyder and her sisters enjoyed playing informally at home on a makeshift court. In May 1913, for instance, Olive recorded that "K" had set up the tennis net for the first time that year. After their match concluded, they enjoyed a cup of tea on the grounds. For the remainder of that summer, Snyder played regularly, both with her sisters and her mixed-sex group of friends.[118]

Physical activity and sports like lawn tennis could help women cope with various maladies, including the rigours of the menstrual cycle. Though references to menstruation are scarce in Victorian and Edwardian literature, personal correspondence provides some insights into women's experiences. In August 1913 Muriel Clark received a letter from her sister, Euphie, in Elora, in which Euphie mentions that though she "was 'sick'" that week she "hadn't a least bit of a cramp. You may be sure I am tickled all over." She goes on to say that same week she participated in the season's first game of mixed doubles tennis, which helped make her feel like she had "come to life again."[119] Between the 1870s and the turn of the century, several unsubstantiated claims about menstruation were made by the medical community, warning that "too much activity or imprudence during menstruation led to illness."[120] While these claims may have kept women from indulging in more aggressive and physically demanding modes of recreation, Euphie writes that participating in the tennis match actually helped relieve her "sickness."

Mixed-doubles matches were an important feature of lawn tennis's evolution in the later years of the nineteenth century, one of the few modes of physical activity where men and women interacted as both partners and adversaries.[121] Like ice skating, lawn tennis was originally the preserve of upper-class males who could display their elitism through "established ideals of 'acceptable' play" such as sportsmanlike conduct.[122] After rules of play

Figure 21. Young Tillsonburg women posing with tennis racquets, c. 1890s. Source: ANHS, Pollard Photo, Photograph Collection.

Figure 22. Two couples in Tillsonburg posing with tennis racquets, early 1900s. Source: ANHS, Photograph Collection.

were codified by the British Lawn Tennis Association in 1888, the sport was considered suitable for women because male players were now subject to codes of "behavioural and emotional self-control when in their presence."[123] More practically, around this time the height of the net was lowered from six feet to three-and-a-half feet, which better accommodated female players and permitted a host of new and different techniques for hitting the ball. Several late nineteenth-century etiquette manuals recommended a friendly match of tennis as an appropriate amusement at morning and afternoon parties during the summer.[124] As noted in Olive Snyder's diary, tennis courts often became picnic grounds, as the players engaged in some social dining after the match. Though lawn tennis required a certain level of physicality, it did not strain the cardiovascular system, so women could enjoy it "without being subjected to insinuations of rompishness."[125] Much like cycling attire, as evidenced by surviving photographs, women's dress on the tennis court remained socially appropriate and comparable to their everyday wear. Many followed the British tradition and donned white linen dresses and low-heeled shoes, which facilitated movement and kept the body cool.

Maintaining the pristine grass of a tennis court or the velvet-like surface of a croquet lawn involved a significant amount of time and labour. Among the upper class, a groomer would have been hired for this purpose. When it came to enjoying lawn sports and other forms of recreation, Adams and other Canadian sport historians have shown that "the play of the few depended on the work of many."[126] Though the Snyders probably oversaw their own maintenance because the family's court was primarily for personal use, the public nature of the Sinclairs' court meant keeping the grounds spotless and well-groomed, a task that would have fallen to a hired labourer.

Conclusion

The period between the 1870s and the beginning of the First World War marked an important era in the growth of sports and opportunities for physical recreation. Over this forty-plus-year period, ideas about gender appropriateness and popular attitudes toward women's bodies and place in public were changing as new ideas emerged about reproductive health and exercise. Though opportunities to engage in sport remained unequal between the sexes in Dresden, Tillsonburg, and Elora, during the period in question there was a marked increase in the amount of time spent discussing women's physical well-being in newspapers, rural and agricultural periodicals, diaries, and letters. Surviving photographs, too, provide important documentation of the shifts occurring in the ways outdoor games and sports were played and by whom. However, the gap between city and country remained stark when it came to sports. In larger urban centres, women were playing on competitive hockey and basketball teams by the 1890s, but the transference of a more competitive and professional sporting culture to small-town Ontario mostly did not occur until after the First World War.

Though opportunities for organized play remained limited, it was still important to recognize that exercise also benefited women physically and emotionally, albeit in gender-specific ways. Despite barriers related to options and spaces for play, middle-class and elite women and girls in Dresden, Tillsonburg, and Elora found ways in all seasons of the year to engage in popular activities like a game of croquet, a spin around the skating rink, or a bicycle ride down a country road. As with all forms of leisure, some activities were marked by their cost and class exclusivity, but overall, the sports and physical recreations that small-town women pursued the most were those that could be played freely and sporadically. Just as women became more visible at public entertainments like minstrel shows and circuses, they also carved a niche for themselves in public spaces where they moved their bodies for recreational purposes. Not only were these women consumers of the new sporting crazes, they were also organizers and promoters, initiating new sports clubs and endorsing the benefits of physical recreation to sisters, daughters, friends, and neighbours.

While women in Dresden, Tillsonburg, and Elora were increasingly becoming more observable in their respective town's public spaces, connections to the private sphere and ideas about social appropriateness never fully disappeared when they entered a public space, be it a theatre or a baseball diamond. A woman's ability to pursue leisure was still conditional upon her responsibilities at home. The Sinclair sisters, for instance, were able to establish and play for the Grasshoppper Tennis Club because their privileged status afforded them greater access to resources such as domestic servants. As a single, middle-class woman who resided with her parents, Olive Snyder was free to play lawn tennis with her sisters and friends once her paid work and household chores were completed. To create "free" time, most women had no choice but to blend labour and leisure or to restrict their activities to ones that could occur around the home. Consequently, as the following chapter demonstrates, small-town women's homes remained an important—if not *the* most important—site for leisure.

FOUR

Crazy Teas and Christmas Trees:
Leisure at Home

Saturday 15 June 1878

Today has been very hot and bright. Since dark it has been
sprinkling rain. This morning I baked bread and scrubbed.
This afternoon I went down to Alfred's to fix Annie's dress
and bring pa home. Mr. & Mrs. Cameron and Miss Bowfield
were there but I did not see them as I did not go into the
room. David went off somewhere to play ball tonight and
did not come home until after nine. George came home
just at nine. Jenny and I watered the garden. Tonight I read
a story aloud.[1]

ETWEEN 1878 AND 1879, twenty-four-year-old Ann Amelia Day of
Eramosa Township, Wellington County, was an avid diarist. At the
time she wrote her 15 June entry, Day was still residing at home, but
less than a year later she married farmer Noah Sunley and established a home
of her own. During this time Day maintained an almost daily record of her
activities, noting matter-of-fact details such as weather patterns, errands,
and domestic chores. The comings and goings of friends and family, her
attendance at public events, and the myriad ways she spent her leisure hours

also receive considerable attention. As a middle-class daughter and later housewife, Day's time was filled with family obligations and domestic duties, though in her spare moments she always made time for small pleasures like diary writing. The very act of keeping a diary signals the importance of setting aside a small block of time to indulge in some fulfilling record keeping. As evidenced in her entries, most of Day's social activities involved spending time with extended networks of kin in her home. Though she often went skating, for a buggy ride or walk, or attended the occasional tea meeting or religious lecture, Day's diary entries signify that the bulk of her "free" time was spent entertaining visitors or visiting others in their homes.

For middle-class women like Ann Amelia Day, the "home was the site of both public and private life: of production and reproduction, of farm work and housework, [...] and of livelihood and leisure."[2] Within the home and its surrounding grounds, women spent time with their parents and siblings, husbands and children, and friends and neighbours. For many women, the home played an integral and pivotal role in the processes by which they maintained important ties to friends, family, communities, and neighbourhoods. As the intimate setting of the turn-of-the-century home underwent structural changes, including more modern and spacious layouts and the addition of labour-saving devices, increasing numbers of women were afforded more time for leisure and new kinds of activities to pursue.

By hosting formal and informal soirées, being visitors in others' homes, or indulging in simple parlour games, small-town women maintained a high level of sociability. This fact complicates some of the more popular perceptions of rural and small-town culture, which is often assumed to be prosaic and unrefined. American historian Ellen M. Plante, for instance, asserts that outside of large cities, women's domestic gatherings were much more informal, simple, and unstructured owing to the lack of "social seasons."[3] Small-town folk may not have socialized according to "seasons" designed by the elite, but such generalizations about their alleged provincialism do not reflect local realities. Class and status were structured according to local circumstances, so analyzing visiting patterns and domestic leisure preferences illuminates the "strategies by which social classes define[d] or consolidate[d] their positions" outside of cities.[4] The pomp and ceremony that increasingly defined women's home gatherings, for instance, points to middle- and upper-class desires to epitomize bourgeois culture and cultivate respectability.

By the turn of the century, notices about women's parties, dances, balls, teas, celebrations, and visits were commonplace and often occupied a substantial amount of space in the social columns of local newspapers. Larger and more elaborate gatherings sometimes elicited a full story on the front page. The respective newspapers of Dresden, Tillsonburg, and Elora functioned as barometers for their communities, indicating when notable events and gatherings would occur and reporting on their success. Though most articles were short accounts of women calling on one another, this seemingly trivial information helps to better reconstruct and determine how age, gender, kinship, community, and class relations impacted women's social time in rural and small-town contexts.[5] Each week, these notices reminded readers that their communities contained tightly defined social circles that selectively chose their leisure activities and who may participate. Naturally, more attention was paid in the press to the grandiose entertainments hosted by wealthier townsfolk, providing a rich archive from which to reconstruct how local elites and some of their middle-class friends spent their free time. It would be remiss not to include their histories here, but it should be clarified that the scope and scale of their sociability was largely confined to their circles alone and does not represent how all residents mingled.

The parties, socials, and entertainments that took place in working-class households were rarely, if ever, mentioned in newspaper social columns. When such an event did enter public discourse, the alleged lawlessness or immoral behaviour resulting from the occasion was often the purpose of the reference. Otherwise, as noted earlier, it has been difficult to locate much about the private and social lives of poorer and marginalized women in these communities. Like their wealthier counterparts, working-class women and girls did visit with one another as often as possible, but they also faced more stringent time and financial constraints. The paucity of information about their domestic recreations in newspapers likely stems from a lack of interest amongst the readership and editors, and not lack of occasions. The nature of working-class women's leisure, which tended to be more informal and unstructured, did not captivate readers the same way that the spectacles taking place in more affluent households did.

Within this chapter, the prescriptive literature found in rural periodicals such as the *Farmer's Advocate* illustrates how domestic leisure activities, particularly after the 1890s, were transforming as middle-class and elite women strove to incorporate elements of modernism into their everyday lives. Advice columns in newspapers and periodicals provide ample evidence of the changes taking place, yet not all female readers blindly followed these directives, which were often disingenuous. Many periodicals, for example, used the advice provided by columnists to pressure women into buying ready-made goods so they could be part of a broader culture of consumption and consumerism.[6] Nevertheless, examining readers' inquiries and editors' responses provides a window into women's concerns regarding home, work, and family.[7] Women's requests for advice demonstrates that they trusted the publications and consulted them regularly. Though columnists aimed to set the standard for what was "proper," not all of the advice was intended for upper-class hostesses. Some offered more practical and frugal suggestions to women with tighter budgets.

The sheer variety of domestic amusements popular around the turn of the century indicates that women, regardless of age, class, or location, were avid and eager consumers of a range of recreational options. From the simple and affordable card games and parlour amusements of the working and middle classes to the costlier masquerades and dinner soirées of the elite, this chapter will show how leisure was a fundamental component of domestic life in Dresden, Tillsonburg, and Elora. Purposely excluded here is a detailed examination of the clubs, charities, and auxiliaries that met in members' homes. Because the growth in club membership was tied to the pursuit of self- and civic improvement outside the home, this sort of leisure was explored in Chapter 2.

Though class and the female life cycle remained integral to the structure, composition, and expansion of domestic leisure activities, between the 1870s and the early 1910s, three important changes occurred that reverberated in the ways that women enjoyed social time at home. First, late nineteenth-century architectural styles and advancements in the mass production of goods provided new mediums in which to enjoy domestic leisure as a family unit. Second, teas, dinners, and holiday parties helped foster both homo- and heterosocial networks of socialization and allowed women to indulge their fondness for entertaining and performing their class privilege. And, finally, the necessity of blending their labour and leisure at times meant less affluent women could still nurture and maintain important bonds of kinship and friendship.

"Happy Homes Make Happy Hearts"

According to figures from the 1891 census, most families in Dresden, Tillsonburg, and Elora lived in modest, single-family detached dwellings constructed of wood or brick, which signalled the occupants' socio-economic status. On average, houses were one or two storeys high and consisted of six to ten rooms and usually a porch of some sort.[8] Most households were conjugal family units, but widowed parents, parents-in-law, and nieces and nephews could also be residents. Domestic servants, nurses, and other full-time help were common in the homes of wealthier citizens. Some middle-class homes operated as boarding houses for male labourers and single working women. Depending on the size of the lot, the lawn surrounding the residence provided space for flower and vegetable gardens, or a small kitchen garden at the very least. As Andrew C. Holman notes, the outward appearance of houses in small-town Ontario reflected the owner's social standing within the community, so careful measures were taken to ensure that homes appeared tidy yet unpretentious. To that end, Holman explains, "a moderate number of bushes of various sizes and neatly mown grass were considered appropriate; a well-pruned tree, even better. A well-kept yard and garden were a credit to the homeowner and the neighbourhood."[9] Around farmhouses, barns and other outbuildings served the function of storing livestock, seed, silage, and equipment.

Of the six to ten rooms located inside homes, generally only two were deemed social spaces: the dining room and the parlour/sitting room/front room.[10] Larger homes, such as those of the affluent Tillson and Sinclair families in Tillsonburg, might contain libraries, smoking rooms, and ballrooms that were constructed for recreational (and gendered) purposes. Outside of these rooms, and apart from the occasional gathering in the kitchen, the home's other rooms were rarely used for leisure.[11] Many middle-class homes had formal dining rooms, but their use was reserved for holidays, family occasions, or parties. Most meals were consumed in the kitchen or breakfast room. Even when a family's residence contained few rooms, it became an important feature of late nineteenth-century home construction to have a special occasion room because, when needed, it provided space to entertain guests.[12]

The parlour occupies a position of great spatial and symbolic importance in the manifold ways women acted as hostesses and organizers of domestic amusements. In most single-family detached homes, when viewing the home from the street, one could easily "read" the parlour's position because it protruded from the front of the home, facing the street or road.[13] It was common to locate a formal front door near the parlour that was restricted to guests' usage; family members and household employees used the more discreet and subtle side and back entrances. Locating semi-public entertainment spaces near the home's front ensured that guests (and the family itself) were not privy to the hustle and bustle of the kitchen and other work rooms in the rear quarters. The specific "location, arrangement, style, and size" of upper-class homes in particular purposely separated spaces where work and play occurred, thus situating "men (and women) in a culture ordered according to class."[14]

By the mid-nineteenth century, parlours and sitting rooms could be found in many Canadian homes. Prior to this, the family's social world was centred in the kitchen because of the ever-present warmth provided by the hearth or cook stove. As the nineteenth century progressed and home heating and lighting systems improved, houses were compartmentalized into areas of work and play and familial roles were redefined, with a greater importance placed on homemaking.[15] Many middle- and upper-class families constructed new homes based on patterns found in home design catalogues and within these predetermined arrangements, rooms were embedded with gendered and recreational meanings. Libraries and game rooms were dubbed masculine domains, while parlours and dining rooms, because of domestic connotations, were more feminine realms.[16] These rooms had dual purposes, however, since they straddled the line between public and private. Because "the house expressed to the public world the aspirations and economic mobility of all its inhabitants,"[17] middle- and upper-class women often hosted entertainments and parties for their husbands' colleagues or potential business partners in the hopes of enhancing the family's financial prospects. In working-class homes, free space was rare, but owing to the importance placed on "giv[ing] social ceremony its due," American historian Katherine C. Grier argues, even poorer families set aside space in the home for recreational purposes.[18] Regardless of their size or arrangement, working-class parlours functioned similarly to those in middle- and upper-class homes: to impart a sense of order, refinement, and respectability to visitors and the public.[19]

In rural and small-town Ontario, evidence from the period suggests that parlours were used sporadically and for a variety of reasons. Some families limited their use to special occasions like weddings or funerals, or used them as temporary guest bedrooms and sickrooms.[20] Some families (and children especially) spent very little time in the parlour.[21] Kate Aitken remembered it as an unwelcoming and uncomfortable space, containing items like photograph albums and stereoscopes that were restricted to guests' use.[22] In many homes, the ornate parlour was primarily used as the setting for parties and dances, because it was "the stage where the family put itself on display."[23] The scope of the leisure activity being hosted certainly defined a woman's standing in the local hierarchy, but the parlour itself also imparted a specific identity to visitors. Some historians have argued that rural families were less concerned with using their parlours to display conspicuous consumption,[24] but periodicals like the *Farmer's Advocate* did encourage women to relocate their entertainments to the parlour because its ambiance created memorable and unique experiences. Though visiting patterns among citizens in Dresden,

Tillsonburg, and Elora tended to be relaxed and informal, many middle- and upper-class women were fond of the sort of genteel leisure that allowed them to showcase their domestic prowess.

No matter how much or how little it was used, the parlour was often *the* showpiece of the home. A typical parlour's walls were constructed from a variety of panelling, woodwork, shelving, and mouldings. Wall coverings, drapes, and carpet added colour and style, complemented by "parlour suites" of chairs, settees, and side tables. Sometimes a large table was centrally located to hold board games or a tea service. Bric-a-brac, pictures, artwork, needlework, books, and small musical instruments were used as decor. Many parlours were "domain[s] for artifactual display" because they held a home's unique (albeit often mass-produced) objects.[25] Some women also used their parlours as makeshift greenhouses to brighten the space on dull winter days. Elora photographer Thomas Connon remarked in 1891 that his wife was "the most successful rose grower in town," citing the exceedingly high quality of her late January "parlor culture" roses.[26]

Industrialization and mass production increased the number and type of items available for parlour decoration. No matter how crowded with curios, the parlour almost always contained a prominently positioned stove or fireplace to dispense heat, and kerosene or gasoline lamps to provide light.[27] Many women took great pride in the arrangement and composition of their parlours. In 1913, Muriel Clark received a letter from her sister, Euphie, in Elora, in which the recent newlywed regaled her sister with the news that she and husband "Spen" were putting the finishing touches on their new sitting room. She writes, "Spen just finished his book shelves for our sitting room today and they look great. There will be plenty of empty space in there of course but we'll maybe get them filled in time. One can't expect to start in with a full library. Suppose Dad told you about my piano. It is a lovely one and I am so glad that we were able to get it."[28]

For families able to afford one, a piano, organ, or melodeon occupied a central and important position in the parlour. In 1877, *Farmer's Advocate* columnist "Minnie Mae"[29] referred to the piano as the "household angel of the period." Mae argued that pianos should be obligatory additions to family homes because when their "liquid harmonies float on the air, there is a spell of refinement, a soothing element to banish discord, and a spirit of magical tenderness."[30] Another *Advocate* article proclaimed in 1884 that "the home is not complete without a musical instrument, piano or organ."[31] In 1899, the *Elora Express* printed the names of two men and one woman who had recently purchased pianos in the vicinity, along with the make of the pianos and where they were purchased.[32] Pianos provided "material proof of middle-class standing,"[33] because they conveyed wealth and knowledge of music theory. Though some social commentators in the 1870s disagreed over whether females should take music lessons,[34] by the turn of the century many women in Dresden, Tillsonburg, and Elora were well-recognized in their communities as piano and organ players. Postings in local newspapers reveal that offering music lessons to children was a source of income for some women.[35]

Gramophones (or phonographs) were also new and popular forms of musical entertainment introduced into rural and small-town homes around the turn of the century. Developed in the late nineteenth century, gramophones were lauded as the first device with the ability to record and play music, thus having the potential to "bring the world of the stage and the concert hall" into the parlour.[36] By 1905, Elorans had become so enamoured with the instrument that the local "Board of Health" expressed concern over the epidemic of "gramophonitis."[37] Though the condition was illusory, the reference reinforces how popular and mainstream technological advancements in the leisure industry were becoming. In Tillsonburg, those citizens without the means to purchase one could rent a "grand concert gram-o-phone" from Wood's Book Store on Broadway Street.[38] More so than other items in the parlour, pianos and other musical instruments functioned as symbols of unity that drew families, neighbours, and friends together.

In many homes, the parlour served as a family's own personal town hall, opera house, lecture hall, theatre, dance hall, and classroom. The extent to which families were encouraged to gather in their parlours is evident in the number of "parlour amusements" that emerged in the later years of the nineteenth century. Printed manuals like Professor Hoffmann's *Parlor*

Figure 23. Man and woman posing with a melodeon in Elora, later nineteenth century. Source: UGASC, Connon Collection, XR1 MS A114_B1F3.

Amusements and Evening Party Entertainments contained sizable lists of card games, "after dinner accomplishments and amusements," theatricals, tableaux vivants, card tricks, coin tricks, and magic tricks, as well as instructions for creating waxwork exhibitions, pantomimes, charades, and conundrums.[39] Even as early as 1871, catalogues such as E.I. Horsman's *Home Amusements Are the Magnets of the Family Circle* advertised popular parlour games and amusements for sale, including Magic Hoops, Parlor Carpet Croquet, Indian clubs, dumbbells, and the Lozo Pendulum Board. According to Horsman, the purchase of such items was requisite for the Victorian family because "Happy Homes Make Happy Hearts."[40] Locally, merchants in Dresden, Tillsonburg, and Elora used newspaper advertisements to announce when their new seasonal stock of parlour games had arrived. A 1905 ad in the *Elora Express*, for instance, noted that local businessman T.P. Smith would be holding an "estate sale" where a variety of games such as dominoes, Parcheesi, bourse, and table tennis could be purchased.[41]

Though some elite families had the means and space to host elaborate theatrical and musical soirées at home, according to personal correspondence and stories in the local press, the favoured parlour amusements of women in Dresden, Tillsonburg, and Elora were card and board games, dancing, singing, giving recitations, listening to lectures, and reading fictional novels and periodicals. The establishment of public libraries across Ontario in the later nineteenth and early twentieth centuries enhanced the popularity of reading for those who were literate, while reading aloud provided illiterate friends and family the opportunity to also join in. Middle-class women also enjoyed hosting house parties, where guests ranged from small groups of female friends to larger assemblages of neighbouring families. During the winter, notices about home parties appeared weekly in newspaper social columns; women's diaries also convey how frequently these gatherings occurred. Playing a variety of board and card games like crokinole, backgammon, checkers, chess, dominoes, and euchre was often the focal point of the evening. One rainy and windy evening in March 1878, for instance, Ann Amelia Day mentions playing four games of "Pannchee" with "Ma," "Bennie," and "David."[42] Here, Day is likely referring to Panchi, a popular board game in North America with origins in India. In February 1914, Olive Snyder recorded that a small group of friends came over to play cards, during which Snyder herself "nearly went to sleep."[43] Board and card games were, for the most part, deemed respectable, though some reformers opposed games of chance because of their associations with gambling and immorality.[44]

By the later years of the nineteenth century, social commentators were emphasizing the importance of enjoying leisure as a family unit. In an article reprinted in the 19 January 1882 edition of the *Rural Canadian*, journalist "Daisy Eyebright" criticized families who spent their leisure hours in separate rooms, far away from one another.[45] She claimed the inevitable consequence was that "sons seek questionable amusements, the daughters make ill-assorted marriages and lead unhappy lives, and the parents find little happiness in their children."[46] Compartmentalizing the home, some historians have argued, led to leisure being segregated based on age, gender, and social appropriateness, and for some this resulted in the unravelling of familial bonds.[47] Eyebright advised parents who desired familial cohesiveness to spend at least one hour a day with their children indulging in some form of wholesome recreation like a sporting activity or any other "good romp." The remainder of the evening might be spent enjoying music, books, and "instructive" yet "amusing" games. According to Eyebright, these pastimes were the best way to avoid monotony and teach rural and small-town children that "they could always be entertained."[48] A father's ability to spend quality time with his children, however, was dependent on the mother, who played the central role in organizing and executing moral, educational, and healthful family-centred recreations. In middle-class households, this required women to oversee cleaning, child-rearing, and other tasks, which produced domestic order and allowed the family to gather once the day's work was complete.[49]

Before it became the primary gathering space for families, the parlour was where many women first met their husbands, spent most of their courtship, and subsequently married. The rigidity that continued to define Victorian and Edwardian rituals of romance meant that once a couple began courting, it was commonplace for the male suitor to visit the woman's home so that her parents could ensure relations between the couple were morally sound.[50] Parties, dances, dinners, and other mixed-sex domestic amusements permitted young people to become acquainted with one another and to develop relationships in a recognized and controlled setting. Prior to her marriage, for instance, Ann Amelia Day's fiancé, Noah Sunley, regularly visited the family home in the evening, often joining the Days for supper and accompanying them to public events.[51] As gatherings became more varied and elaborate, the possibility of meeting a variety of potential partners in a single location increased. For instance, in 1891 a reporter from the *Dresden Times* wrote about the latest social craze, "progressive hammocks." This Victorian incarnation of speed dating involved setting up several hammocks on a home's lawn and inviting "pretty girls" to occupy them. After paying an admission fee, each young man chose one of the hammocks and spent time with the girl occupying it. After a bell rang, the men moved on to another hammock. At the end of the cycle, each man voted for the best "conversationalist" he had encountered. Participants were sternly advised, however, that "any young man found with powder or a long hair on his coat is soaked with a heavy fine."[52]

"True Hospitality": Social Dining

By the later nineteenth century, social dining had become an important way that men and women connected to and spent quality time with friends and family. In this setting, the consumption of food and drink was accompanied by various kinds of entertainment, including play-acting, conversation, music, and games. One of the most ubiquitous forms of social dining to occur in the home was afternoon tea. British immigrants brought the practice with them to North America, and eventually "tea was a core ritual of society" in Canadian communities with British roots.[53] By the turn of the century, however, the simple offering of a cup of tea had evolved into a far more intricate and detailed ritual. In a 1903 article published in the *Tillsonburg Observer*, afternoon tea was deemed "the best method of keeping in touch with one's friends, as well as to introduce a visiting friend to one's general acquaintance."[54] For many, this sentiment held true, based on the number of domestic leisure activities where tea was the focal point around which gathering and socializing occurred. A notable consequence of this evolution was that brewing a pot for family, friends, or neighbours was no longer the straightforward custom it once had been. Holding "a tea," instead, became a way for women to establish or improve their place in the social hierarchy and exhibit a sophisticated sense of domestic refinement.

At almost all home entertainments, regardless of their scope or theme, tea was served because it was available, enjoyable, and a marker of gentility. In his work on country store accounts in Upper Canada, historian Douglas McCalla found that for most families, "tea clearly was a 'necessary.'"[55] When women's auxiliaries held meetings at members' homes, newspaper stories and club records frequently mention that tea or a comparable refreshment was served at the conclusion of the gathering. Some groups, such as the Christ Church Ladies' Guild in Dresden, instead hosted "coffees" when they gathered to discuss fundraising ventures. Some "coffees" were limited to members, while others were communal events. At the guild's May 1891 "coffee," for instance, the entire community was invited to the home of thirty-three-year-old Fanny Rudd, a carriage painter's wife,[56] to enjoy ice cream and cake for the "small sum" of ten cents.[57]

Figure 24. Elizabeth Manson Shand Innes and daughter Mary Ann Innes enjoying tea in a home at Lot 9, Walnut Street, Elora, c. 1900. Source: WCMA, A1998.42, ph 13426.

Party teas became a notable feature of the afternoon tea's evolution during the later Victorian years and were defined by their elaborate themes and get-ups. The "colour tea," for example, was a popular 1890s fad. The hostess chose a colour scheme (such as pink or rainbow) that dictated and inspired the decoration of the tearoom and the presentation and selection of food and drink. By the early 1900s, themed teas were beginning to develop beyond their traditional female-centred approach to better complement the increasingly heterosocial nature of domestic leisure.[58] "Book teas," "hidden treasure teas," and "courtship teas" became trendy among the middle class. At a courtship tea, for instance, the large group of men and women in attendance were asked to answer questions about love, marriage, and romance. The man and woman who scored the highest were dubbed the "bride" and "bridegroom" for the remainder of the soirée and were given flowers to adorn their attire. Arm-in-arm the couple then paraded in front of fellow party guests, who rewarded them with a hearty round of congratulatory applause.[59]

The greater interest being shown in hosting elaborate tea parties was likely influenced by the deluge of advice articles appearing in newspapers, periodicals, and etiquette manuals regarding the proper way to construct the "modern" tea table. According to American historian Beverly Gordon, such "regular helpful features on parties and entertaining" are indicative of how much domestic leisure activities were "an expected and accepted part of community life."[60] In Dresden, Tillsonburg, and Elora, local women both attended and hosted all manner of tea parties ranging from small, intimate gatherings to grand entertainments with music and theatrics. However, as the magnitude of the humble tea party expanded, so too did the expectations for hostesses. In 1892, the *Elora Express* advised women that their summer tea table must be supplied with fine white napery, an abundance of glass, a small arrangement of flowers, dainty slices of ham, thinly sliced buttered toast, berries, cake, and tea with lemon.[61] The *Farmer's Advocate* provided similar counsel to women so that they could "take 'company' a little easier" and ultimately "exercise sociability and true hospitality more frequently."[62] Much of this advice literature, and the experiences of women themselves, reinforces the pivotal role that tea played in the maintenance of social contacts for women across socio-economic strata. The *Advocate* and other periodicals suggested that even the most frugal housewife could still afford to host an elegant tea if she was mindful of prodigal spending. In working-class households, the expense of hosting a formal tea party would have been out of women's reach, but friends and family still gathered informally to chat over tea because of its low cost and availability.

Teas were popular among younger, older, married, and single women alike, but mothers of young children who could not afford to hire a domestic servant faced serious time constraints that affected their ability to entertain. When it came to preparing a well-appointed tea table on one's own, complete with "thin ham sandwiches cut in three-cornered pieces without crust" in addition to "sponge, lady fingers, sugar wafers or macarons" or "any form of cake small and dainty,"[63] a substantial amount of labour was involved, particularly when coupled with women's other daily chores. More extravagant gatherings that personified the ideal soirée were almost entirely the privilege of wealthier women who could afford help or who were beyond their childbearing years. Prior to the guests' arrival, a multitude of tasks, including cleaning, polishing silver, pressing linens, shopping, baking, cooking, setting the tea table, and even attending to the hostess's own physical appearance, had to be accomplished. When less affluent women hosted teas, family members were recruited for their labour. At some nighttime soirées, children might help with welcoming the guests while husbands assisted with dinner service before being banished to other quarters.[64]

Even if the guest list was composed of close friends and neighbours, strict codes of order and etiquette were still followed. Kate Aitken recalls that at her middle-class mother's tea parties, spoons in saucers were always placed parallel to the tea cup's handle, no slurping of tea was ever heard, and guests only engaged in "polite" conversation afterward.[65] Though tea was a much-enjoyed facet of small-town life, when the time came for a woman to host her own event, the amount of time and energy involved to meet the social standards of the day blurred the boundaries between labour and leisure. Undoubtedly, some middle- and upper-class women hosted teas because it was part of their social duty, but others, like Kate Aitken's mother, Ann, revelled in the process. Aitken writes that at the end of the evening, amid the table clearing and washing dishes, "Mother [...] was as gay as a lark. She loved parties."[66] Though preparing and executing a tea party was exhausting and temporarily disrupted the household's rhythm, not all women considered this work, especially when help from domestic servants or family members lightened the load.

Tea was also at the epicentre of one of the most widely recognized domestic leisure activities for Victorian women: the "at home." Beginning roughly in the mid-1880s, this highly structured form of paying social calls became popular in elite and middle-class social circles. Essentially, women planned to be at their residence during a specific time and day of the week, and female friends were invited to drop by and catch up with one another. Though normally designated as single-sex gatherings, in small-town Ontario some "at homes" were advertised to the entire community. Even men's organizations appropriated the "at home" for their own social gatherings. In February 1895, the Tillsonburg Bachelors' Club hosted an elaborate "at home" for 175 male and female guests, including locals and out-of-towners, which the *Observer* dubbed "one of the most fashionable events that has taken place in Tilsonburg for some time."[67]

For the distinguished ladies who represented Tillsonburg's elite, "at homes" were exclusive, insiders-only affairs. Bert Newman was privy to this sort of privileged leisure while employed as a grocery delivery boy in the early 1900s.[68] In his account, Newman recalls that the wives of the "pioneers of our town, the established people" gathered once a month to visit with one another. He vividly recalls the long list of groceries he would deliver to the hostess on the day of her event. These parties, however, were limited to women in town who were of a certain class. To this small-town, working-class youth, the women's affluence was analogous to the Vanderbilts, Astors, and Rockefellers who constituted the richest American families of the Gilded Age. "The parties these ladies used to put on!" Newman remembers. "These parties were a sight to behold!" In winter, members' homes provided the setting, but during the warmer months they entertained one another on manicured lawns lit by Chinese lanterns. Each woman brought her domestic servants along to help serve refreshments, and Newman remembers they were "dressed up in black uniforms with nice little aprons on and white caps on their heads."[69] Details regarding the identities and duties of the help are not provided, however, nor does Newman indicate whether guests contributed anything beyond their servants' labour.

It was not uncommon for rural and small-town women, like their city counterparts, to contact the local newspaper (or have reporters contact them) about their impending soirées and "at homes." The stories vary in length and detail, but class and privilege are evident when specifics like refreshments being served or the entertainment provided afterward are mentioned. Some were simple and succinct: in February 1910, for example, a short notice in the *Elora Express* indicated that Maybell Hall, a twenty-six-year-old bank manager's wife who employed a domestic, would be "at home" at her residence from 3:00 p.m. to 6:00 p.m.[70] On 9 February 1905, the *Tillsonburg Liberal* printed six notices for "at homes" and other women's parties that had been scheduled.[71] Full reports of more elaborate "at homes" were usually published the week following the event. For example, in Tillsonburg in February 1900, sisters Lillie Sinclair and Hattie Harrison (née Tillson) held a joint "at home," entertaining friends with riddles and gifting the winner with a large bouquet of roses and carnations. Given their social status, it is not surprising that the sisters' "at home" was dubbed "one of the largest and most enjoyable of the social events this season" by the *Observer*.[72]

It was not uncommon for middle-class women to occasionally host equally elaborate gatherings despite their more modest household earnings. In May 1895, thirty-five-year-old Dorcas Stinson[73] held an "at home" near Tillsonburg, where she hosted "forty or fifty of her friends, from the hours of five to eight, and proved herself a charming hostess. Refreshments of ice cream, in dainty baskets, cake and other delectable cuisine were provided and musical and social chat made up an enjoyable entertainment."[74] It is unclear if Stinson had any help preparing or executing the elaborate affair, but she and her husband do not appear to have had any children at the time, so she was free to direct more effort toward entertaining. The article's specific mentioning of Stinson as a "charming hostess,"[75] the sizable guest list, and selection of delectable victuals enhanced the glamour of the affair and its hostess. Though being invited to such an event was itself a sign of one's status and acceptance, the official printing of the guest list in the newspaper carried considerable clout and helped guests achieve more "social prominence" in the community.[76]

A clear example of how extravagant gatherings were becoming, Stinson's party was a testament to the middle class's desire to flaunt its disposable wealth and project an image of success. Women were largely responsible for raising or maintaining their family's place in the town's social hierarchy, so when their home parties received "recognition in the local newspaper, the family's social position came to be distinguished from its merely financial status."[77] Prior to the late nineteenth century, female names rarely appeared in newspapers except in connection with birth, marriage, or death, but as the circulation of small-town papers increased, editors focused on publishing stories that appealed to their ever-growing audience of female readers. Using social columns to print detailed accounts of wealthier women's entertainments provided those on the outside with a window into an exclusive and expensive world.

Some "at homes" allowed small-town social climbers to present their daughters as debutantes after turning eighteen, signalling their readiness to accept "social honours" (and male suitors).[78] In February 1905, Minnie Waller, the wife of a well-known manufacturer in Tillsonburg, gave an "at home" in honour of her debutante, Adelaide. Though Mrs. Waller was the host, the event was largely organized and prepared by other local women and their "assistants." The tearoom, the *Tillsonburg Liberal* reported, was "very prettily decorated" with white roses, green tulle, pink carnations, and green ribbon.[79] In communities that lacked the space in which to host the grand "coming out" balls that were popular in larger cities, "at homes" were a suitable country equivalent.

Dinner parties also became popular in Dresden, Tillsonburg, and Elora homes in the late nineteenth and early twentieth centuries. Though the hospitable practice of friends and family gathering for a meal has a long history in rural and small-town Ontario, this type of social dining (often interchangeably called a "tea" or "social") involved careful planning of the guest list, the food, the dishes and glassware with which it would be served, and the entertainment offered after the meal. Though the themes and menus of these new dinner parties were mostly dictated by the seasons, large gatherings of diners were increasingly held beyond calendar holidays and family celebrations.

In more remote areas, where friends and family often had to travel considerable distances to visit one another, women faced immense pressure to execute an evening enjoyable enough to make the long journey worthwhile. In these circumstances, *Farmer's Advocate* contributor "Evelyn L." suggested that tea, coffee, or beef tea be served immediately upon the guests' arrival to warm the body and show gratitude for their travels.[80] Six p.m. was dubbed the ideal hour to commence dinner, so that guests had enough time to engage in some social intercourse before making the journey home. Instead of gathering around a long kitchen table "groaning under the triumphs of culinary skill,"[81] advice columns suggested moving the meal to the more intimate space of the parlour or sitting room and using smaller tables. Circular dining tables were introduced in households around this time which "allowed families to turn in on themselves," thus bringing diners closer together.[82] Each table was to be covered with white linen and adorned with greenery for decorative effect. Considered more refined than the traditional (and often boisterous) gathering around a long bench table, removing the gathering to the parlour again points to the importance of separating work and leisure spaces.

According to "Evelyn L.," an ideal menu consisted of pre-dinner nibbles like pickles, salted almonds, and bread-and-butter sandwiches. An entrée of fried chicken, ham, creamed potatoes, and celery would be followed by cheese, salad, and crackers. If the preferred dessert of ice cream was unavailable, fresh or canned fruit, jellies, and cakes were recommended, accompanied by more tea, coffee, and lemonade in the summer.[83] These offerings represent basic cookery, but such items were not always standard. By and large the choice of dishes was dictated by the cycle of the seasons, the availability of ingredients, dining etiquette, the finances and tastes of the host, ethnic and cultural customs, and the evening's theme. Many women also liked to serve a signature dish they were known for. Though packaged and canned goods were increasingly appearing in turn-of-the-century kitchens, some columnists continued to extol the virtues of home production and scratch cooking because they were indicative of culinary aptitude. When it came to beverages, wine or spirits were rarely mentioned as optimal dinner party refreshments. Their omission is likely a consequence of the hold that the temperance movement had on more rural and conservative regions of the province. But as discussed later in this chapter, it should be assumed that liquor was still enjoyed at some dinner parties.

Though formal dining was originally the preserve of the elite, middle-class men and women in Dresden, Tillsonburg, and Elora were increasingly drawn to the custom of social dining. For families who laboured to harvest, butcher, and preserve most of their own provisions, dinner parties were an opportunity to display their bounty and serve homegrown produce, meats, and dairy products. Only the best and highest quality foodstuffs, however, should be offered to guests. In 1890, when the *Farmer's Advocate* printed Ada Wood's prize-winning essay "A Country Party, and How to Make it Pleasant," the treatise warned hostesses to keep their fare simple because "most people prefer plain, substantial dainties," and "fancy" dishes would do no more than display one's own "vanity and vexation of spirit."[84] Skill and care in this manner were prized over pretension and complexity. Anti-elite discourses such as this were somewhat common in small-town newspapers and rural periodicals. By promoting frugality over flamboyance, authors articulated a moral (and somewhat religious) protest concerning the parties of wealthier folk who displayed excess, gluttony, and conspicuous consumption. Though Wood and others promoted simple dishes, proper execution still mattered. "No dry sponge cake or leathery layer cake with a little jam stretched across it," Wood argued, "should be allowed."[85]

As dining standards rose in the closing years of the nineteenth century, so too did the pressure placed on women to carry out memorable and enjoyable gatherings. Regardless of whether one lived in town or country, the preparation and presentation of food had become a significant marker of gentrification. Rural and small-town women may have lacked some of the modern conveniences and amenities available in large cities, but they still strove to present an air of refinement in their scanty collections of table coverings, dishware, and silver. The links between civility and dining around the turn of the century meant that proper presentation of the table and its contents, no matter how simple, was imperative at all social functions. Such care signalled domestic refinement, an attribute that many rural and small-town women took great pride in.[86]

Along with the attention given to parties, periodicals also suggested that greater care be devoted to the serving of the smallest and humblest of meals. According to an 1886 article in the *Rural Canadian* titled "The Art of Good Dining," even when "no one is present but the home circle," the home's "mistress" and her "maid" ought to treat day-to-day mealtimes as if they were hosting a large affair. Serving the items in a course-by-course fashion was recommended, and all the noise and mess accompanying the service and clean-up of each course should be minimal. For all occasions, grand or small, "the help" must be schooled in the proper techniques to avoid embarrassing the mistress or those around the table.[87] These structured dining practices, however, were unrealistic for most rural and small-town families. It was only the elite and some middle-class citizens in these communities who could afford the variety of food and dinnerware recommended, along with the domestic help necessary to put such effort into daily mealtimes.

The increasing number of notices appearing in small-town newspapers for all manner of household help reinforces how valuable domestic servants had become as the scope of home entertainments expanded. While Myrtle Dreyer (née Morden) was employed as a full-time domestic servant at Annandale House from 1909 to 1911, her responsibilities included preparing meals, serving the table, ironing, and other chores. When interviewed at the age of ninety, Dreyer remembered that she was "restricted" to certain areas of the house, based on her duties. Along with Dreyer, the home's staff included a separate housekeeper to oversee cleaning and laundry and a full-time nurse who cared for an ailing Mary Ann Tillson in her later years.[88] Most women in Dresden, Tillsonburg, and Elora could not afford to hire live-in help, but many posted advertisements for part-time or occasional help. Just as her parlour and tea service reminded guests of a woman's status, the hiring of domestic help also signified her social standing (or where she wished to stand) in the community.

Domestic servants may have lightened women's workloads, but as American historian Ruth Schwartz Cowan notes, even comfortably middle-class women still had plenty of chores,[89] compounded by societal expectations to maintain an orderly, clean, and welcoming home. Middle-class women's diaries attest to the sheer volume of housework that required attention. For instance, Annie Hill mentions in a diary entry from 28 December 1912 that she "swept spare bedroom, hall upstairs & down & stair steps, our bedroom & dining room in morning, dusted pictures, washed off oilcloth in aft." On other days, she took on sizable culinary feats, such as baking several pumpkin and apple pies and one pasty in a single morning. She then carried on with housework and other errands in the afternoon.[90]

When meticulously planned dinner soirées were held, many women desired to serve atypical and stylish cuisine. On a Wednesday evening in mid-February 1892, for example, Mary Ann Tillson hosted a "Crazy Tea" for seventy men and women at Annandale House. Dubbed "A Unique Affair" by the *Tillsonburg Observer* and recognized as "a new feature in social events," the Crazy Tea was distinctly upper class and certainly not the norm outside of the Tillsons' social circle. The evening began with conversation and musical selections from the phonograph. After guests were seated for dinner, they were provided with the evening's menu, composed of word riddles for each of the dishes being served.[91] Akin to themed teas, the use of poetry, verses, puns, and metaphors to introduce dinner items at parties had become a way to make any event special and memorable because, "in this atmosphere, even the most everyday activity or object could be transformed. Everything was given a greater aesthetic charge: the space itself, the table, the menu, the food, and the activities were all made to amuse, delight, and stimulate the senses."[92]

The Crazy Tea was also an opportunity for the Tillsons to exhibit their knowledge of history, the fine arts, and global affairs, all important markers of highbrow culture at the time. Accordingly, the puns were topical and drew on the popular culture and political atmosphere of the day, and the hosts thus appeared worldly and intellectually engaged. Some of the references, according to the *Observer*, were difficult for the partygoers to guess despite the Tillsons' inner circle of friends matching them in terms of background and education (though certainly not wealth). As with other forms of social dining, along with providing nourishment the Crazy Tea and its joyous atmosphere was also meant to test the mind and educate guests.

After being called to the table and receiving the menu, the object of the game was to guess each food riddle in order to receive the dish associated with it. For example, under "Meats" were the clues "A celebrated author" (bacon, a reference to Sir Francis Bacon) and "Women of Grit" (sandwiches, or Sand-Witches). Some of the "Appetizers" were "Tabby's party" (catsup) and "personal howls" (ice cream), and "Beverages" included "Boston's over-throw" (tea) and "Arabian wine" (mocha). Publicly, at least, the Tillsons were temperance people, so no alcohol was served. In total, seventeen menu items were listed in riddle form. The newspaper reported that the puns provoked "laughter and merriment" as well as some controversy, such as the "Women of Grit," which affronted some of the male guests until the dish's identity was revealed. Likely they were Tories and took offence to "Grit" because of the word's association with the Liberal party in the mid-nineteenth century. Each course was served by a team of young men clothed in brightly coloured robes, a role reversal befitting the "crazy" theme. The evening was rounded out by readings and music and was proclaimed by the *Observer* to be "a social event long to be remembered."[93]

In contrast to the Tillsons' extravagant Crazy Tea, typical social dining consisted of small groups of friends, family, and neighbours coming together for the midday meal, particularly after church on Sundays. Annie Hill's diary references how frequently family and friends stayed for dinner and how often she herself went visiting at mealtimes. In many middle-class households, a formal invite was unnecessary. It was not unusual for women and girls to move about so independently because while "women's and children's place may well have been defined as in the home," often "they acted independently of their nuclear families and moved about regularly among a variety of hearths."[94] Olive Snyder recorded such comings and goings in her diary entries. In January 1913, she wrote: "Dads & Mothers golden wedding. Pollie up for dinner and all went to Libs for tea. Very nice quiet day."[95] Neither Hill nor Snyder mention attending or hosting ostentatious dinner parties, but they still found great pleasure in informal modes of social dining because of the interaction that it provided. Indeed, in her diary Snyder expresses exasperation and frustration at large gatherings. She frequently mentions she had a "good time" or "nice time" when in the company of smaller groups.

For both Hill and Snyder, within their tight-knit middle-class social circles there was a constant back and forth between one another's homes, coupled with a regular exchange of goods, services, and assistance. Sickness and hardship were two circumstances that consistently brought women together. While suffering from "la grippe" (influenza) in December 1893, Minnie Smith mentions in consecutive diary entries that she had a "number of callers" to her Norwich home.[96] Illness and "the biological realities of frequent childbirth, nursing, and menopause," historian Theodora Penny Martin explains, "had long drawn women into a physical and emotional supportive network."[97] In rural and small-town Ontario, this practice continued well into the twentieth century. Caring for friends and family or stopping by with an unexpected gift of produce, seeds, or baking not only "reflected reciprocal neighbourhood bonds of exchange, but also feelings of close personal friendship."[98]

Middle-class women also gathered to accomplish their long lists of domestic tasks and responsibilities together. Less affluent women who could not afford domestic help created networks of mutual assistance where, amid the sharing of labour, they used the time together to socialize. The tasks of sewing and quilting, for example, were often completed among groups of women because of the intricacy of the work. Historian Susan Strasser argues that sewing and quilting circles not only allowed women to sew and talk about sewing; here they also "showed off their work, and exchanged ideas, methods, and hints." For some, sewing was just another dreaded yet necessary task, while others "loved the craft itself" and enjoyed "displaying their handicraft privately to the women with whom they sewed, or publicly at country fairs and contests."[99] While needlework was typically completed among women, Catharine Anne Wilson has shown that sometimes neighbourhood parties evolved out of gatherings like quilting bees, where men and women came together for food, social intercourse, and dancing.[100]

Women's daily chores were often structured around a set schedule, but Sunday was the day set aside explicitly for visiting.[101] However, the diaries and reminiscences of Hill, Snyder, and others attest to the fact that such interaction in the home could be, and typically was, enjoyed all days of the week. While each day was often devoted to the completion of a specific domestic chore, women still strove to balance their work and play within the rhythms of daily life. Such a balance was achieved by women coming together and combining work. Sharing responsibilities (and the socializing this prompted) often occurred along gendered lines, creating a sort of female collectivism. The practice is analogous to the "work bees" held throughout rural Ontario at which everything from churches and barns to quilts were constructed collectively to lighten workloads and promote neighbourly togetherness.[102] Snyder's diary entries often discuss the work she accomplished with her sisters and friends: "Kay & I washed as usual and sewed and played tennis. Went to ball game tonight. Also Polly."[103] Annie Hill's days, while much more hectic and labour-filled, were similar: "Made soup, swept bedroom, dining room & hall in morning [...] Jennie & Clarence were here for dinner, Mrs. Moody brought Grandmother here for an hour or so, I washed hall oilcloth & under table in aft. I attended study class at Mrs. Povey's in evening."[104] The diaries of women like Snyder and Hill reveal intertwining notions about work and play, where events flow into each other and cannot be defined as self-contained units.[105] For these women, in the home there was often little differentiation between labour and leisure.

The proclivity for visiting and sharing tasks to ensure that free time was maximized is suggestive of the communal nature of rural and small-town domestic leisure. When time allowed, women made social calls and saw one another as often as possible. In the case of the "at home," for example, when invited to the homes of their friends, women returned the favour by offering comparable hospitality. As historian Jane Pederson has shown in the American context, "the most pronounced character of the country visitor was that they were ubiquitous."[106] In Dresden, Tillsonburg, and Elora, visiting between women was not confined to those living in the same town; quite frequently, women living in the countryside travelled considerable distances to visit with friends in neighbouring towns, and vice versa. Trips to nearby Tillsonburg were weekly if not twice-weekly occurrences for Minnie Smith, though Norwich was over twenty kilometres away. Visiting, however, was dependent on the seasons, time, and availability of transportation. When inclement weather or illness impeded visiting, women often noted this in their diaries. In January 1913, Olive Snyder wrote: "Rained all day so didn't go out and no one came in."[107] When able to, though, women readily sought out companionship with their immediate families, neighbours, or nearby friends. Whether for an extended period or a mere minute or two, the constant patterns of visiting among women in these towns (and their surrounding rural areas) shaped and strengthened emotional bonds of kinship and friendship. The depth and longevity of these bonds, as women's diaries and reminiscences demonstrate, were a source of much-needed assistance, trust, and support.

Holy Days, Hallowe'en, and the Home

By the later years of the nineteenth century, families in Dresden, Tillsonburg, and Elora were eager celebrators of a variety of new holidays alongside the conventional holy days and rites of passage such as baptisms, weddings, and Christmas. Though civic, national, and patriotically themed holidays were habitually celebrated in public spaces with parades and processions, this sort of leisure increasingly came to be seen as disreputable following late nineteenth-century criticisms about raucous behaviour. The result, as Craig Heron and Steve Penfold explain, was that "holidays were slowly transformed into quieter, more privatized, more family-centred occasions with little of the outdoor revelry of the past."[108] For many, the home became the principal (and more respectable) setting in which to enjoy both the traditional Christian celebrations as well as the newly recognized and commercialized holidays like Hallowe'en, Valentine's Day, and birthdays. The implementation of new labour policies that regulated workdays and standardized holiday and vacation time, coupled with greater disposable wealth and improved transportation networks, allowed men and women, more readily than ever before, to host and join in holiday festivities.

As the recognition of both religious and secular holidays became more mainstream, so too did the production of manufactured goods at all price levels so that women could decorate and entertain with gusto. Holiday ephemera like cards, invitations, streamers, and bunting were regularly stocked in rural and small-town book and print shops. In newspaper advertisements, merchants in Dresden, Tillsonburg, and Elora reported with great fanfare when their new stock of seasonal party goods had arrived. In small communities, the promotion and celebration of such holidays helped produce a collective language of sorts through which citizens communicated by attending holiday parties and sharing these experiences with one another.[109] The integrative nature of holiday celebrations helped strengthen "links with others that went beyond kinship ties and beyond geographic proximity."[110] By the 1870s, holidays had become another way to demarcate the seasons,[111] especially among non-farming families. In a practical sense, the impending ritualism associated with holidays made the drudgery of daily tasks a little easier to manage. By the turn of the century, however, holidays and the enlarged expectations attached to their successful execution were creating more worry for middle- and working-class women, who were entrusted with the bulk of the responsibilities attached to celebrating.

The custom of recognizing Hallowe'en is an old one, originating in medieval Ireland and Scotland, where Druids held an annual festival called Samhain to mark the beginning of the Celtic New Year. It was believed to be a time of enhanced paranormal activity because "the boundaries between the living and the supernatural were erased."[112] Cultural historians attribute the growth in Hallowe'en celebrations to Scottish immigrants, who carried the custom with them to North America. Over time, the seriousness attached to the occasion evolved into the more modern appropriation of 31 October where mischief, mayhem, and costumed revellers became the norm.[113]

The timing of Hallowe'en marked the beginning of a new social season in larger cities like Toronto;[114] for rural and small-town folk, the end of

October signalled the near completion of harvest and a last hurrah before the descent into a long winter. Unlike their city counterparts who flocked to streets, theatres, and other public buildings to commemorate the occasion, small-town Ontarians tended to celebrate Hallowe'en in a more private manner, often from the comfort of home. Newspapers printed the occasional story about young ruffians wreaking havoc on public and private property;[115] some residents described the night as a time when "all hell broke loose."[116] By and large, however, "respectable" citizens wishing to celebrate Hallowe'en night attended small parties or gatherings. In 1913, Olive Snyder attended a surprise Hallowe'en party at the home of her friend "Lib," where the group indulged in some taffy making.[117] On Hallowe'en night in 1893, Minnie Smith celebrated at a party with her friend Ginger. Smith recorded that she had a "nice time" as evidenced by the fact that she did not retire until 4:00 a.m.[118]

In 1908, *Farmer's Advocate* reader "Minerva" from Perth County in southern Ontario wrote to columnist "Dame Durden" requesting suggestions for Hallowe'en-themed parties. She was subsequently rewarded with a plethora of tips for hosting the grandest of country "spook" parties. Even in 1908, recommendations were exceedingly elaborate and detailed. Invitations in the shape of pumpkins and decorations of jack-o'-lanterns, sprigs of wheat, rowans, apples, a faux fortune teller, and darkened rooms illuminated with lantern glow were suggested for decorative effect. Though some decor would have been homemade, themed pieces could also be purchased at local stores. Once guests arrived in their masks and costumes, "Dame Durden" suggested they participate in the fortune teller's predictions and in different guessing games. One such game involved inviting guests out to the host's cabbage patch. Each guest was to choose one of the leafy heads, and the size and shape of its stalk, as well as the soil adhering to it, revealed details about their future mate. Parting gifts such as pumpkin-shaped pin cushions and other themed trifles were recommended to lend merriment.[119]

That same year, a young teen named "Ferne" from Norfolk County, located just south of Tillsonburg, also wrote to "Dame Durden" requesting advice. She explained that she and her friends were hosting a Hallowe'en party in the basement of a country church, signifying how much Hallowe'en had evolved beyond its Druid roots. The girls planned to serve tea and play Hallowe'en games and music, but they desired more variety in their festivities. In response, "Dame Durden" suggested cranberries, jack-o'-lanterns, autumn leaves, and oats as decorations, a dim room lit by candlelight, and waiters and waitresses in costume. Also recommended were a variety of games, as well as "Scotch features" such as nuts and scones for refreshment.[120] Other sources of advice, such as Annie Randall White's etiquette guide, suggested that at Hallowe'en parties, "Jack lanterns and tin horns are [...] quite in order. False faces add to the merriment."[121]

Such precise instructions for the perfect party were also doled out to those throwing Valentine's Day soirées. The contrived associations between the medieval St. Valentine and romantic love were first espoused by poets like Geoffrey Chaucer in the early fourteenth century. Like that of Hallowe'en, the celebration of St. Valentine's Day in the early modern and modern periods was part of a new cultural trend that appropriated old-world British folk rituals. By the 1840s, the Valentine's Day cards that were all the rage in fashionable London could also be found in North American book and print shops and dry goods stores because of the "romantic nostalgia for lost folk traditions and festivities."[122] American historian Leigh Eric Schmidt writes that at this time, a Valentine's "mania, craze, rage, or epidemic" developed, a sort of "'social disease' that seemed to recrudesce each year with ever-heightening interest and anticipation."[123]

The mass production of material goods, coupled with an emerging consumer culture, transformed the ways that Victorians and Edwardians celebrated the holiday. By the turn of the century, cards (and the holiday generally) were being marketed specifically to women and children because they were the primary organizers and participants. This fact bestowed on the holiday a "new feminized, domestic luster."[124] Sending the cards that were being stocked by even the smallest of merchants was meant to be a tangible expression of love, but their formulaic verses often reeked of phoniness and sentimentalism. Contrary to popular belief, Valentine's cards did not always signify love. On Valentine's Day 1913, for instance, Olive Snyder wrote in her diary that she had received cards from "Sandy Percy & John."[125] Snyder was unmarried at the time and would remain so the rest of her life, so the cards likely contained platonic messages. Kate Aitken remembered Valentine's Day as an occasion to mail "insulting" and "anonymous" cards, especially to "spinsters, schoolteachers, crabby neighbours, misguided bachelors" and others who were "foolish enough to betray their emotions."[126] Akin to the charivari and other public displays of disapproval, satirical cards sent "under the anonymous cloak of the mail" allowed individuals to express insults and contempt.[127] In the United States, Valentine's Day missives that were lewd, coarse, and mocking actually represented about half the card market.[128]

In 1891, as 14 February drew near, a journalist for the *Dresden Times* wrote that "'Valentine parties' are in order." The *Times* advised those invited to a party to write out their "love missives" prior to the evening of the event. After arriving, guests were instructed to go to the hostess's dressing room and deposit their valentines in carefully designated bags, tie them with a ribbon, and return to the drawing room. Here, two children dressed as Cupid would distribute them.[129] This recommendation was clearly meant for men and women of considerable means, but not all parties were so pretentious. In 1905, thirty-five-year-old Tillsonburg resident Ellen Luke, a labourer's wife who employed a domestic servant,[130] hosted a Valentine's party for "a number of her friends" though specific details of the soirée were omitted from the *Liberal*'s account of the gathering.[131] For those women who could not afford to set aside their chores to celebrate, were not invited to parties, or did not wish to participate, Valentine's Day was not marked by celebration. Farm wife Annie Hill, for instance, spent Valentine's Day of 1913 boiling pumpkins and squash, hosting her husband's friend for tea, and then entertaining a call from a neighbour in the evening.[132]

Throwing elaborate birthday parties for children became another way for small-town middle- and upper-class women to display their class privilege and competence at entertaining, as well as fulfilling the expectation of constructing family-centred leisure activities. The particulars of more affluent children's birthday parties (like the entertainments hosted by their parents) were frequently printed in local newspapers. When Gladys Caverhill of Tillsonburg turned six in May 1895, her parents, John (an accountant) and Francis, hosted a May Day–themed birthday party for twenty-four of her friends, at which the children enjoyed dancing around a maypole and supped on "dainty refreshments [that] tempted the children's palates."[133] In 1890, Ephraim (a liveryman) and Marrilla Becker hosted a surprise birthday party for their daughter, Orpha, on her nineteenth birthday, where twenty young people, including three out-of-town guests, feted the birthday girl. The *Observer* reported that many nice gifts were received, including a gold watch from her parents.[134] In comparison, young Louise Garnham of the small village of Guysboro, just outside of Tillsonburg, celebrated one of her birthdays in a much humbler fashion. The party began with Louise and her friends sewing in the Garnham home's "big parlor," followed by pushing one another on a swing in the orchard and going to the local mill yard, where the girls were allowed to run over the logs and play in the large mounds of sawdust. Finally, everyone gathered back at the Garnham home for the birthday supper consisting of cheese, freshly chipped dried beef, sliced ham, currant buns, doughnuts, and raspberry tarts.[135]

As evidenced in etiquette guides, reminiscences, and newspaper accounts, birthdays generally and children's parties especially had become more complex in terms of the guest list, games, food, and party favours provided. The modern concept of the child's birthday party, consisting of guests other than those of the immediate household, gained prominence in the late nineteenth century. American historian John R. Gillis explains that as Victorians became more child-centred and focused on nurturing familial togetherness, children were treated less as commodities and more as "priceless possessions."[136] In the early nineteenth century, children's birthdays had little significance in the way of established domestic rituals, but by the turn of the century they had become a "cornerstone" of the family's social calendar.[137] In terms of hosting gatherings in the home, particularly when children were involved, one etiquette guide suggested that "birthdays especially should be observed. Even in the house of mourning they may be kept up, for children should not be forced to share in a grief which they cannot understand."[138] Mothers did not require an occasion to throw parties for their children but when they could, one home encyclopedia argued, "life [would] move more smoothly for the whole family."[139]

In the Snyder family, birthdays rarely elicited any sort of grand party or entertainment; when they did occur, they were of a quieter, private, and more family-oriented nature. On her mother's birthday in May 1913, Olive Snyder and her family celebrated with a seasonal rhubarb pie. On one of her sisters' sixteenth birthday, they invited "the families for tea on the lawn."[140] Other rural and small-town women also appear to have spent their own birthdays in a relatively quiet fashion at home. When Francis Poole of Norwich turned twenty-six on 5 April 1904, she wrote in her diary: "I really had help to wash my face this morning—and was it any wonder—it was my birthday. The biggest surprise I had was a visit from Grandma & Sarah who had been to town and came here for dinner. Mrs. Poole also came over this afternoon and we had quite a visit."[141]

In a parallel fashion, while for some families Christmas and New Year's Eve or Day meant large gatherings, for others the holiday season was simply spent in quiet reflection in the company of immediate family at home. The extent to which Christmas was celebrated in rural and small-town Ontario was initially reflective of a community's dominant cultural groups. In mid-nineteenth-century Elora, for instance, since the region was composed of such a strong contingent of first- and second-generation Scottish immigrants, New Year's Day (with its Protestant Scottish roots) was celebrated more fervently than Christmas (notably more Roman Catholic in character and origin). By the 1870s, though, Christmas had become a tradition that virtually all citizens looked forward to. According to Elora historian Stephen Thorning, Santa Claus first visited the town in 1873. As one of the more obvious signs that Christmas was becoming a child-centred holiday, young Elorans were encouraged to visit him at Perry's Drug Store the week prior to 25 December.[142] Across North America, Santa Claus, Christmas trees, gift giving, and other old-world icons of holiday observance had all made their way into upper- and middle-class Christian homes by the later nineteenth century. Christmas was increasingly becoming a "domestic celebration,"[143] even as attending Sunday school concerts and Christmas bazaars remained rituals of the season.

The excitement elicited by Santa Claus and his bountiful bag of gifts is suggestive of the ways that Christmas was being reimagined and transformed in the late nineteenth century, thanks to mass consumption and consumerism. In 1899, Elora proprietor John Gibb announced that his flour and feed store had recently received "Christmas and New Year's fruit" in addition to "fresh family groceries" and a new selection of crockery, glassware, and chinaware that "would make a suitable Christmas present to a friend, and one that would be appreciated as showing the good taste of the giver."[144] As this advertisement suggests, the function of gift giving had evolved beyond an expression of love or gratitude and had become a medium for displaying social status and taste. Gifts increasingly came to symbolize the generosity of the giver rather than appreciation for the receiver. Like the rituals that marked Hallowe'en and Valentine's Day, the number of newspaper advertisements appealing to customers to buy "ideal" Christmas presents, decorations, and other ephemera reflects the growing shift away from holidays being spiritual experiences to more consumer-minded and economically driven practices. Gifts had once been almost wholly homemade, but by the turn of the century middle-class women were less inclined to devote time to such undertakings when presents could easily be purchased from local retailers.

Enticements to purchase seasonal goods provoked a new level of anxiety for women who were tasked with executing the perfect holiday celebration. Though Christmas was a day when families were to gather, the work required for the day's celebration, including preparing dinner, purchasing gifts, and decorating the home, was women's responsibility. Consequently, "Christmas was made by rather than for them."[145] As merchants began catering to female consumers, particularly by feminizing their holiday advertising, this resulted in a "recasting [of] the gendered associations of their stores."[146] The stores dotting small-town main streets, once the locus for male gatherings and exchanges of goods, became sites where middle-class women congregated, browsed, and purchased goods for their families. "The intricate interweaving of romantic sentimentalism, feminization, and consumerism"[147] that became characteristic of holidays bore witness to changes in the ways that women used these celebrations to impart respectability and other markers of middle-class status. Their efforts likely caused angst among less affluent women who could not afford the necessary accoutrements to host the "ideal" celebration. Though Gibb promised Elora shoppers that his holiday goods were so affordable they would "secure ready purchasers,"[148] his customers likely remained middle-class housewives and domestic servants shopping for their wealthier employers.

Despite the growing emphasis on gift giving and decorating, Christmas dinner remained, arguably, *the* cornerstone of the holiday. Suggestions for Christmas menus typically appeared in newspapers and periodicals in the weeks leading up to the holiday. One such proposal suggested beginning with a clear soup followed by toast fingers, salt peanuts, and pickled pears. Roast goose, steamed yams, creamed turnips, jellied apples, orange salad, and celery sticks were suggested for the main course. The traditional British dessert of plum pudding (or Christmas pudding) with a sugar sauce should round out the meal followed by tea or coffee. Recipes for the more popular menu items were included to guide women in preparing the best meal possible.[149] The pressure to fulfill the idyll of a bountiful Christmas feast and perfect presents meant that a significant amount of women's time was spent shopping, which even then could be an exhausting and exasperating experience. Some periodicals reiterated the same anti-elitist discourses they espoused about tea parties, advising rural and small-town hostesses to keep their holiday parties affordable, simple, and small. Thrift was preached as a commendable virtue, but proper execution was still expected. Even as early as 1870, one such article appeared in the *Canada Farmer*, lecturing holiday party-givers about purchasing unnecessary extravagances. The *Farmer* recommended instead that winter pleasures simply involve "friends, mostly young people, meet[ing] at each other's houses, in an informal manner, for music, dancing and various amusements." It was also "stipulated that no other refreshment shall be provided than tea or coffee and bread and butter; and further, that the party shall break up at 12 o'clock."[150]

The Christmas gathering at the home of Robert and Nancy Blackburn in Camden Township near Dresden in 1890 is an example of the extravagance that had, by the late nineteenth century, become a feature of the holiday season. At the time retired farmer Robert was seventy-seven years old and wife, Nancy, seventy-two.[151] Another family member (but not a daughter), twenty-eight-year-old Christy-Ann, also lived in the home, and probably helped in preparing the elaborate holiday soirée. Throughout the female life cycle, as Nancy likely experienced, "the Christmas season lengthened" and "shopping for presents grew in importance, becoming a more absorbing and time-consuming activity."[152] The *Times* reported that apart from three grand-children, all of the Blackburns' immediate family was present for the celebra-tion. After enjoying a hearty Christmas dinner, everyone descended on the parlour and found the day's centrepiece—the Christmas tree—decorated with all manner of fruit that had been hidden as a surprise. The family then indulged in speeches, singing, and recitations. Finally, Santa made his appearance and distributed a grand total of 186 presents.[153] On a slightly less grandiose scale, to celebrate New Year's Eve (or, Hogmanay) in 1910, several men and women from Tillsonburg and the surrounding villages of Ostrander, Mount Elgin, Zenda, Dereham Centre, and Verschoyle descended upon the rural home of James Paisley for a "Scotch Gathering." Adhering to the day's Scottish roots, partygoers enjoyed traditional dances and songs until the wee hours of the morning.[154]

For most rural and small-town women, the holiday season was quietly spent at home in the company of immediate family members. Before her marriage, in 1878 Ann Amelia Day spent a cold and stormy Christmas at home with the "girls," eating apples, drinking cider, and talking "nonsense." At night, they "played quiet games and David displayed his magic lantern."[155] Annie Hill's diary, though written thirty-four years later, is comparable to Day's in terms of the importance placed on the holiday and celebrating at home. To prepare for the Christmas season in 1912, Hill began baking her Christmas cakes on 20 December. On Christmas Day, she and her family travelled to Elora to celebrate at her parents' home.[156] For one anonymous diarist in Wellington County in 1898, after her morning chores of visiting the post office, preparing dinner, and obtaining decorative greenery from a nearby swamp were completed, the rest of her Christmas Day was spent entertaining various visitors who dropped by and enjoying a few games of crokinole in the evening.[157] For Olive Snyder, New

Year's Day in 1913 was a "very nice happy day." She enjoyed the midday meal at a friend's home, followed by the taking of a family portrait in the afternoon and then preparing for the evening's festivities. For her small, mixed-sex circle of friends, Snyder composed a program consisting of "old-fashioned games" in the dining room and dancing that lasted until midnight.[158] The following year, Snyder characterized New Year's Day as a "fine day" and "good time" when, in a similar fashion to the previous year, she visited with friends, neighbours, and family over tea and supper.[159]

Rural and small-town women also enjoyed hosting and attending the occasions of graduations, celebrations, anniversary parties, and weddings in their homes. Agnes McGregor reminisced that during her stint in Tillsonburg, "any event served as an excuse for a party" at the manse. For instance, as a young teen, McGregor hosted a "house-party" after she passed her high school entrance examination. She and her guests played charades, sang ballads and college glee songs around the piano, and dined on ham sandwiches and homemade raspberry vinegar. McGregor expresses that within her circle of friends, most gatherings were held on Friday nights at her home because she had free reign over the home's "living room" and piano.[160] In appreciation of McGregor's frequent hosting, Marguerite Sinclair hosted a tea "in honor" of her friend at the Sinclair home. Many from their inner (and rather affluent) social circle were present for this occasion.[161]

McGregor's penchant for hosting get-togethers at home was partly due to the influence of her parents, who were friendly and popular among her friends. They particularly enjoyed it when Agnes's mother, Jane, accompanied the girls' singing and dancing by playing the piano. Because the McGregors had the help of a domestic servant, Jane McGregor could afford the time away from household duties to entertain her daughter's friends. With such assistance, Agnes was also excused from helping with household chores, apart from keeping her room tidy and running errands. Such freedom allowed Agnes more time to indulge in her favoured pastimes of reading, skating, sleighing, playing with the family's macaw and, of course, hosting parties.[162]

Conclusion

In the last decades of the nineteenth century, domestic leisure activities like teas and dinner parties became events where women could display their class, refinement, and sophistication. The sheer volume of women's domestic leisure activities popular around the turn of the century demonstrates the extent to which women's social lives were undergoing a transformation. As the home itself was altered in the way of labour-saving devices, the accumulation of mass-produced goods, new architectural features, and the expansion of the domestic sphere onto lawns, it became an important setting for men's, women's, children's, and family-centred amusements. By dressing up their parlours, stocking them with all manner of toys and games, and regularly inviting friends and family over for visits, those with the means transformed the space of the home into a temporary world of play. As a result, women were able to strengthen and maintain bonds of friendship and familial togetherness and form networks of mutual assistance that made the accomplishment of laborious domestic tasks a little easier.

The expansion in opportunities for socializing, however, also resulted in greater pressure on women to exhibit exceptional hosting and homemaking skills. Many middle-class women strove to entertain with the same style and gusto as their upper-class counterparts, but their efforts were more about asserting their current position in the socio-economic hierarchy of the town, or improving it if possible. Invoking new themes in home entertainment, such as crazy teas and themed suppers, demonstrated that hosts and participants considered themselves modern and wanted unique and memorable experiences. Unconsciously, they were also performing their class, ethnicity, religious affiliation, and status. As the following chapter will reveal, increasingly after the 1880s some rural and small-town women sought different ways to enliven their home entertainments by incorporating elements of cosmopolitanism in dinner and garden parties. Though taking place on lawns and in parlours and dining rooms, these leisure events allowed rural and small-town women to be temporarily and fictitiously transported to exciting, exotic, and foreign locales.

FIVE

Armchair Tourists:
Fictitious Travel in Tillsonburg

I N THE EARLY 1900s, the Tillsonburg Ladies' Travel Club was a popular and exclusive social organization composed of the town's small yet discernible female elite. Compared to the better-known women's organizations with religious or charitable purposes, the Travel Club's objectives were more idiosyncratic, allowing members to cultivate an appreciation for worldliness, history, and art through fictitious trips to various locales. In the only surviving photograph from the club's early years, six members are posed in front of an ornate, parlour-esque backdrop where they lounge on cushions atop a decorative carpet. The kimonos, hair fans, and tea service suggest Japan was the destination for one of that year's "trips." As the women's positions and appearance suggest, play-acting and costumes were integral to their attempts to interpret and represent the nations, cultures, and people that they "encountered" in their travels and studies.

Beginning in the late nineteenth century, leisure activities became opportunities for small-town Ontarians to momentarily leave their White, Anglo-Celtic identities behind as they adopted self-styled ethnic identities. A popular fundraising bazaar, for example, held intermittently throughout the 1890s in Tillsonburg and nearby Ingersoll, provided an opportunity to visit "all the nations of the earth"[1] and purchase so-called ethnic food and goods from costumed interpreters. In this way, citizens of these towns and

Figure 25. Tillsonburg Ladies' Travel Club, c. 1900–1907. According to Annandale National Historic Site staff, pictured are (left to right) Mabel Borland, Luseilla Harris, Ella Law, Jessie Law, Ethel Ross, and Katie McPhail. The photograph was taken in the front hall of John and Jane Smith's residence, Tillsonburg. Source: ANHS, Pollard Photo, Photograph Collection.

their surrounding rural areas suddenly became members of a broader (but largely imagined) transnational community and affirmed their Whiteness through their appropriations.

As of 2023, the Tillsonburg Ladies' Travel Club was still gathering regularly and was the oldest association of its kind in the community. While there has always been a strong social component to the meetings, "it was and remains a study group,"[2] according to a recent assessment of its activities. When the Travel Club was established in 1900, its focus and objectives were unquestionably linked to a rising consumer consciousness, mass culture, and new modes of consumption. Mass-produced goods and services, more disposable wealth, new transportation infrastructures, improvements in domestic technologies, and diverse options for leisure activities provided opportunities and greater access to material goods that represented White, middle-class gentility and refinement in the Victorian and Edwardian eras. Advice articles appearing in rural and agrarian periodicals, women's magazines, and local newspapers provide evidence that citizens of small-town Ontario, much like their city counterparts, were aware of and willing to engage with modern and novel commodities, services, and activities.

The adoption of this more "cosmopolitan ethos"[3] in leisure activities challenges some of the sweeping generalizations about rural and small-town life that appeared in nineteenth-century poetry and fiction, artwork and photography, and metropolitan newspapers. Residents of large cities were presented as emblems of modernity, while representations of the countryside were often coloured by pre-modern and folk-like associations. While rural and small-town living continued to be defined by idyllic scenes from the province's pastoral past, some reformers and religious officials condemned small communities for being backward, insular, and generally "lacking in social life."[4] This chapter will explore how travellers' clubs and fabricated tours around the world served as important modes of recreation for small-town women who wished to feel and exude modernism.[5] These were activities that allowed partakers to assert their own sense of class and racial superiority while embracing a particular version of global-mindedness. An awareness of the wider world outside one's own geographic confines was a bulwark of the modernist movement, and foreign-themed entertainments provided small-town men and women with the opportunity to engage in this new form of global exploration.

In Tillsonburg, the elite-dominated Travel Club and the community-wide Garden Party of the Nations also demonstrate that the fascination with foreignness transcended class boundaries. Further, though efforts by citizens to appear more cosmopolitan were grounded in an ostensible desire to expand understandings of foreignness, this occurred only on their own terms and in controlled spaces. Conscious choices were made regarding whom locals wished to learn about and how their cultures would be appropriated. Adopting "foreign personae,"[6] whether by drinking tea in a kimono or donning blackface to serve watermelon, communicated that White, Euro-Canadian men and women were aware of and grappling with immigration, miscegenation, and globalization. Though conceptualized as innocent and harmless modes of leisure, the Tillsonburg Ladies' Travel Club and the Garden Party of the Nations exemplify women's desires to expand their geographic knowledge but in a way that reinforced distorted understandings of race, ethnicity, and gender.

While sources confirm the "foreign trend" was popular in other locales, this chapter primarily focuses on examples from Tillsonburg, whose citizens were particularly enamoured with the idea of imaginarily travelling through their leisure. The town's elite and influential members of the middle class, thanks to their wealth and privilege, seem to have led the promotion of this new fad. These citizens had opportunities to travel outside of Ontario and were part of social circles beyond Tillsonburg. Over time, interest in the fictitious travel movement trickled down to the lower middle and working classes. Some examples of foreign-themed entertainments have also been found in Dresden and Elora, but in comparison were much smaller and more infrequent. Ice skating carnivals, Empire Day pageants, and theatrical performances, for instance, were public occasions when locals dressed up and indulged in some play-acting. How to incorporate foreignness in leisure activities was shared through advice and stories in newspapers, periodicals, and women's magazines. Those small-town consumers privileged enough to afford the requisite materials and host or participate in such events could better "demonstrate their gentility and respectability, their cosmopolitanism and modernity."[7] Not all, of course, had the ability to partake; many lacked the means to acquire and purchase the cornucopia of goods being advertised for consumption.[8]

Nevertheless, hints of the "cosmopolitan ethos" were becoming increasingly evident in other ways, through higher standards of education, the organization of various study clubs, and the establishment of public libraries in the later nineteenth century. Rising literacy rates meant citizens had greater access to an array of literary genres,[9] and as reading for pleasure became a popular pastime, works by imperialist writers such as Rudyard Kipling and reprints of fictional classics like *One Thousand and One Nights (The Arabian Nights)* romanticized foreign lands for a new generation of consumers. More tangibly, the appearance of travelling circuses and minstrel shows provided small-town folk an opportunity to gaze at what was positioned as the odd, the exotic, and the foreign, and use them as a means by which to measure their own evolutionary progress. Every day and through a variety of mediums, residents of small-town Ontario consumed images of foreign peoples even as the Canadian government was actively controlling the number of non-White and non-European immigrants entering the country.

Figure 26. Costumed cast of a British/imperial-themed production sponsored by the Mechanics' Institute, Elora, early 1900s. Source: UGASC, Connon Collection, XR1 MS A114_B4.

In the late nineteenth century, popular forms of print media were responsible for transmitting information to small-town readers, and their pages often communicated biased opinions about global politics and affairs. Stories about colonial conflicts like the Boer War, for instance, conveyed specific imperialist values and ideologies to readers. Other articles, such as "Iceland and Its People; The Country That Is Almost Devoid of Comfort," which appeared in the *Tillsonburg Observer* in June 1893, had pedagogical purposes.[10] Some played on widespread fears of the "other"; an 1892 *Observer* article titled "The Wolf Boy of India" described how a missionary claimed to have found an orphaned Indian boy being raised by wolves. Despite retaining his human form, "he bit and scratched with the ferocity of a wild animal, which he was in all respects."[11] Serialized fiction was often strategically printed near these articles, so stories of deceit, intrigue, and scandal reinforced the "othering" of some cultures and exhibited Western jingoism.[12]

Travel lectures were also popular, especially when they professed to have didactic objectives. In October 1893, a missionary physician gave a lecture in Tillsonburg on "China and Its People," at which the audience was "educated" through "graphic pictures of the street life, domestic scenes and other phases of life." To elevate the lecture's "pathetic and repulsive" subject matter, the missionary attempted to infuse his speech with "humourous touches."[13] In endeavouring to "educate" Tillsonburg's citizenry, the lecturer perpetuated the Yellow Peril stereotype and buttressed popular opinions about Chinese people being backward and unassimilable. During this period, such racist attitudes influenced federal immigration policies, like the discriminatory head tax system, in the hopes of curbing the number of Chinese immigrants arriving in Canada.

At the same time, paradoxically, a strong interest in orientalism and sinology developed. Magazines such as the *Ladies' Home Journal* instructed both rural and urban women on how to create "cozy corners," "colonial schemes," and "Oriental booths" in their parlours and sitting rooms.[14] Furniture and goods such as ottomans, Turkish carpets, plush fabrics, and bric-a-brac were suggested to bring hints of colour, texture, and glamour to the home. According to notices in the *Observer* and the *Liberal*, in Tillsonburg outdoor entertainments hosted by elite and middle-class residents often included the wearing of ethnic garb and were illuminated by "Chinese lanterns."[15] Though meant to convey sophistication, most of these decorative pieces were reproductions of original designs and purchased from local shops and mail-order catalogues. Several historians have examined how the introduction of foreign goods into domestic spaces had implicit ties to nationalism and imperialism, allowing affluent city women to distinguish themselves in the "global scheme of things."[16] Rural and small-town women, however, are rarely acknowledged as active participants in this new culture of foreign consumption, though women's magazines and newspaper articles attest to the fact that country women *were* interested in broadening their global consciousness through home decor and entertaining. In this way, they could engage in what Kristin L. Hoganson refers to as the "fictive travel movement."[17] In 1907, for instance, *Ladies' Home Journal* contributor Laura A. Smith advised small-town women unable to travel abroad to gather pamphlets from tour companies and sign out travel books from the local library so they might join the more privileged tourist crowd. For those wishing to incorporate orientalist decoration, Smith recommended constructing a Japanese garden in which "fir trees and a weed-choked rill" and a "miniature pagoda of bamboo fishing-rods" could be installed with only "a little energy."[18]

Around the World in a Day

In towns like Tillsonburg, where Anglo-Celtic ancestry was dominant as a result of contemporary immigration policies, tangible symbols of the British Empire were ubiquitous, from the naming of commercial amusement halls, to the consumption of colonial foodstuffs, to the organization of elaborate Victoria Day celebrations.[19] Just as the local press, literature, and public lectures also "created, interpreted [and] and mediated" national, colonial, and imperial identities,[20] larger visual spectacles such as exhibitions, expositions, and fairs functioned in a similar manner. In his study of modernity and the agricultural fair tradition in Ontario, historian Keith Walden notes, "at the turn of the century, the modern era had become the 'age of the exhibition.'"[21] Most significant were the world's fairs held in Europe, North America, and Australia, followed by the smaller provincial, regional, county, and local fairs. The annual summer or fall agricultural exhibition was a popular social outing for men, women, and families in Dresden, Tillsonburg, and Elora, the crowds gathering at the local fairgrounds to view the horticulture and handicraft submissions on display, participate in sports and games, and catch up with their friends and neighbours. As historian Jodey Nurse explains in her study of Ontario's agricultural fairs, "women benefitted from the multifarious nature of fairs as places where [they] could either support or dismantle notions of feminine behaviour and proper womanhood" by contributing to the displays, sitting on fair boards, or providing entertainment.[22] At the larger exhibitions, alongside the booths advertising domestic goods and agricultural implements, organizers began using midways to showcase carnivalesque attractions such as sideshows, "freak shows," and diorama-like settings of foreign peoples in their so-called natural habitats. Social Darwinist theories and imperial and colonial hierarchies abounded at such displays, which, Walden argues, functioned as "instruments of hegemony" by presenting specific taxonomic orders.[23]

In 1893, the city of Chicago, Illinois, hosted the World's Columbian Exposition to mark the 400th anniversary of Christopher Columbus's initial voyage to the Americas. The official dedication ceremony was held in October 1892 but the fair itself remained closed to the public until May of the following year. According to fair historian Reid Badger, 21.5 million paid admissions were registered over the fair's six-month run.[24] The exposition grounds featured an amalgam of buildings, technological and agricultural exhibits, midway attractions, and ethnographic displays. A significant portion of attendees were Canadians who took advantage of the event's proximity to the border. Beginning in June 1893, the *Tillsonburg Observer* provided weekly reports of those citizens who had left town to visit the "big fair"; the fact that a trip by rail from Tillsonburg to Chicago could be made in just a few days only added to the spectacle's appeal. Advertisements for special fair-bound train and steamer excursions appeared in the *Observer*, along with suggestions for Chicago restaurants and accommodations. Some attended as visitors, while others participated as exhibitors and won prizes for their locally made goods.[25] The costs attached to travelling and attending the fair, including the fifty-cent admission fee, largely relegated attendance to the more privileged.[26] Widespread media coverage, however, allowed those unable to travel to Chicago to experience the fair in print. Near the end of its run, the *Observer* noted that at least seventy-five of Tillsonburg's citizens had graced the "White City," spending an estimated total of $3,000 on travel and other expenses. One reporter pointedly remarked that "a good many hard dollars from Tilsonburg were squandered in taking in the great show before the gates were shut."[27]

Upon their arrival home, fairgoers spoke highly of the sights and sounds they had encountered. Though the fair only lasted for six months, its effects resonated in Tillsonburg for many years after. Some Tillsonburg business owners began renovating their store interiors and window displays, clearly inspired by the exhibits they had viewed on their trip. When dry goods proprietor R.F. Williams returned to Tillsonburg, for example, the *Observer* reported that he was "so loaded up with new ideas that he will hereafter be able to make the store more attractive than ever, which will be pleasing to his many customers and induce others to go inside and take a look around."[28] Similarly, historians have found that American visitors' experiences at the Columbian Exposition precipitated a burst of improvements to residences, businesses, and even entire towns after the fair closed.[29]

In the wake of the 1893 Columbian Exposition, as well as following the 1901 Pan-American Exposition in Buffalo, New York, and the 1904 Louisiana Purchase Exposition in St. Louis, Missouri, miniature exhibitions began appearing in larger towns and cities across North America, held primarily as fundraising fairs for religious auxiliaries and charitable organizations.[30] Eight months after the gates of the Columbian Exposition shut for good, Tillsonburg held its very own version of the fair on a warm Tuesday evening in July 1894. Organized under the auspices of the Methodist church's Epworth League, the event—dubbed the "Garden Party of the Nations"—was held on the vast lawn surrounding E.D. and Mary Ann Tillson's home, Annandale House. Though the attractions and purposes differed, the Garden Party of the Nations was an attempt to mimic the Columbian Exposition's Midway Plaisance with its display of ethnographic villages.[31] Like "sale of work" bazaars and other nineteenth-century fundraising socials, the Garden Party of the Nations was constructed to be both a community-wide social function and a money-making venture. Its unique around-the-world theme was meant to "transport [...] guests beyond the realm of the local."[32] Instead of wasting their money abroad (as the *Observer* remarked), Tillsonburg residents had the world brought to them, enabling them to invest their money in the local economy.

When the Garden Party opened, the *Observer* reported, several booths were set up on Annandale House's manicured lawn, each decorated with colourful flags, bunting, and national symbols indicative of the country or ethnic group being represented. Electric lights strung overhead to illuminate the grounds added to the ambiance. The booths employed popular nineteenth-century motifs to symbolize Canada, the American South, Iceland, China and Japan (homogenized in one booth), Germany, Ireland, Scotland, and England. At each booth White men and women acted as costumed interpreters, doling out "authentic" food, music, and handicrafts for a small fee. Dubbed "the greatest novelty of the season" by the *Observer*, Tillsonburg's inaugural Garden Party of the Nations attracted 800 participants, with receipts totalling $100.[33]

"Belinda," a special correspondent to the *Observer* who occasionally provided readers with a "woman's viewpoint," attended the spectacle and published a thorough report of its attractions. There are no surviving photographs of the event, so it is through Belinda's eyes and words that we gain a visual sense of the party. The first booth she encountered was Canada, with its "pretty Canadian girls dressed in airy, white gowns trimmed in maple leaves" and a flat-roofed wigwam, occupied by an "Indian" who "vigorously" pulled a lunch bell. At the Icelandic booth, she enjoyed a taste of ice cream; at the German booth women with "serious, kindly faces" served pretzels and non-alcoholic beer; upon entering China and Japan, she drank tea and remarked on a table of Asian-themed curiosities. She visited Donegal Castle and the famous Blarney Stone at the Irish booth before finally reaching Great Britain, where the "graceful outlines" of its emblematic lion welcomed her and stood in stark contrast to the "ugly distorted features" of the Japanese deity she had encountered earlier in her "travels." Belinda, however, was most intrigued by the American booth with its depictions of the antebellum South, including a whitewashed cabin, watermelons, and blackfaced interpreters. The event concluded with all the nations marching together away from the grounds where, she remarked, "they [had] met and found one another good fellows."[34]

The event was held again the following year, no doubt inspired by the respectable sum raised in 1894. The 1895 party was the largest and grandest of those held in Tillsonburg in the 1890s.[35] Under the heading "Foreigners in Town; The Nations of the Earth Pitch Their Tents in Tilsonburg," the *Observer* reported that the number of visitors amounted to 1,500, an impressive tally considering the town's population was just over 2,000 people at the time. The 1895 party far surpassed the previous year's receipts with earnings of $300. The nations represented were largely the same, apart from the addition of Italy and a booth dedicated to New England Quakers, where Boston baked beans and pumpkin pie hearkened back to the colonial era and, perhaps, hinted at the strength and resiliency of rural life. In contrast to the previous year's party, the "Indian wigwam" was a booth in and of itself, complete with a "fine collection of relics" and "entertainment [...] provided by a band of most natural looking specimens of the noble red man and woman." Likely, it was White men and women from the town who donned redface to portray the Indigenous people in this booth and at other garden parties. The *Observer* noted that the curiosities on display had been borrowed from a Mr. Scrivens and the costumes deserved "special mention," though details were withheld.[36]

One year later, in June 1896, the town of Ingersoll (located roughly twenty-five kilometres northwest of Tillsonburg) held its version of the Midway Plaisance, dubbed the "Feast of Nations," which lasted for three days. Also organized as a charitable venture, the event was held inside a local arena where, as at Tillsonburg, several booths plastered with national symbols were erected and manned by costumed locals doling out "authentic" dinners for a fee. According to the *Ingersoll Chronicle*, the event was visited by hundreds and considered "an undeniable success, the proceeds netting over $500." The booths were described as "gems of architectural art," and even included massive re-creations of Windsor and Edinburgh Castles. The *Chronicle* declared that the food and costumes of "the various nationalities" present, which included representatives of England, Scotland, Canada, France, New

England, China and Japan, Spain and Italy, and Germany, "were really excellent and true to nature."[37]

Such garden parties remained popular in Oxford County (and presumably other locales) well into the 1910s. Tillsonburg's Red Cross Society revived the event in 1917 as a wartime fundraiser. Mimicking those held in the 1890s, the 1917 affair, described as a "trip around the world," offered 400 "tourists" a glimpse of seven different nations—Great Britain, Ireland, France, Japan, Italy, China, and the United States. For a small sum, citizens purchased a ticket and took a "train" in the form of a donated automobile to the different destinations. The set-up incorporated some of the realities of wartime, including armed guards at the entrance to Great Britain, who demanded visitors show passports "owing to the submarine campaign." Also notable, the only countries included in the "tour" were members of the Allied forces (but not their respective colonies), whereas in the 1890s, Germany had been a mainstay in around-the-world-themed garden parties. Like its predecessors, the 1917 "trip" allowed visitors to experience stereotypical food, drink, attire, and architecture, which blended nostalgia with modernity. While "visiting" the United States, for instance, tourists saw locals in blackface dressed as "Aunt Dinah" and "picaninnies," two prevalent misrepresentations of the antebellum South, alongside White, uniformed members of the armed forces. Despite the considerable sum spent on the event, the net proceeds for the Red Cross only amounted to roughly $200.[38]

Some of the members of the Epworth League and local elites who oversaw the planning, organization, and financing of the original Garden Party of the Nations were part of the large and privileged contingent from Tillsonburg who had experienced the Columbian Exposition first-hand. Though religious and secular organizations were incorporating global themes in their socials and fundraising activities long before North American exhibitions brought the world home to the masses,[39] the Tillsonburg Garden Party was undoubtedly inspired by the organizers' trip to Chicago. Belinda herself said, "National garden party! Midway plaisance! Call it what you will, only let us get into the crowd, mix in and out through it, and be a part of it."[40] Through their personal experiences, organizers served as "conduits of information" for the rest of the town.[41] Additionally, the Epworth League's construction of racialized and ethnic identities at the Garden Party may have been influenced and shaped by missionary efforts during this period. According to historian Rosemary Gagan, White female missionaries in Japan, for instance, "never became completely or comfortably acclimatized," often complaining about "food and domestic habits, politics, morality, and religion."[42] In their attempts to Christianize and Canadianize the so-called heathens of the world, specific colonizer-colonizee relationships were forged through the imperialist gaze,[43] and these biases inevitably travelled back and influenced small-town Ontarians through religious activities like auxiliary fundraisers, Sunday school programs, and public lectures.

Members of the Epworth League did not just mimic the ethnographic villages on display at the Midway Plaisance, they made conscious choices about how foreign peoples would be represented based on their own sensibilities and possibilities. Makeup and costumes, for instance, were necessary to transform locals into foreigners, whereas in Chicago, the reconstructed villages were populated by foreign people who had agreed to be on display for a fee. The original Midway Plaisance consisted of exhibits of people from southern Africa, Asia, and the Middle East. The Garden Party of the Nations, in contrast, was devoid of non-Western representations apart from that of China and Japan. Organizers of the Tillsonburg Garden Party decided not only to include but also to highlight the Canadian, British, and Irish booths, reflecting both their dominant heritage and the boundaries of their cosmopolitanism. Limiting their definition of worldliness to nations that were either predominantly White or celebrated merely for their aesthetic appeal (such as China and Japan) reveals far more about the organizers' sense of their own identity than it does about the people on display. This choice contradicts some of the observations made by historians examining foreign-themed amusements and fundraisers in the United States during the same period. Hoganson, for instance, argues that the choices made regarding which nations and cultures would be appropriated were usually based on the extent of their "foreignness": the more foreign the spectacle, the more likely a profit would be turned. Organizers rarely chose to represent their own ethnicities because they were considered too ordinary and mundane.[44]

The choices made by the Tillsonburg Garden Party's organizers also highlight the strength of imperial sentiment in Canada at the time. As British historians Ashley Jackson and David Tomkins explain, experiencing the empire in "highly visual form[s]" such as expositions and parties was not only a fashionable undertaking but also a "distinctive feature of British culture" and a useful way of presenting its feats to a wider cross-section of the population.[45] In Tillsonburg, the various forms of these visual reminders, such as the use of costumery and preparation of ethnic cuisine, allowed people of White, Anglo-Celtic ancestry to momentarily "play" or "act out" nationalities both similar to and different from their own. Food was often the central focus of fairs, clubs, and parties because the physical act of ingesting atypical food was considered a "cosmopolitan experience" in itself.[46] The kitchen was one of the many stages where women exhibited their cosmopolitanism, reinventing traditional dishes to seem unfamiliar and exotic.

Historians have argued that in the later Victorian period, the appeal of costumery lay in its ability to claim uniqueness and individuality; in small towns like Tillsonburg, incorporating novel forms of individual expression such as racialized attire allowed men and women to stand out against the predominantly White, Anglo-Celtic backdrop of their community. Though costume parties and masquerades were traditionally the preserve of the elite, by the turn of the century middle-class residents were also eagerly donning ethnic garb because of the simple "excitement offered by disguise."[47] For a while they could be someone different, providing a temporary reprieve from the monotony of day-to-day living.

Of all the nations that piqued the curiosity of Westerners at the time, China and Japan were among the most popular to be appropriated in leisure activities because sinology and orientalism were so prominent in Western art and design schemes. Dichotomously, while the so-called Yellow Peril and White slave panic, and "seedy" Chinatowns were provoking anxiety among Westerners and influencing anti-Asian immigration policies, Asian motifs were highly coveted by fashionable members of the middle and upper classes. Aside from capitalizing on its visual appeal, appropriating the Far East theme in everything from leisure activities to parlour decor became a way to curtail fears and misunderstandings over their "otherness."[48] As an example, organizers chose a ten-year-old girl to impersonate a Chinese man at the 1897 Garden Party of the Nations. Her youth and sex had an infantilizing and emasculating effect, downplaying White fears of Chinese men's alleged hypersexuality.[49] The Chinese and Japanese booths at the Garden Party and the portrait of the Tillsonburg Ladies' Travel Club dressed in kimonos show how representations of Asia were usually "limited" to costumery, food, and decorations deemed suitable by Western fashion magazines.[50] Such cultural symbolism became familiar, and as Hoganson suggests, "displaced more complicated or unsettling depictions" of the countries and people being appropriated.[51]

A very small population of Asian immigrants lived in Tillsonburg around the time the Garden Party of the Nations was held. The 1901 census notes three "Chinese and Japanese" people resided in the town, this number increasing to four in 1911. Three of them—Led Sing, Ling Yiu (or Yu), and Lin (or Ling) See—operated a "Laundry Shop" on Broadway Street.[52] Around the turn of the century, hundreds of Chinese laundries could be found across Canada. Once the work of constructing the CPR dried up, many Chinese labourers left Western Canada but struggled to find employment because of language barriers and anti-Asian racism. Some became entrepreneurs and opened laundries, taking advantage of the demand and the small amount of start-up capital required. Customers paid to have their clothing washed by hand, a chore that required long hours and hard labour. Historians note that though laundries were a necessary service, especially among the bachelor population, White citizens were often suspicious of Chinese-owned operations. Like opium dens and gambling halls, laundries operated by Chinese Canadians were assumed to be businesses where nefarious activities occurred.[53] In Tillsonburg, White citizens' understanding of Asian cultures was likely shaped by the presence of the Chinese laundry and popular attitudes around it, in conjunction with the (mis)information they received through novels and "educational" lectures about Asia.

The ways in which the American South was presented at the fairs and garden parties, particularly the use of fictional and racialized characters, echoed discriminatory stereotypes about Black Americans in the wake of Reconstruction and the passage of Jim Crow laws. While some fairs and expositions strove to showcase achievements being made in Black communities, the Garden Party, much like minstrelsy, drew on invented and idyllic images of antebellum plantation life.[54] Though it appears no Black Canadians were living in Tillsonburg in the 1890s, a small group had previously, and the nearby communities of Woodstock, Norwich, and Ingersoll were still home to small populations of Black families who lived and worked alongside the White majority. The presentation of a singular Black culture at the various garden parties, however, was entrenched in White understandings that glorified slavery and the states that condoned it. An image of harmonious subservience was curated for audiences, rather than addressing the systemic racism that existed in Canada and the United States at the time.[55] As with its treatment of China, the Garden Party downplayed White fears of Blackness by cloaking it in the rhetoric of the minstrel show and other forms of postbellum entertainment.[56]

At Tillsonburg's garden parties, the Indigenous people on display were not posed as "savages" or uncivilized warriors, as was common at some American exhibitions. Anthropologist Burton Benedict explains that often the images and objects chosen to depict an all-encompassing Indigenous culture reinforced notions of a primordial and war-like society on the brink of extermination.[57] At the Garden Party of the Nations, choosing to use the "Indian" as the ringer of the lunch bell downplayed personifications of savagery, in this case domesticating him in ways that might quell White fears of violent uprisings.[58] Across Canada, nation-building efforts in the later nineteenth century, especially desires to free up land for White settlement, resulted in the passage of the Indian Act in 1876, the expropriation of Indigenous reserve lands, and the establishment of residential schools. As Indigenous people were increasingly pushed out of sight, they continued to be typecast in familiar ways: brutal and bloodthirsty or primitive and vanquished. By placing the bellringer in a position of servitude and thus a class below their own, the Garden Party organizers who constructed the booth subsequently imparted a White, Canadian nationalism that considered Indigenous people to be second-class citizens. Gendered undertones were also not-so-subtly communicated: the White, Canadian women serving lunch showed the fulfillment of important feminine and domestic duties, while similar behaviour from Indigenous women was noticeably absent.[59]

The organizers' decision to place Canadian and Indigenous people in one booth at the 1894 Garden Party allowed visitors to evaluate cultural "evolution" while presenting the illusion of living cooperatively and benevolently.[60] Whereas the Canadian side was resplendent with symbols of economic progress—sheaves of grain and beavers, for example—the other side, with its flat-topped wigwam shrouded in pine boughs, provided a visual contradiction signalling crudeness. As historian Elsbeth Heaman explains, despite efforts by some exhibitors to present Indigenous peoples as the successful result of government assimilation policies, wigwams and feather headdresses continued to be appropriated and made appearances at turn-of-the-century fairs and exhibitions. The fact remained that "Indians were a spectacle to whites even when they were not behaving spectacularly."[61]

Some of the continental European nations on display at the Tillsonburg garden parties represented the ethnic backgrounds of a handful of the events' organizers, volunteers, and attendees. Filling the booths with folksy, peasant-like interpreters, however, implied that these nations were stuck in some sort of time warp. According to Beverly Gordon, this romanticized vision of Old Europe was a popular one employed at bazaars and fundraising fairs.[62] Here, less-evolved Old World ideals were juxtaposed with the new (and thus better and more progressive) societies that immigrants allegedly found when they arrived in North America. At the same time, hearkening back to an era of pre-industrial simplicity was a cornerstone of anti-modernism, so the ways that continental Europe was imagined by party organizers may have actually been intended to be a positive representation and a valorization of rural life.[63] Because many of the parties' organizers had grown up in the era before modern conveniences complicated the pace of daily life, the use of pastoral symbolism can perhaps be understood as a rejection of some of the less desirable social shifts resulting from industrialization and globalization. In the case of Germany specifically, fears of its rising power in Europe were somewhat nullified by the organizers' presentation of German mannerisms, which Belinda described as "amiable" and "steady."[64] Cloaking Germany in these antiquated characterizations downplayed mounting concerns about its military, economy, and political structure. However, its absence at the 1917 Red Cross fundraiser fair confirmed that Germany was no longer a safe or desired destination.

At the Canadian booth, the imperialist and nationalist sentiments of Tillsonburg's White citizenry were on full display. The young, attractive girls doling out food, resplendent in their white dresses, signified racial and sexual purity and feminine innocence. At other town events where national and imperial themes were prominent, the colour white was used to signify patriotism, particularly when it came to women's and girls' attire. Red and blue accents complemented the white, reminiscent of the Union Jack that bound the nations of the British Empire together. The symbolic maple leaves, snowshoes, and beavers that were woven into Canada's reputation as the "great white north" were also used to their full effect. The combination of so many purportedly Canadian icons with more imperialist ones signified to visitors the dominant Whiteness of the nation's population (illustrated in the girls' white costumes) and the participants' Anglo-Celtic ancestry. Through these specific constructions, organizers reinforced notions of a White Canada that held a superior position in the colonial and racial hierarchy.

The Tillsonburg Ladies' Travel Club

In an 1897 issue of *The Delineator*, a popular American women's magazine, an unnamed columnist mentioned a new social club that was gaining popularity in rural districts—the "travellers' club."[65] Other periodicals with a wide readership, like *Harper's Bazaar,* also published articles with instructions on how to establish a "travel study club" and types of themed events they may enjoy, such as a "purely Italian evening."[66] Travellers' clubs, however, have received little attention in North American studies of leisure, education, and the female club movement. Like the Garden Party of the Nations, travel clubs allowed members to become "armchair tourists" by immersing themselves in foreign cultures without leaving the comfort of home. Despite the moniker, the groups rarely organized actual trips. The imaginary travel theme had become so trendy that this sort of fictitious journeying was sometimes included in the agendas of other social and study clubs.

Though many of the women who composed Tillsonburg's upper class may have had an education and travelled beyond Canada, they still desired a social club that would allow them to "go" further and to exchange stories, as well as share and discuss the local library's holdings of travel literature.[67] For less experienced travellers, membership offered an opportunity to broaden their knowledge of foreign lands, gain an enhanced sense of cultural enlightenment, and engage in an educative (yet sociable) forum. Local histories of Tillsonburg's travel club note that after a "Mrs. Holmstead" from Toronto visited Tillsonburg with the intention of establishing a formal travel club for this group of like-minded women, the Tillsonburg Ladies' Travel Club was founded in 1900. Holmstead may have been invited by a local woman who had recently visited Toronto and after becoming acquainted with a travel club there thought a similar undertaking would flourish in Tillsonburg.[68] Three years earlier in the town of Dundas, near the city of Hamilton, a travel club had been established by Mrs. Wellesley Holmested and Mrs. Gerald Gwyn, both residents of the community. Likely, this is the "Mrs. Holmstead" who visited Tillsonburg and helped to get its travel club off the ground.[69]

According to its constitution, the objective of the Travel Club was to "take trips, in imagination, to different countries and learn all that is possible of the practical details of each tour. To read up-to-date magazine articles and notes from guide books and books of travel. [. . .] It is further the aim of the Club to develop individual talent and to cultivate the appreciation of Art

in its widest sense of the word, at home as well as abroad, therefore committees will be formed for literature, art and music."[70] Initially meetings were
held every Monday from October to April, alternating between afternoon
and evening gatherings at the home of one of the group's members. At the
conclusion of each meeting, it was expected that tea and one kind of cake,
as well as bread and butter, would be served. The yearly membership fee
was fifty cents, though a higher fee could be requested if the club required
additional funds.[71]

The first Travel Club consisted of twelve members, with Mrs. W.W.
(Margaret) Livingstone at the helm as president. The most recent history
of the club, compiled by members in 2000, describes in detail the background of each of the charter members, including information related to
the member's social class (based on her husband's occupation), the location
of the marital home in town, and anyone notable whom the woman was
related to.[72] Based on this information it is clear that the first members
were part of Tillsonburg's elite, a group of White women who oversaw
other social organizations around town and whose husbands were politicians, professionals, and entrepreneurs. It is not surprising, then, that
Article 4 of the constitution contained explicit instructions that "the Club
shall be a limited social one." New offers of membership could be made
only by current members, and the final decision to accept or decline was
made by secret ballot.[73] For this group of affluent women in Tillsonburg,
involvement in the Travel Club further differentiated them from the lower
middle and working classes. Being part of a recognized association such as
the Travel Club bestowed on members the prestige of having the "tourist
outlook." This mentality and the belief that members were more worldly
and refined because they were nurturing their knowledge of politics, history,
and geography set these women apart from those "who were not as attuned
to the culture of travel."[74] A similar outlook existed for the organizers of
the Garden Party of the Nations, whose booth choices and designs had a
pedagogical purpose for the event's visitors.

At the end of each year of study, club members decided the destinations for the coming year by secret ballot. Once agreed upon, a program

committee designed a weekly schedule of activities, with each member in charge of presenting to fellow club members a specific aspect of a certain country or ethnic group's history, culture, society, or political system. This took the form of papers and lectures, photographic and lantern slide shows, illustrated guidebooks, and history lessons. Vocal or instrumental selections, dance, sampling "authentic" cuisine, and wearing ethnic garb were also commonplace. In 1910, when the club "travelled" to Spain, members presented papers and treatises on the Spanish islands, chivalry, Ferdinand and Isabella, *Don Quixote*, sculpture and wood carving, and the customs of Old Madrid. The following year, the club "travelled" to Russia and explored the Kremlin, short poems of Pushkin, and Saint Basil's Cathedral.[75] The choice of destination was often not a coincidence; contemporary developments in politics and world affairs often influenced the destination choices. The Tillsonburg club's yearly agendas share many characteristics with those of the Dundas club as well as the programs recommended in magazines like *Harper's Bazaar*. In 1900, for instance, *Harper's* columnist Margaret Hamilton Welch responded to several clubwomen's requests for planning the perfect "trip" to Russia. Closely resembling what the Tillsonburg club studied ten years later, Welch's recommendations covered a range of study topics, including Pushkin's poetry, Ivan the Terrible, nihilism, and Russian topography.[76]

Aside from being a marker of social status, the appeal of joining the travel club lay in its ability to temporarily transport women away from their everyday lives and familial duties. Indeed, most leisure activities that invoked the foreign theme allowed participants to momentarily adopt habits, speech, style, and mannerisms considered by their White, Anglo-Celtic societies to be strange, subversive, or exotic. According to Hoganson, "travel club members regarded their journeys as hard-earned breaks from daily obligations," and the efforts they put into educating others and expanding their own geographic knowledge became "a source of pride."[77] The ways that these Tillsonburg women attempted to engage with worldliness were not necessarily malicious in their intent, but in reiterating understandings of difference, they reproduced them and concurrently shored up understandings of their own superiority. In this way, their consumption of knowledge operated as a form of power. Leisure activities based on the travel theme forged hierarchies of difference among citizens because they allowed participants to assert their privilege to travel and consume knowledge. The intricate detail that went into constructing these entertainments demonstrates the extent to which participants were interested in their own intellectual gain and creative expression, though the result of their efforts was often the dissemination of racist rhetoric. As Lynne Marks reminds us, small-town Ontario's overwhelmingly White, Anglo-Celtic identity was integral to citizens' "constructions of [. . .] superiority both at home and in the larger world,"[78] resulting in a skewed sense of "ethnographic accuracy."[79]

For less privileged participants, the propensity to use leisure as a way to travel imaginatively can best be understood as a yearning to explore a wider world despite the socio-economic constraints that bound them to home. Though education and literacy rates were rising, only a handful of Tillsonburg's townsfolk were fortunate enough to go abroad and have encounters with the people they read about. By contrast, the price of a single admission to the Garden Party of the Nations or the Feast of Nations provided a condensed version of the world where patrons could make a trip around the globe within a couple of hours. Some visitors were undoubtedly aware of how much the appropriations on display were conjured, based on their own travel experiences or interactions with the groups who were on display. But making money was, above all, the organizers' primary objective when planning the event. For the sake of profits and "entertainment," popular and detrimental understandings about ethnic and cultural difference were reinforced in the events' physical displays and play-acting.

In the face of growing critiques of the staidness of country living, around-the-world themes were increasingly employed by women in patterns of leisure and consumption that reveal desires to exude an aura of cultivation and civilization via expressions and understandings of travel, geography, and foreign peoples. Though women in Dresden and Elora do not appear to have established travel clubs or planned elaborate parties inspired by Chicago's Midway Plaisance, information about cultures outside their own was still disseminated and performed through other modes of leisure such as public lectures, plays, physical activities, and works of fiction. The practice of acquiring a comfortable knowledge of foreign lands and people was a marker of middle-class respectability and contradicted some of the critiques being made by turn-of-the-century social commentators about rural and small-town Ontarians being parochial, uncultured, and backward. The trajectory of the humble garden party, for instance, points to how willing local citizens were when it came to embracing new mediums of modernism. From its beginnings as a large-scale community picnic to the eventual inclusion of foreign themes and motifs, by the turn of the century the garden party was able to fuse pre-modern and modern social practices. Residents of Tillsonburg did not necessarily want to give up their much-enjoyed yet conventional garden party, so instead they revamped and reconciled it within the burgeoning consumption-driven and cosmopolitan world they were a part of. At the same time, the arrangement and content of these events served as an opportunity to assert notions of White, Anglo-Celtic supremacy.

As the Garden Party of the Nations demonstrates, even religious organizations embraced the foreign theme for its alleged educational benefits and ability to turn a profit. In Caroline French Benton's 1912 treatise *Fairs and Fetes*, for instance, she writes that when it came to fundraising, "the old-fashioned fair is a thing of the past."[80] When a 1907 issue of the *Ladies' Home Journal* provided suggestions for religious fundraising fairs, the "fair of the nations" theme was at the top of the list.[81] In a similar vein, the Tillsonburg Ladies' Travel Club's preoccupation with pedagogy and self-improvement demonstrates how diverse women's club work was becoming. Religious auxiliaries, civic improvement societies, and charitable organizations were no less popular at the turn of the century, but the Travel Club's objectives, like so many other women's clubs, underscored the increasing importance of nurturing the need for personal fulfillment and instruction.

Determining whether the displays at the Garden Party of the Nations or the "trips" being organized by members of the Travel Club had any measurable effect on locals' conceptions of their own identities or that of foreign people is challenging. As historian H.V. Nelles reminds us, "simply reading the script" is insufficient because "other meanings can be imparted by performance."[82] By what means the Garden Party was ethnically and spatially constructed, however, does provide us with a glimpse of how the organizers themselves internalized the forces and meanings of imperialism and globalization. Along with the opportunity to visualize imperial and non-imperial entities, around-the-world-themed recreations were meant to be educational, commercial, ambassadorial,[83] and fantastical undertakings for both the producers and the participants. In the imaginary contact zone of the Garden Party, the men, women, and children of Tillsonburg and its surrounding communities encountered highly visual representations of Social Darwinism and the colonialist policies that built the British Empire. A very utopian and united perspective on global relations was offered while racial, ethnic, and colonial hierarchies were simultaneously broadcast to the hundreds of spectators. Whether done consciously or not, "imperial ideas" were still embedded in this sort of popular culture, "even if knowledge and understanding were neither uniform nor erudite."[84]

While these revamped leisure activities were opportunities to reinforce stereotypical perceptions of peoples and cultures (both foreign and domestic), visitors to the Garden Party of the Nations and members of the Travel Club were also urged to consume and absorb tangible signifiers of worldliness, including food, costumes, handicrafts, and other material objects. The very act of going to the fair to see so-called foreign people or dressing up in a kimono and sipping tea was a consumptive process. Even viewing and learning about art, history, culture, and politics was consumption in a metaphysical sense. Consumption and cosmopolitanism coalesced at around-the-world entertainments, where tasting foods and/ or seeing costumes became a way to compare and measure one's own identity with others', as well as amalgamating East and West and modern and anti-modern.[85] The national symbols that were appropriated and the foods and costumes chosen to represent foreignness confirm that Tillsonburg's citizens were willing consumers of ethnicities and cultures outside their own, but in a controlled, distorted, and largely inauthentic way.

Conclusion

By the turn of the century, immigration, urbanization, and a greater sense of globalization meant that late Victorians, including those living outside of larger cities, "could not escape difference and representations of difference";[86] accordingly, this was manifested in a new range of "foreign entertainments" where White, Euro-Canadian men and women, as both hosts and attendees, "could display their privileged positions in the global scheme of things."[87] Mimicking the identity-making practices they had encountered at Chicago's World's Columbian Exposition in 1893, during their travels, or within periodicals and works of fiction, citizens of Tillsonburg used their leisure activities to convey their own understandings of life outside the geographic confines of their town. In this way, they reacted against perceptions that country living was backward and parochial by incorporating modern and unconventional themes and motifs in their domestic spaces and leisure activities. Though most would never leave Canada, learning about and subsequently representing foreign cultures in their play became a satisfying and exciting replacement.

Though the Garden Party of the Nations, Feast of Nations, Tillsonburg Ladies' Travel Club, and other foreign-themed activities may have been attempts to identify with other cultures and show a willingness to accept difference, participants and members simultaneously distanced themselves from the "other" by carefully choosing how they would travel imaginatively and fake their foreignness. At the Garden Party of the Nations and the Feast of Nations, visitors were provided with a particular vantage point of the world that reinforced the dominance of the British Empire. The tourist mentality that elite members of the Travel Club adopted because of their studies separated them from the rest of society thanks to their new-found appreciation for and knowledge of lands beyond North America. Together, events like the Garden Party of the Nations between 1894 and 1897 and the establishment of the Ladies' Travel Club in 1900 provide important and informative glimpses into how elite and non-elite citizens from one small town reconciled their own Anglo-Celtic identities with their desires for knowledge in an increasingly interconnected, consumption-driven, and cosmopolitan world. While Tillsonburg has been chosen as a case study here, print sources from the period demonstrate that this phenomenon of armchair travelling was not unique to Tillsonburg. That is not to say, though, that small-town Ontarians were only fictitious travellers and sought cultural enlightenment from the comfort of home. As the following chapter will reveal, a growing awareness of the wider world prompted many citizens in Dresden, Tillsonburg, and Elora to take advantage of the new transportation networks available to them and venture out of doors to destinations near and far.

SIX

Vacationers and "Staycationers": Leisure Out of Doors

N THE NOVEMBER 1906 issue of the *Ladies' Home Journal,* the fall/ winter edition of Laura A. Smith's column "The Girl in the Small Town" advised young women not to "stand looking out of your window at ground and trees in winter garb and say: 'It is so dull in this town in winter! I just despise being cooped up here. Nothing ever happens.' The social season is at its height in winter in the city; why not among the young people of your town?" In addition to providing ideas for fancy-dress parties, amateur study clubs, and unique holiday events, Smith counselled her readers on the importance of getting outdoors to enliven gloomy winter days.[1] The following year, her spring/summer column declared: "Each golden and each gray day of spring and summer can be crowded with happiness if you, girl in the small town, will appoint yourself a committee of one to set things going." Smith provided tips on constructing entertainment spaces in and around the home, taking excursions to local lakes and rivers, and organizing a "walking party." She concluded by urging women, "Determine to see only the wonders and glories of spring and summer. Be glad you are here to enjoy them. Be as generous as Nature herself in throwing pleasures into the way of others."[2]

Smith's advice to small-town women about spending time outdoors was not unique to the *Ladies' Home Journal.* By the later years of the nineteenth century, the number of newspaper and magazine articles describing the virtues of outdoor play and leisure travel had noticeably increased.[3] Women and girls in Dresden, Tillsonburg, and Elora were amenable to such suggestions, as evidenced by how many of them used their leisure time for the purposes of exploring natural spaces both near and far from home. By the turn of the century, new tourism infrastructures, greater opportunities for non-competitive sports, and more available and affordable modes of travel helped upper-, middle-, and, to a lesser extent, working-class women to participate in a plethora of outdoor leisure activities. Alone, with female friends, or as part of large mixed-sex groups, women engaged in everything from transcontinental and transoceanic jaunts to more local picnicking, boating, and swimming.

This proclivity for touring, day-tripping, and going "back to the land" is indicative of the central role that nature and the environment played as men and women became itinerant leisure seekers in the later nineteenth century. Regions such as the Niagara Peninsula, central Ontario's cottage country, Nova Scotia's Annapolis Valley, Prince Edward Island, and southern British Columbia became renowned for their distinctive geographies.[4] Over time, these locations served as backdrops for lucrative tourist industries that were often developed at the expense of Indigenous people living in the area or nearby. In Jessica Dunkin's work on the history of canoeing, for example, she notes that "summer camps, summer homes, and national parks all provided the impetus for the dispossession of Indigenous peoples."[5] By the postwar period, the availability of air and auto travel allowed vacationing, camping, cottaging, and other outdoor recreational activities to figure more prominently in Canadians' lives and take them further abroad.

This chapter examines the many ways the women of Dresden, Tillsonburg, and Elora traversed the outdoors, first examining the vacation practices of the elite, then exploring the ways middle- and working-class women enjoyed venturing out on excursions and day trips. It also looks at how small towns themselves, such as Elora, developed into and profited from being sought-after tourist destinations. Though much has been written about the desires of urbanites to use outdoor recreational activities as a respite from life in an industrial city, this chapter describes how desires to pursue leisure outdoors, including the quest for the "sublime" and the need to improve one's physical and mental well-being, were not confined to residents of cities.

Most outdoor leisure seekers in Dresden, Tillsonburg, and Elora were day-trippers, excursionists, and "staycationers."[6] In line with previous studies, this chapter separates day-trippers and excursionists from the more elite tourists, based on socio-economic status and the nature of their travel. Indeed, the increasing use of the descriptor "excursion" in the later nineteenth century denoted the temporary jaunts characteristic of middle- and working-class travellers.[7] As opposed to tourists who often departed for significant periods of time and ventured further abroad, day-trippers, as the moniker suggests, generally left home for no more than a day.[8] Excursionists were slightly different in that they were "bent on sightseeing and content with brief stops at settlements along the route, putting up at hotels or staying with acquaintances if more extended visits were made."[9] Excursions involved purchasing a ticket for a train or steamship that provided transportation to a predetermined destination. Day trips, in contrast, were much more spontaneous and informal in their nature and purpose and occurred closer to home.

Sources such as poetry, photographs, letters, diary entries, personal reminiscences, and newspaper coverage of citizens' comings and goings acknowledge and highlight how waterways, shorelines, parks, wooded areas, and other green spaces provided important, unique, and reputable spaces for both homo- and heterosocial leisure activities. As more women explored and interpreted nature and open-air spaces, sites for outdoor leisure were purposefully reconfigured so they could be shared between the sexes and, to an extent, the classes.[10] Just as public entertainment halls were being refitted with the female spectator in mind, greater attention was paid to revitalizing natural spaces and supplying them with amenities suited to feminine and "respectable" tastes. In contrast to the early years of the nineteenth century, when outdoor pursuits were largely the domain of elite men, by the turn of the twentieth century the appeal of spending leisure time outdoors had rapidly spread across gender, cultural, and class divisions.[11] For women, "appropriate" activities popular a generation earlier, such as the occasional ramble in the woods or a berry-picking excursion, had evolved into a much more complex set of activities where heterosocial mixing was common, technological developments provided greater freedom of movement, and spaces (and activities) once deemed masculine and feminine were less rigid and defined. Though financial circumstances continued to limit the range of activities available to some women, tourism companies, civic improvement committees, and municipal councils increasingly acknowledged the growing number of women acting as organizers of, contributors to, and participants in different kinds of outdoor recreation.

The Elite Vacationer

Much like their city counterparts, well-to-do citizens of Dresden, Tillsonburg, and Elora who benefited from substantial disposable incomes, and thus greater opportunities to travel, spent their summers away from town. Though residents travelled throughout the year (Christmas, for example, was a popular time to visit friends and family elsewhere), inclement weather, poor road conditions, and frozen lakes and rivers deterred many from venturing far. Summer, then, was the most popular season for travel. In July 1886, the *Elora Express* remarked that "people are all taking their holidays now. Many a house in the village presents a deserted appearance. In some places the head of the family struggles with fate in the attempt to keep bach. hall; in others the lady of the house is doing vice versa, enjoying the husband's absence and someone else's presence. This is a funny world."[12] In this context "bach. hall," or "bachelor's hall," was a reference to men living alone while a wife was absent.[13] As this article suggests, *both* men and women were taking holidays elsewhere or hosting visitors, and not always doing so together. By the late nineteenth century, newspaper social columns were regularly reporting the comings and goings of residents, regardless of their sex or the duration of the trip. In the 13 September 1888 issue of the *Dresden Times*, for example, it was mentioned that Miss Nellie Wright, Mr. John Jeffs, and Mrs. N. Waffle had just returned from "eastern trips"; Miss Mable Leonard "returned last Saturday from visiting her friends in North Branch, Mich."; and "Miss S.A. Weir, of Port Perry, Ont., and sister of Mr. W.F. Weir, of the Big Axe, is the guest of her cousin, Miss Ida Leaper."[14] Such announcements solidified elite and middle-class residents' positions in the local social hierarchy by publicly proclaiming their privilege to travel and for varying periods of time.

Journeys across the province or to bordering states were the most common destinations. In the summer of 1892, Charles Clarke and family left Elora to visit "Detroit, Duluth and other American cities" in addition to "Decorah, Iowa, to see some relatives."[15] Though the Clarkes had three young children at the time, they employed live-in domestic servants and a nurse who likely accompanied them to oversee childcare responsibilities.[16] Otherwise, travelling with young children was a cumbersome undertaking. Women typically embarked on lengthy trips during singlehood or widowhood, when they had fewer household, familial, financial, and time constraints. The willingness and ability to venture beyond familiar quarters also played a role. The *Tillsonburg Liberal* reported that eighteen-year-old Jessie Hamilton, for instance, spent her "holidays" in July 1910 with "friends" in the villages of Port Royal, Port Rowan, and Rowan Mills along the north shore of Lake Erie.[17] Though these locations were a mere forty or so kilometres southeast of Tillsonburg, for women of lesser means like Hamilton (a farmer's daughter),[18] this relatively short distance encompassed the extent to which they were able to travel.

After 1870, expanded systems of steamship and railway travel, along with the establishment of hotels and restaurants catering to a wider variety of customers, helped facilitate greater interest in short excursions to Ontario's many "wilderness frontiers" in central and northern Ontario, now more affordable, desirable, and accessible to would-be travellers. The story of Muskoka, for example, and its gradual transformation into an outdoor playground for White, urban settlers and tourists is well known.[19] While it is indisputable that Muskoka's distinct cottaging culture was shaped by wealthy urbanites who could afford to go "back to the land" for significant periods of time,[20] there were also affluent rural and small-town Ontarians who vacationed alongside them and contributed to the Euro-Canadian encroachment on the land. Tillsonburg's elite and some middle-class residents enjoyed vacationing in the region so much that a July 1900 issue of the *Observer* called Fairhaven Island on Lake Muskoka a "summer colony" of Tillsonburg citizens. In that issue alone, it was noted that ten local citizens had recently departed for what would become known as "cottage country."[21]

The widespread interest in cottaging and the "great outdoors" is often characterized as a twentieth-century phenomenon but has a much longer and complex history, because "Canadians have been going to summer vacation homes for as long as there has been a country called Canada."[22] By the late nineteenth century, playing along one of the province's many shorelines had become a favoured pastime for men and women of all classes who were drawn to the same cool waters, fresh breezes, and beauteous landscapes that had attracted visitors for centuries; where, why, and for how long they did so, however, depended on social and economic factors. Until 1890, the Tillsons owned a cottage in Port Burwell on the north shore of Lake Erie, located approximately thirty kilometres southwest of Tillsonburg. After famed Methodist evangelists (and Muskoka cottagers) John Edwin Hunter and Hugh Thomas Crossley invited the Tillsons to Fairhaven Island, they fell in love with Muskoka and, in 1894, purchased a parcel of land with an adjacent cottage for $1,400.[23] Though it is unclear why the Port Burwell retreat was abandoned, the establishment of more regular and reliable train service to locales beyond southern Ontario broadened the range of vacation options available.[24] Certainly, relocating to the trendier community of Muskoka better fit the Tillsons' social status. Like Annandale House, the new cottage served as a visual reminder of the family's prestige and affluence. Owning a Muskoka summer home had greater social cachet, which helped the family to make broader social and economic connections beyond Tillsonburg.

The Muskoka district is the territory of the Anishinaabeg, and two sets of treaties—the Robinson-Huron Treaty (1850) and the Williams Treaties (1923)—sought to strip local Indigenous people of their sovereignty so that White settlers could occupy and profit off the land.[25] Efforts to deprive the Anishinaabeg of their territorial rights, along with the establishment of steamship service in 1866, a canal and lock system in 1871, and, most importantly, railway service from Toronto in 1875, provided better access to Muskoka's islands, lakes, and rivers for White Euro-Canadians.[26] By the

1880s, tourism was already well-established in the region.[27] Consequently, more middle- and working-class families from small towns were able to spend considerable time in Muskoka, especially after the first resorts were constructed to accommodate travellers. In 1893, for instance, the *Tillsonburg Observer* mentioned that "the family of Mr. Douglas, cutter in Messrs. Northway & Anderson's tailoring department, returned home Friday, after spending the summer in Muskoka."[28] However, when the *Observer* made its yearly announcement that "the annual summer exodus to the cool wilderness of Muskoka ha[d] begun,"[29] this referred to the town's more affluent residents, because, as historian Peter Stevens notes, "the time and expense of getting there ensured that cottaging during these days remained the preserve of a wealthy, leisured class of people."[30]

The Tillson cottage was in a section of Muskoka nicknamed "Little Pittsburgh," and was part of what locals referred to as the "Beaumaris summer community of Millionaires."[31] In this area, seasonal homes were constructed by a concentrated population of wealthy industrialists from Pittsburgh,

Figure 27. Original Tillson family cottage on Fairhaven Island, Muskoka, c. late 1890s. Pictured are E.D. and Mary Ann Tillson, along with some of their children and grandchildren. Source: ANHS, Photograph Collection.

Pennsylvania, and elsewhere, and the Tillsons were part of a contingent of well-heeled Canadians who purchased property and vacationed among them. The establishment of enclaves such as these was common throughout cottage communities in and around central Ontario, since American vacationers preferred the region's ruggedness over the commercialized pleasure resorts popping up on the East Coast and along the bordering Great Lakes.[32] Muskoka, especially, with its "refreshing waters, beautiful forests, relaxed atmosphere, and fresh, pollution-free air," was the secluded respite that the wealthy desired.[33]

Each summer after the Tillsons purchased the Muskoka cottage, the *Observer* was rife with notices detailing when family members and friends left town for extended holidays at the summer home. The trip involved travelling by private rail car to the port of Gravenhurst and then catching the *R.M.S. Segwun* to Fairhaven Island. The cottage was two storeys high and at the time considered much "grander than most homes in Tillsonburg."[34]

After E.D.'s death in 1902, the original two-storey cottage was dismantled and two separate ones built. Daughter Lillie and her family occupied "Dulce Domum" (Latin for "Sweet Home"), and son E.V. and his family inhabited "Dumbie Dikes" (inspired by the works of Sir Walter Scott). A smaller cottage built earlier, "Rob Roy" (after Scottish hero Robert Roy McGregor), was eventually given to daughter Hattie.[35] The new cottages were not constructed with the red brick available locally but with a special yellow variety produced back in Tillsonburg in the family's brick factory. Family historians note that foodstuffs produced on Annandale Farm in Tillsonburg were regularly shipped by farm labourers to Muskoka while the Tillsons vacationed.

Other prominent families like the Wilsons, Hogarths, and McGregors are also mentioned in the *Observer* as regular visitors to the Muskoka region. The McGregor family was first invited to join the Tillsons at their cottage in 1895. According to Agnes McGregor, E.D. and Rev. McGregor were friends despite the Tillsons being Methodists and the McGregors Presbyterians. Like the Tillsons, most of the cottagers in the Beaumaris community were Methodists. Agnes noted in her autobiography that religious differences aside, "oddly enough, by some sort of spontaneous 'election' my father was always called the chief by the islanders perhaps because of his gift for bringing people of different backgrounds and beliefs together." Initially, the McGregors camped on the Tillsons' property in a large tent, even though E.D. had suggested that Rev. McGregor build his own cottage on a small parcel of the land. Agnes writes that at the time, "this was financially impossible and the kind offer was declined." Instead, for many summers, E.D. leased Rob Roy cottage to the McGregors.[36]

Aside from the one month her father spent at the cottage for his allotted summer vacation, Agnes recalls, Rob Roy was primarily inhabited by her immediate family members, aunts, and grandmother. Along with being a colony for wealthier, influential folks, Muskoka was a colony of women for much of the summer, and especially during the workweek. In an idyllic image of heteronormativity, wives and children eagerly awaited the arrival of "Daddy" via train or steamer on Friday evening.[37] These middle- and upper-class women who employed help at home and did not have the burden of waged labour were afforded greater flexibility when it came to the length and scope of their vacations. Often, domestic servants accompanied their employers to summer homes, or temporary help was secured from the local labour pool.

Having a young family did not keep women away from summer homes, but widows and empty nesters were more likely to be fixtures in cottage country. After the death of her husband in 1903, for instance, Lillie Sinclair spent most summers at Dulce Domum, where she and her female relatives hosted parties for their inner circle. Rarely alone, Lillie was visited by friends from as far away as Calgary, Detroit, and Windsor.[38] Like their hostess, they had the time and money afforded by their social status to undertake lengthy vacations. Even away from home, affluent women maintained high levels of sociability and used their summer homes as they would their primary residences. In some respects, cottage culture was a replica of their lifestyles back home, yet it was also different in the sense that husbands were absent more frequently and the nature-based activities available locally (like swimming and boating) temporarily replaced the club work and fundraisers they typically engaged in.

Figure 28. Marguerite (second from the right) and mother Lillie Sinclair (far right) at cottage "Dulce Domum" in Muskoka, c. late 1910s–early 1920s. Source: ANHS, Photograph Collection.

In the early twentieth-century photographs taken at the Tillson cottages, matriarch Mary Ann, now elderly and using a wheelchair, is shown on the expansive veranda of one of the dwellings (likely Dumbie Dikes), surrounded by her daughters, granddaughters, and a few male relatives. A variety of chairs, including rockers, side tables holding newspapers and a darning basket, and a hammock suggest that a great deal of the family's leisure time was spent in this open-air space facing the water. Though outdoor recreational activities such as hiking and hunting were much enjoyed by cottagers, summertime meant that "the waterfront [...] truly had pride of place," with its "emphasis on fishing, swimming, and boating."[39] Agnes McGregor recalled that during her time spent in Muskoka, she found it to be "a glorious place for sailing and my brother and I soon lost our taste for row boats when we learned how to handle a dinghy."[40]

Grander and more expensive trips taken by citizens to locales outside Canada also received extensive coverage in rural and small-town newspapers. As historian Cecilia Morgan notes in her work on transatlantic tourism, like

Figure 29. Mary Ann Tillson (shown in a wheelchair) at one of the family cottages in Muskoka just prior to her death in 1911. Source: ANHS, Photograph Collection.

their city counterparts, rural and small-town Canadians also began travelling overseas in the later nineteenth century, doing so as individuals, families, or part of large tour groups.[41] Just as the new rail lines criss-crossing the country helped greater numbers of people to move about more freely, new modes of transoceanic travel and the establishment of travel agencies like Thomas Cook helped facilitate tourism on a more global scale. As well, the publication of travel and picture books and the invention of the stereoscope offered enticing glimpses of foreign lands. The Canadian press promoted transcontinental travel and endorsed visits to regions overseas (especially those within the British Empire) for the purposes of maintaining and strengthening "national and imperial memberships."[42] In July 1899, the *Dresden Times* noted that "Squire Chapple and wife returned last Saturday from their extended visit at Paris and other points east. Mrs. Chapple has improved in health."[43] At the time the Chapples undertook their lengthy journey, John (a retired magistrate) was seventy-seven and wife Esther was sixty-seven years old.[44] Based on their ages, it is not surprising that the couple's trip involved seeking out some restorative treatment, on top of the usual cultural enlightenment that elite tourists craved. Throughout Britain and France, a very popular spa culture had developed in the nineteenth century; moneyed travellers like the Chapples often frequented such health resorts for their therapeutic baths and hot springs, thought to cure various maladies.

In June 1889, E.D. and Mary Ann Tillson and daughter Lillie commenced a summer-long trip to Europe, where they intended to visit the Exposition Universelle in Paris.[45] At the time, Lillie was married and the mother of two young daughters, but her family's wealth and extended kinship network granted her the luxury of undertaking such a journey. Likely, husband Lachlin remained in Tillsonburg to tend to his medical practice and daughters Lillian and Marguerite spent the summer in Muskoka with their Tillson cousins. In 1905, Lillie returned to Europe, this time accompanied by twenty-two-year-old Marguerite. According to a newspaper account of the trip, the pair was part of a fifty-eight-member tour group organized by Rev. Dr. W.H. Withrow of Toronto. The tour included "viewing the principal cities of Europe and finest architecture, pictures and antiquities in the world."[46] In Belgium, the Sinclairs attended the Exposition Universelle de Liège, where the famed Tillson Pan-Dried Oats were on display alongside other Canadian goods and foodstuffs.[47]

Just a Train Ride Away: Day-Trippers, Excursionists, and "Staycationers"

Most Canadians could not afford the expense of a summer home or a "grand tour" of Europe, so day trips and excursions were the more realistic alternative, providing middle- and working-class men and women with brief glimpses of beauteous landscapes and rugged wilderness. As Morgan explains, "ideological forces such as romantic ideals of the picturesque and the sublime, antimodern notions of folk culture, and discourses of imperialism and nationalism, combined with either commercial and consumer capitalism or state intervention (or some mixture of both), have played powerful roles in designating and creating certain regions as tourist havens."[48] The eventual extension of a railway and canal system across much of southern Ontario was integral in facilitating the quick and affordable movement of would-be tourists from home to destination and back in less than a day. In the early nineteenth century, outdoor excursions had largely been the privilege of the Upper Canadian elite, but by the turn of the twentieth century, trips to Ontario's many shorelines were being made by visitors from a wider variety of socio-economic backgrounds, prompted by the standardization of vacation days, greater disposable wealth, and a desire to seek out the restorative effects that waterways and green spaces promised.[49]

During this period, living in a larger Canadian city meant that some of the less desirable consequences of industrialization and urbanization such as overpowering stenches, air pollution, and outbreaks of infectious disease were unavoidable during muggy summer days. Money and privilege, however, allowed the wealthy to escape to their country houses and cottages, where slower schedules, cooler waters, and fresher air functioned as antidotes to modern life. Why, then, did women in small towns like Dresden, Tillsonburg, and Elora and their surrounding communities seek out similar reprieves? They may have grappled with the downsides attached to urbanism but on a significantly smaller scale, so when they journeyed about temporarily, was it simply a desire to follow in the fashionable footsteps of city folk? Undoubtedly, yearnings to travel were about needing a change of scenery; nearby beaches and wooded areas held the promise of new surroundings, new people, and novel leisure opportunities. More practically, cool waters and refreshing breezes provided relief from hot kitchens and humid summer weather, but small-town women often did not have to go far for a brief respite. Ann Amelia Day wrote in her diary one sweltering day in July 1878 that while she was sitting outside, friend Mary McCaig stopped by and asked her to go for "a drive," which she happily accepted.[50] As British historian Judith Flanders explains, travelling elsewhere, no matter the destination or distance, was "an end in itself" for Victorians, because the physical act of leaving home was part of a larger social and cultural experience.[51]

In Elora, advertisements for excursions to Hamilton, St. Catharines, and Niagara Falls began appearing soon after regular railway service was established in the early 1870s.[52] Elora itself became a stop on many of the excursions passing through Wellington County, where local passengers joined those already en route to a variety of destinations throughout central and southern Ontario. Companies like the CPR became adamant promoters and sellers of day trips and excursions in the hopes of bolstering sluggish profits.[53] In Elora, the CPR made sure that visually appealing and prominently placed handbills, posters, and newspaper advertisements detailed upcoming journeys. Often, the trips were couched as a must-see opportunity that offered dazzling views of "untouched" landscapes.[54]

Many excursions were organized specifically for fraternal, religious, labour, and charitable organizations.[55] As more branches of these groups were established in Dresden, Tillsonburg, and Elora, their members too became part of the excursion crowd. Usually, excursions were commissioned for registered members only, but sometimes they joined other branches to promote bonding and celebrate loyalty and hard work. The expenses incurred were covered by the sponsoring organization or were offered at a reduced rate for participants, thus allowing greater numbers of working-class men, women, and families to experience the day-tripping phenomenon.

Though Elora itself developed into a sort of tourist hotspot, locals thoroughly enjoyed leaving town to go on excursions (perhaps to avoid the tourists). In 1905, the *Express* noted that a day-long excursion to Niagara Falls was being organized by the Durham Methodist church; the special train commissioned for the trip would be stopping at towns along the way, including Elora, to pick up interested passengers. The advertisement declared that one should "not miss the opportunity of seeing this Great Natural Wonder of the World, now being harnessed by human ingenuity to transfer its illimitable power through electrical energy to distant towns and cities." For Elorans, this trip cost adults $1.75 and children ninety cents.[56] In June 1910, 230 male and female Elora excursionists (approximately 20 percent of the town's population at the time) were dropped off in the small town of Bala in central Ontario and then taken by boat to the lakeside community of Port Carling, where they enjoyed the lush backdrop of Muskoka. The *Express* declared that for all who experienced it, this "ideal water trip" would leave "lasting and most pleasant memories of beautiful natural scenery."[57]

Sometimes the amenities en route were rather lavish, such as the champagne provided during an 1880 excursion that took Elora residents to the Forks of the Credit in southern Ontario.[58] Though regularly advertised as "cheap," excursions often catered to middle- and upper-class passengers. At the turn of the century, when the annual wage of a domestic servant or unskilled labourer was usually less than $400, the purchase of excursion tickets for an entire family took a considerable chunk out of a working-class family's budget.[59]

Newspaper accounts describe how women from Dresden enjoyed travelling by steamer to Detroit and to lakeside retreats such as Walpole Island, located on Lake St. Clair near the Michigan-Ontario border. The steamers picked up passengers at several different docks along the Sydenham River and from Dresden's Green Mountain Hotel. In a July 1888 account of one journey to Walpole, the unidentified author writes that after the steamer left Dresden, on the water "soft winds blew playfully through men's whiskers, and snatched maidens' bonnets and hats and deposited them safely beyond the reach of their owners. Sweet sounds of music proceeded from the hurricane deck."[60] After stopping in the town of Wallaceburg at lunchtime, the party reached Walpole Island in the mid-afternoon and the boat's 935 passengers descended to the grounds. "Soon," the author writes, "every boy and girl had a bow and arrow, or a basket purchased as a souvenir."[61]

The referenced craftwork was likely purchased from the people of Walpole Island First Nation who still occupy the land today and were well-known basket- and matmakers. Walpole (Bkejwanong) is unceded territory and home of the Ojibwe, Potawatomi, and Odawa people who formed the historic Council of Three Fires. Apart from fleeting references to their presence, available sources provide little information about the extent to which the people of Walpole and White excursionists interacted in this contact zone before the twentieth century. However, advertisements for excursions urged Dresden's citizens to "Come or go and have a day with the children of the schools and the 'children of the forest.' Bathing, boat-riding and swinging will be the order of the day."[62] Not only is this description derogatory, it also locks the Walpole Island First Nation in the past as primitive and anti-modern. Despite being acknowledged in this advertisement, it

Figure 30. Dresden Sunday school excursion to Walpole Island, c. 1910. Source: DA, Keith Wells Collection.

is unclear how much of a role Walpole Island First Nation played in the island's early development as a tourist site, and how they were affected by the seasonal influxes of steamer passengers. Whether they were welcome or not, White tourists used the area for its wetlands and its fishing and hunting opportunities.[63]

By the early twentieth century, however, the annual "Walpole Island Indian Fair" or "Great Indian Fair" was drawing thousands of Canadian and American visitors to the region, who desired to see the exhibitions, sports, demonstrations, and musical shows that were organized, hosted, and sponsored by Walpole Island First Nation. Like the American Wild West Show, in the fair's early years the entertainment offered played up the "Indian" stereotypes tourists craved, including sham battles, war dances, and pony races, with the purpose of turning a profit for the community.[64] As historian Daniel Francis explains, the inclusion of Indigenous people in such shows and the

specific events being re-enacted made the spectacles more authentic and "appealed to a nostalgia for the supposed 'good old days.'"[65] Unlike the Wild West Show, however, as hosts, the Walpole Island First Nation controlled the representations on display. Their reasons for participating varied, but likely for some it was a celebration of their culture, while for others it served as an educational opportunity.

The tourism industry that developed in Ontario in the latter part of the nineteenth century, especially for sites like Walpole Island and Niagara Falls, provided "economic opportunities" to local Indigenous people who "were being squeezed out of industry, commerce, and agriculture." Their presence at these sites, according to Morgan, also "offered a chance for them to represent their history."[66] Based on surviving photographs and eventually their hosting of the "Great Indian Fair," the people of Walpole Island First Nation were actively engaged in the local leisure industry, performing the "Indianness" that visitors desired.[67] Historian Andrew Watson describes a similar practice taking place in Muskoka, where Indigenous women "dressed themselves and their daughters in regalia and travelled to central locations, such as Port Carling, where their crafts were guaranteed to sell."[68] The commodification of Indigenous culture, especially the purchase of craftwork, allowed White women the opportunity to materially commemorate their trips to tourist sites like Walpole. While historians have noted that some Victorians were clear about their desires to see "authentic Indians" while travelling,[69] the degree to which Dresden residents also wished to "gaze" at local Indigenous people while excursioning is unknown. When such cultural encounters did happen at tourist sites, historian Patricia Jasen notes, they were usually "brief and mainly voyeuristic."[70]

According to one newspaper advertisement, a round-trip excursion from Dresden to Walpole Island cost around sixty cents for adults and twenty-five cents for children.[71] Ticket prices for excursions were often on par with or cheaper than the commercial entertainments and religious fundraisers offered in towns. The services on board varied from trip to trip, but a ticket generally covered all the day's transportation and sometimes a free lunch and musical entertainment. On one excursion from Dresden, the events on board became so "boisterous" that some passengers fell overboard.[72] It is not surprising, then, considering the sheer size of these vessels and the fact that many boasted they could hold up to 1,000 passengers "with ease and safety,"[73] that excursions sometimes turned deadly. One notably tragic incident was the sinking of the steamer *Victoria* on 24 May 1881 in London, Ontario. When the overloaded boat capsized in the Thames River, 182 excursionists (mostly women) perished, representing the single largest loss of life in that city's history.[74]

A popular passenger and freight steamer, the *Byron Trerice*, was commissioned by lumberman Alexander Trerice while mayor of Dresden in 1882 and named after his son. For its maiden voyage to Detroit, a grand unveiling was planned, and "the boat was gaily decked with British and American colours, while, rolled up in a ball shape was a flag bearing the concealed name of the new boat." Trerice's wife, Elizabeth, and Miss E. Watson were invited to participate in the ceremony and given the honour of christening the new vessel with the "customary bottle of wine," while the many spectators who had gathered cheered heartily. It was noted that the boat would be "supplied with all modern improvements, ample staterooms, and the cabins finished in exquisite style." At the time, Captain Asa Ribble oversaw a crew of sixteen.[75] Along with trips to Detroit, the *Byron Trerice* also took passengers to Walpole Island, where they disembarked for a day of fun at Highbanks Dock. The *Byron Trerice* was marred by misfortune, however, enduring several accidents and then an untimely fire that led to its demise and the deaths of three crewmembers in 1893.

The 'City of Chatham' and the 'Byron Trerice' at Highbanks dock, on Walpole Island.

Figure 31. Passenger steamers *City of Chatham* (left) and the *Byron Trerice* (right) at Highbanks Dock, Walpole Island, c. 1880s–1890s. Source: DA, Photograph Collection.

Excursions from Dresden were also offered on rail lines. In 1888, one could travel from Dresden to Toronto to attend the "Fair" for the sum of $4.20.[76] In this context, the fair was the Canadian National Exhibition (CNE), which Keith Walden notes was a popular destination for residents of Ontario's outlying areas who could afford the expense.[77] In a letter to her daughter Muriel in September 1913, Elora's Georgina Clark mentions that husband Frank took sons Keith and George and daughter Jean to Niagara and the Exhibition in Toronto, where "they had a high time" and stayed four nights.[78] At all times of the year, regular journeys to neighbouring towns and cities were commonplace. For Elorans, and others living in rural Wellington County, trips to Guelph occurred regularly and for a variety of reasons. In her diary, Ann Amelia Day mentions travelling from Eramosa Township to nearby Guelph (a few kilometres away) in 1878 to attend an "Exhibition" and in 1879 to purchase her wedding clothes.[79] In November 1913, Georgina Clark noted in a letter to daughter Muriel that she was planning to travel to Guelph the next morning, as the "Presbyterial" was meeting.[80] For Tillsonburg residents, several larger urban centres were just a short train or stagecoach ride away. According to Mary Ann Tillson's great-granddaughter Margaret Draper Jansen, Mary Ann "made up her mind very quickly" to "take the train to Brantford or Woodstock or Ingersoll." On the way to the station, she would pick up granddaughter Lillian Sinclair and then proceed to stop every man they met and ask him for the sum of his pocket money. It seems that the decision to leave was made so quickly that Mary Ann consistently forgot to bring money along or needed to supplement what was in her possession at the time. A testament to the Tillsons' reputation in town (and an example of Mary Ann exercising her class privilege), the workers would agree to loan her their money. Jansen says, "She would count it carefully—tell the man to go to The Tillson Counting House and say that Mrs. Tillson had borrowed it and get his money back." Jansen remembers that "buying material for clothes, having lunch at the hotel, looking at hats, new styles, etc." were the order of the day.[81]

In the 1890s, the E&H Railway offered Dresden residents "special weekly excursions" to Detroit every Wednesday and Saturday at 8:15 a.m. at a cost of one dollar.[82] After a more efficient rail system was established through the town, the novelty of boat travel largely fell out of style because of the convenience, affordability, and excitement of riding the train.[83] When the E&H Railway started offering four daily runs to the lakeside community of Rondeau, located approximately fifty kilometres southeast of Dresden, women and their families came to favour these "'lake district' holidays" that were often mentioned as ideal vacation spots by the local press. Like Walpole

Island, Rondeau's amenities, including its sandy beaches and refreshing waters, made it a popular spot for excursionists and day-trippers. According to Jeffrey Carter and Marie Carter, "in the time it took to travel to Walpole Island for a picnic, the train could take you to Rondeau, in little more than an hour, for a full day of swimming, picnicking, sports and dancing."[84]

Other choice "lake district" spots, such as Port Burwell and Port Stanley along Lake Erie, were popular destinations for Tillsonburg residents seeking a few hours of rest, relaxation, and lakeside scenery. Photographs of women gazing across the shoreline and mixed-sex groups in canoes confirm the appeal of visiting Erie's cool waters. Getting to beaches, however, posed an issue prior to the establishment of daily railway service, as residents were forced to rely on poor roads and bumpy, time-consuming stagecoach and carriage rides. By the mid-1870s, though, more reliable (and regular) train services to destinations further away allowed greater numbers of leisure seekers to leave town for waterfront picnics and fishing excursions. During this period, references to day trips and excursions increased substantially in the *Observer* and other small-town newspapers. Depending on the destination and activities being offered, a single excursion from Tillsonburg to one of the port towns on Lake Erie could include upward of 500 passengers, not including those already on board from other towns.[85] This number constitutes a substantial proportion of residents leaving town for the day, especially considering the population of Tillsonburg was just over 2,000 around the turn of the century.

Women also sought recreation spots in town, choosing to make use of Big Otter Creek and various mill ponds for their picnics and water sports. In 1891, the Tillsonburg Boating Club was established on the banks of Lake Joseph, where young, affluent men could pay a one-dollar annual fee to hang out in a specially designed boathouse, outfitted with amenities such as a reading room. One of the perks of joining the Boating Club was being able to take one's sweetheart out for a canoe ride.[86] Bert Newman recalled that "all the young bloods" in Tillsonburg had canoes at their disposal. Newman himself did not own one, but he and his friends often borrowed them. When young women were invited along, they usually brought a picnic lunch or

Figure 32. Canoeing near Port Burwell, c. 1890s. Source: ANHS, Pollard Photo, Photograph Collection.

Figure 33. Woman gazing over the Lake Erie shoreline, later nineteenth century. Source: ANHS, Pollard Photo, Photograph Collection.

Figure 34. Canoeists in Tillsonburg, c. 1890s. Based on the presence of British and American flags, this picture was taken around Independence Day and Dominion Day in the first week of July. Source: ANHS, Pollard Photo, Photograph Collection.

supper to be enjoyed during a break in the ride. Newman says, "On a nice, soft, balmy evening in the month of June under the silvery moon you could take your sweetie out for a canoe ride. What is more romantic than that?"[87] In her diary, Minnie Smith of Norwich mentions having the "Kellett girls" over for tea and then going boating as a group afterward. Smith also went for boat rides with Elmer Lossing, who may have been a suitor, judging from recurring references to him and his family in her diary.[88]

In the early 1880s, special "moonlight" train excursions began being offered to Tillsonburg citizens. Historian Dale Barbour recounts a similar practice at Winnipeg Beach, Manitoba, where these unique jaunts, or "moonlight specials,"[89] were commissioned to accommodate working men's and women's schedules. The efforts of rail and steam companies to gain the business of the working class reveals the potential market they saw in them, as well as working-class desires to pursue the same activities that more privileged citizens were participating in. Typically, the specials left town on weekdays around suppertime, destined for the nearby lakeshore, and returned near midnight. Some provided musical entertainment upon arrival,[90] while others simply dropped the excursionists off to entertain themselves. Compared to excursions that ran on weekends and catered more to middle-class families, moonlight specials were "conceptualized as a heterosocial affair,"[91] where social and sexual mores among single men and women were often contested. On one moonlight excursion carrying Tillsonburg passengers in July 1880, an altercation erupted between a drunk man and a "respectable lady" from Brantford. It was reported that the man, who "had soaked his brains in bad whiskey" for much of the day, "insulted and slightly injured" the woman on the ride home.[92] Some religious officials and reformers opposed moonlight specials because the darker and more inconspicuous setting might prompt passengers to engage in violent, rough, or sexual behaviour. Such incidents, however, appear to have been rare on excursion trains from Tillsonburg. Aside from the assault on the "respectable lady," the *Observer* boasted that "there was not the slightest necessity for the general charge of rowdyism made in the telegraphic correspondence of the city dailies."[93]

"O, lovely Elora!": Marketing the Small Town

In the latter half of the nineteenth century, alongside the growing popularity of vacation destinations like the Niagara region and Muskoka, more "off the beaten track" locales like Elora also became tourist destinations because of their ruggedness and their proximity to larger industrial centres in southern Ontario. Elora's location at the junction of the Grand and Irvine Rivers, its imposing gorge, and mythologized Indigenous landmarks drew local and visiting pleasure-seekers alike. Thanks in part to aggressive beautification and marketing campaigns by civic leaders hoping to profit from the burgeoning vacation industry, the town annually welcomed hundreds of tourists who dabbled in various leisure activities on the banks of the river system. In this way, Elora became a contact zone of sorts. Here, both residents and visitors enjoyed the various leisure activities that developed out of Elora's natural surroundings, though sometimes conflict erupted between the two groups, especially when disrespectful behaviours or damage to property occurred.

The frequency with which Elora welcomed visitors is evident in the nineteenth-century poems that paid homage to the town. Most were composed by amateurs and often published anonymously in newspapers to tempt prospective visitors.[94] In 1880, for instance, the poem of one anonymous "lady who [was] charmed" by Elora was submitted to the *Lightning Express* and published.[95] Even the professionals were lured by Elora's beauty. Celebrated Canadian poet Alexander McLachlan published a piece titled "ELORA" in his 1874 volume, *Poems and Songs*. Characterized as the "Burns of Canada,"[96] McLachlan remarked that of the many sights he had seen nationwide, none could compare: "O, lovely Elora! thou-rt queen of them all."[97] If ever he was to encounter a great life misfortune, McLachlan proclaimed, he would "commune with Nature till death set me free, And rest then for ever, Elora, in thee."[98] In 1879, this poem was reprinted in the *Tillsonburg Observer* after several of its citizens visited Elora during a Great Western Railway (GWR) picnic outing.[99]

Hoping to profit from day-trippers' and excursionists' desires for a temporary escape (and buoy the town's fledgling economy), local promoters began marketing Elora in the early 1870s as *the* tourist destination in southern Ontario. At the time, however, the local landscape was in such poor shape that it required extensive remodelling to meet visitors' expectations. The first European settlers had recognized the region's water-power potential, but by the late 1860s Elora's coveted waterways had become a "dumping ground" and the town emitted a rather foul odour. So much garbage, sewage, and decomposing livestock had accumulated in the rivers that the refuse caught fire during a dry spell in the summer of 1868. The overfished waters kept anglers and naturalists away, and the once lush and abundant vegetation on the riverbanks dried up. The first excursion train to the town arrived via the GWR in 1873, but visitors were disgusted and disappointed with the conditions and amenities they found. For Elora to continue being included on the excursion circuit, an organized clean-up effort was mandated by railway officials. Three years later, the Elora Rivers' Improvement Committee

(ERIC) was formed to spearhead a reconstruction of the town's "natural" beauty. The committee oversaw the building of steps and a footbridge around the gorge, wooden benches for resting, and a fountain complete with an iron drinking cup; vegetation was also restored, and the rivers restocked with game fish. A sausage-on-a-bun vendor even established business to feed hungry pleasure-seekers.[100] Elora photographers Thomas Connon and John R. Connon, renowned for their patenting of new photographic technologies, set up a portable darkroom on a rocky cliff near the gorge so they could take scenic snapshots as well as capture Elora's visitors in various states of play to sell as mementoes.

Figure 35. Professor David Ritchie's pleasure boat tour on the Grand River, Elora, c. 1900. Source: WCMA, A2008.122, ph 29601.

Elora newspapers frequently reported on the progress of the ERIC, as well as the increasing numbers of pleasure-seekers arriving daily throughout the summer months. In 1879, the *Lightning Express* provided day-trippers with a list of must-see attractions in town. In addition to seeing the gorge, visitors were urged to visit local sites steeped in White settler lore, such as the Indian Bridge, Wampum Cave, and Lover's Leap.[101] By the end of the 1870s, the *Lightning Express* was reporting that in just a few years, Elora had been visited by men and women "of travelled experience" from as far away as New York City, Rochester, Detroit, Montreal, Toronto, Hamilton, and scores of other places.[102]

While small-town men and women sought brief escapes from their daily routines by travelling to larger urban centres and resort areas, many city dwellers chose to spend their summers in less populated locales. This movement of people from cities to the countryside and vice versa was, by and large, seasonal in nature.[103] Some went to small towns and rural areas to aid friends and family who owned farms, while for others the visit was purely recreational.[104] In the same way that Torontonians and Hamiltonians escaped to the resorts and cottages dotting the shores of the Great Lakes and Georgian Bay, retreating to a farm or more secluded town promised fresh air, cool breezes, and open spaces. Though newly created green spaces in cities were meant to provide a safe and reputable space for play,[105] sites like Elora drew large crowds because the supposed "goodness" and simplicity inherent in rural life was such a popular cultural and literary motif.[106] Disenchanted with the trials and tribulations of their modern lifestyles, city tourists travelling out to the country were driven by a nostalgic thirst for authenticity and the "sublime,"[107] traits which Elora's boosters claimed the famous gorge offered. These characterizations almost exoticized small towns by presenting them as counterpoints to industrialization and urbanization. This is ironic, however, considering how small towns at the time were selectively replicating urban behaviours in their quest to appear attractive, modern, and progressive.

As more Canadians travelled, desires to document their experiences through photography also grew. By the 1850s and 1860s, the daguerreotype of the early nineteenth century had been replaced by the collodion process that imprinted a photographic negative onto a glass plate, allowing for duplication of the image. The new process required less skill and less financial investment in equipment.[108] The real revolution in photographic technology occurred in the 1870s and 1880s, with the advent of the gelatin dry plate process, which produced an image much faster than the collodion.[109] These templates offered greater durability and portability. The dry plate process also prompted the invention of the first "hand-held" camera that could be taken out of the photographer's studio and used in a more casual manner.[110] A parallel development of this evolution was the emergence of stereo photography in the 1860s and 1870s, which involved the production of an enlarged and wider view of a landscape or attraction. Such alterations to photographic technology in the later decades of the nineteenth century resulted in a surge of amateur and professional photographers setting up business across Canada and capturing the leisure practices of Canadians.

Figure 36. Group picnicking in Elora, 30 July 1885. Source UGASC, Connon Collection, XR1 MS A114059_B1F1.

Renowned for their landscape portraits, the father-son duo of Thomas Connon and John R. Connon of Elora became one of the best-known professional photography teams in the province for capturing hundreds of photographs of men, women, and children playing in and around local waterways. Having a photograph taken was almost requisite for picnic parties or day-trippers who visited the town.[111] In 1878, for instance, the *Lightning Express* mentioned that amid their picnic supper and games, a group of twenty young men and women sat for a photograph on some fallen rocks in the bed of the Irvine River. The article noted that the photograph would make a handsome addition to the Connons' growing series of stereoscopes.[112] Though photographs captured a brief and curated moment from an excursion, the growing desire to document a trip (no matter the destination) was an important part of the travel experience for Canadians. Vacation photographs became a fixture in well-to-do homes in the late nineteenth century, a signal to visitors that their occupants had joined the sophisticated tourist crowd.

Compared to sites like Niagara Falls and Muskoka, Elora could not offer the same amenities that the *haute bourgeoisie* expected or were used to. But at the same time, Elora's simplicity was what contributed to its reputation for being a charming and accessible space. Consequently, it became a destination for various religious auxiliaries, such as one youth group from nearby Berlin (present-day Kitchener), whose day trip to the town was captured in a lengthy poem titled "Our Picnic at Elora." The author, twenty-three-year-old Mary Woods, writes that early in the morning, the group of fifteen young men and women set out in wagons and on the way met a similar convoy of pleasure-seekers, so a playful race to the town ensued. After Woods and her group reached Elora, they unloaded their wagons and, not wasting any time, eagerly descended on a rocky pathway that would lead them to their first view of the Elora Gorge, a sight that provoked "exclamations of delight." Woods and her friends then dispersed into smaller groups and engaged in more gendered activities, the men enjoying some hiking and climbing while the women admired the scenery and picked flowers. At noon they reconvened for lunch, enjoying sandwiches, eggs, pickles, ham, cakes, pies, and lemonade from their picnic baskets. After quickly washing their dishes and packing the baskets away, they went off as a group in search of the waterfalls and rock formations, each taking a rock chip as a souvenir. Woods remarked that it would take much space to describe "each place [their] merry footsteps fell" that day, but they made sure to have a group photo taken on a "rocky nook" in the afternoon. At suppertime, they once again gathered at the picnic area to polish off their provisions before leaving for home. When some of the young women began to drift off to sleep, Woods playfully implies that this became an opportunity to engage in some light flirting. She writes, "Here the boy's kindness was again plainly seen. / As they asked us our heads on their shoulders to lean. / And tho' it was hardly the thing we knew, / We were awfully tired, what else could we do?" Woods concludes by declaring that "Since then we've met often and many have said 'More fun in one day we could not have had.'"[113] The poem was never published (and likely never intended to be), but within its cheerful stanzas it is clear that the author and her group had a lively time experiencing all that Elora offered to day-trippers.

Comparable praise from other groups brought recognition and tourist dollars to the town. Certainly, some local men and women welcomed the tourist industry because it provided employment opportunities in the service sector; others, however, loathed the leisure seekers invading their town. Conversely, some tourists complained of the treatment they received from locals; damage to personal property was one such concern.[114] In 1886, a troubled day-tripper wrote to the editor of the *Express* asking for better surveillance after reports surfaced of local boys stealing picnic baskets, vandalizing conveniences, and smashing stoves meant for day-trippers' use.[115] In 1892, it was reported that some lacrosse sticks and a pair of kid gloves were stolen from a visitor's wagon.[116] Mary Woods and her group also experienced an irksome run-in with the locals: while packing up to leave, some Elora boys who were watching them began chanting "E-L-O-R-A," followed by loud cheers as the wagons left town. Woods and her friends retorted back with "RATS, RATS, RATS!"[117] Local officials, realizing that potential visitors might be dissuaded by reports of rude receptions, eventually enacted a law that required "young rowdies" to pay a hefty fine if found guilty of harassment and/or theft.[118] When similar tensions erupted between guests and hosts at other destinations such as Niagara Falls, ethnicity and class divisions figured prominently in those disputes.[119] Such divisive forces do not have appear to have caused conflict in Elora; rather, locals wished to reinforce their status as permanent citizens of the town and assert their authority as "owners" of its lands and waters.

Though the restoration of the local landscape was responsible for creating a lucrative tourist industry in town, it also prompted greater numbers of native-born Elorans (both male and female) to make use of local waterways and rock formations for their own leisure activities, celebrations, and family get-togethers. In addition to photographs of visiting picnickers, dozens of images of local female pleasure-seekers were captured by photographers, helping us to better understand and map how, where, and why women became avid outdoor pleasure-seekers in the town. These photographs show how the female subjects' composition, actions, and demeanour undergo noticeable transformations between the late nineteenth and early twentieth centuries. Though the images generally indicate that a meaningful amount of leisure time was spent outdoors, they also communicate some of the shifts that were occurring in terms of the use of space, gender relations, and leisure habits. Connon photographs from the 1860s and 1870s, for instance, are characterized by the sitters' stiff and sedate poses in front of backdrops in a photography studio. By the 1880s and 1890s, the photographer's studio had moved outdoors; many Connon prints from this later period consist of large groups of men, women, and children perched on Elora's rocky crags.

Most importantly, after the turn of the century, more women became the focus of the photographs, often shown dabbling in the rivers or walking along their banks. They also increasingly began appearing in more candid shots and were photographed alone. By the 1910s, some were shown engaging in more traditionally masculine pursuits like public swimming and fishing. As American historian Glenda Riley explains in her study of Western conservationism, despite perceptions that they belonged in "safe" domestic spaces and not the "dangerous" outdoors, women played an active role in restoring and feminizing nature. They did so, Riley contends, by "arguing that their domestic domain included any place their husbands and children dared to go. In these women's eyes, their roles as wives and mothers were just as valid outdoors as they were indoors."[120] The power of maternalism may explain why Elora's waterways also became more of a mixed-sex territory. In this context, women's innate role as caregiver and protector also applied to nature, permitting an evolution in gendered leisure practices and hetero- and homosocial relations to occur. As photographs from Elora suggest, distinctions between areas and actions once constructed as "masculine" or "feminine" were less

Figure 37. Six women on the banks of the Elora Gorge, later nineteenth century. Source: UGASC, Connon Collection, XR1 MS A114_B1F4.

stark than they had been; instead, both men and women experienced nature and stewarded the land for their own purposes.

In addition to indulging in the customary picnic and viewing the Elora Gorge, locals and visitors also used the waterways to enjoy various water sports like canoeing and swimming. Prior to the manufacture of personal flotation devices, learning to swim was an important safety precaution for pleasure-seekers, whether they were swimming informally or navigating

Figure 38. Three people in Elora Gorge with Irvine Bridge in the background, c. 1910. Source: WCMA, A1978.223, ph 6299.

watercraft. At the turn of the century, reports of drownings were common, as most men and women did not receive formal instruction and education about swimmer safety. Day-trippers and tourists were especially susceptible, but locals also succumbed to the dangers of the waterways at their doorsteps. In May 1886, while playing near the Irvine River, three young Elora girls were swept away when they attempted to cross the water using wooden planks. The *Elora Express* reported that the girls were able to crawl out of the river, but

Figure 39. Woman fishing in Elora Gorge, c. 1909. Source: WCMA, A2006.112, ph 20835.

Figure 40. Tillsonburg women swimming in Lake Erie at Port Dover, 1913. Source: ANHS, Photograph Collection.

the incident left them chilled and one of the girls had to be carried home.[121] Before the widespread construction of community swimming pools in the early twentieth century, lakes, rivers, and ponds served swimmers' needs. In cities, pools could be found at many of the newly established associations for young working-class people, such as the Young Men's Christian Association (YMCA) and Young Women's Christian Association (YWCA), where activities like swimming were offered as a distraction from seedier forms of urban leisure. In Elora, the possibility of swimming in local waters was contingent on the clean-up efforts of the ERIC. Around the same time, other waterside communities initiated restoration efforts so that their natural spaces could be used safely; in Hamilton, for instance, the Lake Ontario shoreline was cleaned up and vegetation restored, enabling better access for locals and visiting pleasure-seekers alike.[122]

Beaches and swimming holes came to represent a contested space between male and female swimmers. Though some men bathed and swam in the nude, women were expected to be more modestly clothed in heavy, cumbersome bathing costumes. An 1871 Elora bylaw concerning "Public Morals" deemed any sort of "indecent" washing or bathing in public waters a criminal offence that carried upwards of a fifty-dollar fine.[123] Stephen Thorning writes, however, that male workers at a local carpet factory still enjoyed stripping down and taking a dip during their lunch break. Some citizens were outraged by this behaviour while others simply chose not to look.[124] As beaches and embankments were constructed (or re-constructed) into heterosocial spaces, all swimmers were expected to remain fully clothed to protect feminine modesty.[125] Despite bylaws and strict codes regarding appropriate bathing attire, some women disobeyed orders. In Elora in 1886 a petticoat, bustle, and a pair of lady's gloves were found on the banks of the Irvine River; evidently a woman had been enjoying a private swim and was forced to make a quick exit before being seen by an approaching party.[126] Though feminine propriety and modesty remained of utmost importance, women were encouraged to frolic outdoors for their constitutions, for the maintenance of healthy hair and skin,[127] and for the personal pleasure that nature-based activities such as swimming, "rambling," and canoeing provided.

Conclusion

The history of women's forays into nature tourism and outdoor leisure has only recently received attention from Canadian social, feminist, and environmental historians, yet this sort of leisure played an important role for women living in turn-of-the-century rural and small-town Ontario. The idea that being ladylike was incompatible with outdoor recreation has resulted in skewed depictions of how much women actively engaged in such leisure. Though the anxieties attached to city life account for why so many privileged urbanites flocked to lakeside resorts and tourist hotspots, the motives of rural and small-town Ontarians, while occasionally converging with those of city folk, were tied more to the desire to see new landscapes, coupled with a growing recognition of the physical and emotional benefits of water, sunshine, and fresh air. Along with indulging in new types of public, commercial, and domestic entertainments, women's enthusiasm for spending time outdoors was also part of a broader and more modern leisure culture that was increasingly being promoted to and embraced by them. Out of doors, women exercised independence by traipsing through the woods, travelling abroad, or taking the "moonlight special" to a beach town. In nature, spaces for socialization became broader and less defined by constructs about gender and propriety.

Though time, money, and work obligations acted as deterrents to engaging in leisure activities away from and outside of the home, the sheer variety of outdoor recreational options available by the First World War demonstrates that these pleasures were no longer the exclusive privilege of the upper class as they had been half a century earlier. Affluence may have allowed elite women to spend considerable time touring Europe or vacationing at a summer home, but for most others, outdoor recreation could be readily found in day trips to local beaches or excursions on steamers or trains. When examining the leisure habits of women from Dresden, Tillsonburg, and Elora, we see that by and large, many similarities existed in their use of outdoor spaces. The implementation of regular and reliable transportation services through these towns, a wider variety of local options for those who could not travel away from home, and desires to explore the world beyond their community's boundaries motivated more women to move about independently and with more freedom than ever before. Though Elora certainly stands out because of the tourist industry that developed there, in the late nineteenth century the landscapes of Dresden and Tillsonburg and nearby areas also benefited from the greater attention paid to beautifying the local environment.

The various ways that rural and small-town women incorporated nature and landscapes (both natural and human-made) into their outdoor leisure activities also evolved in the later years of the nineteenth century. Just as public buildings were being refitted with women's interests in mind, local green spaces, parks, and waterways underwent restorations that created more options for leisure activities outside of the home and the entertainment hall. However, women's increasing visibility in public spaces also provoked new worries as the gap between activities once regarded as "masculine" and "feminine" narrowed, and more spaces were refitted for activities that allowed heterosocial mixing. As the following chapter will reveal, sometimes venturing out of doors could have grave consequences for a woman's reputation, especially if she was seen indulging in activities considered improper or unlawful.

SEVEN

Bad Girls in the Country? When Leisure Slipped from Reputable to Disreputable

C AREFULLY TUCKED AWAY in one of the storage rooms at Annandale National Historic Site, the Tillson family scrapbook is one of the most valued pieces in the museum's collection of local keepsakes. Between its black leather covers are pasted various mementoes related to the family's past, especially the Tillsons' role in establishing the town's first permanent settlement. The settler folklore that permeates the book, such as memories of Grandma Tillson making sausage in her mid-nineteenth-century kitchen, contributes to the source's significance, according to family members and staff at Annandale National Historic Site. One handwritten page, however, hints that the Tillsons may not have been as respectable as local mythology suggests. An undated letter, written by "A friend," admonishes the addressee, "Mrs. Tilsen," for her alleged "evile" leisure habits. The anonymous author writes:

> I hope you will eccsuse me riting too you with led pensil as I never spell verry well when I use pen and inck. This is a delli-kite matter I want too speek too you about but I feal it is my dewty. Don't you thinck you are to good a wuman too waist so mutch time at the moovys and plaing cards. Them others yeu mock around with are not worth anythink anyway but

it is difernt with yew. We woud luv to hav yeu work with us in the salvacion army. There is so much too bee done.

Anuther thing aren't yeu afrade of lusing your husbinds trust and affection by making him so lonly knites.

I hav herd that yew play cards for money but I knew yeu wasent that far sunk in evile. Befor it is to late I emploor yeu too give it all up and forsaik yeur disrepertabel assoshiates. Let them go to perdition whear they are heded ass they aint wurth savin. I aint sining my naim too this ass am just a common woman and yeu aint never hurd of me anyway but even if I aint hed know edicashun Im just as good as that bunsh yeur so cagy with.[1]

It is unclear how the writer acquired such intimate knowledge of Mrs. Tillson's activities, but the claims likely originated in town gossip circles. Though it is not stated which Mrs. Tillson the letter was meant for or who "A friend" was,[2] this working-class critique of elite culture, grounded in strong feelings about piety and femininity, reveals that any woman, regardless of her social standing, was subject to observation and scrutiny, even in small communities. The fact that the letter was written from the perspective of a self-professed uneducated and "common" woman alerts us to the complicated intersections of gender, class, morality, and religion, which greatly influenced how leisure and social habits were perceived. Though the constraints placed on public behaviour and recreation around the turn of the century were generally based on "classed notions of social order and fueled by the ideologies of dominant groups,"[3] when a leisure activity was deemed disreputable, the offenders did not always represent the "standard" groups of deviants—men, immigrants, and the working class—so often cited by nineteenth-century contemporaries and historians thereafter. The letter to Mrs. Tillson suggests that religious and class-based notions of appropriateness were integral in constructing definitions of reputable and disreputable. It also reverses the conventional expectation of the elite criticizing the immorality of the lower orders and prompts a broader discussion about the importance of non-legal modes of authority in small towns.

This chapter explores women's leisure practices that slipped from reputable to disreputable, from acceptable to deviant, in Dresden, Tillsonburg, and Elora, identifying the more prominent unsanctioned activities that women and girls engaged in and the conversations that erupted over how "bad" some of these amusements were. The diverse modes of regulation that sought to curtail such behaviour show that the later nineteenth- and early twentieth-century phenomenon known as the "girl problem" was also experienced (to an extent) in the countryside, but unlike the urban "bad girls" examined by some Canadian and American historians,[4] the females in Dresden, Tillsonburg, and Elora whose "acting out" appears in diverse historical records represented a broader (and much more varied) cross-section of the population. Recreational activities provided one opportunity for women to circumvent prescribed gender norms in these communities, and mannerisms that straddled the line between reputable and disreputable often occurred in these contexts.

In small towns and rural areas, behavioural codes of order were enforced by several governing bodies. In the earlier part of the nineteenth century, churches once had the authority to excommunicate parishioners for participating in unseemly leisure activities.[5] While clergymen continued to exercise some influence through sermons and surveillance, by the latter part of the century, family, neighbours, town or municipal bylaws, and the criminal justice system had arguably become more powerful arbitrators. In her formative study on the history of sexual deviancy in Ontario, historian Karen Dubinsky recognizes families, community members, and the legal system as the three most important enforcers of moral behaviours in rural areas and small towns.[6] This chapter builds on the work of Dubinsky and others by assessing how modes of surveillance functioned in Dresden, Tillsonburg, and Elora. In addition to the control exercised by familial, community, and legal authorities, I consider how the press and local gossip also contributed to wider discourses about acceptable behaviour. In particular, the way that journalists publicized specific infractions to function as cautionary tales illuminates the dominant social attitudes in these towns, and confirmed the presence of a "girl problem" (albeit a small one).

For the purposes of this examination, "bad" behaviour and "acting out" are defined as acts that were self-directed and in which women and girls willingly participated. Card games, celebratory drinking, unchaperoned walks, merry-go-round rides, and courting rituals might all be innocent, acceptable leisure and recreational activities; they might also slip into gambling, public drunkenness, vagrancy, theft to secure the price of admission, or objectionable sexual behaviours. Discreet scolding of local lawbreakers and delinquents often occurred through private reprimands at home, letters couched in religious rhetoric (as the Salvation Army "friend" did), or public shaming in the print media. Arguably the most powerful regulator and chastiser of women's actions, slanderous gossip was a mechanism that constrained and shaped women's choices in small communities. Lesser crimes like public drunkenness and gambling were largely controlled by local bylaws, while other bothersome "moral infractions"[7] such as petty theft were generally handled by the lower-level courts. Depending on how and where women and girls acted out, along with their age, reputation, class, and ethnicity, they could face a gauntlet of regulatory systems ranging from watchful parents and neighbours to defamation by local newspapers to the authority of the police and court systems.

Leisure practices that transgressed moral and social boundaries have, unfortunately, left few traces in the historical records of these three towns. As a result, uncovering the extent to which women and girls "misbehaved" in Dresden, Tillsonburg, Elora, and the surrounding rural areas poses several investigative challenges. Some county records, like those in Oxford, are rich with archival material in the form of jail registers, judge's bench books, and court transcripts. Similar records for the counties or districts that administered Dresden and Elora are sporadic at best, though newspapers occasionally printed year-end reports and statistics from the county jail. To some extent, as Dubinsky argues, legal documents can "provide a window into instances of personal life" we may not otherwise be privy to,[8] but the view provided by these texts "is rarely clear and therefore must be wiped clean," as historian

Steven Maynard reminds us.[9] To gain a better sense of the motives and truth behind these alleged crimes, it is necessary to read against the grain and pay careful attention to the perspectives, objectives, and biases of male judges who decided the fate of female defendants and the court-appointed recorders who composed these sources.

Minor offences like public drunkenness and gambling were usually handled by the local police magistrate (if one was present) or justice of the peace. Serious criminal cases like murder or abortion were tried in front of the periodic assize court. It is unclear if formal records were kept, but little evidence from the police courts in Dresden, Tillsonburg, and Elora has survived. In her experience researching female criminality, legal historian Constance Backhouse concedes that even in larger cities, evidence of women's entanglements with the law is difficult to find because of the absence of surviving records from the lower courts.[10] Though small-town weeklies published reports of varying lengths from all levels of the judicial system, the high-profile cases being tried at the assizes garnered the most attention. These newspaper stories, when paired with jail registers and quantitative data found in the nominal census, hold the richest information about female criminal behaviour. Census records sometimes offer complementary information about the women involved, but they are seldom helpful in identifying disreputable behaviour linked to leisure activities. Women who earned money through unlawful occupations such as sex work or running gambling dens, for instance, did not disclose such personal information to census enumerators.[11]

When women's behaviour led to an arrest or jail time, their visibility in the historical record becomes much clearer. Yet compared with large cities like Toronto, where sources from that city's jails often include each inmate's age, place of birth, city of residence, occupation, social habits, marital status, and other personal details,[12] Oxford County's jail register, for example, provides little beyond the detainee's name, date of admittance, reason for detention, length of incarceration, and occasionally a note about their fate, such as commitment to an asylum or a reformatory.[13] But the data contained within these records do aid in "flesh[ing] out the identities and circumstances of women in conflict with the law."[14] During the period under examination here, nearly forty different offences were committed by women though some, such as sex work and vagrancy, were marked by various descriptions. This was common, Backhouse explains, because the wording of the charge was left to the discretion of the presiding jail clerk.[15] The records also indicate that charges against women began to drop off after the late 1880s, possibly coinciding with the establishment of police constabularies and county poor houses.

The Rural-Urban Dichotomy

In the latter part of the nineteenth century, concerned about "the vulnerability and moral irresponsibility of young working women in the city," some social reformers believed that a "girl problem" was emerging.[16] As young women relocated to North America's urban centres seeking employment, adventure, or escape from the drudgery of agricultural labour, their independence and separation from family allegedly made them susceptible to a seedy underbelly of sex, pleasure, and leisure. Most of the scholarship on the "girl problem" focuses on female offenders with similar characteristics—typically young, single, immigrant, working-class city dwellers. The trifecta of urbanization, industrialization, and immigration, which provoked overcrowding, poverty, and higher crime rates, was thought to be the root cause of their poor behaviour. These explanations highlight the ways rural and urban were historically understood to be mutually constitutive. The more the crowded, dirty city was recognized as immoral and bad, the more the surrounding countryside and its service centres were idealized as tranquil and wholesome; each defined and gave meaning to the other. Author and historian Canniff Haight, for instance, characterized Canadian women as "pure, modest, [and] affectionate. They made good wives [and] were the best and most thoughtful mothers that ever watched over the well-being of their children."[17] The assumption that rural and small-town women were paragons of virtuous femininity was closely aligned with the widely held belief about patriarchal authority; to question the moral purity of a community's female population was to question the effectiveness of its patriarchal structure.[18]

With respect to the Canadian context, historians like Dubinsky and Lynne Marks have addressed the presence of "bad girls" in rural and small-town Ontario,[19] while urban historians, including Carolyn Strange, Tamara Myers, and Amanda Glasbeek, have explored the "girl problem" in cities like Toronto and Montreal. Though circumstances varied depending on location, the extent to which small-town leisure activities were regulated and the ways that women became entangled with the criminal justice system were not altogether different than in larger cities, though variations in modes of policing, population, systems of labour, and proximity to family and neighbours existed. Records suggest that regulation within the confines of home, church, and the immediate community played a more integral role in small towns, where people knew each other and were privy to each other's personal business. At the same time, between 1870 and 1914, more public attention was being paid to so-called disreputable modes of recreation that women and girls were increasingly engaging in as a result of greater opportunities for leisure activities in these towns. The ways that women became entangled with systems of authority in Dresden, Tillsonburg, and Elora and the frequency with which leisure was suggested as a catalyst for their "bad" behaviour reveals how much communal censure and moral regulation were involved in controlling citizens' social habits. The females in these towns and their surrounding areas were rarely depicted as the sort that would "engage in acts of prostitution, theft, and violence,"[20] but available sources suggest that some did indulge in activities considered beyond the bounds of appropriateness. Like their city counterparts, some rural and small-town girls and women convicted of crimes were sent to reformatories and asylums to serve their sentences and receive instruction on proper female decorum. These female delinquents counter the popular belief that Ontario's smaller communities had developed effective systems of regulation that kept women and girls protected from dangerous situations.[21] Indeed, "a brick farmhouse [or] a village home," Kate Aitken recalled, could "carry under its wide and spreading roof the same violent passions, the same deep-seated resentments as are known in any city."[22]

Forging the Rural "Girl Problem"

In the mid-to-late nineteenth century, Ontario politicians, social reformers, and evangelicals began demonstrating a greater desire to shield citizens from the immorality they believed was a consequence of the vast socio-economic changes occurring nationwide. The growth in leisure and recreational activities and the alleged dangers they posed to young people was a key area of concern. Rural periodicals and small-town newspapers increasingly voiced reformers' preoccupation with maintaining a strict moral code and reducing instances of bad behaviour. Their readers were exposed to debates about decency, sexuality, and lawlessness, which intensified anxieties that local citizens might be showing signs of such corruption. Many feared that the bad behaviour permeating cities would trickle down to the outlying, smaller communities.

Several town and municipal councils passed regulatory bylaws in the latter third of the nineteenth century, suggesting that disreputable leisure practices were very real (and troubling) concerns for local officials. By 1859, the Municipal Council of Oxford County had instituted a "ByLaw to enforce the observance of Public Morals" that prohibited, among other actions, the construction of bowling alleys for amusement, profit, or hire.[23] In 1874, another set of morality bylaws were passed in Oxford that outlawed (among other indiscretions) drunk and disorderly conduct around streets and public spaces, the use of profane or blasphemous language, any "indecent or immoral behavior," and the "[keeping] of a bawdy house or house of ill fame or frequent[ing] the same."[24] Some of these bylaws were likely reactions to specific cases and scandals occurring in the county's midst, while others were anticipatory. The fact that several morality bylaws were passed at a time in Oxford County's history when the Euro-Canadian population was still relatively small suggests the importance of constructing a convincing image of a law-abiding and morally upstanding populace for prospective settlers.

In many communities, large and small, sex work prompted immense anxiety. Historical analyses of the female sex trade traditionally frame it within larger, more urbanized contexts, but small towns were also home to communal brothels or independent sex workers. In Elora, for instance, "Sophie's Hotel" was a recreational and "lively spot for gentlemen wishing to become better acquainted with Sophie's numerous 'nieces.'"[25] Between 1870 and 1914, approximately three dozen women were incarcerated in the Oxford County jail for crimes associated with sex work.[26] At least sixteen of the accused kept houses of "ill fame,"[27] though most likely operated out of their own homes and engaged in sex work themselves. One of them, twenty-three-year-old Clarissa Lambert, was charged in 1900 with keeping a house of ill fame. According to the 1901 census, Lambert lived in Tillsonburg with her young daughter and made $700 as a charwoman that year.[28] At the time, a twenty-something male head of household earned an average income of $500 annually,[29] so Lambert likely lied to census enumerators about her occupation, or her wages were supplemented by the money she earned prostituting herself and/or others.

In the nineteenth century, sex work—and fornication generally—was habitually associated with cities, arising from the widespread belief that young, unassuming females adrift in metropolitan areas were more susceptible to immoral pleasures.[30] Dubinsky notes that most females who admitted to trading sexual acts for a little pocket money or gifts were providing favours to suitors, not strangers.[31] Though the number of "private bargains amicably struck" and the degree to which leisure influenced women's and girls' decisions to sell sexual favours cannot be quantified, historian Francis Swyripa points out that in more rural contexts, "casual sex was perhaps the only way for girls to acquire money and goods independently of the family."[32] In towns like Dresden, Tillsonburg, and Elora, wage-earning opportunities for women were limited and rarely paid well, and that fact may have increased the temptation to trade sex for money or other items of value.

Regardless of whether she resided in a rural or urban area, a woman who was known to be engaging in pre- or extra-marital sex was deemed "fallen" because she had "transgressed the bounds of respectable womanhood" and thus was "beyond the pale" and "could never be fully redeemed."[33] Instead, it was the "good" and "respectable" young girls and teens who needed to be safeguarded from disreputable pleasures. As historian Mariana Valverde explains, early twentieth-century investigations into the causes of "social vice" claimed that young girls who frequented sites of leisure and engaged in premarital sex with male companions, while not sex workers in practice, were just as demoralized as sex workers.[34]

Familial Regulation of Youth and Its Limits

When it came to controlling and preventing instances of crime and deviance in small towns, considerable attention was paid to children and adolescents because of the belief that prevention began with the discipline, monitoring, and control of youthful behaviour.[35] Parents were expected to play a key role in shaping the sexual and moral development of the next generation. Consequently, the family served as "the most immediate watchdog regulating social life and sexual behaviour" in the later nineteenth and early twentieth centuries.[36] Though some politicians, civic boosters, and journalists steadfastly denied that their towns contained even a fragment of the moral deprivation believed to be rampant in cities, the print media still provided parents with advice and information on how to keep boys entertained and girls "good."[37] One reporter from the *Dresden Times* argued that when girls acted out, parents ought to be blamed for their unruly behaviour, because they had been allowed "to run wild on the streets and cultivate habits of looseness and to associate without restraint with companions of the lowest type."[38] Popular among Methodist auxiliaries, a Canadian periodical called the *Missionary Outlook* also called attention to the need to keep girls away from "utter ruin." In an article published in 1905, author Mrs. John Dennison argued that in addition to being aware of the "young man problem" and the need to "keep a 'Grip on Harry,'" it was equally important that mothers "keep a 'Grip on Susan.'"[39]

When families were successful in their role of moral regulator, their actions left few records beyond memories of childhood. Dresden's Inez

B. (Eagleson) Perrin remarked of her upbringing that most children were "kept too busy to find much time for mischief." She admits that the youth in her community were certainly not "angels in any sense of the word," while explicitly noting that the concept of juvenile delinquency was not one that she and her contemporaries were aware of. She rather righteously suggests that children in her day understood the importance of respecting their elders, and that parents stayed home at night to watch their children. Perrin recalls that "the only family courts we know of were across our father's knee and his hand applied to our birthday suit and the only suspended sentence received was a reprimand from mother."[40]

The informal nature of parental discipline described by Perrin is difficult to measure because it tends to be invisible in the historical record. We also know little about the places female children went to escape surveillance. Outside of the city, where commercial amusement halls and public parks were less abundant, the countryside, wooded areas, and waterways offered a variety of potential playgrounds and locations for misbehaviour that were beyond parents' sight. Like Perrin, Tillsonburg's Bert Newman remarked that during his childhood, "no one had ever heard the words 'juvenile delinquency'" in town,[41] because children were too busy playing outside or helping their families to get into mischief. The reason for this, Newman remembers, was because children were forced to be creative and make their own fun, and children rarely found amusement in seriously breaking the law. Small towns may have lacked the spaces and anonymity that allowed urban children a greater degree of freedom, but arguably children were more likely to get away with breaking the law in smaller communities because the small local police force (if one was present) could not adequately patrol public spaces.[42]

As discussed in Chapter 2, by the 1880s females in Dresden, Tillsonburg, and Elora were becoming fixtures on their respective town's streets and sidewalks and in entertainment halls and other sites of leisure. Most young women resided with their families until marriage, and though this living arrangement was thought to shield girls from trouble, the constant monitoring and pressure to uphold their families' notions of respectability likely prompted many to seek leisure beyond the home. Some girls took to the streets to "elude overzealous [...] surveillance,"[43] while others tried to escape abusive and tyrannical fathers, and "took extra risks and were left more vulnerable than they might otherwise have been."[44] Young women and their parents were warned how quickly seemingly harmless leisure activities could transform from reputable to disreputable outside the home. In 1887, a piece appeared in a widely read Oxford County newspaper, the *Woodstock Sentinel-Review*, about the popularity of kissing games in smaller communities in the United States. The author writes that "perhaps it cannot be called immoral; but when society has reached a certain stage of refinement these games vanish."[45] When reports of women carousing with men or indulging in alcohol were published, they were often framed within a cautionary discourse that associated women's engagement in "rough" leisure with the breakdown of home, family, and Victorian and Edwardian notions of respectability and femininity.

When children exhibited the sort of bad behaviour that constituted a punishable offence, it was usually relatively minor in nature. In contrast to Perrin's and Newman's assertions that children in Dresden and Tillsonburg were too preoccupied to get into trouble, Stephen Thorning writes that Elora certainly had its "gangs of youth" who, similar to their counterparts in cities like Hamilton,[46] dabbled in petty crimes like vandalism, loitering, shoplifting, and making suggestive comments to pedestrians.[47] As described in Chapter 6, bothersome antics like damaging property, harassment, and petty theft troubled locals and the picnic parties and day-trippers visiting Elora. In February 1890, Elora photographer Thomas Connon mentioned in a letter to his son, John, that a local girl named Alberta had recently been found shoplifting,[48] so "her parents have put her away some place [but] nobody seems to know where."[49] In 1899, a story in the *Elora Express* detailed how fifteen-year-old Martha Busch from nearby Woolwich stole "two handkerchiefs, five yards of print and $2 in money." Referring to it as a "sad case," the *Express* stated that Busch had previously served six months in jail for theft. When asked to speak about her daughter's actions, Busch's mother told the police court she was "incorrigible" and needed to be sent to a reformatory, suggesting Busch had a penchant for deviance. She was eventually sentenced to a three-year stay in Toronto's Andrew Mercer Reformatory for Women.[50]

The concern expressed by Busch's mother contrasts with the assertions made by Perrin and Newman about the importance of family discipline and children being kept busy. These differences also reinforce the intersections and shifting relations between families and other institutions, notably the criminal justice system. By the mid-nineteenth century, a child-saving movement was taking shape, driven by reformers' belief that there was a crisis of degeneracy among youth. In 1851, the first reformatories were established to handle juvenile delinquents in the Province of Canada. The Youthful Offenders Act of 1894 mandated that juvenile delinquents not be treated as adults but rather as "misdirected and misguided child[ren]" before the courts.[51] The 1908 federal Juvenile Delinquents Act defined juvenile delinquents as persons between the ages of seven and sixteen "who had contravened any federal, provincial, or municipal law, or ordinance, who were liable by reason of any act to be committed to an industrial school or reformatory, or who were guilty of 'sexual immorality or any similar form of vice.'"[52]

Prior to this legislation, children had faced the full brunt of the law when they committed crimes. In Oxford County, for instance, two girls—Minnie Church and Annie Dawson—aged nine and ten years old, respectively, were incarcerated for "prostitution and street walking" and "disorderly conduct" in the 1880s.[53] According to the jail register, which neglected to include details about the nature of their arrests, Church spent one month in the county jail while Dawson was incarcerated for almost three months. Defining juvenile delinquency and placing children in a separate judicial category was a response to claims by politicians, physicians, and social reformers that children needed specific modes of rehabilitation when they "acted out." Additionally, it kept children away from the dangers of the overcrowded city and county jails.

The 1908 Juvenile Delinquents Act contained a "local option" component that provided districts with the authority to set up juvenile courts and modes of regulation as they saw fit.[54] As a result, treatment of juvenile delinquency varied from community to community. In 1912, Tillsonburg's town council enacted a curfew bylaw that sought to control the number of children seen in "public place[s] at night without proper guardianship."[55] According to its provisions, all children under the age of fourteen were to remain in their homes after 9:00 p.m. If they contravened the law, they could be "warned to go home by any constable or peace Officer and if after such warning the child is found loitering in a public place such child may be taken by the Constable or officers to its home or to the Children's Shelter."[56] When violations occurred, the parents were held accountable and fined one dollar for the child's first offence, two dollars for the second, and five dollars for any subsequent ones. Working-class families would have struggled to pay these substantial fines, so the curfew bylaw provided even more incentive to curb children's behaviour. Aside from creating a financial responsibility, "an errant daughter [also] reflected badly on a parent's reputation."[57]

Other pieces of legislation endeavoured to keep children away from disreputable pleasures. In Oxford County (which applied to Tillsonburg) various bylaws passed between the 1850s and 1890s forbade the distribution or sale of alcohol to any child, minor, or apprentice under the age of twenty-one without written consent from the parents, guardian, or master.[58] In 1899, children living in the "East Riding of Wellington" (near Elora) were prohibited from frequenting barrooms and from being a "lounger" or "idler" near such establishments.[59] In Dresden, a bylaw "Respecting the issue of Licenses for Public Shows etc." contained a subsection that barred children's presence at local bowling alleys, billiard and bagatelle tables, or roller-skating rinks if they had been "forbidden" to do so by a parent or guardian.[60]

The passage of these local bylaws suggests that historians' assertions about juvenile delinquency being more prevalent in cities could benefit from greater consideration of how rural and small-town parents and the judiciary dealt with similar "problem" children. When courts deemed caregivers incapable of acting as a reforming influence, juveniles like Martha Busch were sent to youth correctional facilities. The Oxford County jail registers between 1870 and 1914 note that two young women, ages unknown, were sent to the Mercer Reformatory, one in 1909 for "keeping a house of ill fame" and one in 1912 for "walking the streets at night." Others were "sent to the hospital," which may be a reference to the county's House of Refuge, built in 1893 and located on the outskirts of Woodstock.[61]

Other measures to control wayward children, including the establishment of branches of the Children's Aid Society (CAS), were meant to end "such glaring evils as street begging, peddling of small wares, [and] youthful immorality and truancy."[62] Between 1891 and 1912, sixty CAS branches were established in cities and small towns across Ontario.[63] In Dresden, a local CAS was launched in October 1898 in conjunction with the branch in Chatham.[64] It is unclear whether Tillsonburg and Elora had their own CAS branches or were part of larger county-wide initiatives. If children could not be kept in the home, efforts were made to at least keep them off the streets. In 1910, a "department of games" was constructed in Tillsonburg's St. Paul Public Library. After its opening, the *Liberal* mentioned that such an initiative might prove useful in keeping children off the streets in similar towns, by offering them "checkers, chess, jackstraws and such like, instead of books, for their amusement during winter evenings."[65] As this proposal illustrates, family regulation during this period was increasingly subject to oversight and intervention through directives enacted at the local and, sometimes, provincial and national levels.

Communal Censure: From Informal Reprimands to Town and Municipal Bylaws

The Salvation Army "soldier" who chastised Mrs. Tillson about her gambling and movie-watching is an example of the sort of censure that was exercised informally in private communication. Middle-class observers may have viewed the Salvation Army as "devoid of the trappings of respectability" because of the controversial nature of their conversion tactics,[66] but the anonymous author's consternation over Mrs. Tillson's conduct suggests that this working-class critic's notions of respectability and religiosity clashed with those of the local elite when it came to leisure. Such community censure took a variety of forms, including gossip, private reprimand, exposure in local newspapers, and the passage of bylaws aimed at curtailing certain behaviours. Often, these intersected and happened concurrently.

Earlier in the nineteenth century, churches in rural and small-town Ontario had the authority to excommunicate parishioners for participating in "unseemly" leisure activities like play-acting,[67] but this form of censure seems to have been practised less as the century went on. During her teenage years, Agnes McGregor recalled, she and three of her school friends in Tillsonburg agreed to join the chorus of a local production of Gilbert and Sullivan's comic opera *Trial by Jury*. Though McGregor enjoyed being on stage and was enthralled by the opportunity to wear makeup as one of the play's "witnesses," she writes that this display was "much to the disapproval of some of the town prudes," who likely initiated gossip about her participation. Rev. McGregor actually supported his daughter's role in the opera because he and his wife enjoyed attending the theatre.[68] Clearly, the attitudes of the previous half century were shifting as more liberal ideas about how to spend one's "free" time were adopted and accepted by church officials and affluent citizens. Perhaps it was to counter the socio-economic power that elites exercised in small communities that some working-class evangelists, like Mrs. Tillson's critic, spoke out against such secular leisure practices by asserting their greater sense of moral and religious superiority.

The desire to enjoy many of the new leisure options available in and around small towns prompted some men and women of lesser means to commit petty offences such as theft, deceit, and trespassing. In July 1892, the *Elora Express* thought it necessary to inform the public that a young man "forgot" to pay for the ice cream that he purchased for himself and his "best girl" at a local shop.[69] A rather substantial article appeared in the *Tillsonburg Observer* in 1894, detailing how eighteen-year-old Emma Cooper, a domestic servant in the home of dentist Melvin D. Crooker, had stolen fifteen dollars from the purse of a house guest and was found to be "indulging extensively in rides on the merry-go-round and other luxuries." Rather than being sent to jail (which the police magistrate deemed more harmful than helpful), the girl was reinstalled in her former position and her wages used as restitution for the stolen money.[70] Cooper's actions—both the theft of the money and the use of it to finance her leisure—reinforce how domestic servants were both poorly paid and forced to adhere to their employers' definitions of respectability. For Cooper, this meant not spending the little money she earned on "frivolous" amusements. Just as socially unacceptable behaviour from a son or daughter could impact the social standing of their parents, the disreputable actions of an employee could affect the reputation of the employer. The way that the case was eventually handled, with Cooper returning to her job in the Crooker home, underpins the belief that domestic service was considered a redeeming occupation for working-class women and had the power to inculcate middle-class notions of respectability in those who were judged to be more susceptible to dissolute pleasures.[71]

Like their more youthful counterparts, women in Dresden, Tillsonburg, Elora, and their surrounding communities "defied social convention and conducted their social lives in public,"[72] but traversing these traditionally male-dominated spaces was not always easy, uneventful, or safe. Occasionally, the greater variety of leisure activities available and the heterosocial nature of some of those pursuits resulted in public spaces (and the activities that occurred within their boundaries) becoming "new terrains of struggle."[73] Not surprisingly, as women became more visible in public spaces, arrests for vagrancy rose considerably throughout the later years of the nineteenth century. Because it was defined by a multiplicity of "deviant acts," a vagrancy charge permitted "the net of the criminal justice system" to be "cast over a large number of women who could be arrested for a variety of reasons."[74] For a woman, the simple act of loitering "on any street, road, highway or public place" or "wander[ing] in the fields, public streets or highways, lanes or places of public meeting or gathering of people [without giving] a satisfactory account" of her actions constituted vagrancy and called for a fine upwards of fifty dollars or jail time.[75]

Gendered meanings and double standards were embedded in the many definitions of vagrancy and expose contemporary "social anxieties about women's sexuality, respectability, and increasingly public role."[76] In her work on vagrancy in early nineteenth-century Montreal, historian Mary Anne Poutanen describes how public areas functioned as an extension of the home, and were spaces where working-class women socialized, performed labour, and irritated elites with their "idleness."[77] Vagrancy charges were often laid in conjunction with other crimes and actions occurring in public, particularly sex work and drunkenness. As evidenced by the data from the Oxford County jail register, the number of women arrested simultaneously for vagrancy and sex work suggests that they were using public spaces for multiple purposes, including leisure and employment. In both rural and urban contexts, "concerned" citizens questioned women who cavorted in public alone or at night, so reporting female vagrants to local authorities was a form of punishment for those who "stepped outside prescribed roles as private, domestic, and mannerly citizens."[78] This pattern, and the frequency with which women were arrested for vagrancy, differed little between the city and the countryside. In Oxford County, vagrancy represented the fourth most common charge levied against women and girls who were sent to the county jail,[79] while in Montreal, vagrancy was one of the "largest crime categories for female offenders," according to Tamara Myers.[80] Among the women who appeared in front of the Toronto Women's Court, one in five had been arrested for vagrancy.[81]

When a serious crime like sexual assault was committed against a woman, the print media typically characterized this as evidence that women required greater protection in public. As rural and small-town Ontario underwent vast socio-economic changes, including the constant appearance of travelling entertainers, pedlars, immigrants, and agricultural labourers, local citizens were advised to be wary of unfamiliar individuals.[82] Anyone who seemed incompatible with small-town Ontario's predominantly White, Christian, and Anglo-centric culture could be scapegoated when reprehensible behaviour occurred. In the rural Prairie West, itinerant labourers travelling around the countryside were often cast as the seducers and corrupters of innocent young women, provoking them into participating in unseemly activities. One *Farmer's Advocate* article from 1908 suggested that mounting crime rates in rural Canada were due to "hobos; the large importation of undesirable immigrants of the submerged and criminal classes; and [...] the increasing number of gangs of Italians and other foreigners employed by the railways and other public enterprises on construction work."[83] Historically, crimes and behaviours such as vagrancy, sex work, and drunkenness were racialized to a greater degree than others because of their associations with idleness, moral depravity, and biological inferiority. Farm wives and their daughters, and rural women generally, were advised to stay away from these "dangerous" passersby and avoid going outdoors without a male chaperone.

The *Advocate*'s contention that rural crime was increasing contrasts with a piece published in the *Tillsonburg Observer* in 1900. According to James Noxon, provincial Inspector of Prisons and Public Charities, instances of crime still posed a significant issue in cities (especially among young women and girls working in factories and shops), but in rural districts rates were dropping.[84] Retrospectively, it is difficult to determine whether Noxon's assertion was true: were men and women acting out less, or were their actions being scrutinized and controlled to a lesser degree?[85] As both men and women in Dresden, Tillsonburg, and Elora became more mobile, they found ways to escape the constant scrutiny and constraints being imposed on their behaviour. Though sometimes communal watchfulness thwarted plans to engage in disreputable leisure, new transportation options like trains and bicycles could more ably transport citizens away from town, allowing them greater freedom to indulge in the sorts of activities considered intolerable by more conservative community members. Just because "bad" behaviour was not occurring within the vantage point of local morality enforcers does not mean that women were not exhibiting it.

Evidence of increased watchfulness may be explained by the number of police constabularies installed in small towns throughout southern Ontario in the late nineteenth century. In Tillsonburg, Police Chief Archie Pow was widely recognized by the *Observer* and *Liberal* for his efforts to curb local crime. Elora's citizens, however, had little faith in the constables hired by the town. According to Stephen Thorning, in the 1880s, one "was suspended on several occasions for drinking while on duty, and for public drunkenness."[86] As a result, some citizens continued to initiate their own forms of justice when lawlessness occurred.[87] Despite concerns about the ineptitude of constabulary members, their installation was an acknowledgement that small towns were disorderly and had evolved beyond the safety provided by a tight-knit group of community members. Whether local police forces had a direct impact on declining crime rates, however, is unclear. By the 1880s, when several constabularies had been established across Oxford County, there was a noticeable drop in the number of females arrested for vagrancy.[88] The establishment of formalized policing systems and the presence of officers out on patrol may have deterred women from engaging in "bad" or criminal behaviour, but this does not mean that illegal activities ceased. Likely, many moved indoors to avoid public scrutiny and the police.

When women and girls were known to be engaging in concerning behaviours in the public spaces of small towns, the practice of public shaming without naming was invoked to coerce guilty parties into correcting their transgressions. The local newspaper was usually the chosen medium for this message. When the *Tillsonburg Observer* mentioned in May 1895 that some local boys and girls had "disgraced themselves" by stealing flowers from the gardens of prominent men, the children's names were withheld "for the sake of the parents."[89] Chief Pow, however, was aware of the guilty parties and warned that if any more "depredations" occurred, the flower stealers' identities would be revealed. Paul Voisey writes that in the small town of High River, Alberta, where a similar practice was employed, the "editors of weeklies disagreed on whether or not to publish the names of local offenders since it would upset and humiliate their families."[90]

The social and sexual lives of local citizens provided fodder for reporters who enjoyed publishing veiled critiques of dubious behaviours occurring in their midst. In the early 1880s, the *Sarnia Sun* reported that boys from Dresden had a "sneaking regard" for girls from the nearby town of Wallaceburg, as evidenced by the numbers of them returning home in the early morning hours after "meandering" up there.[91] Though physical intimacy between young people was frowned upon in this period (and especially in public), in 1875 the *Tillsonburg Observer* reported that lately some unidentified courting couples had been seen around town "wrapping their heads in a shawl when they kiss each other at the gate to deaden the smacking."[92] In an era when chaperonage was still considered necessary when courting, especially among the middle and upper classes, young women who ignored such etiquette and spent time alone with men (especially at night) risked ruining their and their family's reputations.[93]

In a case where such dating decorum was disregarded, Henry Davidson of the rural township of West Zorra in Oxford County was charged with trespassing in 1891 because of a false promise. Dubbed "A Persistent Lover" by the *Guelph Weekly Herald*, Davidson was alleged to have asked a female companion to accompany him to a party, and though she agreed to do so, when he arrived at her home on the day of the event, he found the residence shrouded in darkness. Eventually let in by the girl's uncle, Davidson forced his way up to her bedroom so that "he might talk with her and endeavor to persuade her to fulfill her promise."[94] This case, and those of Emma Cooper and the ice cream "dine and dashers," are examples of minor infractions that were associated with desires to participate in specific leisure activities and social events. These instances and others showcase how rules regarding propriety were often contested or ignored when less affluent citizens did not have the money or means to participate. Sometimes watchful members of the community stepped in and restrained pleasure-seekers' zealous desires, but not always.

In the scathing critique of Mrs. Tillson's alleged gambling habits, the author was not so concerned that she was "plaing [*sic*] cards" but rather that she was gambling. Throughout the later nineteenth and early twentieth centuries, despite its reputation of being uncouth, gambling was common in businesses such as taverns, barrooms, billiard halls, and sports venues, as well as in the private spaces of members-only associational clubs and the family home. The first piece of federal legislation outlawing gambling in Canada was passed in 1875, providing local law enforcement officials with the power to stem the illegal establishment of gaming houses in their communities.[95] In 1892, the newly amended Criminal Code of Canada defined common gaming houses and betting houses as unlawful and "disorderly." Whether it was games of chance, cards, or betting, all manner of public gambling was considered illegal.[96] Evidence of dissolute gaming, including the presence of "cards, dice, balls, counters, tables or other instruments of gaming," playing or looking on in a gaming house, gambling on a public conveyance (such as a boat or train), or holding a lottery or raffle without consent could result in significant fines or prison time depending on the offence.[97]

The little information uncovered about rural and small-town lady gamblers indicates that most of their participation occurred in domestic spaces for two reasons: first, because "respectable women" were not welcome in the public venues where gambling usually occurred; and second, because in the home they were shielded from the scrutiny of the town's more evangelical citizenry. Cards were a popular parlour amusement among all classes because they were enjoyable and affordable. Historians Frances Hoffman and Ryan Taylor claim that card playing was a "universal passion" among Ontarians around the turn of the century.[98] Various games were played in both single-sex and mixed-sex groups of friends, family, and neighbours. In her diary, Olive Snyder mentions playing cards both at home and at her friends' homes in Elora.[99] Card clubs also became popular in the late nineteenth century, with women as the "prime factors" in these groups.[100] In 1894 the *Farmer's Advocate* provided a list of "Amusing Parlor Games for Winter Evenings," recommending a "good card game" alongside crokinole, "tiddledy-winks hopscott [*sic*]," and the "Christmas tree game."[101] Even board games sometimes provoked friendly competition. At a party hosted by George and Gertrude Tillson in 1903, a crokinole tournament was held where "there was close competition for first place."[102]

It is impossible to determine how many women played cards and other games for profit, but in 1895 one story in the *Tillsonburg Observer* suggests a group of local women were doing so. In the town's "social circles," players of the card game "Pedro" were warned to keep an eye out for a "certain young lady, who had been a steady loser for some time," but now suddenly had "commenced to rake in all the spoils."[103] Some women and girls made it clear that no money was exchanged in their homes or in the games they played. Kate Aitken, for example, fondly remembered "the table which stood in the centre of the dining-room was usually occupied by a long Mississippi board, the Presbyterian version of a billiard table and *not* considered sinful." Aitken's father owned a general store attached to the family home, and "during the slack periods," Aitken recounts, "my father would bring in his cronies for a game of Mississippi, played with cues and balls, but with no betting allowed."[104]

In the few works by Canadian historians that address the history of gambling prior to the 1920s, female gamblers have received considerably less attention than their male counterparts. When it came to engaging in "rough" behaviour in public spaces, some women frequented public drinking establishments, but beyond that we know little about their presence at gambling dens, racetracks, or billiard halls. Robert Brandon writes that there were "six hotels and three billiard halls in full swing" in Dresden in the 1870s, so "one can easily picture that much time was spent in these places as these beverages were then reasonable in price."[105] These establishments would have catered to male patrons as the only women on the premises were usually employed as table girls or chambermaids.[106] In her examination of turn-of-the-century New York City, Kathy Peiss acknowledges that working-class women gambled, "but the context in which they did so differed significantly from the male rituals of shooting pool, rolling dice, and betting on cards." This sort of gaming was endemic in more masculine settings, while women's preferred modes of gambling were "impersonal and abstract system[s] of chance" such as lotteries.[107]

While reformers tried to discourage all from gambling, women's participation was monitored more closely because of the consequences such debauchery might impose on maternal well-being. When women did participate, contemporaries felt that they "needed more protection from their own folly than did men."[108] Protective advice could be found in local newspapers and rural periodicals where prescriptive literature and cautionary tales were published in the hopes of curbing desires to partake. In 1905, a piece appeared in the *Tillsonburg Liberal*, written by an anonymous detractor from St. Clair, Michigan, who acknowledged the prevalence of gambling in family homes and questioned the sort of example women set for their sons when they indulged in a hand of euchre or poker. Whether the stake was "money, jewels, real estate, or merely bric-a-brac, books, music, pocket books, or any other 'old thing,'" women were asked to seriously consider, as the "Professed Christians" they claimed to be, how God would judge such behaviour.[109] Like the letter to Mrs. Tillson, the article is another example of how religious rhetoric was employed to admonish women's recreational choices that contradicted Christian principles.

Two pieces published in the *Elora Lightning Express* and *Elora Express* in the 1880s drew upon popular constructions of class and gender to argue that gambling was the antithesis of refinement and femininity. The first article, titled "Aristocratic Lady Gamblers," recalled how one after-dinner game of baccarat among a high-society group in the town of Newmarket erupted into a verbal brawl akin to the "manners of scullery-maids and the language of coal-heavers."[110] The second article, "Women Who Play Poker," described how women in Washington, DC, were taking up gambling as a form of recreation during Lent because other amusements (such as dancing) were forbidden. Poker was their preferred game, and though at some tables bets were limited to twenty-five cents, one "young society belle" managed to lose $200 over the course of five sittings. Less affluent women who had a "moderate amount of pin money" also played but were limited to what was known as "penny ante 5 cent limit." The article also details how heterosocial poker parties were "all the rage," though "vulgar" chips and money were largely absent from these festivities. Though the article does not overtly condemn female gamblers, the sub-headline warns the *Express*'s readers that the details "may make the hair stand on end."[111] Within such stories that appeared in the print media, strong messages were conveyed to women about the harms of gambling, particularly when played for profit.

Though views differed over whether cards and other games were appropriate leisure activities, the consensus was that gaming slipped from reputable to disreputable when money was exchanged. One article from an 1870 issue of the *Canada Farmer* reinforced this, stating that "once the element of gambling is introduced, the play, be it what it may, passes out of the range of recreation and becomes vice."[112] Otherwise, another commentator wrote, "a pack of cards is as harmless as a croquet set or a box of dominoes."[113] Observers urged players to consider whether gambling was necessary to enhance a game's appeal. One writer suggested awarding prizes to game winners in lieu of betting on the outcome. As Chapter 4 described, at many small-town women's social events, prizes such as bouquets of flowers were awarded to winners of parlour games.

Because disreputable activities were rarely acknowledged in women's letters and diaries, it is difficult "to quantify the amount of card betting and gaming which occurred indoors, in pubs and clubs or at home."[114] This is especially true when assessing the playing habits of women. Donald G. Wetherell and Irene Kmet argue that in small-town Alberta, the population of public poolrooms and other gaming establishments was "wholly male."[115] Because of their reputation for immorality, it is difficult to uncover concrete information about the sorts of customers who patronized gaming halls and the ancillary activities that occurred within their walls. Local bylaws, however, provide some revealing information. In Dresden, the proprietors of bowling alleys, billiard and bagatelle tables, and roller-skating rinks were not authorized to "permit any tippling or gambling of any kind to be carried on therein or thereupon."[116] County jail registers also provide brief glimpses of women's involvement with gambling rings. In 1880, Hattie Harvey and Ignahus Balentin were remanded to the Oxford County jail for almost two months for "keeping a gambling house."[117] Where the house was located, the sort of clientele it catered to, and Harvey's and Balentin's reputations, however, are unknown.

As forms of disreputable leisure, gambling and drinking share several traits. For the most part, both were recognized components of masculine culture in rural and small-town Ontario. Both were also viewed by religious officials and reformers as demoralizing forms of amusement when engaged in by members of the "lower orders," women, or to the point of overindulgence. Alcohol was consumed both publicly and privately, ranging from the male ritual of congregating in a tavern to grab a pint,[118] to the liquor purchases that appear in household and general store account books.[119] In turn-of-the-century Tillsonburg, Bert Newman recalled that the town's four hotels had "wide-open bars," where "whiskey was 10 cents a glass, and fellows drank it straight. There were no tables or chairs in the barrooms; instead, the bar had a foot railing, and you stood up to the bar to drink."[120] Apart from instances when excessive drinking provoked violent or indecent behaviour, alcohol was an accepted means of fostering sociability among men in both public and private spaces. In contrast, when women participated in this sort of disreputable leisure, they were viewed as "de-womanized" and as "exhibiting features of a 'bastardized masculinity.'"[121] Drinking, and other forms of vice it was associated with (such as sex work), sharply diverged from the ideal conduct of the pious and pure woman.

Men's consumption of alcohol occurred everywhere and at all times of the year in rural and small-town Ontario, while women's drinking tended to be more covert and contained. However, holidays and public celebrations were occasions when both men and women drank. In 1892, the *Elora Express* stated rather matter-of-factly that Victoria Day celebrations in town prompted "subject[s] who [were] 'trooly loil'" to get drunk after the day's games, activities, and anthem-singing had concluded.[122] In his personal correspondence, Thomas Connon remarked that "the only stir to be seen in Elora" on Victoria Day in 1890 consisted of excursion parties who "never fail" to make it to the town, "passing through sober going, drunk getting back."[123] Kate Aitken remembered that though they "weren't a drinking household, there was always good liquor for the grown-ups Christmas afternoon."[124] Drinking was monitored and regulated by local bylaws designed not to condemn drinkers but to censure instances of overindulgence or public intoxication. An 1874 bylaw in Oxford County, for example, stipulated that any person found drunk or guilty of any disorderly conduct on any streets, highways, or public places faced a fine upwards of fifty dollars or time in jail if the fine was not paid.[125] According to an 1899 ordinance enacted in Eastern Wellington County (that likely applied to Elora), no alcoholic beverage could be sold or served to "any person who has the habit of drinking intoxicating liquor to excess" or "to the child, servant, wife or agent of any known habitual drunkard."[126]

Between 1870 and 1914, of the forty-plus crimes women were jailed for in Oxford County, "drunk and disorderly" charges were the second-most common (insanity/feeblemindedness being the first). Statistically, this pales in comparison to the number of men similarly charged, but drunkenness was so closely aligned with rough masculinity that the rates of arrest among women reinforce that they did not always obey gendered prescriptions for appropriate womanly behaviour. Similarly, many of the women tried before the Toronto Women's Court also faced drunk and disorderly charges. In total, this represented one in four arrests.[127] In that court the women tended to be over the age of thirty, Roman Catholic, and itinerant, seeking occasional employment as domestic servants or sex workers.[128] Based on the minimal personal information available, the women charged with drunkenness in Oxford County were of Anglo-Celtic descent, between the ages of twenty and forty, mostly Protestant, and a mix of married and unwed. In both Oxford County and Toronto, several of the women accused of drunkenness were, much like vagrants, reoffenders and often arrested for committing simultaneous crimes. Mary Sommers, for instance, appears in the Oxford County jail register four times between 1876 and 1880 for drinking and vagrancy charges. Recidivists like Sommers are a reminder of how common drinking was,[129] and how an arrest, conviction, or even a brief incarceration could not temper some women's desires to drink.

Aside from those whose arrests left a scanty record of their activities, little is known about how much (or how little) women in Dresden, Tillsonburg, and Elora routinely imbibed. Cautionary reports in local newspapers about incidents such as deaths or injuries associated with intoxication attempted to deter "good" women from drinking. Because of the harsh criticisms doled out to those who indulged in the traditionally male pleasures of drinking and gambling, when those women did participate in so-called dissolute practices, they tended to do so more discreetly and privately. Upper- and middle-class men and women were no more or less virtuous than their working-class counterparts, but their limited interactions with the legal system "fits into wider class-based patterns of privacy."[130] It is also likely that their privilege, visibility, and power meant that the well-to-do were publicly appraised to a lesser degree and application of the law occurred more sporadically (if at all). Small communities meant greater familiarity among citizens, so respectable women who entered masculine domains like barrooms, hotels, billiard halls, and the like risked becoming the source of local gossip. And there were certainly class dimensions attached to hiding disreputable behaviour. Largely, female elites were just as susceptible to censure from the community as anyone else, and failing to adhere to prescribed notions of appropriateness (which they also had a hand in constructing) could have dire socio-economic consequences.

When it came to taking a public stance on socio-political issues like temperance, in smaller communities such as Elora these crusades were led by "high-profile men" and, to a lesser degree, women, but many felt conflicted over their views on the "liquor question" for fear that they might affront a person of affluence and "consequently [. . .] hurt business."[131] In Tillsonburg, E.D. Tillson and family professed to be staunch temperance advocates despite the fact that E.D. supported the building of hotels in town; furthermore, liquor purchases are recorded in the household's account books, and a wine cellar was in the basement of Annandale House.[132] But when the *Observer* and *Liberal* published details of the family's rather elaborate dinner parties, alcohol was never mentioned in the refreshment lists. While publicly elite families such as the Tillsons may have professed to be dry, references to booze in cookbooks and etiquette guides reinforce that alcohol *was* permitted in so-called "dry" homes, ranging in form from patent medicines to the spirits reserved for guests and dinner parties.[133] A former domestic servant at Annandale House, Myrtle Dreyer (née Morden), remembers making a "very rich Christmas cake, wrapping it in a brandy soaked cloth and storing it in the basement."[134] Kate Aitken recalls that drinking "dandelion wine" was considered "highly respectable" among residents in Beeton. Even her mother, "who never touched anything stronger than tea," enjoyed "her glass of dandelion wine with visiting neighbours."[135]

Self-righteous teetotallers, who often hobnobbed with the local elites and middle-class citizens who hosted the elaborate (and sometimes boozy) dinner parties and socials, tended to be members of local chapters of the Woman's Christian Temperance Union (WCTU). While their purpose was to reform society by stemming alcohol consumption, as Chapter 2 detailed, the women who joined Tillsonburg's WCTU were also interested in the "distinct women's middle-class culture" that developed through membership.[136] While temperance never fully disappeared from their agenda, the Tillsonburg WCTU's meetings around the turn of the century, for example, began to include more social components.[137] According to historian Sharon Anne Cook, social endeavours "became a mainstay of the women's social interaction, which kept the group convivial and united."[138] From its founding, the WCTU was interested in philanthropic work and over time this gradually replaced the cause of temperance.

For women wishing to indulge, liquor-laced patent medicines could be readily purchased from grocers and druggists in Dresden, Tillsonburg, and Elora. The consumption of these "tonics" was an accepted practice in Victorian and Edwardian society, offering women a measure of discretion when purchasing them for their alcoholic properties. Shopkeepers wishing to sell alcoholic beverages that were not masquerading as patent medicines were often required to purchase a special liquor permit to do so. The passage of local bylaws that oversaw the distribution of permits was meant to control the number of businesses that could sell alcohol and thus regulate its availability. At a municipal council meeting in Dresden in 1877, for example, it was decided that only two shopkeepers per year could purchase permits allowing them to exclusively sell liquor.[139] Town historian Helen Burns writes that at one point upwards of six establishments were allowed to have licences, and they sold whiskey from a barrel for five cents a glass. Over time, fewer permits were distributed, possibly because they were so expensive; at one point, shopkeepers were charged the immense sum of $500.[140]

Within the criminal justice system, even if a woman herself was not on trial, her reputation and the various forms of disreputable leisure she was known to participate in always were. Women who drank, for instance, were "assumed to be prostitutes or gin-shop derelicts."[141] In one such case, a Wellington County man, Daniel Heffernan, appeared before the police magistrate in 1868, accused of indecently assaulting Mrs. Ellen Lawlor in a rural area between Guelph and Fergus. Though the *Guelph Herald* reported that the evidence from the two parties was "contradictory," the counsel for the accused argued that his client could prove Lawlor was seen drinking with a man on the day of the alleged incident. The case was remanded to the

Quarter Sessions for further adjudication and Heffernan was released on $400 bail.[142] Drawing attention to her suspect behaviour not only buttressed the defendant's alibi, but insinuating that Lawlor lacked morals by drinking and carousing with men also invalidated her story. In the late nineteenth century, evidence that a woman was drinking was often accompanied by the stereotypes of "fallen woman" or "bad mother," or was equated with participation in the sex trade. Such opinions about women's drinking remained unchanged until roughly the First World War, when the rules regarding female decorum relaxed ever so slightly.

Sex and the Criminal Justice System

Many of the transgressions that women and girls committed in Dresden, Tillsonburg, and Elora were relatively minor infractions, lapses in moral judgement, or bothersome nuisances. When females faced heavier repercussions such as jail time or a monetary fine, it was usually for a crime involving inappropriate sexual behaviour. Despite the "simplicity, innocence, and solid family values" allegedly associated with small-town and country living, "the farmhouse and farmyard could [also] serve as a setting for acts of sexual violence, seduction, and strife."[143] Forms of seemingly innocent rural and small-town leisure activities that were part of the courting process—skating, dancing, attending the theatre, cycling, going out walking, or buggy rides—provided avenues for couples to meet, flirt, and engage in sexual activity. Certainly, women and girls in Dresden, Tillsonburg, and Elora tested the boundaries of respectable womanhood by exploring sexuality for personal pleasure. While some were victims of brutal acts of sexual violence, most women who appeared in front of the local courts or were chastised for immoral behaviour in newspapers were there because of offences involving consensual sex.

The *Tillsonburg Observer* reported on 9 April 1880 that according to data compiled by the Registrar-General, one in every sixty-five children born in Oxford County in 1878 was illegitimate.[144] While this statistic, perhaps published as a warning, is by no means shocking, it is a reminder that sexual activity was not always restricted to the marital bed. When a pregnancy resulted, many rural and small-town families did not turn their errant daughters out on the streets; in many cases illegitimate offspring were accepted as full-fledged members of the family. Though earlier in the nineteenth century "deviant" sexual acts such as fornication and adultery could result in excommunication or disciplinary action from church officials,[145] publishing the illegitimacy rate from 1878 suggests that the public desired to know the intimate details of their neighbours' sex lives. The increasing number of seduction cases brought before the courts in this period also points to a growing awareness of couples having premarital sex. Typically, seduction cases involved a young, unmarried girl who had been debauched by a male (regardless of whether the sex was consensual or forced). In addition to prosecuting the accused, fathers often requested restitution for the loss of the daughter's innocence. Except for cases where the female had a "reputation," blame was usually placed on the male seducer, who was obliged to provide redress to the victim so that her and her parents' names could be cleared.[146]

Especially when it came to crimes involving sex, knowledge of a woman's alleged habits prior to conviction became increasingly important when assessing wrongdoings and meting out punishment. The early twentieth-century judicial minute books from the county-wide criminal court in Kent, which administered the Dresden area, attest to this fact. Alongside each offender's name, age, and other personal details, the minute books contain a category for "Habits," which fall under the broad and undefined descriptors of "good," "fair," or "bad." Though some wrongdoers were listed as having "good" or "fair" habits, in the estimation of the minute book's recorder(s) most of the women listed displayed "bad" ones.[147] Predictably, their crimes almost always resulted in guilty verdicts.

While some families may have accepted illegitimate children, women were still considered to have fallen into disrepute when they admitted to engaging in premarital sex, or worse, having a child out of wedlock. In small towns and rural areas, it was difficult if not impossible for a woman to hide her pregnancy unless she was sent away for the duration of her confinement. As a consequence, women sometimes resorted to drastic measures:

several stories printed in the *Woodstock Sentinel-Review* detail how women in Oxford County disposed of their babies in wooded areas, stove pipes, trash cans, and railway stations.[148] Such shocking acts made good copy for newspapers, as well as serving as morality lessons. Local newspapers were "important purveyor[s] of information and opinion on sexual crime," often playing up and sensationalizing the cases on the docket at the assize court. Though, as Dubinsky notes, the amount of attention paid to sex crimes in newspapers varied from place to place, turn-of-the-century reporters at the *Sentinel-Review* were the sort that "gave ample space to the crime, the investigation, and the trial and did not hesitate to create heroes and villains in the process."[149] Not surprisingly, the activities receiving the most coverage were those that provided readers with scandalous details. While Glasbeek warns that crime stories in early twentieth-century newspapers were generally "glib," "formulaic," and carefully chosen,[150] the cases often involved very private matters (such as lewdness or sexual activity), and publication in the local paper pushed these events to the forefront of community commentary. The amount of attention paid to "bad" females in the newspaper, the pejorative ways they were described, and the inclusion of other disreputable activities they were known to dabble in inevitably had social consequences. Often, the more unfortunate a woman's financial situation, the more harm was done to her reputation.

Parents may not have always turned their wayward daughters out, but neighbours and other members of the community often had little patience for disreputable behaviour, especially when it came to illicit or premarital sex. According to Peter Ward, "gossip there no doubt would be, and likely a woman's marriage prospects would be blackened as well."[151] Even if the case was being handled by the courts, local citizens still felt the need to be involved, as evidenced by how many enjoyed attending hearings and trials, especially those of higher profile cases. In this sense, the courthouse itself became a site of leisure. In 1895, a courtroom full of spectators gathered in Woodstock to hear a fifteen-year-old mixed-race girl describe her entire romantic history after her suitor, a young Black man named Thomas Marshall, was charged with seduction. Beatrice "Maud" Anderson, described by the *Sentinel-Review* as a "prepossessing mulatto,"[152] told the court how she and Marshall engaged in consensual sex outside her father's home. In her deposition, Anderson recounted the events that occurred while the couple was out enjoying some leisure time together: "The intercourse took place at night. I guess I was out walking with him he met me at our house and we went up town." She also noted that it "took place standing" and Marshall was the only man she had allowed to have intercourse with her.[153] Anderson admitted that she was now "in the family way" and though the couple wished to marry, they were forbidden to do so by her father, who disapproved of the match. When called as a witness, Marshall Anderson (a well-respected watchman in Woodstock) stated that prior to his daughter's relationship with the accused, he believed her to be of "pure character."[154] The jury rendered a verdict of guilty, but mercy was recommended and the sentence postponed. Though seduction cases were common in rural and small-town Ontario, the fact that the court-room was crowded with spectators suggests the interplay of race, age, and illicit sex served as a spectacle for the larger White population. Even though both Beatrice and her father called attention to her formerly "pure character," she was still deemed "fallen" by community members.[155]

Conclusion

When women and girls "acted out" and exhibited "bad behaviour" in rural areas and smaller towns like Dresden, Tillsonburg, and Elora, the criminal justice system was one of many regulatory bodies that censured leisure activities deemed suspect and in need of regulation. Parents, neighbours, and other community monitors also enforced middle-class standards of morality, respectability, and appropriateness that dictated how women should behave. Even the print media's strategy of public shaming without naming alerted readers to the fact that local women and girls were circumventing ideals of feminine decorum. The increased regulation of female activities and conduct shows the permeation of moral reform discourses into more remote locations, and the extent to which this influenced locals' intolerance of activities that allowed women to step outside the bounds of respectability and femininity.

While previous studies have made inroads toward debunking the myth that rural areas and small towns were morally upstanding and comparatively crime-free when judged against cities, this chapter has shown how women's and girls' engagement in so-called bad behaviour often occurred while pursuing different modes of leisure that straddled the line between reputable and disreputable. Indeed, moral panic and fears of deviancy *were* present in the countryside, as evidenced by the degree to which females were scrutinized. During the period examined here, parents, community members, and a surge of new town and municipal bylaws demonstrated greater interest in the social and sexual worlds of women and girls, often exposing the private areas of their lives and subjecting them to public examination.

Whether it was minor transgressions like stealing money for merry-go-round rides or private indiscretions involving consensual sex, the line between reputable and disreputable grew increasingly blurred as more options for leisure became available in these communities. Agreement over what constituted appropriate behaviour could vary depending on age, gender, class, ethnicity, religious devotion, and modes of regulation. The critique of Mrs. Tillson's "bad" behaviour by the Salvation Army "friend" is a reminder that any woman, even a member of an affluent family, was not exempt from the judgement of more evangelical neighbours. The occasional ways that ostensibly personal and private matters (such as sex work and alcoholism) entered public discourse provide a small window into the more intimate recreational activities of citizens, particularly women. Perhaps most importantly, their alleged involvement in criminal activities sheds some light on public opinion toward working-class women and girls whose leisure, social and sexual lives, and family dynamics are less visible in the historical record. When they "acted out," various forms of punishment were imposed, ranging from monetary fines to public shaming to rehabilitation in reformatories.

CONCLUSION

THROUGHOUT ONTARIO'S HISTORY, the social and cultural activities (or lack thereof) in small towns and their surrounding rural areas have provided fodder for critics who believe that life beyond city borders is boring, backward, and conservative. Today, rural Ontario continues to be plagued by such judgements, despite the endurance of established recreational opportunities, such as agricultural fairs and associations, travel clubs, choirs, and the Women's Institutes. A well-known treatise on this topic was published by Presbyterian minister John MacDougall in 1913 titled *Rural Life in Canada: Its Trend and Tasks*. Though his book focused primarily on rural areas, MacDougall argued that one of the most pressing "problems" in the countryside was that the "means of social life, in the ordinary acceptance of that term, are lacking."[1] While insufficient leisure offerings were one concern of rural critics, Ruth Sandwell notes that the "rural problem," historically, was also about needing "modernized and improved" ways of living, "in many of the same ways that applied to urban and industrial areas."[2] Rural depopulation was, undeniably, a reality in early twentieth-century Canada, but the extent to which out-migration was caused by anti-modernism and inadequate leisure pursuits was unfairly exaggerated by MacDougall and other naysayers. Historians of rural Canada have shown that desires to pursue post-secondary education and the mechanization of agricultural production, for example, had an enormous impact on young men's and women's decisions to leave small towns and farms. Though caution has been exercised throughout this book in using Dresden, Tillsonburg, and Elora as examples of rural and small-town Ontario as a whole, if their stories and trajectories are in any way similar to those of other communities, we can conclude that in these towns and beyond, options for leisure and amusement were actually increasing in scope and variety in the years approaching the First World War. This reality, then, stands in stark contrast to MacDougall's and other critics' concerns about the dearth of social opportunities in less populated areas.

Indeed, as early as 1875, the *Tillsonburg Observer* was boasting about the abundant options for recreation that were available; a brief note in the social column of the 26 November issue declared: "Plenty of amusement in Tilsonburg now. Tea meetings, concerts, and other things too numerous to mention."[3] Published thirty-eight years prior to MacDougall's *Rural Life in Canada*, this particular report suggests that citizens of Tillsonburg had no shortage of fun activities to participate in. The fact that a social column existed at that point meant that enough of the paper's readership was involved with or desired to know what was happening around town. What constituted "amusement" for residents of Tillsonburg was probably different from what it meant for others, but the publication of this brief note about the town's social offerings signified to anyone outside of Tillsonburg that its citizens were respectable, social, and enlightened people. When compared with the variety of leisure activities available at the outset of the First World War, the selection identified in 1875 is a mere drop in the bucket of what was to come. Though brief, this piece from the *Observer* points to the necessity of rethinking how leisure in rural and small-town Ontario has been misrepresented in both the past and present.

The "tea meetings, concerts, and other things too numerous to mention" that existed in Tillsonburg in 1875 were typical of the activities that could be found in most small southern Ontario towns at the time. It was common practice on a weeknight, for instance, for local citizens and those from the countryside to gather in town at a church or concert hall in support of a local charitable or religious cause, paying their small admission fee to listen to a musical performance or poetry recitation. At the conclusion of the entertainment, the patrons congregated around tables laden with snacks, tea, and coffee and then, vittles in hand, divided into smaller groups, typically separated by sex. Topics of conversation included the merit and quality of the past two hours' entertainment, news about crops and yields, anecdotes on child rearing, or a hushed tête-à-tête about a piece of local gossip. The guests then headed for home, usually around 10:00 p.m. or so, and retired to their beds. The women hosting the event remained to clean up plates, rearrange chairs and tables, and count the receipts before they, too, could go home and rest their weary bodies.[4]

Such a scenario, repeated across small-town Ontario in the late nineteenth century, is what social commentators and others bemoaned when they talked about "stereotypes of dour Protestant small-town life."[5] The supposition that most (if not all) small-town leisure activities occurred in and around churches was largely true in 1870s Dresden, Tillsonburg, and Elora, but it does not account for the trajectory that leisure took as the end of the century approached. As this study has argued, many women's social lives were multifaceted, diverse, and full of goings-on. Although the church and its ancillary activities remained a cornerstone of small-town life well into the twentieth century, many clergymen became promoters of "rational recreation" to keep parishioners connected to the church. As a result, offerings for leisure became more varied, complex, and secular. Available sources suggest that the middle- and upper-class women who complemented their church-based activities with secular ones found just as much (if not more) enjoyment in them.

In the years approaching the First World War, new and popular modes of leisure that historians often identify with industrialization, new transportation infrastructures, a growing consumer culture, and desires for self-improvement were not confined to cities, as this book has shown. City and country may have "travelled inseparably" in literature, newspapers, and social reform discourses, but they continued to be juxtaposed by some reformers and social critics: cities were extolled as "seats of government, learning, civilization, and commerce," while the countryside was "backward and unwashed."[6] In reality, literate middle- and upper-class women from Dresden, Tillsonburg, Elora and their surrounding rural areas were avid subscribers and readers of magazines and periodicals from near and far, so naturally their leisure activities began to mimic the fads developing elsewhere. In the late nineteenth century, cosmopolitan leisure habits had a noticeable trickle-down effect, as small-town women became eager followers and consumers of fashions, interior design trends, ideas for social clubs, and other modes of recreation that signified modernism and a willingness to engage in a broader culture of consumption and cosmopolitanism.

Not all activities, however, could be translated from the big city to small towns, which were constrained by finances, smaller populations, deficiencies in local transportation and communication systems, and ill-equipped buildings. At the same time, though, activities with roots in rural and farming communities, like fairs and exhibitions, were refashioned into spectacles that communicated modernity and progress to larger, more urbanized audiences. On a more localized level, rural inhabitants typically pursued formal leisure offerings in the service centre of the nearby small town, while town-dwellers also used the countryside for its wooded areas, waterways, and more diverse range of agrarian-focused clubs. When examining leisure, we see that the sharp cultural divergences that supposedly existed between "urban" and "rural" and "city" and "country" were far narrower than often believed.

Leisure, in many ways, acted as a bridge between rural and urban. Over time, railways, steamships, and bicycles became a tangible link between city, town, and country, and facilitated travel to different regions of Ontario. Clubs, societies, and associations that were branches of larger national organizations connected rural and small-town women with their city counterparts, especially when province-wide conferences were held. Mail-order catalogues brought the urban department store to country women unable to travel afar, and reading about or purchasing a variety of domestic goods allowed them to emulate urban, middle-class patterns of consumption and consumerism. When moving between regions, whether from town to city or vice versa, women sought modes of recreation that they could not find at home or were a new variation of activities they already enjoyed. As women pursued leisure activities to a greater degree, there was flow and movement between not only the countryside and small towns but also towns and cities.

The spaces and places around Dresden, Tillsonburg, and Elora are undeniably significant when thinking through the continuities and changes occurring in women's social lives. But the dynamics of spatial occupation cannot be understood without acknowledging that alterations to townscapes and green spaces were necessary to facilitate women's movement from the "private" to the "public" sphere. The young women careening down sidewalks on bicycles and the groups of adolescent girls enjoying matinee performances at the local opera house were partly there because town councils and proprietors of amusement halls had realized that females were an untapped financial resource. Especially, middle- and upper-class women and girls had more time and disposable wealth to spend on leisure. As a result, public spaces like concert halls, sidewalks, and waterways became more accessible and amenable to respectable, feminine tastes, thus prompting more women and girls to seek leisure outside the home.

While public spaces were being built or refurnished into socially acceptable venues for leisure, the home remained an important focal point of women's social lives. This reality was pragmatic, as most of women's daily responsibilities occurred in the home. In less affluent households, however, boundaries between labour and leisure were often fluid and indefinable, so women combined their work and play to maximize available social time together. When domestic servants and expensive labour-saving devices were unattainable, women shared their work to ensure that households continued to run smoothly. In public, members of religious, charitable, and benevolent organizations did much the same by organizing dinners, socials, and fundraisers that guaranteed that institutions like churches and libraries stayed open. Inevitably, the time they spent together in their own and others' homes forged important friendships, strengthened ties among family members, and prompted sociability beyond the task at hand.

Concurrently, notions of "work" and "play" and a growing awareness of the need to curtail idleness through modes of "rational recreation" resulted in a reordering of the ways that homes were arranged and occupied. Rooms with specific leisured purposes, like parlours, became a fixture among the middle and upper classes, though working-class women, too, used their limited means to carve out spaces designated for leisure. Even areas surrounding homes, like lawns and verandas, had important social functions when the weather cooperated. Beyond the structure of rooms, a wider variety of games, toys, books, and musical instruments increasingly found their way into domestic spaces. These goods could be acquired from local merchants or mail-order catalogues, and female consumers were targeted in their advertising campaigns. "Eaton's mail order was an especially powerful civilizing agent," historian Donica Belisle writes, because the company believed that "rural customers could impose order on uncivilized territories" when they bought its products.[7] Like their city counterparts, small-town women were swayed by the forces of consumerism and consumption. These gendered practices not only influenced how women lived, looked, and acted, they also affected the family because women "supervised most of the consumption taking place in their households."[8] Increasingly, material objects that suggested worldliness and geographic knowledge, like Turkish rugs and culinary delicacies, made their way into homes, though the women displaying or serving these curiosities typically had little to no first-hand knowledge of the lands and cultures they were purporting to represent.

A noticeable continuity in the ways that women pursued leisure in these towns concerns sport. Until just after the First World War, women, and to an extent the working class and people of colour, remained barred from professional and amateur sports teams and leagues, which were exclusively White and male. Sports such as baseball, football, and lacrosse, along with the concept of women competing against men, were off limits because of widespread beliefs about their ability to foster masculine qualities such as "physical courage, strength, stamina, will power, and self-control."[9] Concerns over feminine frailty and the masculinization of the female body were potent forces that contributed to keeping women on the sidelines. Small-town boosters in the late nineteenth century presented the successes of local sports teams as a reflection of the town's character, and women were considered incapable of withstanding the fierce competition that developed between rival communities. By the 1890s, some local sporting organizations that lacked the competitive atmosphere of professional teams, such as bicycle clubs, had begun inviting women to join their ranks. Anxieties around female cyclists and the increasingly heterosocial nature of physical activity, however, remind us that not all community members were comfortable with the idea of women occupying public spaces for the purposes of leisure.

Like cycling, lawn tennis had once been the preserve of upper-class male players, but the barriers that initially kept women away from participating were altered, ushering in a new era of the game. How and where tennis was played, however, confirms that class was integral in shaping women's options for physical activity. There are no indications that the Grasshopper Tennis Club was exclusively composed of elites, but founders Lillian Sinclair and Marguerite Sinclair had a backyard tennis court at their disposal, which greatly enhanced their ability to pursue the sport and manage the club. Middle-class women like Elora's Olive Snyder also played tennis (though on a more modest scale), but many of the new leisure activities that women began engaging in required money in the way of equipment, fees, or admission costs. Some leisure activities, then, did separate the classes, and excluded those who did not have the time, money, or knowledge with which to participate. While some working-class women and girls found ways around financial constraints, overall we know less about how they pursued "reputable" modes of leisure in Dresden, Tillsonburg, and Elora. Their absence, however, reinforces how much the middle and upper classes used leisure (and especially activities that cost money) to cultivate social selectiveness. The Tillsonburg Ladies' Travel Club, for instance, had no qualms about advertising itself as a "limited" organization and promoted its role as an arbiter of worldliness and sophistication. Several community-wide events and parties advertised themselves as open to the public, but admission fees and expectations regarding appearance undeniably prevented the working class from participating, creating a wedge between them and everyone else. Public entertainments and parties where ethnic and religious stereotypes were invoked can also be considered modes of leisure that cultivated exclusivity in the ways they "othered" non-White people and celebrated White, Anglo-Celtic, and Christian ideals and traditions.

Although as Nancy B. Bouchier reminds us, "no single community is representative of the province or nation," a microhistorical approach that examines how gender, leisure, culture, and class intersect "broadens the perspectives drawn from studies done on the national and provincial levels."[10] This book has endeavoured to use Dresden, Tillsonburg, and Elora as examples of how smaller communities underwent immense physical, political, social, cultural, economic, and religious transformations that affected the provisioning of leisure activities for all citizens, and women especially. While Dresden and Tillsonburg experienced measured population growth between 1870 and 1914, Elora shrank. Dresden, once a sizable community of formerly enslaved and mixed-race people, had become by 1914 a community of mostly White, Anglo-Celtic Protestants. All three communities evolved from Indigenous-occupied territories to a scattering of settlers and then bustling (albeit small) agro-industrial centres before 1914. The broader social dynamics occurring in each town unquestionably shaped the ways that their citizens pursued leisure. In Tillsonburg, for example, class divisions were more prominent thanks to a larger population and the presence of a recognized grouping of elites, so we see more women's leisure activities marked by social exclusion and cosmopolitanism compared to the other two towns. Though most of Dresden's earlier Black settlers had left by 1914, the importance of race is more pronounced there than in Tillsonburg and Elora, as evidenced by references to citizens' skin colour, prejudicial attitudes about the Black community, and White citizens' encroachment on the territory of Walpole Island First Nation. In Elora more so than in Dresden and Tillsonburg, the local landscape played a significant role in shaping outdoor recreational offerings in the town. The Elora Gorge and the river system brought countless day-trippers to the town and boosted the local economy. Over time, the refurbishment of the town's natural environment also provided locals with more options for recreation.

Within these three towns, however, more commonalities than differences have been revealed concerning the ways that local women pursued leisure. In all three communities much the same trajectory unfolded. In the 1870s and early 1880s, men and women tended to occupy separate social spaces, with men being afforded more freedom in the way of public socializing, while women's activities (like auxiliary membership) were generally confined to home and church. These opportunities were complemented by newer and more secular offerings in the late 1880s and 1890s (such as community-wide socials and dances), though many continued to be sex-specific. By the early 1900s and 1910s, formal and informal groupings of women remained popular, but heterosocial mixing had become more common as men and women sought more androgynous pastimes like moving picture shows, bicycle riding, and performances by amateur theatre groups. Throughout the period examined here, we also see the extent to which leisure served to regulate and censure women and girls, as parents, concerned community members, local governments, and the criminal justice system increasingly monitored disreputable behaviour. Some families struggled to offer "healthful" modes of recreation to children and adolescents; resultingly, leisure could slip from being reputable to disreputable very easily. The working-class women of these communities faced considerable scrutiny as they sought ways to have fun that were affordable and socially appropriate according to middle-class norms of respectability.

Though variations between towns certainly existed, the leisure activities of women in Dresden, Tillsonburg, and Elora likely mimicked those occurring elsewhere across Ontario, and even in the province's larger urban centres and cities to a degree. It is clear that women in the communities examined here had a wide-ranging, diverse, and complex set of options for leisure activities at their disposal by the First World War. This recognition complicates popular characterizations of late nineteenth- and early twentieth-century women's lives by offering some novel and important insights into small-town culture, specifically regarding relations between the sexes and tensions among the classes. Perhaps most importantly, the activities described here demonstrate that desires to engage in leisure and the spaces and places where such activities were pursued were increasingly coming under women's control by the late 1890s and early 1900s. Whereas in the 1870s and 1880s what constituted "suitable" masculine and feminine behaviour was socially constructed, by the early 1900s and 1910s more elite and middle-class women were demonstrating choice and agency in their leisure pursuits. The Elora Spinsters' Convention, for instance, was an opportunity for local women to engage in a dialogue about feminist and socio-political issues, albeit only in the "safe" space of a satirical fundraiser.

As events in Dresden, Tillsonburg, and Elora suggest, women's social lives underwent immense change in small-town Ontario, and a dichotomy slowly emerged about who should pursue leisure and how. By the early 1900s, newspapers were (largely) praising the virtues and activities of women-specific and mixed-sex clubs, societies, gatherings, and sporting organizations that promoted acceptable, feminine, and middle-class norms. But only thirty or so years earlier, in the *Tillsonburg Observer*'s short exposé, "How Very Lady-Like,"[11] the five young women caught spying on the men's literary association were ridiculed and mocked for daring to show curiosity about this new group. As this example demonstrates, between the late nineteenth and early twentieth centuries, popular perceptions about what "ladylike" meant were shifting. Women played an active role in this process by carving a space for themselves and their mutual interests, both in public and in private. It was a gradual and at times difficult undertaking, marred by detractors who questioned and condemned women who exhibited "indecent" behaviours like cycling, drinking, or gambling. Concerns that leisure might be detrimental to home, family, work, and community meant that turn-of-the-century women had to demonstrate that they could capably "do it all"—nurture a happy home life, earn a living (if necessary), embody respectability, act charitably, *and* engage in "appropriate" modes of leisure that supported their physical, intellectual, and emotional well-being.

ACKNOWLEDGEMENTS

T HE RESEARCH AND writing of this book took place on the ancestral lands of the Anishinaabeg, Attawandaron, and Haudenosaunee peoples in southern Ontario. As a descendant of settlers on those lands, I recognize and honour the Indigenous ancestors who stewarded that territory. I wish to thank those living there today for the privilege of residing, working, and pursuing play among them.

I did not know it at the time, but the inspiration for this book can be traced to the summer of 2003 when I was hired as a research assistant at Annandale National Historic Site (or, "Annandale House") in Tillsonburg, Ontario. One of the projects assigned to me by then curator Rita Corner was refiling and reorganizing the museum's documentary artifact collection. In doing so, I became acquainted with the fonds of the town's namesake, the Tillson family. I was surprised to find that the collection of newspaper clippings, letters, photographs, reminiscences, and other mementoes painted a very vivid picture of the family's female members. Until that point, my understanding of women's history in small-town Ontario was that it was subordinate to men's. Especially, the files highlighted the diverse social lives of the Tillson women, which motivated me to learn more about how other women in Tillsonburg and beyond were spending their free time in the later nineteenth and early twentieth centuries. Since then, I have maintained a close relationship with staff at Annandale House and have been buoyed by their enthusiasm for this work. Patricia Phelps's knowledge of Tillsonburg's history was exceptionally helpful during the research process and Jen Gibson went out of her way to provide me with dozens of photographs from the museum's collection. I cannot thank Rita Corner enough for giving me that initial research assistant job and teaching me the fundamentals of working in a historic house museum.

This work began as a doctoral dissertation completed at York University in Toronto, Ontario. My brilliant supervisor, Bettina Bradbury, was a constant source of intellectual support and inspiration. When I needed it, she always provided that necessary boost of confidence. Her compassion and willingness to open her home made my life as a commuting graduate student so much easier. During the writing process, committee members Craig Heron and Jennifer Stephen shared their expertise in Canadian history and pushed me to think differently about my sources. Linda Ambrose, Marcel Martel, and Eva C. Karpinski willingly participated in the dissertation defence and offered valuable suggestions for revisions. During my time in the history graduate program, financial support was provided by the Faculty of Graduate Studies, the Department of History, CUPE local 3903, and the United Empire Loyalists' Association of Canada (Toronto branch). Friends in my PhD reading group—Kristine Alexander, Stacey Alexopoulos, Jarett Henderson, Dan Horner, and Angela Rooke—read early iterations of some of this book's chapters and offered thoughtful suggestions for improvement. As a graduate student, I also benefited from the opportunity to present my research to members of the Rural History Roundtable at the University of Guelph. Roundtable convenor Cathy Wilson has become a cherished mentor over the years. Her transformative work on the history of rural Canadian communities and cultures pushes me to be a better historian every day.

Over the past fifteen years, I have had the pleasure of meeting many researchers, museum professionals, archivists, librarians, bloggers, and local historians who listened patiently while I described the project and helped me think through the dynamics of small-town life. At the County of Oxford Archives, archivists Mary Gladwin and Liz Dommasch were incredibly helpful when it came to suggesting and locating relevant sources. Historian Marie Carter was a wonderful resource concerning Dresden's history. Her work and the records available at the Dresden Archives certainly enriched this study. Professors Nina Reid-Maroney and Deirdre McCorkindale graciously answered questions and helped fill some gaps concerning Black history in southwestern Ontario. Historians Stacey Alexopoulos and Ian Mosby generously shared their knowledge of treaty history, which enhanced several areas of this book. I am also indebted to staff at the Archives of Ontario, Norwich District Museum and Archives, University of Guelph Archival & Special Collections, and the Wellington County Museum and Archives for all the assistance provided during the research process.

While preparing this book for publication, I had the pleasure of working with several fantastic people at the University of Manitoba Press. The process could not have been easier for a first-time author. Thank you to David Carr for sending that initial email back in 2013, indicating interest in my doctoral research, and to Glenn Bergen for supporting my proposal submission. Jill McConkey's unwavering kindness and thoughtfulness during manuscript revisions meant the world to me. Thank you, Jill, for believing in me and helping to see this through. In reviewing the manuscript, the anonymous readers and copy editor Maureen Epp were a tremendous help. Thanks, also, to Sarah Ens and Barbara Romanik for all they have done to bring this book to life.

I am incredibly lucky to have the steadfast support of my parents, Albert and Debbie Beausaert, who always nurtured my love of local history. Because of them, I had the privilege of growing up surrounded by farmland in Norfolk County, which inspired me to tell the stories of other rural and small-town people. Thank you for teaching me the importance of hard work and perseverance. I tried to carry those lessons with me through this process.

For many years and throughout various iterations of this work, my husband Rob Miller has been a tireless source of positivity and encouragement. Thank you, Rob, for helping me navigate the ups and downs of teaching, research, and publishing. This would not have been possible without your patience, technological know-how, and willingness to talk through the writing roadblocks. Everything you did made this book stronger.

In 2018, our world was turned upside down when our son Bentley unexpectedly joined us fifteen weeks before his due date. Bentley, being your mommy has been my greatest challenge and greatest joy. Despite a rough start and uncertain prognosis, you have defied the odds. Watching you navigate the challenges of being micropremature has motivated me to see this project through to the end. The world needs more of your joyful spirit and sweet nature.

This book is dedicated to Rob and Bentley, the two loves of my life.

NOTES

Introduction

1   University of Guelph, Archival & Special Collections (hereafter UGASC), s0131b25, Olive Anderson Snyder, *Little Towns* (n.p., 1900), unpaginated.

2   UGASC, Marston-Archibald Collection, XR1 MS A371, "Photographs, genealogy, Olive Snyder poetry," newspaper article (date and name unknown).

3   Jane H. Hunter, "Inscribing the Self in the Heart of the Family: Diaries and Girlhood in Late-Victorian America," *American Quarterly* 44, no. 1 (March 1992): 52.

4   UGASC, s0131b25, Olive Anderson Snyder, *Little Towns* (n.p., 1900), unpaginated.

5   Paula M. Nelson, "'Do Everything'—Women in Small Prairie Towns, 1870–1920," *Journal of the West* 36 (October 1997): 52.

6   Keith Walden, *Becoming Modern in Toronto: The Industrial Exhibition and the Shaping of a Late Victorian Culture* (Toronto: University of Toronto Press, 1997), 333.

7   David B. Danbom, *Born in the Country: A History of Rural America*, 2nd ed. (Baltimore: Johns Hopkins University Press, 2006); Janet Galligani Casey, *A New Heartland: Women, Modernity, and the Agrarian Ideal in America* (Oxford: Oxford University Press, 2009); Ronald R. Kline, *Consumers in the Country: Technology and Social Change in Rural America* (Baltimore: Johns Hopkins University Press, 2000); Thomas J. Schlereth, "Country Stores, County Fairs, and Mail-Order Catalogues: Consumption in Rural America," in *Consuming Visions: Accumulation and Display of Goods in America, 1880–1920*, ed. Simon J. Bronner (New York: W.W. Norton, 1989), 339–75.

8   Kline, *Consumers in the Country*, 7–8.

9   Walden, *Becoming Modern in Toronto*, 334.

10   Lynne Marks, *Revivals and Roller Rinks: Religion, Leisure, and Identity in Late-Nineteenth-Century Small-Town Ontario* (Toronto: University of Toronto Press, 1996), 4.

11   Dresden was initially part of Kent County but after it was dissolved in 1998, its towns and townships were amalgamated into the municipality of Chatham-Kent.

12   These are the modern-day counties or municipalities that Dresden, Tillsonburg, and Elora are currently part of.

13   See Joy Parr, *The Gender of Breadwinners: Women, Men and Change in Two Industrial Towns, 1880–1950* (Toronto: University of Toronto Press, 1990).

14   Hugh Cunningham, *Leisure in the Industrial Revolution: 1780–1880* (London: Croom Helm, 1980), 140.

15   See, for example, Julia Roberts, *In Mixed Company: Taverns and Public Life in Upper Canada* (Vancouver: University of British Columbia Press, 2009); Catharine Anne Wilson, "Reciprocal Work Bees and the Meaning of Neighbourhood," *Canadian Historical Review* 82, no. 3 (September 2001): 431–64; Catharine Anne Wilson, *Being Neighbours: Cooperative Work and Rural Culture, 1830–1960* (Montreal and Kingston: McGill-Queen's University Press, 2022); Colin D. Howell, *Blood, Sweat, and Cheers: Sport and the Making of Modern Canada* (Toronto: University of Toronto Press, 2001).

16   See, for example, Françoise Noel, *Family and Community Life in Northeastern Ontario: The Interwar Years* (Montreal and Kingston: McGill-Queen's University Press, 2009); Cynthia Comacchio, *The Dominion of Youth: Adolescence and the Making of Modern Canada, 1920–1950* (Waterloo, ON: Wilfrid Laurier University Press, 2008); Kyle Andrew Rich, Larena Hoeber, and Anne Weisgerber, "The Battle of Little Big Puck: Narratives of Community, Sport, and Relationships in Rural Canada," *Journal of Rural and Community Development* 15, no. 3 (2020): 45–64; and Carly Adams and Darren J. Aoki, "'Hey, Why Don't We Have a Bonspiel?' Narrating Postwar Japanese Canadian Experiences in Southern Alberta through Oral Histories of Curling," *International Journal of the History of Sport* 37, no. 16 (2020): 1715–33.

17   Donald G. Wetherell and Irene Kmet, *Useful Pleasures: The Shaping of Leisure in Alberta, 1896–1945* (Regina: Canadian Plains Research Center, 1990), xxiii.

18   Quote from Gary S. Cross, *A Social History of Leisure since 1600* (State College, PA: Venture Publishing, 1990), 2. See also Cunningham, *Leisure in the Industrial Revolution*; Peter Bailey, "'A Mingled Mass of Perfectly Legitimate Pleasures': The Victorian Middle Class and the Problem of Leisure," *Victorian Studies* 21, no. 1 (Autumn 1977): 7–28; Peter Bailey, *Leisure and Class in Victorian England* (London: Methuen, 1987); Peter Bailey, *Popular Culture and Performance in the Victorian City* (Cambridge: Cambridge University Press, 1998); Alan Delgado, *Victorian Entertainment* (Newton Abbot, UK: David and Charles, 1971); Roy Rosenzweig, *Eight Hours for What We Will: Workers and Leisure in an Industrial City, 1870–1920* (Cambridge: Cambridge University Press, 1983); James Walvin, *Leisure and Society, 1830–1950* (London: Longman, 1978).

19   See, for example, Sharon Anne Cook, *"Through Sunshine and Shadow": The Woman's Christian Temperance Union, Evangelicalism, and Reform in Ontario, 1874–1930* (Montreal and Kingston: McGill-Queen's University Press, 1995); Wendy Mitchinson, "Aspects of Reform: Four Women's Organizations in Nineteenth-Century Canada" (PhD diss., York University, 1976); Katie Pickles, *Female Imperialism and National Identity: Imperial Order Daughters of the Empire* (Manchester: Manchester University Press, 2002; distributed exclusively

in the USA by Palgrave); Carmen Nielson Varty, "'A Career in Christian Charity': Women's Benevolence and the Public Sphere in a Mid-Nineteenth-Century Canadian City," *Women's History Review* 14, no. 2 (2005): 243–64; Carmen Nielson Varty, "The City and the Ladies: Politics, Religion, and Female Benevolence in Mid-Nineteenth-Century Hamilton, Canada West," *Journal of Canadian Studies* 38, no. 2 (Spring 2004): 151–71; Marilyn Färdig Whiteley, "'Doing Just About What They Please': Ladies' Aids in Ontario Methodism," *Ontario History* 83, no. 4 (December 1990): 289–304.

20   See Cross, *A Social History of Leisure since 1600.*

21   James Opp and John C. Walsh, eds., *Home, Work, and Play: Situating Canadian Social History, 1840–1980* (Don Mills, ON: Oxford University Press, 2006), 241.

22   Walvin, *Leisure and Society*, viii.

23   Robert J. Lake, "Social Class, Etiquette and Behavioural Restraint in British Lawn Tennis, 1870–1939," *International Journal of the History of Sport* 28, no. 6 (2011): 878.

24   M. Ann Hall, *The Girl and the Game: A History of Women's Sport in Canada*, 2nd ed. (Toronto: University of Toronto Press, 2016), xix.

25   Ruth Sandwell, "Notes toward a History of Rural Canada, 1870–1940," in *Social Transformation in Rural Canada: Community, Cultures, and Collective Action*, ed. John R. Parkins and Maureen G. Reed (Vancouver: University of British Columbia Press, 2013), 23.

26   Stephen Thorning, *The Model Village and the Struggle for Success: A History of Elora, Ontario* (Fergus, ON: Wellington County Historical Society, 2023), 205–6.

27   Historian Alison Norman, for instance, notes that though there were branches of clubs formed specifically for Haudenosaunee women on the Six Nations of the Grand River reserve, some chose to join the reform-minded charity and voluntary associations run by local non-Indigenous women. See Norman, "Race, Gender and Colonialism: Public Life among the Six Nations of Grand River, 1899–1939" (PhD diss., Ontario Institute for Studies in Education, University of Toronto, 2010), 253.

28   Margaret Kechnie, *Organizing Rural Women: The Federated Women's Institutes of Ontario, 1897–1919* (Montreal and Kingston: McGill-Queen's University Press, 2003), 10. For a more in-depth discussion of the problem of defining rural, see R.W. Sandwell, introduction to *Canada's Rural Majority: Households, Environments, and Economies, 1870–1940* (Toronto: University of Toronto Press, 2016), 3–28.

29   W.H. Graham, *Greenbank: Country Matters in 19th Century Ontario* (Peterborough, ON: Broadview Press, 1988), 5.

30   Marguerite Van Die examines mid-nineteenth-century Brantford and the various ways women exercised their piety in public, such as overseeing Sunday schools, taking care of and raising money for church buildings, and the moral surveillance

of disreputable behaviours; see Van Die, "Revisiting 'Separate Spheres': Women, Religion, and the Family in Mid-Victorian Brantford, Ontario," in *Households of Faith: Family, Gender, and Community in Canada, 1760–1969*, ed. Nancy Christie (Montreal and Kingston: McGill-Queen's University Press), 234–63; quote from p. 256.

31 See, for example, Dale Barbour, *Undressed Toronto: From the Swimming Hole to Sunnyside, How a City Learned to Love the Beach, 1850–1935* (Winnipeg: University of Manitoba Press, 2021).

32 Deirdre McCorkindale, "Black Education: The Complexity of Segregation in Kent County's Nineteenth-Century Schools," in *Unsettling the Great White North: Black Canadian History*, eds. Michele A. Johnson and Funké Aladejebi (Toronto: University of Toronto Press, 2022), 335.

33 Dresden Archives (hereafter DA), Dresden Area Schools; Nina Reid-Maroney, *The Reverend Jennie Johnson and African Canadian History, 1868–1967* (Rochester, NY: University of Rochester Press, 2013), 43.

34 The diary entry is quoted in Reid-Maroney, *The Reverend Jennie Johnson*, 46.

35 "Base Ball and a Baser Umpire," *Dresden Times*, 13 September 1888, 4.

36 See Ron W. Shaw, *London Ontario's Unrepentant Confederates, the Ku Klux Klan and a Rendition on Wellington Street* (Carleton Place, ON: Global Heritage Press, 2018).

37 "Dresden and Racial Discrimination," Canada's Human Rights History, accessed 25 January 2024, https://historyofrights.ca/encyclopaedia/main-events/dresden-racial-discrimination/.

38 Donald G. Wetherell and Irene R.A. Kmet, *Town Life: Main Street and the Evolution of Small Town Alberta, 1880–1947* (Edmonton: University of Alberta Press and Alberta Community Development, 1995), 69.

39 As George S. Hage similarly found when examining newspapers in Minnesota, by the later nineteenth century, "sports coverage had staked its claim to newspaper space, and that claim could only grow more insistent in the years ahead." See Hage, "Games People Played: Sports in Minnesota Daily Newspapers 1860–1890," *Minnesota History* 47, no. 8 (Winter 1981): 328.

40 Paul Voisey, *High River and the Times: An Alberta Community and Its Weekly Newspaper, 1905–1966* (Edmonton: University of Alberta Press, 2004), xxviii.

41 Hereafter it will be referred to as the *Farmer's Advocate* or *Advocate*.

42 Marks, *Revivals and Roller Rinks*, 20.

43 Wilson, *Being Neighbours*, 10.

44 J.I. Little, *Reading the Diaries of Henry Trent: The Everyday Life of a Canadian Englishman, 1842–1898* (Montreal and Kingston: McGill-Queen's University Press, 2021), 4.

45 Gayle R. Davis, "Women's Frontier Diaries: Writing for Good Reason," *Women's Studies: An Inter-Disciplinary Journal* 14, no. 1 (1987): 8.

46 Marilyn Ferris Motz, "Folk Expression of Time and Place: 19th-Century Midwestern Rural Diaries," *Journal of American Folklore* 100, no. 396 (April–June 1987): 133.

Chapter 1. Situating the Small Town

1   Peter Baskerville, *Sites of Power: A Concise History of Ontario* (Don Mills, ON: Oxford University Press, 2005), 55.

2   This number is for the Attawandaron, Wendat, and Tionontati people. See Bruce G. Trigger, "The Original Iroquoians: Huron, Petun, and Neutral," in *Aboriginal Ontario: Historical Perspectives on the First Nations*, ed. Edward S. Rogers and Donald B. Smith (Toronto: Dundurn Press, 1994), 41.

3   Baskerville, *Sites of Power*, 58.

4   John McCallum, *Unequal Beginnings: Agriculture and Economic Development in Quebec and Ontario until 1870* (Toronto: University of Toronto Press, 1980), 3.

5   Library and Archives Canada (hereafter LAC), Census of Canada, 1871, accessed 22 September 2022, https://www.bac-lac.gc.ca/eng/census/1871/Pages/about-census.aspx.

6   McCallum, *Unequal Beginnings*, 55.

7   Baskerville, *Sites of Power*, 68. "British Isles" refers to England, Scotland, and Wales.

8   Cecilia Morgan, *Building Better Britains? Settler Societies in the British World, 1783–1920* (Toronto: University of Toronto Press and the Canadian Historical Association, 2017), 40.

9   David Gagan, *Hopeful Travellers: Families, Land, and Social Change in Mid-Victorian Peel County, Canada West* (Toronto: University of Toronto Press, 1981), 12.

10   Lynne Marks, *Revivals and Roller Rinks: Religion, Leisure, and Identity in Late-Nineteenth-Century Small-Town Ontario* (Toronto: University of Toronto Press, 1996), 16. Elora's population was slightly below at 1,304.

11   Nancy B. Bouchier, *For the Love of the Game: Amateur Sport in Small-Town Ontario, 1838–1895* (Montreal and Kingston: McGill-Queen's University Press, 2003), 18.

12   Elizabeth Jane Errington, *Wives and Mothers, School Mistresses and Scullery Maids: Working Women in Upper Canada, 1790–1840* (Montreal and Kingston: McGill-Queen's University Press, 1995), 9.

13   Andrew C. Holman, *A Sense of Their Duty: Middle-Class Formation in Victorian Ontario Towns* (Montreal and Kingston: McGill-Queen's University Press, 2000), 8.

14   Gilbert A. Stelter, "Combining Town and Country Planning in Upper Canada: William Gilkison and the Founding of Elora," in *The Country Town in Rural Ontario's Past: Proceedings of the Sixth Annual Agricultural History of Ontario Seminar, October 31, 1981*, ed. A.A. Brookes (Guelph, ON: University School of Part-time Studies and Continuing Education, University of Guelph, 1981), 1.

15   See Errington, *Wives and Mothers*, 13.

16   Statistics Canada, Census Profile, 2016 Census, Dresden https://www12.statcan.gc.ca/census-recensement/2016/dp-pd/prof/details/page.

cfm?Lang=E&Geo1=POPC&Code1=0238&Geo2=PR&Code2=35&Search-Text=Dresden&SearchType=Begins&SearchPR=01&B1=All&GeoLevel=PR&GeoCode=0238&TABID=1&type=0.

17   "Explore Dresden," Downtown Dresden Business Improvement Area (B.I.A) and Dresden Community Development Association, accessed 25 January 2024, http://www.dresden.ca.

18   Government of Ontario—First Nations, Inuit, and Métis, "Map of Ontario Treaties and Reserves," accessed 25 January 2024, https://www.ontario.ca/page/map-ontario-treaties-and-reserves.; see also Daniel Palmer, "The McKee Treaty of 1790: British-Aboriginal Diplomacy in the Great Lakes" (PhD diss., University of Saskatchewan, 2017), https://harvest.usask.ca/server/api/core/bitstreams/0d8047b0-baa5-4baf-b4e8-5f4621b66488/content.

19   The original mandate of the British-American Institute included educating "Indians." Local historians note that Indigenous people attended religious campground meetings in the Dresden area into the 1830s. See Marie Carter and Jeffrey Carter, *Stepping Back in Time: Along the Trillium Trail in Dresden* (Dresden, ON: Catherine McVean Chapter IODE, 2003), 14–15.

20   Ontario Heritage Trust Plaque, "The Founding of Dresden," accessed 25 January 2024, https://www.heritagetrust.on.ca/plaques/founding-of-dresden. Local historians Robert Brandon and Helen Burns refer to Jared Lindsley as "Gerald" and "Gerard" Lindsley; see Brandon, *The History of Dresden* (Dresden, ON: Dresden Centennial Committee, 1982); and DA, 2021.88, Helen Burns Papers, Handwritten, "Dresden's Early Years."

21   DA, 2021.88, Helen Burns Papers, Handwritten, "Dresden's Early Years."

22   Carter and Carter, *Stepping Back in Time*, 16. The hesitation to recognize Willoughby and Harris as founders may be tied to their Black American ancestry.

23   For more, see Carter and Carter, *Stepping Back in Time*, 24.

24   The origins of the name Dawn Township have not been uncovered, but "Dawn" may have signified freedom and liberty for the free and enslaved Black people who settled in the area.

25   Harriet Beecher Stowe, *Uncle Tom's Cabin; or, Life among the Lowly* (Boston: John P. Jewett; Cleveland: Jewett, Proctor & Worthington, 1852). *Uncle Tom's Cabin* was the second best-selling book of the nineteenth century, after the Bible.

26   Brandon, *The History of Dresden*, 28.

27   See Jacqueline Tobin, with Hettie Jones, *From Midnight to Dawn: The Last Tracks of the Underground Railroad* (New York: Doubleday, 2007), 31.

28   Carter and Carter, *Stepping Back in Time*, 35.

29   Brandon, *The History of Dresden*, 20.

30   Conversation between Marie Carter and the author, August 2022.

31   Carter and Carter, *Stepping Back in Time*, 38.

32   Ibid.

33 Michael Wayne, "The Black Population of Canada West on the Eve of the American Civil War: A Reassessment Based on the Manuscript Census of 1861," *Histoire sociale/Social History* 28, no. 56 (1995): 477.

34 Carter and Carter, *Stepping Back in Time*, 42.

35 For more on Whipper's businesses and land ownership, see Marie Carter, "William Whipper's *Lands along the Sydenham*," in *The Promised Land: History and Historiography of the Black Experience in Chatham-Kent's Settlements and Beyond*, ed. Boulou Ebanda de B'béri, Nina Reid-Maroney, and Handle Kashope Wright (Toronto: University of Toronto Press, 2014), 73–90.

36 Brandon, *The History of Dresden*, 29.

37 Donald Wetherell, "Making New Identities: Alberta Small Towns Confront the City, 1900–1950," *Journal of Canadian Studies* 39, no. 1 (Winter 2005): 181.

38 Carter and Carter, *Stepping Back in Time*, 33.

39 Ibid., 66.

40 *Province of Ontario Gazetteer and Directory, Including the City of Montreal, P.Q., 1895* (Toronto: Might Directory Co., 1895), 249.

41 Ibid.

42 *Fifth Census of Canada, 1911*, Vol. I (Ottawa: C.H. Parmelee, 1913), 78.

43 *Fifth Census of Canada, 1911*, Vol. II (Ottawa: C.H. Parmelee, 1913), 220–21.

44 Some sources refer to her as "Mrs. White."

45 Brandon, *The History of Dresden*, 30.

46 Ibid., 32.

47 Statistics Canada, Census Profile, 2016 Census, Tillsonburg, Ontario, accessed 25 January 2024, https://www12.statcan.gc.ca/census-recensement/2016/dp-pd/prof/details/Page.cfm?Lang=E&Geo1=CSD&Code1=3532004&Geo2=PR&Code2=35&SearchText=tillsonburg&SearchType=Begins&SearchPR=01&B1=All&type=0.

48 Stompin' Tom Connors, "Tillsonburg," *My Stompin' Grounds*, © 1971, Boot Records, BOS 7103.

49 Edward Dunsworth, *Harvesting Labour: Tobacco and the Global Making of Canada's Agricultural Workforce* (Montreal and Kingston: McGill-Queen's University Press, 2022), 29.

50 Government of Ontario—First Nations, Inuit, and Métis, "Map of Ontario Treaties and Reserves."

51 Ellen H. Eff, *Hamlet on the Otter: A Historical Sketch of Tillsonburg, Its First Hundred Years, 1815–1915* (Tillsonburg, ON: News Printing, 1963). According to local historian Ellen H. Eff, "the mistake of spelling 'TILLSONBURG' with one 'L' was made when drafting the Act of Incorporation. Somebody made the fatal mistake and there was considerable indignation among the town citizens when the error was discovered, and while it was agreed that 'something must be done about it,' nobody did anything to rectify the error until 1902 when several public spirited citizens petitioned the Assembly to restore the name to its correct spelling in consideration of the many valuable and enduring services rendered by the TILLSON family." For the purposes of consistency, the proper spelling of

Tillsonburg with two l's has been used throughout except when quoting primary sources.

52 John Irwin Cooper, "George Tillson," *Dictionary of Canadian Biography Online, 1861–1870*, vol. 9, *1861–1870*, accessed 25 January 2024, http://www.biographi.ca/009004-119.01-e.php?&id_nbr=4746.

53 Matthew G. Scholtz and Anna M. Bailey, *Tillsonburg Diary: A Chronological History, 1824–1994* (Tillsonburg, ON: Tillsonburg District Chamber of Commerce, 1995), 1.

54 Bruce Richard, "Edwin Delevan Tillson," *Dictionary of Canadian Biography Online*, vol. 13, *1901–1910*, accessed 11 February 2009, http://www.biographi.ca/009004-119.01-e.php?&id_nbr=7106; Scholtz and Bailey, *Tillsonburg Diary*, 3. Tillson's foray into oat milling was prompted by the digestive issues he suffered after a bout of typhoid fever. He desired a palatable breakfast cereal with healthful properties, and the Tillson Pan-Dried Oats product was created.

55 Gagan, *Hopeful Travellers*, 7.

56 "Tilsonburg. A Brief Business Review of Our Enterprising Town," *Tillsonburg Liberal*, 3 March 1887, 2.

57 *Ontario Gazetteer and Business Directory 1884–5* (Toronto: R.L. Polk and Co., 1884), 875–76.

58 Donald G. Wetherell and Irene R.A. Kmet, *Town Life: Main Street and the Evolution of Small Town Alberta, 1880–1947* (Edmonton: University of Alberta Press and Alberta Community Development, 1995), 159.

59 *Province of Ontario Gazetteer and Directory*, 753.

60 *Fifth Census of Canada, 1911*, Vol. I (Ottawa: C.H. Parmelee, 1913), 85.

61 "Tilsonburg. A Brief Business Review of Our Enterprising Town," *Tillsonburg Liberal*, 3 March 1887, 2.

62 "Elora's Summer Resort," *Elora Lightning Express*, 29 August 1878, 2.

63 In the most recent 2016 census, Elora was enumerated as part of Centre Wellington township. Figures compiled by the County of Wellington note that the towns of Elora and Salem had a combined population of 7,565 in mid-2016. See Wellington County, Wellington County 2016 Population Estimates, accessed 25 January 2024, https://www.wellington.ca/en/resident-services/resources/Planning/Population-Housing-Employment/Mid-2016-Population-And-Households.pdf.

64 Kenneth Westhues and Peter R. Sinclair, *Village in Crisis* (Toronto: Holt, Rinehart and Winston of Canada, 1974), 15–16.

65 John Robert Connon, *The Early History of Elora, Ontario and Vicinity*, 2nd rev. printing, reissued with introduction by Gerald Noonan (Waterloo, ON: Wilfrid Laurier University Press, 1975), 46.

66 Ibid., 58.

67 Stelter, "Combining Town and Country Planning in Upper Canada," 8, 11.

68   Nina Perkins Chapple, *A Heritage of Stone: Buildings of the Niagara Peninsula, Fergus and Elora, Guelph, Region of Waterloo, Cambridge, Paris, Ancaster-Dundas-Flamborough, Hamilton and St. Marys* (Toronto: J. Lorimer, 2006), 29.

69   Elizabeth Waterston and Douglas Hoffman, eds., *On Middle Ground: Landscape and Life in Wellington County, 1841–1891* (Guelph, ON: University of Guelph, 1974), 5.

70   Wellington County Museum and Archives (hereafter WCMA), A1982.13, Elora Women's Institute Tweedsmuir History, 61.

71   Ibid.

72   UGASC, XR1 MS A192067, Elora Women's Institute Tweedsmuir History.

73   Roberta Allan, *History of Elora* (Elora, ON: The Institute, 1982), 7.

74   UGASC, Marston-Archibald Collection, XR1 MS A371, Photographs, genealogy, Olive Snyder poetry, Olive Anderson Snyder – Poetry, "A Saga of Elora."

75   See Michelle Filice, "Haldimand Proclamation," *Canadian Encyclopedia*, accessed 25 January 2024, https://www.thecanadianencyclopedia.ca/en/article/haldimand-proclamation. For more, see Susan M. Hill, *The Clay We Are Made Of: Haudenosaunee Land Tenure on the Grand River* (Winnipeg: University of Manitoba Press, 2017).

76   Westhues and Sinclair, *Village in Crisis*, 6, 17.

77   *Lovell's Province of Ontario Directory for 1871* (Montreal: John Lovell, 1871), 361.

78   Ibid., 344.

79   Ibid., 806.

80   "The City of the Rocks. Elora Is One of the Most Picturesque Spots in the Dominion," *Guelph Herald*, Special Illustrated Edition, December 1895, 18.

81   Westhues and Sinclair, *Village in Crisis*, 16.

82   Stelter, "Combining Town and Country Planning in Upper Canada," 11.

83   *Census of Canada, 1880–81*, Vol. I (Ottawa: Maclean, Roger, and Co., 1882), 212–13.

84   Westhues and Sinclair, *Village in Crisis*, 22–23.

85   In 1873, Elora was home to four different newspapers that were formed by competing politicians hoping to influence the electorate. The phenomenon was short-lived, however, because the town was back to just one newspaper by 1877. See Stephen Thorning, "Elora Once Had Four Newspapers Serving 1,600 People," *Elora Sentinel*, 13 November 1990, 6.

86   *Province of Ontario Gazetteer and Directory*, 271.

87   Bouchier, *For the Love of the Game*, 28.

88   *Census of Canada, 1880-81*, Vol. I, 79.

89   Total populations were found in the federal censuses conducted between 1871 and 1911.

90   For similar examples, see McCallum, *Unequal Beginnings*, 65. Ruth Sandwell also discusses the decline of industries and populations in rural Ontario; see Sandwell,

Canada's Rural Majority: Households, Environments, and Economies, 1870–1940 (Toronto: University of Toronto Press, 2016).

91   Jacob Spelt, *The Urban Development in South-Central Ontario* (Assen, Netherlands: Van Gorcum, 1955), 157.

92   *First Report of the Bureau of Labor of the Province of Ontario for the Year Ending December 31st 1900* (Toronto: L.K. Cameron, 1901), 18.

93   *Fifth Census of Canada, 1911*, Vol. I, 94.

94   Westhues and Sinclair, *Village in Crisis*, 21.

95   According to the Ontario Bureau of Labor's Report from 1902, Dresden was home to a branch of the American Federation of Labor. No unions are listed in Tillsonburg and Elora in the early 1900s. Information about Dresden found in *Third Report of the Bureau of Labor for the Year Ending December 31st 1902* (Toronto: L.K. Cameron, 1903), 62.

96   Linda Ambrose, "Cartoons and Commissions: Advice to Junior Farmers in Postwar Ontario," in *People, Places, and Times: Readings in Canadian Social History*, vol. 2, *Post-Confederation*, ed. Cynthia R. Comacchio and Elizabeth Jane Errington (Toronto: Thomson Nelson, 2006), 279.

97   "The Lower Classes," *Rural Canadian* 1, no. 3 (December 29, 1881): 13.

98   Errington, *Wives and Mothers*, 15

99   Paul Voisey, *Vulcan: The Making of a Prairie Community* (Toronto: University of Toronto Press, 1988), 215.

100 Holman, *A Sense of Their Duty*, 7.

101 LAC, Census of Canada, 1911, Schedule No. 1, Ontario, Centre Wellington, Elora Village, accessed 17 July 2023, http://central.bac-lac.gc.ca/.redirect?app= census&id=36831276&lang=eng.

102 "Instructions to Officers," 1901 Census of Canada, accessed 25 January 2024, https://www.nappdata.org/napp/resources/enum_materials_pdf/enum_ instruct_ca1901a.pdf.

103 Voisey, *Vulcan*, 204.

104 Kenneth M. Sylvester, "Household Composition and Canada's Rural Capitalism: The Extent of Rural Labor Markets in 1901," *Journal of Family History* 26, no. 2 (April 2001): 290.

105 For more on seasonality and how it contributed to occupational pluralism, see Peter Baskerville and Eric W. Sager, *Unwilling Idlers: The Urban Unemployed and Their Families in Late Victorian Canada* (Toronto: University of Toronto Press, 1998), 83–85.

106 Ruth Sandwell discusses a similar practice occurring on Salt Spring Island, British Columbia; see Sandwell, *Contesting Rural Space: Land Policies and the Practice of Resettlement on Salt Spring Island, 1859–1891* (Montreal and Kingston: McGill-Queen's University Press, 2005), 128.

107 Sylvester, "Household Composition and Canada's Rural Capitalism," 292.

108   See Glenda Strachan, Ellen Jordan, and Hilary Carey, "Women's Work in a Rural Community: Dungog and the Upper Williams Valley, 1880–1900," *Labour History* 78 (May 2000): 47–50.

109   *Province of Ontario Gazetteer and Directory*, 271.

110   LAC, Census of Canada, 1901, Schedule No. 1, Ontario, Centre Wellington, Elora Village, accessed 17 July 2023, https://recherche-collection-search.bac-lac.gc.ca/eng/home/record?app=census&IdNumber=36844513.

111   Leo Johnson, "The Political Economy of Ontario Women in the Nineteenth Century," in *Women at Work: Ontario, 1850–1930*, ed. Janice Acton, Penny Goldsmith, and Bonnie Shepard (Toronto: Canadian Women's Educational Press, 1974), 14.

112   Sherri Pettit, *The Van Norman Genealogy: Descendants of Joseph and Elizabeth (Wybern) Van Norman, 1772–1996* (n.p., 1996), 143–44.

113   "Our First Citizen 'At Rest,'" *Tillsonburg Liberal*, 6 February 1902, 1.

114   "A Beautiful Home," *Tillsonburg Observer*, 6 May 1887, 1.

115   "Improvements in Tilsonburg," *Tillsonburg Observer*, 17 June 1880, 5.

116   Annandale National Historic Site (hereafter ANHS), Documentary Artifact Collection, Laurel's Booklets, *E.D. & Mary Ann* original drafts file, letter from Margaret D. Jansen, great-granddaughter of E.D. and Mary Ann, to Laurel Beechey, dated 5 February 1986; ANHS, Documentary Artifact Collection, Catherine Marilla Tillson file, letter from Margaret Draper Jansen to Laurel Beechey, 20 June 1986.

117   "Improvements in Tilsonburg," *Tillsonburg Observer*, 17 June 1880, 5.

118   Carter and Carter, *Stepping Back in Time*, 80.

119   Ibid.

120   Marie Carter, *Building Heritage: A Guide to the Historical Houses of Dresden, Ontario* (Chatham, ON: Chamberlain/Mercury Printing, 2004), unpaginated.

121   Holman, *A Sense of Their Duty*, 7.

122   Ibid., 10.

123   E.P. Thompson, *The Making of the English Working Class* (London: Gollancz, 1963).

124   Marks, *Revivals and Roller Rinks*, 4.

125   Holman, *A Sense of Their Duty*, 14.

126   Waller told interviewer Laurel Beechey she was born in 1888, but that date is inconsistent with data found in the census. According to various censuses, Alice Agnes Waller was born in 1880 in Norwich. See LAC, Census of Canada, 1901, Schedule No. 1, Ontario, Norfolk North, Tilsonburg, accessed 17 July 2023, https://recherche-collection-search.bac-lac.gc.ca/eng/home/record?app=census&IdNumber=37026368.

127   ANHS, Documentary Artifact Collection, Laurel's Booklets, *E.D. & Mary Ann* original drafts file.

128   See Bert Newman, *Reminiscences about Tillsonburg*, ed. Dave Stover (Tillsonburg, ON, 1986), 27.

129 Bert Newman, *Once Upon a Time: Further Reminiscences about Tillsonburg*, ed. Dave Stover (Tillsonburg, ON: Otter Printing, 1988), 91.

130 Kenneth C. Dewar, *Charles Clarke, Pen and Ink Warrior* (Montreal and Kingston: McGill-Queen's University Press, 2002), 267.

131 Ibid., 152.

132 Ibid., 204.

133 Ibid., 212–13.

134 LAC, Census of Canada, 1891, Schedule No. 1, Ontario, Centre Wellington, Village of Elora, accessed 17 July 2023, https://recherche-collection-search.bac-lac.gc.ca/eng/home/record?app=census&IdNumber=26844404.

135 Dewar, *Charles Clarke*, 232.

136 Magda Fahrni, "'Ruffled' Mistresses and 'Discontented' Maids: Respectability and the Case of Domestic Service, 1880–1914," *Labour/Le Travail* 39 (Spring 1997): 72.

137 Ibid., 71.

138 LAC, Census of Canada, 1901, Schedule No. 1, Ontario, Centre Wellington, Elora Village, accessed 25 January 2024, https://recherche-collection-search.bac-lac.gc.ca/eng/home/record?app=census&IdNumber=36279461; Census of Canada, 1901, Schedule No. 1, Ontario, Bothwell, Town Dresden, accessed 25 January 2024, https://recherche-collection-search.bac-lac.gc.ca/eng/home/record?app=census&IdNumber=36355846.

139 *Tillsonburg Observer*, 22 July 1892, 1.

140 LAC, Census of Canada, 1901, Schedule No. 1, Ontario, Bothwell, Town Dresden, accessed 25 January 2024, https://recherche-collection-search.bac-lac.gc.ca/eng/home/record?app=census&IdNumber=36355765.

141 Monda Halpern, *And on That Farm He Had a Wife: Ontario Farm Women and Feminism, 1900–1970* (Montreal and Kingston: McGill-Queen's University Press, 2001), 39–40.

142 LAC, Census of Canada, 1901, Schedule No. 1, Ontario, Centre Wellington, Elora Village, accessed 25 January, 2024, https://recherche-collection-search.bac-lac.gc.ca/eng/home/record?app=census&IdNumber=35436370.

143 Holman, *A Sense of Their Duty*, 8.

144 Bouchier, *For the Love of the Game*, 29.

145 Ibid.

146 Wetherell and Kmet, *Town Life*, 120.

147 Charlotte M. Canning, *The Most American Thing in America: Circuit Chautauqua as Performance* (Iowa City, IA: University of Iowa Press, 2005), 194.

148 Wetherell and Kmet, *Town Life*, 99.

149 Ibid., 175.

150 Stephen Thorning, "Elora Rifles Called to Fight Invasion That Never Happened," *Wellington Advertiser*, 8 March 2019, https://www.wellingtonadvertiser.com/elora-rifles-called-to-fight-invasion-that-never-happened/.

151   Stephen Thorning, *The Model Village and the Struggle for Success: A History of Elora, Ontario* (Fergus, ON: Wellington County Historical Society, 2023), 203.

152   Historic Sites and Monuments Board of Canada, "Elora Drill Shed," accessed 25 January 2024, https://www.pc.gc.ca/apps/dfhd/page_nhs_eng.aspx?id=369.

153   Stephen Thorning, "The Elora Armoury Hall: Some Historical Notes," *Wellington County History* 3 (1990): 68.

154   *Elora Express*, 1 July 1886, 1.

155   Stephen Thorning, "The Drill Shed Was Elora's Own 'Theatre on the Grand,'" *Elora Sentinel and Fergus Thistle*, 15 June 1993, 6–7.

156   Brandon, *The History of Dresden*, 30.

157   According to Robert Brandon, Shaw's was located on the top floor of the building at the corner of Lindsley and St. George Streets where Foster's Creamery was in the mid-twentieth century; see Brandon, *The History of Dresden*, 33, 74.

158   Russell Lynes, *The Lively Audience: A Social History of the Visual and Performing Arts in America, 1890–1950* (New York: Harper and Row, 1985), 130.

159   Information found in various issues of the *Tillsonburg Observer*.

160   *Tillsonburg Observer*, 9 April 1880, 1.

161   Laurel A. Beechey, *Tillsonburg's Town Hall* (Tillsonburg, ON: Tillsonburg Architectural Conservation Advisory Committee, 1997), 4.

162   "The New Opera House," *Tillsonburg Observer*, 1 April 1898, 4.

163   Beechey, *Tillsonburg's Town Hall*, 16.

164   See John MacDougall, *Rural Life in Canada: Its Trend and Tasks*, with introduction by Robert Craig Brown (Toronto: University of Toronto Press, 1973).

165   David Mizener, "Furrows and Fairgrounds: Agriculture, Identity, and Authority in Twentieth-Century Rural Ontario" (PhD diss., York University, 2009), 16.

166   Kate Aitken, *Never a Day So Bright* (New York: Longmans, 1957), 161.

167   Mizener, "Furrows and Fairgrounds," 17.

168   Randy William Widdis, "Belleville and Environs: Continuity, Change and the Integration of Town and Country during the 19th Century," *Urban History Review* 19, no. 3 (February 1991): 207.

Chapter 2. A Reconnaissance of Recreation

1   "How Very Lady-Like," *Tillsonburg Observer*, 21 December 1871, 2.

2   Heather Murray, *Come, Bright Improvement!: The Literary Societies of Nineteenth-Century Ontario* (Toronto: University of Toronto Press, 2002), 107.

3   Jeanne Halgren Kilde, "The 'Predominance of the Feminine' at Chautauqua: Rethinking the Gender-Space Relationship in Victorian America," *Signs* 24, no. 2 (Winter 1999): 453.

4   Margaret C. Kechnie, *Organizing Rural Women: The Federated Women's Institutes of Ontario, 1897–1919* (Montreal and Kingston: McGill-Queen's University Press, 2003); Linda Ambrose, "Ontario Women's Institutes and the Work of Local History," in *Creating Historical Memory: English-Canadian Women and the*

Work of History, ed. Beverly Boutilier and Alison Prentice (Vancouver: University of British Columbia Press, 1997), 75–100; Linda Ambrose, "Our Last Frontier: Imperialism and Northern Canadian Rural Women's Institutes," *Canadian Historical Review* 86, no. 2 (June 2005): 257–84; Linda Ambrose, "The Women's Institutes in Northern Ontario," in *Changing Lives: Women in Northern Ontario*, ed. Margaret Kechnie and Marge Reitsma-Street (Toronto: Dundurn Press, 1996), 263–74; Linda Ambrose, "'What Are the Good of Those Meetings Anyway?': Early Popularity of the Ontario Women's Institutes," *Ontario History* 87, no. 1 (March 1995): 1–20; Linda Ambrose, *For Home and Country: The Centennial History of the Women's Institutes in Ontario* (Erin, ON: Boston Mills Press, 1996); Linda Ambrose, *A Great Rural Sisterhood: Madge Robertson Watt and the ACWW* (Toronto: University of Toronto Press, 2015); Linda Ambrose and Margaret Kechnie, "Social Control or Social Feminism?: Two Views of the Ontario Women's Institutes," *Agricultural History* 73, no. 2 (Spring 1999): 222–37; Amy Parker, "'Making the Most of What We Have': The Women's Institutes of Huron County, Ontario during the Inter-War Period" (MA thesis, University of Guelph, 2007).

5   David Nasaw, *Going Out: The Rise and Fall of Public Amusements* (Cambridge, MA: Harvard University Press, 1999), 25–26.

6   Ibid., 26.

7   Keith Walden, *Becoming Modern in Toronto: The Industrial Exhibition and the Shaping of a Late Victorian Culture* (Toronto: University of Toronto Press, 1997), 249.

8   UGASC, Marston-Archibald Collection, XR1 MS A371, Box 1, Olive Snyder diary, 1913.

9   Mary Neth, *Preserving the Family Farm: Women, Community, and the Foundations of Agribusiness in the Midwest, 1900–1940* (Baltimore: Johns Hopkins University Press, 1995), 248–49.

10   Though adored throughout town and beyond, the Dresden Concert Band struggled to support itself financially and regularly petitioned the town council for funding, hoping to receive pay for its playing and to purchase uniforms. See Robert Brandon, *The History of Dresden* (Dresden, ON: Dresden Centennial Committee, 1982), 44.

11   Ambrose, "'What Are the Good of Those Meetings Anyway?'" 8.

12   Amanda Vickery, "Historiographical Review: Golden Age to Separate Spheres? A Review of the Categories and Chronology of English Women's History," *Historical Journal* 36, no. 2 (June 1993): 400.

13   Donald G. Wetherell and Irene Kmet, *Useful Pleasures: The Shaping of Leisure in Alberta, 1896–1945* (Regina: Canadian Plains Research Center, 1990), 74.

14   "Street Preaching in Elora," *Elora Lightning Express*, 31 May 1872, 2.

15   Neil Semple, *The Lord's Dominion: The History of Canadian Methodism* (Montreal and Kingston: McGill-Queen's University Press, 1996), 337.

16 See William Westfall, *Two Worlds: The Protestant Culture of Nineteenth-Century Ontario* (Montreal and Kingston: McGill-Queen's University Press, 1989), 128–30.

17 For more, see Frank Abbott, "Cold Cash and Ice Palaces: The Quebec Winter Carnival of 1894," *Canadian Historical Review* 69, no. 2 (1988): 197–98.

18 John S. Moir, *Enduring Witness: A History of the Presbyterian Church in Canada* (Canada: Bryant Press, n.d.), 24.

19 Lynne Marks, "Religion, Leisure, and Working Class Identity," in *Labouring Lives: Work and Workers in Nineteenth-Century Ontario*, ed. Paul Craven (Toronto: University of Toronto Press, 1995), 291.

20 "Politics and the Franchise. What Tilsonburg Women Say about Them," *Tillsonburg Observer*, 22 February 1895, 4.

21 Paul Voisey elaborates on this in *Vulcan: The Making of a Prairie Community* (Toronto: University of Toronto Press, 1988).

22 WCMA, A1996.112, Diary of Annie Hill (née Drury) of Fergus, Ontario, 1912–1923.

23 Kate Aitken, *Never a Day So Bright* (New York: Longmans, 1957), 30.

24 UGASC, Marston-Archibald Collection, XR1 MS A371, Box 1, Olive Snyder diary, 1913.

25 UGASC, Marston-Archibald Collection, XR1 MS A371, Box 1, Olive Snyder diary, 1914–1917.

26 WCMA, A1981.92, Ann Amelia Day/Sunley Diary, Eramosa Township, 1878–1879.

27 My thanks to Craig Heron for coining this term and bringing it to my attention.

28 County of Oxford Archives (hereafter COA), Series 2, By-Laws (1850–1867), No. 59 By Law No. 2, By Law for the purpose of protecting and enforcing the observance of Public Morals within the County of Oxford, 1859.

29 Semple, *The Lord's Dominion*, 355.

30 See Christopher Armstrong and H.V. Nelles, *The Revenge of the Methodist Bicycle Company: Sunday Streetcars and Municipal Reform in Toronto, 1888–1897* (Toronto: Peter Martin Associates, 1977), 50.

31 Lynne Marks, *Revivals and Roller Rinks: Religion, Leisure, and Identity in Late-Nineteenth-Century Small-Town Ontario* (Toronto: University of Toronto Press, 1996), 103.

32 "The Lord's Day Alliance," *Tillsonburg Observer*, 6 December 1900, 1.

33 The Tweedsmuir History states this information was taken from the 10 July 1870 issue of the *Elora Observer*. See UGASC, XR1 MS A192067, Elora Women's Institute Tweedsmuir History.

34 *Tillsonburg Observer*, 31 May 1895, 1.

35 See Paul Laverdure, *Sunday in Canada: The Rise and Fall of the Lord's Day* (Yorkton, SK: Gravel Books, 2004), 17, 75.

36 Francis Hoffman and Ryan Taylor, *Much to Be Done: Private Life in Ontario from Victorian Diaries* (Toronto: Natural Heritage/Natural History, 1996), 196.

37   ANHS, Documentary Artifact Collection, Thomson Family file, "Mrs. Charles
      Thomson Recalls Yesteryears," *Tillsonburg News* article, 19 February 1942, 12.

38   Mrs. Tilton, "Compilation," in *Women of Canada: Their Life and Work*, com-
      piled by the National Council of Women of Canada at the request of the Hon.
      Sydney Fisher, Minister of Agriculture, for distribution at the Paris International
      Exhibition, 1900, 304.

39   For more, see Lucille Marr, "Sunday School Teaching: A Women's Enterprise,"
      Histoire sociale/Social History 26, no. 52 (November 1993): 332.

40   Marks, *Revivals and Roller Rinks*, 75.

41   Laurel Beechey, *The Father of Tillsonburg, Edwin Delevan Tillson and Mary Ann
      Tillson* (Tillsonburg, ON, n.d.), 18. Fredericksburg was once the name of the
      town of Delhi, located about twenty kilometres east of Tillsonburg.

42   In many small towns, renting pews in the local church was not only a status
      symbol but also an "important means of revenue for the church. The Tillson
      family paid an annual pew rent, and according to [Laurel] Beechey, the Tillsons'
      rental of a church pew in 1902 amounted to $6.50. These pew rents, however,
      reinforced class lines within the church and by extension the community.
      Pew rents traditionally reflected class boundaries due to their cost, but in the
      late-nineteenth century, skilled and even some semi-skilled workers were paying
      such rents as a means of establishing a more respectable position for themselves
      within society. The distinction, however, was maintained through the location of
      the pew; those nearer to the front were more expensive and therefore affordable
      for only the wealthiest families." See Rebecca Beausaert, "'The Parties These
      Ladies Used to Put On!': Class and the Formation of Women's Leisure Activities
      in Tillsonburg, Ontario, 1881–1911" (MA thesis, Western University, 2006),
      20–21; see also Marks, *Revivals and Roller Rinks*, 63. In her work, Marguerite
      Van Die also discusses how pew renting was an important source of revenue for
      churches. See Van Die, *Religion, Family, and Community in Victorian Canada:
      The Colbys of Carrollcroft* (Montreal and Kingston: McGill-Queen's University
      Press, 2005), 137–39.

43   Marks, *Revivals and Roller Rinks*, 70.

44   The example used is May Oliver, who lived in Dresden. See LAC, Census
      of Canada, 1901, Schedule No. 1, Ontario, Bothwell, Town Dresden,
      accessed 25 January 2024, http://central.bac-lac.gc.ca/.redirect?app=cen-
      sus&id=36500812&lang=eng. In 1913, the ten members of Dresden's Christ
      Church Ladies' Guild contributed $9.55 in dues, on top of handiwork and culin-
      ary donations. See Western University, Archives and Special Collections (here-
      after WUASC), Christ Church Dresden Papers, 1859–1935.

45   According to Lynne Marks, when compared to their male counterparts, work-
      ing-class women were much more involved in the church; see Marks, *Revivals and
      Roller Rinks*, 50.

46   Benjamin Fish Austin, *Woman; Her Character, Culture and Calling. A Full
      Discussion of Woman's Work in the Home, the School, the Church and the Social*

Circle; With an Account of her Successful Labors in Moral and Social Reform, her Heroic Work for God and Humanity in the Mission Field, her Success as a Wage-Earner and in Fighting Life's Battle Alone; With Chapters on all Departments of Woman's Training and Culture, her Claims to the Higher Education, and the Best Methods to be Pursued Therein (Brantford, ON: Book and Bible House, 1890), 89.

47   ANHS, Documentary Artifact Collection, Thomson Family Files, Obituary, *Tillsonburg News* article, Ada Thomson (born in Tillsonburg 8 April 1888, life-long resident of the town), date unknown.

48   UGASC, Marston-Archibald Collection, XR1 MS A371, Box 1, Olive Snyder diary, 1914–1917.

49   Marks, *Revivals and Roller Rinks*, 65.

50   Stephen Thorning, *The Model Village and the Struggle for Success: A History of Elora, Ontario* (Fergus, ON: Wellington County Historical Society, 2023), 83.

51   For more on the history of Methodist Ladies' Aids, see Marilyn Färdig Whiteley, *Canadian Methodist Women, 1766–1925: Marys, Marthas, Mothers in Israel* (Waterloo, ON: published for Canadian Corporation for Studies in Religion by Wilfrid Laurier University Press, 2005); Marilyn Färdig Whiteley, "'Doing All the Rest': Church Women of the Ladies' Aid Society," in *Framing Our Past: Canadian Women's History in the Twentieth Century*, ed. Sharon Anne Cook, Lorna R. McLean, and Kate O'Rourke (Montreal and Kingston: McGill-Queen's University Press, 2001), 18–21; and Marilyn Färdig Whiteley, "'Doing Just About What They Please': Ladies' Aids in Ontario Methodism," *Ontario History* 83, no. 4 (December 1990): 289–304.

52   Archives of Ontario (hereafter AO), F 373, Tweedsmuir Histories Collection, Kent County: Dresden (Molly Creek), 48.

53   WUASC, Christ Church Dresden Papers, 1859–1935.

54   Nancy Grey Osterud, *Bonds of Community: The Lives of Farm Women in Nineteenth-Century New York* (Ithaca, NY: Cornell University Press, 1991), 292.

55   Hannah M. Lane, "'Wife, Mother, Sister, Friend': Methodist Women in St. Stephen, New Brunswick, 1861–1881," in *Separate Spheres: Women's Worlds in the 19th-Century Maritimes*, ed. Janet Guildford and Suzanne Morton (Fredericton, NB: Acadiensis Press, 1994), 95.

56   WUASC, Christ Church Dresden Papers, 1859–1935.

57   Marks, *Revivals and Roller Rinks*, 65.

58   The guild's schedule deviated slightly during times of the year (such as summer) when participants may have been busy with familial obligations or were out of town.

59   WUASC, Christ Church Dresden Papers, 1859–1935.

60   Whiteley, "'Doing Just About What They Please,'" 295.

61   Norwich and District Museum and Archives (hereafter NDMA), 2002.62.1, Minnie Smith Collection.

62   *Elora Lightning Express*, 11 July 1872, 2.

63 Whiteley, "'Doing Just About What They Please,'" 296, 300.

64 ANHS, Documentary Artifact Collection, Marguerite Sinclair Scrapbook, 30; see also "Conundrum Social," *Tillsonburg Observer*, 26 February 1903, 1.

65 See, for example, *Dresden Times*, 22 November 1888, unpaginated; *Tillsonburg Observer*, 26 November 1875, 2; *Tillsonburg Observer*, 20 June 1872, 3.

66 Information about Edward Huston found in Marie Carter and Jeffrey Carter, *Stepping Back in Time: Along the Trillium Trail in Dresden* (Dresden, ON: Catherine McVean Chapter IODE, 2003), 76, 84. Quote from *Dresden Times*, 2 July 1891, 1.

67 Bert Newman, *Reminiscences about Tillsonburg*, ed. Dave Stover (Tillsonburg, ON, 1986), 27.

68 *Elora Express*, 5 July 1905, 8.

69 Dresden Public Library (hereafter DPL), *Saint Andrew's Presbyterian Church, Dresden, Ontario, One Hundredth Anniversary 1872–1972*, 6.

70 "The Catholic Concert in Elora," *Elora Lightning Express*, 16 February 1872, 2.

71 *Census of Canada, 1870–71*, Vol. I (Ottawa: I.B. Taylor, 1873), 107.

72 Marks, *Revivals and Roller Rinks*, 38.

73 Wetherell and Kmet, *Useful Pleasures*, 120.

74 Amenzo J. Herrick, "The Church and Entertainments," *Tillsonburg Liberal*, 4 January 1910, 2.

75 Nevill L. Ward, "Correspondence; To the Editor of 'The Liberal,'" *Tillsonburg Liberal*, 21 July 1910, 4.

76 Kathryn H. Fuller, *At the Picture Show: Small-Town Audiences and the Creation of Movie Fan Culture* (Washington, DC: Smithsonian Institution Press, 1996), 86.

77 Lawrence W. Levine, *Highbrow/Lowbrow: The Emergence of Cultural Hierarchy in America* (Cambridge, MA: Harvard University Press, 1988), 231–34; see also Russell Lynes, *The Lively Audience: A Social History of the Visual and Performing Arts in America, 1890–1950* (New York: Harper and Row, 1985), 35. Nan Enstad's work examines the significance of early motion pictures for young working-class women in urban America, arguing that new genres that appealed to working-class women resulted in their greater presence at the theatre; see Enstad, *Ladies of Labor, Girls of Adventure: Working Women, Popular Culture, and Labor Politics at the Turn of the Twentieth Century* (New York: Columbia University Press, 1999), 161–200.

78 Brandon, *The History of Dresden*, 50.

79 "Elora Walking Tour: North of the Grand River," *Wellington County History* 17 (2004): 39.

80 Fuller, *At the Picture Show*, 87.

81 Tillsonburg's first theatre, established sometime in the late 1900s or early 1910s, was called the Bijou and was located on Broadway Street. See ANHS, Documentary Artifact Collection, Social History Files, Theatres.

82 Kathryn Helgesen Fuller, "'You Can Have the Strand in Your Own Town': The Marginalization of Small Town Film Exhibition in the Silent Film Era," *Film History* 6 (1994): 169.

83 Ibid., 170.

84 Semple, *The Lord's Dominion*, 410–11.

85 Mariana Valverde, *The Age of Light, Soap, and Water: Moral Reform in English Canada, 1885–1925*, with a new introduction (Toronto: University of Toronto Press, 2008), 52–53.

86 The show was based on an 1897 novel by Social Gospeller Charles Monroe Sheldon called *In His Steps: What Would Jesus Do?*

87 *Tillsonburg Observer*, 2 April 1903, 1; *Tillsonburg Observer*, 9 April 1903, 1.

88 Town of Tillsonburg, 1800–1909 By-Laws, By-Law No. 0594 of the Corporation of the Town of Tillsonburg to amend By-Law No. 146 for licensing Circuses and other Exhibitions, Effective Date: 04/06/1909, accessed 25 January 2024, https://lfpp.oxford-county.ca/WebLink/DocView.aspx?id=37650&dbid=0&repo=Tillsonburg-Public.

89 Marks, *Revivals and Roller Rinks*, 111.

90 "Bachelors' Ball," *Tillsonburg Observer*, 8 February 1872, 2. In Bert Newman's reminiscences, he states that the Bachelors' Club balls in Tillsonburg were generally an invite-only sort of event.

91 "The Bachelors' Party," *Tillsonburg Observer*, 8 February 1895, 1; "A Masquerade," *Tillsonburg Observer*, 1 March 1895, 4. Peter Ward discusses the importance of formal balls organized by bachelors' clubs in smaller communities, though primarily in the pre-Confederation period; see Ward, *Courtship, Love, and Marriage in Nineteenth-Century English Canada* (Montreal and Kingston: McGill-Queen's University Press, 1990), 66–71.

92 DPL, Inez (Eagleson) Perrin, "Call Back Yesterday," *North Kent Leader Centennial Edition*, 23 June 1982, E-27.

93 DA, Dresden Area Schools.

94 Marks, *Revivals and Roller Rinks*, 133.

95 Craig Heron, *Lunch-Bucket Lives: Remaking the Workers' City* (Toronto: Between the Lines, 2015), 359.

96 Jane Nicholas, *Canadian Carnival Freaks and the Extraordinary Body, 1900–1970s* (Toronto: University of Toronto Press, 2018), 35.

97 Carolyn Strange and Tina Loo, "Spectacular Justice: The Circus on Trial, and the Trial as Circus, Picton, 1903," *Canadian Historical Review* 77, no. 2 (June 1996): 174; see also Mary M. Brown, "Entertainers of the Road," in *Early Stages: Theatre in Ontario, 1800–1914*, ed. Ann Saddlemyer (Toronto: University of Toronto Press, 1990), 125.

98 Gerald Lenton-Young, "Variety Theatre," in *Early Stages: Theatre in Ontario, 1800–1914*, ed. Ann Saddlemyer (Toronto: University of Toronto Press, 1990), 166.

99 "Van Amburgh's Menagerie," *Tillsonburg Observer*, 30 May 1872, 2.

100 *Elora Express*, 11 July 1872, 2.

101 ANHS, Documentary Artifact Collection, Thomson Family Files, "Mrs. Charles Thomson Recalls Yesteryears," *Tillsonburg News* article, 19 February 1942, 12.
102 Thorning, *The Model Village*, 204.
103 This information has been taken from a variety of sources such as newspapers and Bert Newman's reminiscences.
104 DPL, *North Kent Leader Centennial Edition*, 23 June 1982.
105 Thorning, *The Model Village*, 208.
106 Quote from Jane Nicholas, *Canadian Carnival Freaks*, 29; see also Linda Scarangella McNenly, "Foe, Friend, or Critic: Native Performers with Buffalo Bill's Wild West Show and Discourses of Conquest and Friendship in Newspaper Reports," *American Indian Quarterly* 38, no. 2 (Spring 2014): 147.
107 Strange and Loo, "Spectacular Justice," 180.
108 *Tillsonburg Observer*, 24 May 1900, 4.
109 NDMA, X79A-XX1-15, Francis Poole Diary, 1904.
110 *Tillsonburg Observer*, 7 June 1895, 1.
111 Newman, *Reminiscences about Tillsonburg*, 28.
112 ANHS, Documentary Artifact Collection, "William Harcourt Popham Remembers."
113 J.M.S. Careless, "The Cultural Setting: Ontario Society to 1914," in *Early Stages: Theatre in Ontario, 1800–1914*, ed. Ann Saddlemyer (Toronto: University of Toronto Press, 1990), 39.
114 "S.S." refers to school section, Sunday school, or Sabbath school.
115 ANHS, Documentary Artifact Collection, Marguerite Sinclair Scrapbook, pamphlet, "Empire Day Concert in Tillsonburg," 23 May 1899.
116 Lynes, *The Lively Audience*, 130.
117 Ibid., 132.
118 D. Layne Ehlers, "This Week at the Opera House: Popular Musical Entertainment at Great Plains Opera Houses, 1887–1917," *Great Plains Quarterly* 20 (Summer 2000): 189.
119 *Dresden Times*, 27 December 1888, special supplement.
120 DPL, Inez (Eagleson) Perrin, "Call Back Yesterday," *North Kent Leader Centennial Edition*, 23 June 1982, E-27.
121 Information taken from various issues of the *Elora Express*, *Elora Lightning Express*, and *Elora News*. Church and associational entertainments and meetings left the Drill Shed because they found homes elsewhere, including recently built church auditoriums or, in the case of associational meetings, members' homes.
122 Neth, *Preserving the Family Farm*, 245.
123 See Robertson Davies, "The Nineteenth-Century Repertoire," in *Early Stages: Theatre in Ontario, 1800–1914*, edited by Ann Saddlemyer (Toronto: University of Toronto Press, 1990), 90–122.
124 William F. Condee, "*Hamlet*, Sunday School, *Zarrow's Pig Revue*: Cultural Regulation in America's Opera Houses," *Journal of American Culture* 22, no. 2 (1999): 59.

125 Ibid.
126 Town of Tillsonburg, 1800–1909 By-Laws, By-Law 0312 Amend By Law 146 Re: Licences—Theatrical Troups, Effective Date: 02/06/1894, accessed 25 January 2024, https://lfpp.oxfordcounty.ca/WebLink/DocView.aspx?id= 42340&dbid=0&repo=Tillsonburg-Public.
127 *Elora Lightning Express*, 27 May 1875, unpaginated.
128 Ehlers, "This Week at the Opera House," 188.
129 ANHS, Documentary Artifact Collection, Marguerite Sinclair Scrapbook, pamphlet—programme at the Opera House, 11 December 1903, "The Merchant of Venice."
130 See Susan Torrey Barstow, "'Hedda Is All of Us': Late-Victorian Women at the Matinee," *Victorian Studies* 4, no. 3 (Spring 2001): 393.
131 *Tillsonburg Liberal*, 5 May 1910, 5.
132 Cheryl Thompson, "*Black* Minstrelsy on Canadian Stages: Nostalgia for Plantation Slavery in the Nineteenth and Twentieth Centuries," *Journal of the Canadian Historical Association* 31, no. 1 (2021): 69. For more on racial stereo-types, see Cheryl Thompson, *Uncle: Race, Nostalgia, and the Politics of Loyalty* (Toronto: Coach House Books, 2021).
133 It is often not specified which kind of minstrel show (White or Black) was performing. Quote from Joan Nicks and Jeannette Sloniowski, "Entertaining Niagara Falls, Ontario: Minstrel Shows, Theatres, and Popular Pleasures," in *Covering Niagara: Studies in Local Popular Culture*, ed. Joan Nicks and Barry Keith (Waterloo, ON: Wilfrid Laurier University Press, 2010), 305. See also Wetherell and Kmet, *Useful Pleasures*, 215–16.
134 *Elora Express*, 22 February 1905, 8.
135 Email from Dr. Nina Reid-Maroney to author, 8 July 2010. Notice appeared in the *Dresden Times*, 2 March 1893.
136 "Guy Brothers Minstrels," *Tillsonburg Liberal*, 15 December 1910, 1.
137 Newman, *Reminiscences about Tillsonburg*, 28–31.
138 ANHS, Documentary Artifact Collection, "William Harcourt Popham Remembers."
139 Nasaw, *Going Out*, 54.
140 See, for example, Afua Cooper, *The Hanging of Angélique: The Untold Story of Canadian Slavery and the Burning of Old Montreal* (Toronto: HarperCollins, 2006); Barrington Walker, ed., *The History of Immigration and Racism in Canada: Essential Readings* (Toronto: Canadian Scholars' Press, 2008); Constance Backhouse, *Colour-Coded: A Legal History of Racism in Canada, 1900–1950* (Toronto: University of Toronto Press, 1999); Thompson, *Uncle*.
141 Thompson, "*Black* Minstrelsy on Canadian Stages," 71.
142 Nicks and Sloniowski, "Entertaining Niagara Falls," 305.
143 "Guy Brothers Minstrels," *Tillsonburg Liberal*, 15 December 1910, 1.
144 Quote from David R. Roediger, *The Wages of Whiteness: Race and the Making of the American Working Class* (London: Verso, 1991), 120. See also Stephanie Dunson, "The Minstrel in the Parlor: Nineteenth-Century Sheet Music and

the Domestication of Blackface Minstrelsy," *American Transcendental Quarterly* 16, no. 4 (December 2002): 241–56; and Eric Lott, *Love and Theft: Blackface Minstrelsy and the American Working Class* (New York: Oxford University Press, 1995).

145 Roediger, *The Wages of Whiteness*, 121.

146 Dunson, "The Minstrel in the Parlor," 246.

147 ANHS, Documentary Artifact Collection, Marguerite Sinclair Scrapbook, 34; see also ANHS, Documentary Artifact Collection, "William Harcourt Popham Remembers."

148 AO, F 26, Charles Clarke Fonds, MS 76 (2), Clarke Papers, 1880–1940, Spinsters' Convention handbill.

149 AO, F 26, Charles Clarke Fonds, MS 76 (2), Clarke Papers, 1880–1940, Supplement to the *Elora Express* by Rose Clarke, vol. 30, no. 45, Elora, 25 November 1903.

150 Craig Heron and Steve Penfold, *The Workers' Festival: A History of Labour Day in Canada* (Toronto: University of Toronto Press, 2005), 17; see also Susan G. Davis, *Parades and Power: Street Theatre in Nineteenth-Century Philadelphia* (Philadelphia: Temple University Press, 1986), 47.

151 Belinda, "Politics and the Franchise. What Tilsonburg Women Say about Them," *Tillsonburg Observer*, 22 February 1895, 4.

152 See Halpern, *And on That Farm He Had a Wife;* and Jodey Nurse, *Cultivating Community: Women and Agricultural Fairs in Ontario* (Montreal and Kingston: McGill-Queen's University Press, 2022).

153 AO, F 26 Charles Clarke Fonds, MS 76 (2), Clarke Papers, 1880–1940, Supplement to the *Elora Express* by Rose Clarke, vol. 30, no. 45, Elora, 25 November 1903.

154 *Fourth Census of Canada, 1901,* Vol. I (Ottawa: S.E. Dawson, 1902), 87.

155 AO, F 26 Charles Clarke Fonds, MS 76 (2), Clarke Papers, 1880–1940, Supplement to the *Elora Express* by Rose Clarke, vol. 30, no. 45, Elora, 25 November 1903.

156 See Michele Stairs, "Matthews and Marillas: Bachelors and Spinsters in Prince Edward Island in 1881," in *Mapping the Margins: The Family and Social Discipline in Canada, 1700–1975*, ed. Nancy Christie and Michael Gauvreau (Montreal and Kingston: McGill-Queen's University Press), 247–70; see also Halpern, *And on That Farm He Had a Wife*, 41–43.

157 AO, F 26 Charles Clarke Fonds, MS 76 (2), Clarke Papers, 1880–1940, Supplement to the *Elora Express* by Rose Clarke, vol. 30, no. 45, Elora, 25 November 1903.

158 *Farmer's Advocate and Home Magazine* 18, no. 11 (November 1883): 347.

159 Bonnie Huskins, "The Ceremonial Space of Women: Public Processions in Victorian Saint John and Halifax," in *Separate Spheres: Women's Worlds in the 19th-Century Maritimes*, ed. Janet Guildford and Suzanne Morton (Fredericton, NB: Acadiensis Press, 1994), 145.

160   Davis, *Parades and Power*, 16.

161   See Jody Baltessen and Shelagh J. Squire, "Winnipeg Women Getting Together:
Study Groups and Reading Clubs, 1900–1940," in *Framing Our Past: Canadian
Women's History in the Twentieth Century*, ed. Sharon Anne Cook, Lorna
R. McLean, and Kate O'Rourke (Montreal and Kingston: McGill-Queen's
University Press, 2001), 10–14; Gail Cuthbert Brandt, "Organizations in
Canada: The English Protestant Tradition," in *Women's Paid and Unpaid Work:
Historical and Contemporary Perspectives*, ed. Paula Bourne (Toronto: New
Hogtown Press, 1985), 79–96; J.C. Croly, *The History of the Woman's Club
Movement in America* (New York: H.G. Allen, 1898); Lori D. Ginzberg, *Women
and the Work of Benevolence: Morality, Politics, and Class in the Nineteenth-
Century United States* (New Haven, CT: Yale University Press, 1990); Kristin
L. Hoganson, *Consumers' Imperium: The Global Production of American
Domesticity, 1865–1920* (Chapel Hill: University of North Carolina Press,
2007); Anne Meis Knupfer and Christine Woyshner, eds., *The Educational Work
of Women's Organizations, 1890–1960* (New York: Palgrave Macmillan, 2008);
Alison Prentice et al., *Canadian Women: A History*, 2nd ed. (Toronto: Harcourt
Brace, 1996).

162   *Tillsonburg Observer*, 26 July 1895, 1.

163   List of members found in *Tillsonburg Observer*, 23 August 1895, 1; information about husbands' occupations found in LAC, Census of Canada, 1891,
Schedule No. 1, Ontario, Norfolk North, Tilsonburg, accessed 25 January 2024,
https://recherche-collection-search.bac-lac.gc.ca/eng/Home/Search?DataSo
urce=Genealogy%7CCensus&ApplicationCode=27&YearOfImmigration-
slider=0&Age-slider=0&YearOfBirth-slider=0&ProvinceCode=ON&Place=T
ilsonburg&.

164   Sharon Anne Cook, *"Through Sunshine and Shadow": The Woman's Christian
Temperance Union, Evangelicalism, and Reform in Ontario, 1874–1930*
(Montreal and Kingston: McGill-Queen's University Press, 1995), 152.

165   *Tillsonburg Observer*, 8 February 1900, 1.

166   Baltessen and Squire, "Winnipeg Women Getting Together," 10.

167   Ambrose, "'What Are the Good of Those Meetings Anyway?'" 8.

168   Neth, *Preserving the Family Farm*, 136.

169   Carly Adams, "Supervised Places to Play: Social Reform, Citizenship, and
Femininity at Municipal Playgrounds in London, Ontario, 1900–1942," *Ontario
History* 10, no. 1 (Spring 2011): 63.

170   *Tillsonburg Observer*, 17 May 1895, 1.

171   "An Ideal Rural Club," *Farmer's Advocate and Home Magazine* 44, no. 901 (30
December 1909): 2080–81.

172   "Literary Societies and Rural Clubs," *Farmer's Advocate and Home Magazine* 44,
no. 1050 (7 November 1912): 1933.

173   Augusta H. Leypoldt and George Iles, eds., *List of Books for Girls and Women and Their Clubs with Descriptive and Critical Notes and a List of Periodicals and Hints for Girls' and Women's Clubs* (Boston: The Library Bureau, 1895), 144.

174   WCMA, A1952.225.1, Man 18, Mu 3, Diary of an unidentified student, likely in Elora, some local and family names references, 1898–1900, 1915.

175   *Dresden Times*, 29 November 1888, 5.

176   *Dresden Times*, early November 1888 (date and page number illegible).

177   *Dresden Times*, 22 November 1888, unpaginated.

178   Baltessen and Squire, "Winnipeg Women Getting Together," 11.

179   Ambrose, "'What Are the Good of Those Meetings Anyway?'" 3.

180   WCMA, A1981.92, Ann Amelia Day/Sunley Diary, Eramosa Township, 1878–1879.

181   Linda M. Ambrose, "'Forever Lunching': Food, Power, and Politics in Rural Ontario Women's Organizations," in *Women in Agriculture: Professionalizing Rural Life in North America and Europe, 1880–1965*, ed. Linda M. Ambrose and Joan M. Jensen (Iowa City, IA: University of Iowa Press, 2017), 176.

182   Elise Chenier, "Class, Gender, and the Social Standard: The Montreal Junior League, 1912–1939," *Canadian Historical Review* 90, no. 4 (December 2009): 671–710.

183   *Fifth Census of Canada, 1911*, Vol. I (Ottawa: C.H. Parmelee, 1913), 327.

184   DA, Marie Carter, *100 Years of IODE, Catherine McVean Chapter originally Sydenham Chapter 1914–2014 Dresden, Ontario*, 57, 68.

185   Carter and Carter, *Stepping Back in Time*, 128–29; *100 Years of IODE in Dresden 1914–2014*, accessed 22 August 2022, http://dresden.ca/wp-content/uploads/2015/02/IODEbooklet.pdf.

186   Katie Pickles, *Female Imperialism and National Identity: Imperial Order Daughters of the Empire* (Manchester: Manchester University Press, 2002; distributed exclusively in the USA by Palgrave), 16.

187   Ibid., 23.

188   Katie Pickles, "Forgotten Colonizers: The Imperial Order Daughters of the Empire (IODE) and the Canadian North," *Canadian Geographer* 42, no. 2 (1998): 193.

189   AO, F 373, Tweedsmuir Histories Collection, Kent County: Dresden (Molly Creek), unpaginated.

190   Kechnie, *Organizing Rural Women*, 3.

191   For a thorough history of how the Women's Institute was established, see Ambrose, *For Home and Country*.

192   Ambrose and Kechnie, "Social Control or Social Feminism?" 224.

193   Ambrose, *For Home and Country*, 26.

194   WUASC, Women's Institute, Tweedsmuir History, Tillsonburg Branch (Oxford County, Ontario), #M1472.

195   UGASC, XRI MSA 564, Box 5, Folder #4, F.W.I.O. Membership in Wellington.

196 WCMA, A1996.112, Diary of Annie Hill (née Drury) of Fergus, Ontario, 1912–1923.

197 AO, F 373, Tweedsmuir Histories Collection, Kent County: Dresden (Molly Creek), unpaginated.

198 See Ambrose and Kechnie, "Social Control or Social Feminism?"; Ambrose, "The Women's Institutes in Northern Ontario," 263–74; Kechnie, *Organizing Rural Women*.

199 *Tillsonburg Observer*, 27 February 1908, 1.

200 See Donica Belisle, *Purchasing Power: Women and the Rise of Canadian Consumer Culture* (Toronto: University of Toronto Press, 2020), 98–123.

201 "Farmers' Institute," *Tillsonburg Observer*, 19 February 1903, 4.

202 WUASC, Women's Institute, Tweedsmuir History, Tillsonburg Branch (Oxford County, Ontario), #M1472, Tillsonburg Women's Institute—Sixtieth Anniversary 1903–1963, "A Short History of the Tillsonburg Women's Institute written for The Tweedsmuir Book, 1947."

203 WUASC, Women's Institute, Tweedsmuir History, Tillsonburg Branch (Oxford County, Ontario), #M1472, Tillsonburg Women's Institute—Sixtieth Anniversary 1903–1963, Newspaper article—"Tillsonburg Senior Women's Institute Celebrates 60th Anniversary."

204 WCMA, A1996.112, Diary of Annie Hill (née Drury) of Fergus, Ontario, 1912–1923.

Chapter 3. Safeties, Skates, and Sleds

1 "Physical Exercise," *Farmer's Advocate and Home Magazine* 27, no. 317 (May 1892): 196.

2 M. Ann Hall, *The Girl and the Game: A History of Women's Sport in Canada*, 2nd ed. (Toronto: University of Toronto Press, 2016), 19.

3 Ibid., 34.

4 Don Morrow and Kevin B. Wamsley, *Sport in Canada: A History*, 3rd ed. (Don Mills, ON: Oxford University Press, 2013), 179.

5 Colin D. Howell, *Blood, Sweat, and Cheers: Sport and the Making of Modern Canada* (Toronto: University of Toronto Press, 2001), 90.

6 See "Female Cyclists," *Dominion Medical Monthly and Ontario Medical Journal* 7, no. 3 (September 1896): 255–56.

7 Peter F. Radford discusses female foot racing from the perspective of nineteenth-century Britain; see Radford, "Women's Foot-Races in the 18th and 19th Centuries: A Popular and Widespread Practice," *Canadian Journal of History of Sport* 25 (1994): 57.

8 Nancy B. Bouchier, *For the Love of the Game: Amateur Sport in Small-Town Ontario, 1838–1895* (Montreal and Kingston: McGill-Queen's University Press, 2003), 48.

9   Glen Norcliffe, *The Ride to Modernity: The Bicycle in Canada, 1869–1900*
     (Toronto: University of Toronto Press, 2001), 30. Sheila Hanlon provides a thor-
     ough analysis of how gender shaped the mechanics of cycling; see Hanlon, "The
     Lady Cyclist: A Gender Analysis of Women's Cycling Culture in 1890s London"
     (PhD diss., York University, 2009), 49–98.

10   Norcliffe, *The Ride to Modernity*, 31.

11   Some historians note that tricycles, or three-wheeled bicycles, as well as tandem
     bikes were popular prior to the safety bicycle and were much enjoyed by women.

12   Robert S. Kossuth and Kevin B. Wamsley, "Cycles of Manhood: Pedaling
     Respectability in Ontario's Forest City," *Sport History Review* 34 (2003): 171.

13   Bouchier, *For the Love of the Game*, 43, 46.

14   *Tillsonburg Observer*, 16 August 1895, 1.

15   See Philip Gordon Mackintosh, "A Bourgeois Geography of Domestic Cycling:
     Using Public Space Responsibly in Toronto and Niagara-on-the-Lake, 1890–
     1900," *Journal of Historical Sociology* 20, nos. 1/2 (March/June 2007): 132.

16   Clare S. Simpson, "Capitalising on Curiosity: Women's Professional Cycling
     Racing in the Late-Nineteenth Century," in *Cycling and Society*, ed. Dave Horton,
     Paul Rosen, and Peter Cox (Aldershot, UK: Ashgate Publishing, 2007), 49–50.

17   Norcliffe, *The Ride to Modernity*, 53–57.

18   Ibid., 31.

19   *Tillsonburg Observer*, 8 April 1892, 5.

20   Mackintosh, "A Bourgeois Geography of Domestic Bicycling," 127.

21   For more on women's participation in high-wheel bicycle racing, see M. Ann Hall,
     *Muscle on Wheels: Louise Armaindo and the High-Wheel Racers of Nineteenth-
     Century America* (Montreal and Kingston: McGill-Queens University Press, 2018);
     and Roger Gilles, *Women on the Move: The Forgotten Era of Women's Bicycle Racing*
     (Lincoln, NE: University of Nebraska Press, 2018).

22   Bert Newman, *Once Upon a Time: Further Reminiscences about Tillsonburg*, ed.
     Dave Stover (Tillsonburg, ON: Otter Printing, 1988), 156.

23   *Tillsonburg Observer*, 3 May 1895, 4.

24   In May 1895, F.J. Frank of Bidwell Street, Tillsonburg, offered a "first-class, high
     grade bicycle for sale cheap." See *Tillsonburg Observer*, 17 May 1895, 1.

25   *Tillsonburg Observer*, 21 August 1891, 1.

26   *Tillsonburg Observer*, 31 May 1895, 1.

27   ANHS, Documentary Artifact Collection, Agnes McGregor File, "Memories" by
     Agnes Christine McGregor (an autobiography), written 20 April 1959.

28   *Tillsonburg Observer*, 25 September 1891, 1.

29   Town of Tillsonburg, 1800–1909 By-Laws, By-Law 0439 Driving Park To Regulate
     and Manage, Effective Date: 07/06/1900, accessed 27 July 2023, https://lfpp.oxford-
     county.ca/WebLink/DocView.aspx?id=42400&dbid=0&repo=Tillsonburg-Public.

30   AO, GS 111, Dresden, Kent Co., Council Minutes 1872–1899, By-Laws 1882–
     1899, Municipal Council Meeting November 6, 1903, By Law 303; WCMA,

A1985.54, Series 2: By-Laws, 1858–1927, File 2: By-Laws April 16, 1861–March 1927 (WCA 233), By Law Number 392.

31 *Tillsonburg Observer*, 20 April 1894, 1.

32 *Tillsonburg Observer*, 29 June 1894, 1.

33 *Tillsonburg Observer*, 7 September 1894, 1.

34 Town of Tillsonburg, 1800–1909 By-Laws, By-Law 0521 Bicycling and Riding On Sidewalks, Effective Date: 04/04/1905, accessed 27 July 2023, https://lfpp.oxford-county.ca/WebLink/DocView.aspx?id=42477&dbid=0&repo=Tillsonburg-Public.

35 For more about the Tillsonburg Rover and Ingersoll Meteor bicycle clubs, see Rebecca Beausaert, "'Young Rovers' and 'Dazzling Lady Meteors': Gender and Bicycle Club Culture in Turn-of-the-Century Small-Town Ontario," *Scientia Canadensis: Canadian Journal of the History of Science, Technology and Medicine* 36, no. 1 (2013): 33–61.

36 The name of the club was likely an homage to the widely popular Rover Safety Bicycle.

37 *Tillsonburg Observer*, 9 May 1890, 5.

38 *Canadian Wheelman* 1, no. 9 (16 March 1896): 33.

39 *Canadian Wheelman* 13, no. 12 (4 May 1896): 30.

40 *Tillsonburg Observer*, 10 May 1895, 1.

41 *Tillsonburg Observer*, 19 July 1895, 1.

42 *Canadian Wheelman* 13, no. 12 (4 May 1896): 44.

43 Fiona Kinsey, "Reading Photographic Portraits of Australian Women Cyclists in the 1890s: From Costume and Cycle Choices to Constructions of Feminine Identity," *International Journal of the History of Sport* 28, nos. 8–9 (May–June 2011): 1127.

44 Bouchier, *For the Love of the Game*, 46.

45 Barbara E. Kelcey, "Dress Reform in Nineteenth-Century Canada," in *Fashion: A Canadian Perspective*, ed. Alexandra Palmer (Toronto: University of Toronto Press, 2004), 230.

46 For more on the dangers of fashion, see Alison Matthews David, *Fashion Victims: The Dangers of Dress Past and Present* (London: Bloomsbury Visual Arts, 2015).

47 See Kelcey, "Dress Reform in Nineteenth-Century Canada."

48 *Ingersoll Chronicle*, 7 May 1896, 10.

49 *Tillsonburg Observer*, 17 May 1895, 1.

50 *Tillsonburg Observer*, 17 May 1895, 1.

51 "Rusty," "Meteor Flashes from Ingersoll," *Canadian Wheelman* 1, no. 16 (1 July 1895): 22.

52 ANHS, Documentary Artifact Collection, Overview of Tillsonburg Sports and Recreation Highlights, 1900 to Present.

53 Karen Dubinsky, *Improper Advances: Rape and Heterosexual Conflict in Ontario, 1880–1929* (Chicago: University of Chicago Press, 1993), 115–19. Peter Ward discusses new sites for courtship, including the use of new modes of transportation; see Ward, *Courtship, Love, and Marriage in Nineteenth-Century English*

328 | Notes to Pages 130-133

Canada (Montreal and Kingston: McGill-Queen's University Press, 1990), 86–92. Dan Azoulay examines rules of courting in public spaces, including advice to female cyclists; see Azoulay, *Hearts and Minds: Canadian Romance at the Dawn of the Modern Era, 1900–1930* (Calgary: University of Calgary Press, 2011), 106–10.

54   Hanlon, "The Lady Cyclist," 66.

55   Newman, *Once Upon a Time*, 156.

56   Dave Brown, "The Northern Character Theme and Sport in Nineteenth-Century Canada," *Canadian Journal of History of Sport* 20, no. 1 (1989): 47–56.

57   WCMA, A2002.51 MU 437, Emma Clarke Files, letter, 1869.

58   *Tillsonburg Observer*, 14 February 1890, 1.

59   "Sleighing Party," *Tillsonburg Observer*, 22 February 1895, 4.

60   For more, see Ward, *Courtship, Love, and Marriage*, 91.

61   "Minnie May's Department," *Farmer's Advocate and Home Magazine* 19, no. 218 (February 1884): 52.

62   ANHS, Documentary Artifact Collection, "William Harcourt Popham Remembers."

63   Hall, *The Girl and the Game*, 2nd ed., 40. Historian Allan Downey discusses a similar process occurring for lacrosse; see Downey, *The Creator's Game: Lacrosse, Identity, and Indigenous Nationhood* (Vancouver: University of British Columbia Press, 2018). Nancy B. Bouchier explores how lacrosse played a role in the process of identity formation in the communities of Ingersoll and Woodstock in the later nineteenth century; see Bouchier, "Idealized Middle-Class Sport for a Young Nation: Lacrosse in Nineteenth-Century Ontario Towns, 1871–1891," *Journal of Canadian Studies* 29, no. 2 (Summer 1994): 89–110.

64   ANHS, Documentary Artifact Collection, Thomson Family Files, "Mrs. Charles Thomson Recalls Yesteryears," *Tillsonburg News* article, 19 February 1942.

65   ANHS, Documentary Artifact Collection, Social History Files—Sports History, File—Sports: Sports Misc.

66   ANHS, Documentary Artifact Collection, Agnes McGregor File, "Memories" by Agnes Christine McGregor (an autobiography), written 20 April 1959.

67   "Health Amusements for Children," *Farmer's Advocate and Home Magazine* 1, no. 9 (August 1880): 186.

68   Julia McNair Wright, *The Complete Home: An Encyclopaedia of Domestic Life and Affairs. The Household, in its Foundation, Order, Economy, Beauty, Healthfulness, Emergencies, Methods, Children, Literature, Amusements, Religion, Friendships, Manners, Hospitality, Servants, Industry, Money, and History. A Volume of Practical Experiences Popularly Illustrated* (Philadelphia; Brantford, ON: Bradley, Garretson, 1879), 562.

69   M. Ann Hall, *The Girl and the Game: A History of Women's Sport in Canada* (Peterborough, ON: Broadview Press, 2002), 7.

70   Despite the popularity of ice skating, Canadian environmental and sport historians have largely ignored its significance for rural and small-town Ontarians.

Mary Louise Adams's work primarily examines the history of ice skating through the lens of gender, while Don Morrow and David Young address the establishment of figure skating clubs as a product of a more professionalized, urban sporting culture. Lynne Marks's study of Ingersoll, Thorold, and Campbellford does acknowledge the enthusiasm for ice skating in small-town Ontario, but as an activity that prompted questions about respectability and affordability. See Mary Louise Adams, *Artistic Impressions: Figure Skating, Masculinity, and the Limits of Sport* (Toronto: University of Toronto Press, 2011); Mary Louise Adams, "Freezing Social Relations: Ice, Rinks, and the Development of Figure Skating," in *Sites of Sport: Space, Place, Experience*, ed. Patricia Vertinsky and John Bale (London: Routledge, 2004), 57–72; Mary Louise Adams, "From Mixed-Sex Sport to Sport for Girls: The Feminization of Figure Skating," *Sport in History* 30, no. 2 (June 2010): 218–41; Mary Louise Adams, "The Manly History of a 'Girls' Sport: Gender, Class and the Development of Nineteenth-Century Figure Skating," *International Journal of the History of Sport* 24, no. 7 (2007): 872–93; Don Morrow et al., *A Concise History of Sport in Canada* (Toronto: Oxford University Press, 1989); David Young, *The Golden Age of Canadian Figure Skating* (Toronto: Summerhill Press, 1984); Lynne Marks, *Revivals and Roller Rinks: Religion, Leisure, and Identity in Late-Nineteenth-Century Small-Town Ontario* (Toronto: University of Toronto Press, 1996). Though figure skating is not directly addressed, see also Alan Metcalfe, *Canada Learns to Play: The Emergence of Organized sport, 1807–1914* (Toronto: McClelland and Stewart, 1987).

71 Hall, *The Girl and the Game*, 24; Marks, *Revivals and Roller Rinks,*127.
72 Adams, *Artistic Impressions*, 139.
73 Adams, "The Manly History of a 'Girls' Sport," 877.
74 "Physical Exercise," *Farmer's Advocate and Home Magazine* 27, no. 317 (May 1892): 196.
75 Edna Wallace Hopper, "The Value of Physical Training for Women," *Elora Express*, 1 February 1905, 5.
76 Adams, *Artistic Impressions*, 118–20.
77 "Bad Weather for the Devil," *Tillsonburg Observer*, 10 March 1882, 1.
78 DPL, Inez (Eagleson) Perrin, "Call Back Yesterday," *North Kent Leader Centennial Edition*, 23 June 1982, E-27.
79 Young, *The Golden Age of Canadian Figure Skating*, 23. Prior to Forbes's invention, the earliest forms of skates were fashioned out of bone and wood and used by Haudenosaunee hunters to stalk their prey. Awkward and weighty skates were introduced in seventeenth-century Europe and used until lighter ones were constructed almost a century later.
80 *Canada's Greatest Store: Christmas Catalogue, 1897, the T. Eaton Co. Limited* (Toronto: D.E. Scott, 1897), 19.
81 DPL, Inez (Eagleson) Perrin, "Call Back Yesterday," *North Kent Leader Centennial Edition*, 23 June 1982, E-27.

82   Stephen Thorning, "First Elora Ice Rink Was Constructed in 1879," *Elora Sentinel*, 22 October 1991, 6.

83   UGASC, Marston-Archibald Collection, XR1 MS A371, Box 1, Olive Snyder diary, 1914–1917.

84   *Elora Express*, 1 February 1905, 8.

85   Stephen Thorning, "Competitive Speed Skating Became a Local Fad in 1899," *Wellington Advertiser*, 8 July 2011, 10.

86   *Tillsonburg Observer*, 3 December 1880, 1.

87   Adams, *Artistic Impressions*, 111–12.

88   Benjamin Fish Austin, *Woman; Her Character, Culture and Calling. A Full Discussion of Woman's Work in the Home, the School, the Church and the Social Circle; With an Account of her Successful Labors in Moral and Social Reform, her Heroic Work for God and Humanity in the Mission Field, her Success as a Wage-Earner and in Fighting Life's Battle Alone; With Chapters on all Departments of Woman's Training and Culture, her Claims to the Higher Education, and the Best Methods to be Pursued Therein* (Brantford, ON: Book and Bible House, 1890), 224.

89   Dorotea Gucciardo, "The Powered Generation: Canadians, Electricity, and Everyday Life" (PhD diss., Western University, 2011), 27, https://ir.lib.uwo.ca/cgi/viewcontent.cgi?article=1376&context=etd.

90   Donald G. Wetherell and Irene R.A. Kmet, *Town Life: Main Street and the Evolution of Small Town Alberta, 1880–1947* (Edmonton: University of Alberta Press and Alberta Community Development, 1995), 248, 273.

91   Kate Aitken, *Never a Day So Bright* (New York: Longmans, 1957), 61.

92   "Lorne Skating and Curling Rink," *Tillsonburg Observer*, 15 December 1882, 1.

93   Marks, *Revivals and Roller Rinks*, 128.

94   Hall, *The Girl and the Game*, 24.

95   ANHS, Documentary Artifact Collection, Folder: Laurel's Booklet *E.D. & Mary Ann* original drafts.

96   Bouchier, *For the Love of the Game*, 80–81.

97   Young, *The Golden Age of Canadian Figure Skating*, 24.

98   UGASC, XR1 MS A192067, Elora Women's Institute Tweedsmuir History, 73.

99   Aitken, *Never a Day So Bright*, 78.

100   *Elora Express*, 15 February 1905, 8.

101   "The Carnival," *Tillsonburg Observer*, 29 January 1903, 4; ANHS, Documentary Artifact Collection, Marguerite Sinclair Scrapbook.

102   Marks, *Revivals and Roller Rinks*, 128.

103   WCMA, A2004.91 MU 513, File 3, Muriel Clark, Elora, letters, 1914.

104   WCMA, A1996.129 MU 312, Margaret A. Templin diary, 1920.

105   *Elora Express*, 6 December 1899, 1.

106   *Elora Express*, 2 December 1903, 8.

107   *Dresden Times*, 19 February 1891, 5.

108 ANHS, Documentary Artifact Collection, "William Harcourt Popham Remembers."

109 *Tillsonburg Observer*, 5 November 1875, 3.

110 ANHS, Documentary Artifact Collection, "William Harcourt Popham Remembers."

111 See Gerald Pocius, *A Place to Belong: Community Order and Everyday Space in Calvert, Newfoundland* (Montreal and Kingston: McGill-Queen's University Press, 1991), 254–58.

112 Quote from "Women in the Garden," *Rural Canadian* 1, no. 3 (29 December 1881): 6. For more on gardening as a "useful" activity, see Linda J. Borish, "Benevolent America: Rural Women, Physical Recreation, Sport and Health Reform in Ante-Bellum New England," *International Journal of the History of Sport* 22, no. 6 (2005): 946–73.

113 Stephen Thorning, *The Model Village and the Struggle for Success: A History of Elora, Ontario* (Fergus, ON: Wellington County Historical Society, 2023), 195–96.

114 See David C. Jones, "'From Babies to Buttonholes': Women's Work at Agricultural Fairs," *Alberta History* 29, no. 4 (1981): 26–32; Ellen M. Plante, *Women at Home in Victorian America: A Social History* (New York: Facts on File, 1997), 171–76; Jodey Nurse, *Cultivating Community: Women and Agricultural Fairs in Ontario* (Montreal and Kingston: McGill-Queen's University Press, 2022).

115 Interestingly, a men's lawn tennis club was not formed in Elora until May 1910, according to the *Elora Express*.

116 ANHS, Documentary Artifact Collection, Marguerite Sinclair Scrapbook.

117 *Elora Express*, 24 May 1905, 8.

118 UGASC, Marston-Archibald Collection, XR1 MS A371, Box 1, Olive Snyder diary, 1913.

119 WCMA, A2004.91, MU 513, File 1, Muriel Clark, Elora, Letters, 1910, 1912.

120 Wendy Mitchinson, *The Nature of Their Bodies: Women and Their Doctors in Victorian Canada* (Toronto: University of Toronto Press, 1991), 91. For a much more detailed discussion about historical perceptions of menstruation as a "disability," see Cheryl Krasnick Warsh, *Prescribed Norms: Women and Health in Canada and the United State since 1800* (Toronto: University of Toronto Press, 2010), 3–46.

121 Robert J. Lake, "Gender and Etiquette in British Lawn Tennis, 1870–1939: A Case Study of 'Mixed Doubles,'" *International Journal of the History of Sport* 29, no. 5 (2012): 692.

122 Robert J. Lake, "Social Class, Etiquette and Behavioural Restraint in British Lawn Tennis, 1870–1939," *International Journal of the History of Sport* 28, no. 6 (2011): 881.

123 Ibid., 882.

124 See *The Home Treasury of Useful and Entertaining Knowledge on the Art of Making Home Happy, and an Aid in Self-Education; the Laws of Etiquette and Good Society; Home Amusements; Out-Door Sports; And Other Interesting Matter of Social and Educational Value.* (Toronto, London, ON, Brockville, ON, and St. John, NB: J.S. Robertson and Bros., 1883), 247.

125 Margery A. Bulger, "American Sportswomen in the 19th Century," *Journal of Popular Culture* 16, no. 2 (Fall 1982): 5.

126 See Adams, "Freezing Social Relations," 65.

Chapter 4. Crazy Teas and Christmas Trees

1 WCMA, A1981.92, Ann Amelia Day/Sunley Diary, Eramosa Township, 1878–1879.

2 Monda Halpern, *And on That Farm He Had a Wife: Ontario Farm Women and Feminism, 1900–1970* (Montreal and Kingston: McGill-Queen's University Press, 2001), 7.

3 Ellen M. Plante, *Women at Home in Victorian America: A Social History* (New York: Facts on File, 1997), 124.

4 Jane Marie Pederson, *Between Memory and Reality: Family and Community in Rural Wisconsin, 1870–1970* (Madison: University of Wisconsin Press, 1992), 187.

5 Ibid., 186.

6 Ellen Gruber Garvey, *The Adman in the Parlor: Magazines and the Gendering of Consumer Culture, 1880s to 1910s* (New York: Oxford University Press, 1996), 136.

7 Angela E. Davis, "'Country Homemakers': The Daily Lives of Prairie Women as Seen through the Woman's Page of the Grain Growers' Guide 1908–1928," in *Canadian Papers in Rural History*, vol. 8, ed. Donald H. Akenson (Gananoque, ON: Langdale Press, 1992), 163–74.

8 *Census of Canada, 1890–91*, Vol. I (Ottawa: S.E. Dawson, 1893), 36, 39, 58–89, 70–71.

9 Andrew C. Holman, *A Sense of Their Duty: Middle-Class Formation in Victorian Ontario Towns* (Montreal and Kingston: McGill-Queen's University Press, 2000), 167.

10 References are made in the primary and secondary literature to various names for the room, but "parlour" is most frequently used. Some historians argue, however, that in rural homes one cannot classify parlours in the same manner as one would for an urban home because of function, contents, and layout.

11 In the absence of a formal dining room, the kitchen was used to entertain guests; see John R. Gillis, *A World of Their Own Making: Myth, Ritual, and the Quest for Family Values* (New York: Basic Books, 1996), 120.

12 Peter Ward, *A History of Domestic Space: Privacy and the Canadian Home* (Vancouver: University of British Columbia Press, 1999), 61.

13 Sally McMurry, "City Parlor, Country Sitting Room: Rural Vernacular Design and the American Parlor, 1840–1900," *Winterthur Portfolio* 20, no. 4 (Winter 1985): 262.

14 Annmarie Adams, "Female Regulation of the Healthy Home," in *Home, Work, and Play: Situating Canadian Social History, 1840–1980*, eds. James Opp and John C. Walsh (Don Mills, ON: Oxford University Press, 2006), 6.

15 According to John R. Gillis, homemaking was a "labor of love involving the creation of the symbols, myths, and rituals that made a house a home. And from the very beginning the use of the term 'homemaking' was gendered, based on the assumption that a man could build and repair a house but only a woman could make a home." See Gillis, *A World of Their Own Making*, 122.

16 For more on space and gender segregation in the home, see Jane Hamlett, "'The Dining Room Should Be the Man's Paradise, as the Drawing Room Is the Woman's': Gender and Middle-Class Domestic Space in England, 1850–1910," *Gender and History* 21, no. 3 (November 2009): 576–91.

17 Adams, "Female Regulation of the Healthy Home," 6.

18 Katherine C. Grier, "The Decline of the Memory Palace: The Parlor after 1890," in *American Home Life, 1880–1930: A Social History of Spaces and Services*, ed. Jessica H. Foy and Thomas J. Schlereth (Knoxville: University of Tennessee Press, 1992), 53.

19 Gillis, *A World of Their Own Making*, 127.

20 Ruth Sandwell, *Canada's Rural Majority: Households, Environments, and Economies, 1870–1940* (Toronto: University of Toronto Press, 2016), 87.

21 American historian Sally McMurry argues that during the Progressive Era, many rural families abandoned the characteristically urban formal parlour in favour of the informal sitting room because it better reflected and accommodated their more casual social patterns. A similar principle appears to have been adopted in many rural and small-town Ontario homes; see McMurry, *Families and Farmhouses in Nineteenth-Century America: Vernacular Design and Social Change* (New York: Oxford University Press, 1988), 135.

22 Kate Aitken, *Never a Day So Bright* (New York: Longmans, 1957), 28–30.

23 Gillis, *A World of Their Own Making*, 127.

24 McMurry, *Families and Farmhouses*, 147.

25 Gerald Pocius, *A Place to Belong: Community Order and Everyday Space in Calvert, Newfoundland* (Montreal and Kingston: McGill-Queen's University Press, 1991), 239–48, quote on p. 242.

26 WCMA, A1977.67, Connon family correspondence, 1852–1930 (microfilm), letter from Thomas Connon to John R. Connon, 1 February 1891. For more on the history of ornamental house plants, see Cheryl Lyon-Jenness, "Bergamot Balm and Verbenas: The Public and Private Meaning of Ornamental Plants in the Mid-Nineteenth-Century Midwest," *Agricultural History* 73, no. 2 (Spring 1999): 201–21.

27   Dorotea Gucciardo, "The Powered Generation: Canadians, Electricity, and Everyday Life" (PhD diss., Western University, 2011), 38-39, https://ir.lib.uwo.ca/cgi/viewcontent.cgi?article=1376&context=etd.

28   WCMA, A2004.91, MU 513, File 1, Muriel Clark, Elora, Letters, 1910, 1912.

29   Sometimes she is referred to as "Minnie May" in the *Farmer's Advocate and Home Magazine*.

30   "Use of Music," *Farmer's Advocate and Home Magazine* 12, no. 10 (October 1877): 244.

31   "Home Attraction," *Farmer's Advocate and Home Magazine* 19, no. 2 (February 1884): 56.

32   *Elora Express*, 8 November 1899, 1.

33   Stephanie Dunson, "The Minstrel in the Parlor: Nineteenth-Century Sheet Music and the Domestication of Blackface Minstrelsy," *American Transcendental Quarterly* 16, no. 4 (December 2002): 245.

34   "Shall Girls Play the Piano," *Tillsonburg Observer*, 22 August 1872, 2.

35   In the column containing advertisements for professional services in Tillsonburg, Miss Mary Widner offered "Piano Teaching. Pupils prepared for Toronto College or Conservatory of Music." In that same issue, Miss M.R. Murray, the organist at Avondale Presbyterian church and pupil of Mr. A.S. Vogt of the Toronto Conservatory of Music, also offered piano and organ lessons. Both advertisements appeared in the *Tillsonburg Observer*, 29 January 1903, 4.

36   Russell Lynes, *The Lively Audience: A Social History of the Visual and Performing Arts in America, 1890–1950* (New York: Harper and Row, 1985), 31.

37   *Elora Express*, 24 May 1905, 8.

38   *Tillsonburg Observer*, 29 November 1900, 1.

39   Professor Hoffmann, *Parlor Amusements and Evening Party Entertainments* (London: G. Routledge and Sons, 18–?).

40   E.I. Horsman, *Home Amusements Are the Magnets of the Family Circle* (New York: H.C. Stoothoff, 1871), title page.

41   *Elora Express*, 6 December 1905, 1.

42   WCMA, A1981.92, Ann Amelia Day/Sunley Diary, Eramosa Township, 1878–1879.

43   UGASC, Marston-Archibald Collection, XR1 MS A371, Olive Snyder diary, 1914–1917.

44   "Games, Harmless, and Otherwise," *Tillsonburg Liberal*, 4 May 1905, 7.

45   "Daisy Eyebright" seems to be the pseudonym of American author Sophia Orne Edwards Johnson, who wrote for several American magazines, including rural and agricultural periodicals, in the later nineteenth century. See "S.O. Johnson," https://en.wikipedia.org/wiki/S._O._Johnson.

46   "How to Spend Winter Evenings," *Rural Canadian* 1, no. 4 (19 January 1882): 12.

47   Donna R. Braden, "'The Family That Plays Together Stays Together': Family Pastimes and Indoor Amusements, 1890–1930," in *American Home Life*,

1880–1930: A Social History of Spaces and Services, ed. Jessica H. Foy and Thomas J. Schlereth (Knoxville: University of Tennessee Press, 1992), 146–47.

48   "How to Spend Winter Evenings," *Rural Canadian* 1, no. 4 (19 January 1882): 12.

49   Gillis, *A World of Their Own Making*, 95.

50   Peter Ward, "Courtship and Social Space in Nineteenth-Century English Canada," *Canadian Historical Review* 68, no. 1 (1987): 37–38; Constance Backhouse, *Petticoats and Prejudice: Women and Law in Nineteenth-Century Canada* (Toronto: Osgoode Society by Women's Press, 1991), 40–41.

51   WCMA, A1981.92, Ann Amelia Day/Sunley Diary, Eramosa Township, 1878–1879.

52   *Dresden Times*, n.d. (likely sometime around end of July 1891), unpaginated.

53   Keith Walden, "Tea in Toronto and the Liberal Order, 1880–1914," *Canadian Historical Review* 93, no. 1 (March 2012): 2.

54   "Concerning Afternoon Teas," *Tillsonburg Observer*, 5 February 1903, 1.

55   Douglas McCalla, "Seeing Pioneers as Modern: Rural Upper Canadians Go Shopping," in *Temps, espace, et modernités: Mélanges offerts à Serge Courville et Normand Séguin*, ed. Brigitte Caulier and Yvan Rousseau (Quebec: Les Presses de l'Université Laval, 2009), 143. McCalla also discusses purchases of tea in rural Upper Canada in his longer monograph, *Consumers in the Bush: Shopping in Rural Upper Canada* (Montreal and Kingston: McGill-Queen's University Press, 2015).

56   LAC, Census of Canada, 1891, Schedule No. 1, Ontario, Bothwell, Dresden Town, accessed 17 July 2023, https://recherche-collection-search.bac-lac.gc.ca/eng/home/record?app=census&IdNumber=24992963.

57   *Dresden Times*, 21 May 1891, 5.

58   See Walden, "Tea in Toronto and the Liberal Order."

59   "Conversation as Entertainment," *Farmer's Advocate and Home Magazine* 43, no. 806 (5 March 1908): 406. Joy Parr discusses similar "mock weddings" occurring in the small industrial towns of Paris and Hanover in the 1920s and 1930s. The events described by Parr, however, were more satirical in nature, consisting of sex and age reversals meant to parody traditional marriage practices; see Parr, *The Gender of Breadwinners: Women, Men and Change in Two Industrial Towns, 1880–1950* (Toronto: University of Toronto Press, 1990), 30–32.

60   Beverly Gordon, *The Saturated World: Aesthetic Meaning, Intimate Objects, Women's Lives, 1890–1940* (Knoxville: University of Tennessee Press, 2006), 68.

61   "The Summer Tea Table," *Elora Express*, 21 July 1892, 6.

62   "Modern Tea Parties," *Farmer's Advocate and Home Magazine* 22, no. 258 (June 1887): 182.

63   Ibid.

64   For example, see Aitken, *Never a Day So Bright*, 212–14.

65   Ibid.

66   Aitken, *Never a Day So Bright*, 215.

67   "The Bachelors' Party," *Tillsonburg Observer*, 8 February 1895, 4.

68   Bert Newman, *Once Upon a Time: Further Reminiscences about Tillsonburg*, ed. Dave Stover (Tillsonburg, ON: Otter Printing, 1988), 91.

69   Ibid. This special group, according to Newman, was composed of women from elite Tillsonburg families such as the Tillsons, Sinclairs, Browns, Jacksons, Maddocks, Joys, Bennetts, Lukes, Thomsons, Raynes, and Hogarths.

70   LAC, Census of Canada, 1911, Schedule No. 1, Ontario, Wellington South, Elora, accessed 17 July 2023, https://recherche-collection-search.bac-lac. gc.ca/eng/home/record?app=census&IdNumber=13739442; *Elora Express*, 2 February 1910, 5.

71   *Tillsonburg Liberal*, 9 February 1905, 1.

72   *Tillsonburg Observer*, 22 February 1900, 1.

73   According to the 1891 census, thirty-five-year-old Dorcas was married to Gilbert Stinson, a fifty-year-old lime burner. Though the lime-burning business was considered a laborious and often thankless industrial occupation, its manufacturers had the potential to make a considerable sum of money, explaining why Dorcas may have had the means with which to throw such an elaborate party. See LAC, Census of Canada, 1891, Schedule No. 1, Ontario, Oxford South, Oxford North, accessed 17 July 2023, https://recherche-collection-search.bac-lac.gc.ca/eng/ home/record?app=census&IdNumber=26274768.

74   *Tillsonburg Observer*, 3 May 1895, 1.

75   Ibid.

76   Marjory Lang, *Women Who Made the News: Female Journalists in Canada, 1880–1945* (Montreal and Kingston: McGill-Queen's University Press, 1999), 202.

77   Ibid., 196.

78   Annie Randall White, *Twentieth Century Etiquette: An Up-to-Date Book for Polite Society* (Chicago: Wabash Publishing House, 1900), 108.

79   *Tillsonburg Liberal*, 2 February 1905, 1.

80   Beef tea was the broth produced from boiling lean pieces of beef. It was often used as an appetite stimulant and given to invalids for its nutritional value.

81   Evelyn L., "A Few Suggestions for Entertaining," *Farmer's Advocate and Home Magazine* 27, no. 324 (December 1892): 491.

82   Gillis, *A World of Their Own Making*, 90.

83   Evelyn L., "A Few Suggestions for Entertaining," 491.

84   Miss Ada Wood, "Prize Essay, A Country Party, and How to Make It Pleasant," *Farmer's Advocate and Home Magazine* 25, no. 290 (February 1890): 53. At work bees in rural Ontario, Catharine Anne Wilson notes, portion sizes were prized over "fancy" dishes when workers were treated to meals. To show thanks for their efforts, hosts cooked hearty (yet tasty) fare that was filling and attainable; see Wilson, *Being Neighbours: Cooperative Work and Rural Culture, 1830–1960* (Montreal and Kingston: McGill-Queen's University Press, 2022), 200–201.

85 Miss Ada Wood, "Prize Essay, A Country Party, and How to Make It Pleasant," *Farmer's Advocate and Home Magazine* 25, no. 290 (February 1890): 53.

86 Andrea G. Radke, "Refining Rural Spaces: Women and Vernacular Gentility in the Great Plains, 1880–1920," *Great Plains Quarterly* 24 (Fall 2004): 227, 235, 240.

87 "The Art of Good Dining," *Rural Canadian* 9, no. 1 (January 1886): 28.

88 ANHS, Documentary Artifact Collection, Annandale House maid, Myrtle Dreyer (née Morden), born 8 July 1894, interview conducted 24 July 1984.

89 Ruth Schwartz Cowan, *More Work for Mother: The Ironies of Household Technology from the Open Hearth to the Microwave* (New York: Basic Books, 1983), 158–59.

90 WCMA, A1996.112, Diary of Annie Hill (née Drury) of Fergus, Ontario, 1912–1923.

91 ANHS, Documentary Artifact Collection, Tillson Family Scrapbook, Newspaper article, "A Unique Affair."

92 Gordon, *The Saturated World*, 104.

93 ANHS, Documentary Artifact Collection, Tillson Family Scrapbook, Newspaper article, "A Unique Affair."

94 Pederson, *Beyond Memory and Reality*, 198.

95 UGASC, Marston-Archibald Collection, XR1 MS A371, Box 1, Olive Snyder diary, 1913.

96 NDMA, 2002.62.1, Minnie Smith Collection.

97 Theodora Penny Martin, *The Sound of Our Own Voices: Women's Study Clubs 1860–1910* (Boston: Beacon Press, 1987), 30.

98 Mary Neth, *Preserving the Family Farm: Women, Community, and the Foundations of Agribusiness in the Midwest, 1900–1940* (Baltimore: Johns Hopkins University Press, 1995), 61.

99 Susan Strasser, *Never Done: A History of American Housework* (New York: Pantheon Books, 1982), 133–34.

100 Wilson, *Being Neighbours*, 114–16.

101 Halpern, *And on That Farm He Had a Wife*, 24. Nancy Grey Osterud states that planned social events such as parties were never held on Sundays; see Osterud, *Bonds of Community: The Lives of Farm Women in Nineteenth-Century New York* (Ithaca, NY: Cornell University Press, 1991), 234. See also Neth, *Preserving the Family Farm*, 26–28.

102 See Catharine Anne Wilson, "Reciprocal Work Bees and the Meaning of Neighbourhood," *Canadian Historical Review* 82, no. 3 (September 2001): 431–64; and Wilson, *Being Neighbours*.

103 UGASC, Marston-Archibald Collection, XR1 MS A371, Box 1, Olive Snyder diary, 1913. For more on the importance of sisterly bonds in the rural context, see Halpern, *And on That Farm He Had a Wife*, 64.

104 WCMA, A1996.112, Diary of Annie Hill (née Drury) of Fergus, Ontario, 1912–1923.

105 Marilyn Ferris Motz, "Folk Expression of Time and Place: 19th-Century Midwestern Rural Diaries," *Journal of American Folklore* 100, no. 396 (April–June 1987): 140, 144.

106 Pederson, *Between Memory and Reality*, 188.

107 UGASC, Marston-Archibald Collection, XR1 MS A371, Box 1, Olive Snyder diary, 1913.

108 Craig Heron and Steve Penfold, *The Workers' Festival: A History of Labour Day in Canada* (Toronto: University of Toronto Press, 2005), 30.

109 Gordon, *The Saturated World*, 29.

110 Neth, *Preserving the Family Farm*, 63.

111 Heron and Penfold, *The Workers' Festival*, 29.

112 Nicolas Rogers, "Halloween in Urban North America: Liminality and Hyperreality," *Histoire sociale/Social History* 29, no. 58 (November 1996): 463; see also Rogers, *Halloween: From Pagan Ritual to Party Night* (Oxford: Oxford University Press, 2002).

113 Keith Walden, "Respectable Hooligans: Male Toronto College Students Celebrate Hallowe'en, 1884–1910," *Canadian Historical Review* 68, no. 1 (1987): 6; see also Rogers, "Halloween in Urban North America," 461–77.

114 Walden, "Respectable Hooligans," 6.

115 See Stephen Thorning, "Elora Woman Left Town after Two-Day Charivari," *Wellington Advertiser*, n.d., unpaginated.

116 Aitken, *Never a Day So Bright*, 199.

117 UGASC, Marston-Archibald Collection, XR1 MS A371, Box 1, Olive Snyder diary, 1913.

118 NDMA, 2002.62.1, Minnie Smith Collection.

119 "A Hallowe'en Party," *Farmer's Advocate and Home Magazine* 43, no. 835 (24 September 1908): 1489.

120 "A Hallowe'en Social," *Farmer's Advocate and Home Magazine* 43, no. 835 (24 September 1908): 1489.

121 White, *Twentieth Century Etiquette*, 53.

122 Leigh Eric Schmidt, "The Fashioning of a Modern Holiday: St. Valentine's Day, 1840–1870," *Winterthur Portfolio* 28, no. 4 (Winter 1993): 214.

123 Leigh Eric Schmidt, *Consumer Rites: The Buying and Selling of American Holidays* (Princeton, NJ: Princeton University Press, 1995), 39.

124 Quote from Schmidt, *Consumer Rites*, 71. Peter Ward writes that in addition to adults, male and female children and adolescents also enjoyed sending valentines to one another; see Ward, *Courtship, Love, and Marriage in Nineteenth-Century English Canada* (Montreal and Kingston: McGill-Queen's University Press, 1990), 92–98.

125 UGASC, Marston-Archibald Collection, XR1 MS A371, Box 1, Olive Snyder diary, 1913.

126 Aitken, *Never a Day So Bright*, 199.

127 Schmidt, *Consumer Rites*, 81.

128 Ibid., 77.
129 *Dresden Times*, 19 February 1891, 5.
130 LAC, Census of Canada, 1901, Schedule No. 1, Norfolk North, Tilsonburg, accessed 17 July 2023, https://recherche-collection-search.bac-lac.gc.ca/eng/home/record?app=census&IdNumber=36143638.
131 *Tillsonburg Liberal*, 16 February 1905, 1.
132 WCMA, A1996.112, Diary of Annie Hill (née Drury) of Fergus, Ontario, 1912–1923.
133 *Tillsonburg Observer*, 10 May 1895, 1.
134 *Tillsonburg Observer*, 28 February 1890, 1.
135 ANHS, Documentary Artifact Collection, "A Tillsonburg Woman's Memory of a Party of the Days of Confederation Mrs. Joel Bate, One of the Garnhams of Guysboro, Recalls Early Days By A.S. Paragus."
136 Gillis, A *World of Their Own Making*, 72.
137 Ibid., 72.
138 White, *Twentieth Century Etiquette*, 53.
139 Julia McNair Wright, *The Complete Home: An Encyclopaedia of Domestic Life and Affairs. The Household, in its Foundation, Order, Economy, Beauty, Healthfulness, Emergencies, Methods, Children, Literature, Amusements, Religion, Friendships, Manners, Hospitality, Servants, Industry, Money, and History. A Volume of Practical Experiences Popularly Illustrated* (Philadelphia; Brantford, ON: Bradley, Garretson, 1879), 562.
140 UGASC, Marston-Archibald Collection, XR1 MS A371, Box 1, Olive Snyder diary, 1913.
141 NDMA, X79A-XX1-15, Francis Poole Diary, 1904.
142 Stephen Thorning, "Santa Claus First in Elora in 1870s," *Elora Sentinel*, 17 December 1991, 6.
143 Schmidt, *Consumer Rites*, 124. For more on the expansion of Christmas rites and rituals, see Mark Connelly, *Christmas: A Social History* (London: I.B. Tauris, 1999).
144 *Elora Express*, 13 December 1899, 1.
145 Gillis, *A World of Their Own Making*, 104.
146 Schmidt, *Consumer Rites*, 73.
147 Ibid., 102.
148 *Elora Express*, 13 December 1899, 1.
149 Thorning, "Santa Claus First in Elora in 1870s."
150 "Recreation," *Canada Farmer* 2, no. 1 (25 January 1870): 33.
151 LAC, Census of Canada, 1891, Schedule No. 1, Ontario, Bothwell, Dresden Town, accessed 17 July 2023, https://recherche-collection-search.bac-lac.gc.ca/eng/home/record?app=census&IdNumber=24978763.
152 Schmidt, *Consumer Rites*, 151.
153 "Pleasant Gathering," *Dresden Times*, 1 January 1891, 1.
154 *Tillsonburg Liberal*, 4 January 1910, 1.

155   WCMA, A1981.92, Ann Amelia Day/Sunley Diary, Eramosa Township, 1878–1879.
156   WCMA, A1996.112, Diary of Annie Hill (née Drury) of Fergus, Ontario, 1912–1923.
157   WCMA, A1952.225.1, Man 18, Mu 3, Diary of an unidentified student, likely in Elora, some local and family names references, 1898–1900, 1915.
158   UGASC, Marston-Archibald Collection, XR1 MS A371, Box 1, Olive Snyder diary, 1913.
159   UGASC, Marston-Archibald Collection, XR1 MS A371, Box 1, Olive Snyder diary, 1914–1917.
160   ANHS, Agnes McGregor File, "Memories" by Agnes Christine McGregor (an autobiography), written 20 April 1959.
161   ANHS, Documentary Artifact Collection, Marguerite Sinclair Scrapbook.
162   ANHS, Agnes McGregor File, "Memories" by Agnes Christine McGregor (an autobiography), written 20 April 1959.

Chapter 5. Armchair Tourists

1   *Tillsonburg Observer*, 13 July 1894, 1.
2   "Tillsonburg Ladies Travel Club Focuses on Alaska, Hawaii," *Norfolk and Tillsonburg News*, 11 November 2015, https://www.norfolkandtillsonburgnews.com/2015/11/11/tillsonburg-ladies-travel-club-focuses-on-alaska-hawaii/wcm/e344b5e5-2340-c9fb-286e-842afe089c6c.
3   Kristin L. Hoganson, *Consumers' Imperium: The Global Production of American Domesticity, 1865–1920* (Chapel Hill: University of North Carolina Press, 2007), 14.
4   John MacDougall, *Rural Life in Canada: Its Trend and Tasks*, with introduction by Robert Craig Brown (Toronto: University of Toronto Press, 1973), 131; see also Co-Operating Organizations of the Presbyterian and Methodist Churches, County of Huron, Ontario, *Report on a Rural Survey of the Agricultural, Educational, Social, and Religious Life*. Prepared for the Huron Survey Committed by the Department of Temperance and Moral Reform of the Methodist Church, the Board of Social Service and Evangelism, and the Board of Sabbath Schools and Young People's Societies of the Presbyterian Church (December–January 1913–1914). Throughout the late nineteenth and early twentieth centuries, rural and agrarian periodicals such as the *Farmer's Advocate and Home Magazine*, *Canada Farmer*, and *Rural Canadian* published various advice articles on ways to enliven rural and small-town social gatherings, ways to keep boys and girls on farms, and more "modern" methods for improving social relations.
5   Sections of this chapter were previously published in Rebecca Beausaert, "'Foreigners in Town': Leisure, Consumption, and Cosmopolitanism in Late-Nineteenth and Early-Twentieth Century Tillsonburg, ON," *Journal of the Canadian Historical Association* 23, no. 1 (2012): 215–47.

6 Hoganson, *Consumers' Imperium*, 137.

7 Thomas J. Schlereth, "Country Stores, County Fairs, and Mail-Order Catalogues: Consumption in Rural America," in *Consuming Visions: Accumulation and Display of Goods in America, 1880–1920*, ed. Simon J. Bronner (New York: W.W. Norton, 1989), 347.

8 David B. Danbom, *Born in the Country: A History of Rural America*, 2nd ed. (Baltimore: Johns Hopkins University Press, 2006), 133.

9 See Adam Crerar, "Writing across the Rural-Urban Divide: The Case of Peter McArthur, 1909–24," *Journal of Canadian Studies* 41, no. 2 (Spring 2007): 131n25.

10 "Iceland and Its People," *Tillsonburg Observer*, 9 June 1893, 7.

11 "The Wolf Boy of India," *Tillsonburg Observer*, 22 July 1892, 7.

12 For example, see "A Remarkable Oriental Experience. A Thrilling Story of Chinese Treachery," *Tillsonburg Observer*, 17 March 1893, 7.

13 "Lecture on China," *Tillsonburg Observer*, 13 October 1893, 1.

14 John Sparrowhawk, "Divans and Cozy Corners," *Ladies' Home Journal* 13, no. 11 (October 1896): 17.

15 See "Eleven Years Old," *Tillsonburg Observer*, 16 August 1895, 4; "Japanese Garden Party," *Tillsonburg Liberal*, 13 July 1905, 1; Bert Newman, *Once Upon a Time: Further Reminiscences about Tillsonburg*, ed. Dave Stover (Tillsonburg, ON: Otter Printing, 1988), 91.

16 Hoganson, *Consumers' Imperium*; Beverly Gordon, *The Saturated World: Aesthetic Meaning, Intimate Objects, Women's Lives, 1890–1940* (Knoxville: University of Tennessee Press, 2006); Catherine Hall and Sonya O. Rose, eds., *At Home with the Empire: Metropolitan Culture and the Imperial World* (Cambridge: Cambridge University Press, 2006); Kristin Hoganson, "The Fashionable World: Imagined Communities of Dress," in *After the Imperial Turn: Thinking with and through the Nation*, ed. Antoinette Burton (Durham, NC: Duke University Press, 2003), 260–78; Susan Nance, *How the Arabian Nights Inspired the American Dream, 1790–1935* (Chapel Hill: University of North Carolina Press, 2009).

17 Hoganson, *Consumers' Imperium*, 157.

18 Laura A. Smith, "The Girl in the Small Town: Spring and Summer Pleasures She May Enjoy," *Ladies' Home Journal* 24, no. 6 (May 1907): 26.

19 See Joanna de Groot, "Metropolitan Desires and Colonial Connections: Reflections on Consumption and Empire," in *At Home with the Empire: Metropolitan Culture and the Imperial World*, ed. Catherine Hall and Sonya O. Rose (Cambridge: Cambridge University Press, 2006), 166–90.

20 Peter H. Hoffenberg, *An Empire on Display: English, Indian, and Australian Exhibitions from the Crystal Palace to the Great War* (Berkeley: University of California Press, 2001), 27.

21   Keith Walden, *Becoming Modern in Toronto: The Industrial Exhibition and the Shaping of a Late Victorian Culture* (Toronto: University of Toronto Press, 1997), 15.

22   Jodey Nurse, *Cultivating Community: Women and Agricultural Fairs in Ontario* (Montreal and Kingston: McGill-Queen's University Press, 2022), 250.

23   Walden, *Becoming Modern in Toronto*, 15; see also Robert W. Rydell and Rob Kroes, *Buffalo Bill in Bologna: The Americanization of the World, 1869–1922* (Chicago: University of Chicago Press, 2005).

24   Reid Badger, *The Great American Fair: The World's Columbian Exposition and American Culture* (Chicago: Nelson Hall, 1979), 109. Elsbeth Heaman notes that total attendance was around 27.5 million, while Philip Deloria argues 27 million attended; see Heaman, *The Inglorious Arts of Peace: Exhibitions in Canadian Society during the Nineteenth Century* (Toronto: University of Toronto Press, 1999), 234 and Philip Deloria, *Indians in Unexpected Places* (Lawrence, KS: University Press of Kansas, 2004), 61.

25   In July 1896, the *Tillsonburg Observer* announced that Mrs. A.M. Croley finally received the award she had won at the 1893 World's Columbian Exposition in Chicago for her exhibit of natural specimens; see *Tillsonburg Observer*, 10 July 1896, 1. In October 1893, the *Observer* reported that "Mr. E.D. Tillson has been notified that flour exhibited by him at the World's Fair was awarded a medal on Wednesday"; see *Tillsonburg Observer*, 20 October 1893, 1.

26   Badger, *The Great American Fair*, 109.

27   *Tillsonburg Observer*, 3 November 1893, 1.

28   *Tillsonburg Observer*, 1 September 1893, 4.

29   Badger, *The Great American Fair*, 115.

30   Gordon, *The Saturated World*, 114. Modupe Labode, for instance, has examined the 1906 Carnival of Nations held in Denver, Colorado, that was spearheaded by local socialite Margaret Brown, later immortalized as the "Unsinkable Molly Brown" after the sinking of the *R.M.S. Titanic*; see Labode, "A Carnival for a Cathedral: The 1906 Carnival of Nations in Denver," *Colorado Heritage* (Autumn 2008): 14–25.

31   Jane Nicholas explores the rise of exhibitionary culture at North American fairs and shows and how exhibits of "freaks," people with disabilities, people of colour, and others were tied to consumers' interest in Social Darwinism, categorizations of difference, consumerism, and empire; see Nicholas, *Canadian Carnival Freaks and the Extraordinary Body, 1900–1970s* (Toronto: University of Toronto Press, 2018).

32   Hoganson, *Consumers' Imperium*, 140.

33   *Tillsonburg Observer*, 13 July 1894, 1.

34   Belinda, "The National Garden Party," *Tillsonburg Observer*, 24 July 1894, 4.

35   Issues of the *Tillsonburg Observer* are missing for July and August 1896, so it is unclear whether a "Garden Party of the Nations" was held that year.

36   "Foreigners in Town," *Tillsonburg Observer*, 19 July 1895, 4.

37　"The Feast of Nations; One of the Most Successful Affairs Ever Held Here,"
　　Ingersoll Chronicle, 25 June 1896, 1. Details were also provided in "Feast of
　　Nations," *Ingersoll Chronicle*, 18 June 1896, 1.

38　"Tillsonburg Tourists Take Trip around the World," *Tillsonburg Observer*, 22
　　November 1917, 3.

39　Beverly Gordon, *Bazaars and Fair Ladies: The History of the American
　　Fundraising Fair* (Knoxville: University of Tennessee Press, 1998), 131.

40　"The National Garden Party," *Tillsonburg Observer*, 24 July 1894, 4.

41　Hoganson, *Consumers' Imperium*, 24.

42　Rosemary R. Gagan, *A Sensitive Independence: Canadian Methodist Missionaries
　　in Canada and the Orient, 1881–1925* (Montreal and Kingston: McGill-Queen's
　　University Press, 1992), 66.

43　Thanks to Adam Crerar for bringing this possibility to my attention. For female
　　missionaries' constructions of the Indigenous "other," see Myra Rutherdale,
　　*Women and the White Man's God: Gender and Race in the Canadian Mission
　　Field* (Vancouver: University of British Columbia Press, 2002), 28–49.

44　Hoganson, *Consumers' Imperium*, 139.

45　Ashley Jackson and David Tomkins, *Illustrating Empire: A Visual History of
　　British Imperialism* (Oxford: Bodleian Library, University of Oxford, 2011), 174.

46　Hoganson, *Consumers' Imperium*, 143.

47　Ibid., 138.

48　For example, see Florence Pegg Taylor, "Some Oriental Ideas," *Ladies' Home
　　Journal* 20, no. 4 (March 1903): 36.

49　*Tillsonburg Observer*, 9 July 1897, 1.

50　Hoganson, "The Fashionable World," 270.

51　Hoganson, *Consumers' Imperium*, 146.

52　Due to the census enumerator's handwriting, two of the first names are dif-
　　ficult to read, so possibilities have been noted. See LAC, Census of Canada,
　　1911, Schedule No. 1, Ontario, Oxford South, Tillsonburg, accessed 17
　　July 2023, https://recherche-collection-search.bac-lac.gc.ca/eng/home/
　　record?app=census&IdNumber=15276330.

53　For more on Chinese laundries in Canadian history, see Ban Seng Hoe, *Enduring
　　Hardship: The Chinese Laundry in Canada* (Gatineau, PQ: Canadian Museum of
　　Civilization, 2003).

54　Labode, "A Carnival for a Cathedral," 19–21; Gordon, *The Saturated World*, 115.

55　Burton Benedict, "Rituals of Representation: Ethnic Stereotypes and Colonized
　　Peoples at World's Fairs," in *Fair Representations: World's Fairs and the Modern
　　World*, ed. Robert W. Rydell and Nancy E. Gwinn (Amsterdam: VU University
　　Press, 1994), 31.

56　Hoganson, *Consumers' Imperium*, 146–48.

57　Benedict, "Rituals of Representation," 32.

58   Dominic David Alessio, "Domesticating the 'Heart of the Wild': Female Personifications of the Colonies, 1886–1940," *Women's History Review* 6, no. 2 (1997): 259.

59   I am grateful to my friend and fellow historian Stacey Alexopoulos for bringing this observation to my attention.

60   Robert W. Rydell, *All the World's a Fair: Visions of Empire at American International Expositions, 1876–1916* (Chicago: University of Chicago Press, 1984), 228.

61   Heaman, *The Inglorious Arts of Peace*, 307.

62   Gordon, *Bazaars and Fair Ladies*, 131.

63   Hoganson, "The Fashionable World," 272.

64   Belinda, "The National Garden Party," *Tillsonburg Observer*, 24 July 1894, 4.

65   "State Federation of Women's Clubs," *Delineator* 49, no. 2 (February 1897): 234.

66   "Our Home Study Club: Conducted by E.B. Cutting," *Harper's Bazaar* 46, no. 3 (March 1912): 149; "Good Form and Entertainment," *Harper's Bazaar* 42, no. 11 (November 1908): 1158.

67   ANHS, Documentary Artifact Collection, Box—Travel Club (Tillsonburg Ladies' Travel Club), G.E. Grieve, Seventy-Five Years of Travel Club, April 1976; Tillsonburg Public Library (hereafter TPL), *A Century of Travel 1900–2000 Tillsonburg Ladies' Travel Club Established 1900* (n.p., 2000).

68   Earlier unpublished histories of the Travel Club refer to a Mrs. Holmstead, while a later one calls her Mrs. Olmstead. See ANHS, Documentary Artifact Collection, Box, Travel Club (Tillsonburg Ladies' Travel Club), G.E. Grieve, Seventy-Five Years of Travel Club, April 1976, and the Tillsonburg Ladies' Travel Club 1961–62; TPL, *A Century of Travel 1900–2000 Tillsonburg Ladies' Travel Club Established 1900* (n.p., 2000).

69   The Dundas Travel Club, like the Tillsonburg Travel Club, is still in existence today. The information about the establishment of the Dundas club was found in Joann MacLachlan, *The Dundas Travel Club: Documenting a Journey* (Hamilton, ON: Lavender Hill Publishers' Services, 2021).

70   ANHS, Documentary Artifact Collection, Box, Travel Club (Tillsonburg Ladies' Travel Club), Tillsonburg Branch of the Travel Club Constitution and By-Laws.

71   Ibid.

72   TPL, *A Century of Travel 1900–2000 Tillsonburg Ladies' Travel Club Established 1900* (n.p., 2000).

73   ANHS, Documentary Artifact Collection, Box, Travel Club (Tillsonburg Ladies' Travel Club), Tillsonburg Branch of the Travel Club Constitution and By-Laws.

74   Hoganson, *Consumers' Imperium*, 187.

75   ANHS, Documentary Artifact Collection, Box, Travel Club (Tillsonburg Ladies' Travel Club), Tillsonburg Branch of the Travel Club Constitution and By-Laws.

76   In the 1900s and 1910s, *Harper's Bazaar* contained a column called "Our Home Study Club," where clubwomen wrote to columnist E.B. Cutting for advice and inspiration to take back to meetings. The information about Russia was taken

from an earlier column by Margaret Hamilton Welch called "Club Work in Summer." See Welch, "Club Work in Summer: Plan for Club Work," *Harper's Bazaar* 33, no. 38 (22 September 1900): A1346.

77 Hoganson, *Consumers' Imperium*, 60.

78 Lynne Marks, *Revivals and Roller Rinks: Religion, Leisure, and Identity in Late-Nineteenth-Century Small-Town Ontario* (Toronto: University of Toronto Press, 1996), 13.

79 Gordon, *The Saturated World*, 114.

80 Carolyn French Benton, *Fairs and Fetes* (Boston: Dana Estes and Company, 1912), vii.

81 "The Minister's Social Helper: Suggests Some Fairs and Booths to Those Who, Working Socially in the Churches, Plan to Raise Money by Annual Sales," *Ladies' Home Journal* 24, no. 11 (October 1907): 31.

82 H.V. Nelles, *The Art of Nation-Building: Pageantry and Spectacle at Quebec's Tercentenary* (Toronto: University of Toronto Press, 1999), 169.

83 Labode, "A Carnival for a Cathedral," 18–19.

84 Jackson and Tomkins, *Illustrating Empire*, 150.

85 Hoganson, *Consumers' Imperium*, 143.

86 Ibid., 137.

87 Ibid., 146–49.

Chapter 6. Vacationers and "Staycationers"

1 Laura A. Smith, "The Girl in the Small Town: Fifth Article: Winter Pleasures She May Have," *Ladies' Home Journal* 23, no. 12 (November 1906): 40.

2 Laura A. Smith, "The Girl in the Small Town: Spring and Summer Pleasures She May Enjoy," *Ladies' Home Journal* 24, no. 6 (May 1907): 26.

3 Faye Hammill and Michelle Smith note that travel advertising was commonplace in Canadian periodicals well into the twentieth century, conveying the same messages about class, identity, and cosmopolitanism to readers; see Hammill and Smith, *Magazines, Travel, and Middlebrow Culture: Canadian Periodicals in English and French, 1925–1960* (Liverpool: Liverpool University Press, 2017).

4 See Dale Barbour, *Winnipeg Beach: Leisure and Courtship in a Resort Town, 1900–1967* (Winnipeg: University of Manitoba Press, 2011); Claire Campbell, *Shaped by the West Wind: Nature and History in Georgian Bay* (Vancouver: University of British Columbia Press, 2005); Michael Dawson, *Selling British Columbia: Tourism and Consumer Culture, 1890–1970* (Vancouver: University of British Columbia Press, 2004); Karen Dubinsky, *The Second Greatest Disappointment: Honeymooning and Tourism at Niagara Falls* (New Brunswick, NJ: Rutgers University Press, 1999); Patricia Jasen, *Wild Things: Nature, Culture, and Tourism in Ontario, 1790–1914* (Toronto: University of Toronto Press, 1995); Ian McKay, *In the Province of History: The Making of the Public Past in Twentieth-Century Nova Scotia* (Montreal and Kingston: McGill-Queen's

University Press, 2010); Cecilia Morgan, *"A Happy Holiday": English Canadians and Transatlantic Tourism, 1870–1930* (Toronto: University of Toronto Press, 2008); Peter A. Stevens, "Getting Away from It All: Family Cottaging in Postwar Ontario" (PhD diss., York University, 2010); Alan MacEachern and Edward MacDonald, *The Summer Trade: A History of Tourism on Prince Edward Island* (Montreal and Kingston: McGill-Queen's University Press, 2022).

5   Jessica Dunkin, *Canoe and Canvas: Life at the Encampments of the American Canoe Association, 1880–1910* (Toronto: University of Toronto Press, 2019), 187.

6   "Staycation" is a more modern term to describe those who, as a result of various constraints, choose to spend their vacation time near or at home. Though rooted in late twentieth- and early twenty-first-century meanings, I believe it also applies to the experiences of those living a century earlier.

7   According to Dale Barbour, excursions were defined as "a short trip to a place and back, for pleasure or a purpose; a group of people taking a short trip; or a temporary deviation from a regular course or pattern." See Barbour, *Winnipeg Beach*, 35.

8   See John Towner, *An Historical Geography of Recreation and Tourism in the Western World, 1540–1940* (Chichester, UK: John Wiley and Sons, 1996); Marguerite S. Shaffer, *See America First: Tourism and National Identity, 1880–1940* (Washington, DC: Smithsonian Institution Press, 2001); Jasen, *Wild Things*.

9   Patricia Jasen, "Native People and the Tourist Industry in Nineteenth-Century Ontario," *Journal of Canadian Studies* 28, no. 4 (Winter 1993/1994): 16.

10 David McMurray, "Rivaling the Gentleman in the Gentle Art: The Authority of the Victorian Woman Angler," *Sport History Review* 39 (2008): 114.

11 Judith Flanders, *Consuming Passions: Leisure and Pleasure in Victorian Britain* (London: Harper Press, 2006), 211–12.

12 *Elora Express*, 22 July 1886, 1.

13 *Merriam-Webster Dictionary*, s.v. "bachelor's hall," accessed 26 July 2023, https://www.merriam-webster.com/dictionary/bachelor%27s%20hall.

14 *Dresden Times*, 13 September 1888, 5.

15 *Elora Express*, 21 July 1892, 1.

16 LAC, Census of Canada, 1891, Schedule No. 1, Ontario, Centre Wellington, Village of Elora, accessed 17 July 2023, https://recherche-collection-search.bac-lac.gc.ca/eng/home/record?app=census&IdNumber=26844405.

17 *Tillsonburg Liberal*, 7 July 1910, 5.

18 LAC, Census of Canada, 1911, Schedule No. 1, Ontario, Oxford South, Tillsonburg, accessed 17 July 2023, https://recherche-collection-search.bac-lac.gc.ca/eng/home/record?app=census&IdNumber=13308728.

19 For more on Muskoka's resettlement and evolution into a popular cottaging destination, see Andrew Watson, *Making Muskoka: Tourism, Rural Identity, and Sustainability, 1870–1920* (Vancouver: University of British Columbia Press, 2022).

20 Barbour discusses how a similar phenomenon happened somewhat later at Winnipeg Beach, Manitoba; see Barbour, *Winnipeg Beach*.

21 *Tillsonburg Observer*, 26 July 1900, 1.

22 Stevens, "Getting Away from It All," 2.

23 Laurel Beechey, *Tillson Family Homes* (Tillsonburg, ON, n.d.), 15. The cottage was previously owned by Hugh Thomas Crossley and John Edwin Hunter.

24 Email from Patricia Phelps to author, 6 July 2012: "It would have either been by train or horse & buggy, as people did 'drive' down to Burwell. If they were going for their vacation with lots of luggage they could have gone by train as there was one that ran to Port Burwell from Tillsonburg, I think daily."

25 Government of Ontario—First Nations, Inuit, and Métis, "Map of Ontario Treaties and Reserves," accessed 25 January 2024, https://www.ontario.ca/page/map-ontario-treaties-and-reserves.

26 Stevens, "Getting Away from It All," 60.

27 See Watson, *Making Muskoka*.

28 *Tillsonburg Observer*, 8 September 1893, 4.

29 *Tillsonburg Observer*, 17 July 1896, 1.

30 Stevens, "Getting Away from It All," 63.

31 ANHS, Documentary Artifact Collection, Lillie File, Tillson Newsletter, written by Laurel Beechey, addressed to Mrs. Kay Clark in Brampton, Ont., 24 May 1990.

32 Stevens, "Getting Away from It All," 64.

33 Andrew Hind and Maria Da Silva, *Muskoka Resorts: Then and Now* (Toronto: Dundurn Natural Heritage, 2011), 19.

34 Laurel Beechey, *The Father of Tillsonburg, Edwin Delevan Tillson and Mary Ann Tillson* (Tillsonburg, ON, n.d.), 24.

35 Beechey, *Tillson Family Homes*, 15. All of the names are derived from works by Sir Walter Scott.

36 ANHS, Documentary Artifact Collection, Agnes McGregor File, "Memories" by Agnes Christine McGregor (an autobiography), written 20 April 1959, 14–15.

37 Barbour, *Winnipeg Beach*, 38; see also Cindy S. Aron, *Working at Play: A History of Vacations in the United States* (New York: Oxford University Press, 1999), 85.

38 ANHS, Documentary Artifact Collection, Lillie File.

39 Stevens, "Getting Away from It All," 64.

40 ANHS, Documentary Artifact Collection, Agnes McGregor File, "Memories" by Agnes Christine McGregor (an autobiography), written 20 April 1959, 14–15.

41 Morgan, "*A Happy Holiday*," 9.

42 Ibid., 25.

43 DPL, *North Kent Leader Centennial Edition*, 23 June 1982, B 19, reference to *Dresden Times* article from 18 July 1899, 1.

44 LAC, Census of Canada, 1891, Schedule No. 1, Ontario, Bothwell, Dresden Town, accessed 17 July 2023, https://recherche-collection-search.bac-lac.gc.ca/eng/home/record?app=census&IdNumber=24991731.

45   Laurel Beechey, *Edwin Delevan Tillson and Mary Ann Tillson* (Tillsonburg, ON, 2000), 26.

46   Laurel Beechey, *E.D. Tillson: His Children and Their Grandchildren* (Tillsonburg, ON, 1991), 32.

47   Ibid.

48   Cecilia Morgan, *Creating Colonial Pasts: History, Memory, and Commemoration in Southern Ontario, 1860–1980* (Toronto: University of Toronto Press, 2015), 115.

49   See Towner, *An Historical Geography of Recreation and Tourism*, 167–212.

50   WCMA, A1981.92, Ann Amelia Day/Sunley Diary, Eramosa Township, 1878–1879.

51   Flanders, *Consuming Passions*, 219.

52   UGASC, XR1 MS A192067, Elora Women's Institute Tweedsmuir History, 232.

53   Dawson, *Selling British Columbia*, 24. For more on marketing Canada, see E.J. Hart, *The Selling of Canada: The CPR and the Beginnings of Canadian Tourism* (Banff, AB: Altitude Publishing, 1983).

54   See *Elora Express*, 5 July 1905, 8; "The Bala Excursion," *Elora Express*, 29 June 1910, 5.

55   Jasen, *Wild Things*, 127.

56   *Elora Express*, 5 July 1905, 8.

57   "The Bala Excursion," *Elora Express*, 29 June 1910, 5.

58   *Elora Lightning Express*, 13 May 1880, 2.

59   Data about annual wages of working-class citizens found in censuses conducted in Dresden, Tillsonburg, and Elora in 1901.

60   AO, F 373, Tweedsmuir Histories Collection, Dresden (Molly Creek).

61   Ibid.

62   DPL, *North Kent Leader*, Centennial Edition, 23 June 1982.

63   While tourism is not addressed directly, Rick Fehr examines government-sponsored agricultural and industrial initiatives on Walpole Island as part of an assimilationist project in early twentieth-century Ontario. See Fehr, "Who Has Traded Cash for Creation? Approaching an Anishinaabeg Informed Environmental History on Bkejwanong Territory" (PhD diss., York University, 2010), https://central.bac-lac.gc.ca/.item?id=NR80527&op=pdf&app=Library&oclc_number=1019480965.

64   The "Anishinaabe Fair—Bkejwanong Territory" Facebook profile contains several historical newspaper articles that detail the evolution of the Walpole Island fair and its events. See https://www.facebook.com/BkejwanongAnishinaabeFair/.

65   Daniel Francis, *The Imaginary Indian: The Image of the Indian in Canadian Culture* (Vancouver: Arsenal Pulp Press, 1992), 94.

66   Cecilia Morgan, *Commemorating Canada: History, Heritage, and Memory, 1850s–1990s* (Toronto: University of Toronto Press, 2016), 154.

67   Several photos demonstrating how Walpole Island residents participated in the local leisure industry are available at University of Michigan, "Neat Old Pictures," accessed 24 July 2012, http://www.personal.umich.edu/~ksands/pictures.html.

68 Watson, *Making Muskoka*, 71–72.

69 See Jasen, "Native People"; Paige Raibmon, "Living on Display: Colonial Visions of Aboriginal Domestic Spaces," in *Home, Work, and Play: Situating Canadian Social History, 1840–1980*, eds. James Opp and John C. Walsh (Don Mills, ON: Oxford University Press, 2006), 18–32. For more on Indigenous peoples' engagement with tourist industries and the repurposing of Indigenous lands, see Helen Agger, *Dadibaajim: Returning Home through Narrative* (Winnipeg: University of Manitoba Press, 2021); and Courtney W. Mason, *Spirits of the Rockies: Reasserting an Indigenous Presence in Banff National Park* (Toronto: University of Toronto Press, 2014).

70 Jasen, "Native People," 16. For more on the development of tourism in Canada and tourists' interest in Indigenous people, see Morgan, *Commemorating Canada*.

71 DPL, *North Kent Leader*, Souvenir Centennial Edition, 23 June 1982.

72 Marie Carter and Jeffrey Carter, *Stepping Back in Time: Along the Trillium Trail in Dresden* (Dresden, ON: Catherine McVean Chapter IODE, 2003), 87.

73 DPL, *North Kent Leader*, Souvenir Centennial Edition, 23 June 1982.

74 After spending the day enjoying Victoria Day celebrations at a park on the city's outskirts, 600 excursionists embarked on the homeward journey on the *Victoria*. It was so overloaded with passengers that their weight and movements caused the vessel to capsize. One hundred and eighty-two excursionists lost their lives, many of whom were female passengers who could not swim and whose heavy skirts and petticoats weighed them down. See Ontario Heritage Trust Plaque, "The 'Victoria' Boat Disaster 1881," accessed 25 January 2024, https://www.heritagetrust.on.ca/plaques/victoria-boat-disaster-1881; and Kenneth D. McTaggart, *The Victoria Day Disaster* (London, ON: McTaggart, 1978). For more on how the sinking of the *Victoria* affected Springbank Park's popularity, see Robert S. Kossuth, "Spaces and Places to Play: The Formation of a Municipal Parks System in London, Ontario, 1867–1914," *Ontario History* 97, no. 2 (Autumn 2005): 160–90. For the impact on women aboard the *Victoria*, see Robert S. Kossuth, "Dangerous Waters: Victorian Decorum, Swimmer Safety, and the Establishment of Public Bathing Facilities in London (Canada)," *International Journal of the History of Sport* 22, no. 5 (2005): 801.

75 DA, Helen Burns Papers, 2021.90, Shipping History, "Launching of the 'Byron Trerice' . . . May 4th, 1882."

76 *Dresden Times*, 13 September 1888, 4.

77 Keith Walden, *Becoming Modern in Toronto: The Industrial Exhibition and the Shaping of a Late Victorian Culture* (Toronto: University of Toronto Press, 1997), 190.

78 WCMA, A2004.91, MU 513, File 1, Muriel Clark, Elora, Letters, 1910, 1912.

79 WCMA, A1981.92, Ann Amelia Day/Sunley Diary, Eramosa Township, 1878–1879.

80 WCMA, A2004.91, MU 513, File 1, Muriel Clark, Elora, Letters, 1910, 1912.

81   ANHS, Documentary Artifact Collection, Folder: Laurel's Booklets, *E.D. & Mary Ann* original drafts, Letter from Margaret D. Jansen, great-granddaughter of E.D. and Mary Ann, to Laurel Beechey, dated 5 February 1986.

82   *Dresden Times*, 28 May 1891, 5.

83   Carter and Carter, *Stepping Back in Time*, 89.

84   Ibid., 118.

85   *Tillsonburg Observer*, 25 July 1890, 1.

86   *Tillsonburg Observer*, 5 June 1891, 1.

87   Bert Newman, *More Reminiscences about Tillsonburg*, ed. Dave Stover (Tillsonburg, ON: Otter Printing, 1987), 144.

88   NDMA, 2002.62.1, Minnie Smith Collection. For more on the complicated history of canoeing in Canada, see Bruce Erickson and Sarah Wylie Krotz, eds., *The Politics of the Canoe* (Winnipeg: University of Manitoba Press, 2021).

89   See Barbour, *Winnipeg Beach*.

90   *Tillsonburg Liberal*, 13 July 1905, 1.

91   Barbour, *Winnipeg Beach*, 40.

92   "The Moonlight Excursion," *Tillsonburg Observer*, 23 July 1880, 1.

93   Ibid.

94   Stephen Thorning, "Elora Gorge Was a Big Tourist Attraction Over 100 Years Ago," *Wellington Advertiser*, 28 June 1999, 10.

95   "'Elora.' For the *Lightning Express*," *Elora Lightning Express*, 26 August 1880, 2.

96   *Selections from Scottish Canadian Poets being a collection of the best poetry written by Scotsmen and their descendants in the Dominion of Canada* (Toronto: Imrie, Graham and Company, 1900), 71.

97   Alexander McLachlan, *Poems and Songs* (Toronto: Hunter, Rose and Company, 1874), 83.

98   Ibid., 84.

99   "Elora Appreciated," *Elora Lightning Express*, 11 September 1879, 2.

100   Stephen Thorning, "River Cleanup and Tourism Went Hand in Hand in 19th Century," *Elora Sentinel*, 25 May 1993, unpaginated.

101   "Elora Visitors' Guide," *Elora Lightning Express*, 14 August 1879, 2.

102   *Elora Lightning Express*, 29 August 1878, 2.

103   Towner, *An Historical Geography of Recreation and Tourism*, 35.

104   Roy I. Wolfe, "The Summer Resorts of Ontario in the Nineteenth Century," *Ontario History* 54 (1962): 149. For more on "work vacations" to rural areas, see Aron, *Working at Play*, 234–35.

105   Sharon Wall, *The Nurture of Nature: Childhood, Antimodernism, and Ontario Summer Camps, 1920–55* (Vancouver: University of British Columbia Press, 2009), 27; see also Towner, *An Historical Geography of Recreation and Tourism*, 35, 240.

106   Towner, *An Historical Geography of Recreation and Tourism*, 240.

107   Courtney W. Mason, "Rethinking the Revival of the Glengarry Highland Games: Modernity, Identity, and Tourism in Rural Canada," *Sport History Review*

36, no. 2 (2005): 146. For more, see Gary S. Cross and John K. Walton, *The Playful Crowd: Pleasure Places in the Twentieth Century* (New York: Columbia University Press, 2005), 117.

108 Diana Pedersen and Martha Phemister, "Women and Photography in Ontario, 1839–1929: A Case Study of the Interaction of Gender and Technology," *Scientia Canadensis: Canadian Journal of the History of Science, Technology and Medicine* 9, no. 1 (28) (1985): 29.

109 Ibid., 37.

110 Lily Koltun, ed., *Private Realms of Light: Amateur Photography in Canada, 1839–1940* (Markham, ON: Fitzhenry and Whiteside, 1984), 15.

111 Lindy Mechefske has compiled a series of picnic photographs taken across Ontario in the later nineteenth and early twentieth centuries; see Mechefske, *Ontario Picnics: A Century of Dining Outdoors* (Lunenburg, NS: MacIntyre Purcell Publishing, 2021).

112 *Elora Lightning Express*, 26 September 1878, 2.

113 University of Waterloo Special Collections & Archives (hereafter UWSCA), Schantz Russell Family Fonds, GA 91-1-8, Schantz, Florence Annie Catherine 1880–[19--?], Manuscript: Poem: Our Picnic at Elora, 1894.

114 For more on this, see Towner, *An Historical Geography of Recreation and Tourism*, 236.

115 *Elora Express*, 22 July 1886, 1.

116 "Local News," *Elora Express*, 28 July 1892, 1.

117 UWSCA, Schantz Russell Family Fonds, GA 91-1-8, Schantz, Florence Annie Catherine 1880–[19--?], Manuscript: Poem: Our Picnic at Elora, 1894.

118 "Local News," *Elora Express*, 28 July 1892, 1.

119 Dubinsky, *The Second Greatest Disappointment*, 75.

120 Glenda Riley, "Victorian Ladies Outdoors: Women in the Early Western Conservation Movement, 1870–1920," *Southern California Quarterly* 83, no. 1 (Spring 2001): 63.

121 *Elora Express*, 20 May 1886, 1.

122 In the context of industrial Hamilton, historians Ken Cruikshank and Nancy B. Bouchier note the great lengths taken by city officials to clean up shorelines to provide a more "respectable" site in which to enjoy swimming, because as a sport "it offered a positive alternative to the other attractions associated with the city." They also elucidate how swimming was tied to concerns over hygiene and health; taking a quick dip not only provided exercise, but unlike other sports it also cleansed its participants. For more, see Ken Cruikshank and Nancy B. Bouchier, "Dirty Spaces: Environment, the State, and Recreational Swimming in Hamilton Harbour, 1870–1946," *Sport History Review* 29 (1998): 59–76; Ken Cruikshank and Nancy B. Bouchier, "'The Heritage of the People Closed against Them': Class, Environment, and the Shaping of Burlington Beach, 1870s–1980s," *Urban History Review* 30, no. 1 (October 2001): 40–55; and Ken Cruikshank and

352 | Notes to Pages 249–256

Nancy B. Bouchier, *The People of the Bay: A Social and Environmental History of Hamilton Harbour* (Vancouver: University of British Columbia Press, 2016).

123   WCMA, A1985.54, Series 2: By-Laws, 1858–1927, File 2: By-Laws April 16, 1861–March 1927 (WCA 233), By-Law Number 108.

124   Stephen Thorning, "Elora Promoted Tourism and Fishing to Support the Village—in the Early 1900s," *Elora Sentinel*, n.d, unpaginated.

125   Barbour, *Winnipeg Beach*, 107; see also Dale Barbour, *Undressed Toronto: From the Swimming Hole to Sunnyside, How a City Learned to Love the Beach, 1850–1935* (Winnipeg: University of Manitoba Press, 2021).

126   *Elora Express*, 8 July 1886, 1.

127   "Air and Sunshine for the Hair," *Elora Express*, 19 May 1892, 3.

Chapter 7. Bad Girls in the Country?

1   ANHS, Documentary Artifact Collection, Tillson Family Scrapbook, hand-written letter, dated Thursday afternoon, other date unknown.

2   Both Patricia Phelps, former curator at Tillsonburg's Annandale National Historic Site, and Laurel Beechey, Tillson family historian, are unsure which Mrs. Tillson the letter was addressed to. Based on the critiques made in the letter, it was likely written sometime in the late 1910s or 1920s.

3   Kevin B. Wamsley, "State Formation and Institutionalized Racism: Gambling Laws in Nineteenth and Early Twentieth Century Canada," *Sport History Review* 29 (1998): 78.

4   See Ruth Alexander, *The Girl Problem: Female Sexual Delinquency in New York, 1900–1930* (Ithaca, NY: Cornell University Press, 1995); Tamara Myers, *Caught: Montreal's Modern Girls and the Law, 1869–1945* (Toronto: University of Toronto Press, 2006); Mary Odem, *Delinquent Daughters: Protecting and Policing Adolescent Female Sexuality in the United States, 1885–1920* (Chapel Hill: University of North Carolina Press, 1995); Joan Sangster, *Girl Trouble: Female Delinquency in English Canada* (Toronto: Between the Lines, 2002); Carolyn Strange, *Toronto's Girl Problem: The Perils and Pleasures of the City, 1880–1930* (Toronto: University of Toronto Press, 1995).

5   Lynne Marks, "No Double Standard?: Leisure, Sex, and Sin in Upper Canadian Church Discipline Records, 1800–1860," in *Gendered Pasts: Historical Essays in Femininity and Masculinity in Canada*, ed. Kathryn McPherson, Cecilia Morgan, and Nancy M. Forestell (Toronto: University of Toronto Press, 2003), 52.

6   Karen Dubinsky, *Improper Advances: Rape and Heterosexual Conflict in Ontario, 1880–1929* (Chicago: University of Chicago Press, 1993), 119–26.

7   Ibid., 125.

8   Karen Dubinsky, "'Maidenly Girls' or 'Designing Women'?: The Crime of Seduction in Turn-of-the-Century Ontario," in *Gender Conflicts: New Essays in Women's History*, ed. Franca Iacovetta and Mariana Valverde (Toronto: University of Toronto Press, 1992), 29.

9   Steven Maynard, "'Horrible Temptations': Sex, Men, and Working-Class Male Youth in Urban Ontario, 1890–1935," *Canadian Historical Review* 78, no. 2 (June 1997): 197.

10   Constance Backhouse, "Nineteenth-Century Canadian Prostitution Law: Reflections of a Discriminatory Society," *Histoire sociale/Social History* 18, no. 36 (November 1985): 396.

11   For more on the fallibility of the census, see Patrick A. Dunae, "Sex, Charades, and Census Records: Locating Female Sex Trade Workers in a Victorian City," *Histoire sociale/Social History* 42, no. 84 (November 2009): 267–97.

12   Amanda Glasbeek, *Feminized Justice: The Toronto Women's Court, 1913–1934* (Vancouver: University of British Columbia, 2009), 21.

13   COA, RG2, Series 6 Treasurer, Box 1, Subseries A, Administration of Justice 1850–1887; Box 2, Subseries A, Administration of Justice, 1887–1907; Box 3, Subseries A, Administration of Justice, 1908–1925.

14   Glasbeek, *Feminized Justice*, 21.

15   Backhouse, "Nineteenth-Century Canadian Prostitution Law," 396n7.

16   Strange, *Toronto's Girl Problem*, 23.

17   Canniff Haight, *Country Life in Canada*, with a new introduction by Arthur R.M. Lower (Belleville, ON: Mika Publishing, 1971), 48.

18   Dubinsky, *Improper Advances*, 152.

19   Dubinsky, *Improper Advances*; Marks, "No Double Standard?"; Lynne Marks, *Revivals and Roller Rinks: Religion, Leisure, and Identity in Late-Nineteenth-Century Small-Town Ontario* (Toronto: University of Toronto Press, 1996).

20   Lesley Erickson, *Westward Bound: Sex, Violence, the Law, and the Making of a Settler Society* (Vancouver: University of British Columbia Press, 2011), 111.

21   Dubinsky, *Improper Advances*, 122.

22   Kate Aitken, *Never a Day So Bright* (New York: Longmans, 1957), 204.

23   COA, Series 2, By-Laws (1850–1867), No. 59 By Law No. 2, By Law for the purpose of protecting and enforcing the observance of Public Morals within the County of Oxford, 1859.

24   COA, Series 2, By-Laws, Box 2, File 7#11, By-Law No. 189, By-Law to enforce the observance of Public Morals in the County of Oxford.

25   "Elora Walking Tour: South of the Grand River," *Wellington County History* 17 (2004): 48.

26   COA, RG2, Series 6 Treasurer, Box 1, Subseries A, Administration of Justice 1850–1887; Box 2, Subseries A, Administration of Justice, 1887–1907; Box 3, Subseries A, Administration of Justice, 1908–1925.

27   The charges included "keeping a bawdy house," "keeping a house of ill fame," keeping a house of ill fame and being an inmate," and "keeping a house of prostitution and ill fame."

28   A charwoman was someone hired to do cleaning, usually taking care of a larger building. See LAC, Census of Canada, 1901, Schedule No. 1, Ontario, Norfolk North, Tilsonburg, accessed 17 July 2023, https://recherche-collection-search.

bac-lac.gc.ca/eng/home/record?app=census&IdNumber=36053532. "Clarina" is listed as the first name by LAC, but I believe it is written as "Clarissa."

29   See Peter Baskerville and Eric W. Sager, *Unwilling Idlers: The Urban Unemployed and Their Families in Late Victorian Canada* (Toronto: University of Toronto Press, 1998), 115.

30   Erickson, *Westward Bound*, 93.

31   Dubinsky, *Improper Advances*, 78–79. According to Mariana Valverde, the "finery-to-fall" narrative, which middle-class observers constructed to link working-class women's love of finery with their alleged engagement in sex work, was a pervasive one in the nineteenth century; see Valverde, "The Love of Finery: Fashion and the Fallen Woman in Nineteenth-Century Social Discourse," *Victorian Studies* 32, no. 2 (Winter 1989): 169–88.

32   Frances Swyripa, "Negotiating Sex and Gender in the Ukrainian Bloc Settlement: East-Central Alberta between the Wars," in *Home, Work, and Play: Situating Canadian Social History, 1840–1980*, ed. James Opp and John C. Walsh (Don Mills, ON: Oxford University Press, 2006), 53.

33   Marks, *Revivals and Roller Rinks*, 90.

34   Mariana Valverde, *The Age of Light, Soap, and Water: Moral Reform in English Canada, 1885–1925*, with a new introduction (Toronto: University of Toronto Press, 2008), 83.

35   Donald G. Wetherell and Irene R.A. Kmet, *Town Life: Main Street and the Evolution of Small Town Alberta, 1880–1947* (Edmonton: University of Alberta Press and Alberta Community Development, 1995), 237.

36   Dubinsky, *Improper Advances*, 119.

37   Similar prescriptions for boys also appeared, but they primarily dealt with how to keep boys on the farm and were tied more to fears over rural depopulation than to boys' raucous behaviour.

38   "Immorality," *Dresden Times*, 23 July 1891, 4.

39   Mrs. John Dennison, "The Young Woman Problem," *Missionary Outlook* (June 1905): 139.

40   DPL, Inez (Eagleson) Perrin, "Call Back Yesterday," *North Kent Leader Centennial Edition*, 23 June 1982, E-27.

41   Bert Newman, *Reminiscences about Tillsonburg*, ed. Dave Stover (Tillsonburg, ON, 1986), 27.

42   D. Owen Carrigan, *Juvenile Delinquency in Canada: A History* (Concord, ON: Irwin Publishing, 1998), 24.

43   Mary Anne Poutanen, "The Homeless, the Whore, the Drunkard, and the Disorderly: Contours of Female Vagrancy in the Montreal Courts, 1810–1842," in *Gendered Pasts: Historical Essays in Femininity and Masculinity in Canada*, ed. Kathryn McPherson, Cecilia Morgan, and Nancy M. Forestell (Toronto: University of Toronto Press, 1999), 46.

44   Dubinsky, *Improper Advances*, 120.

45   "Dancing vs. Kissing," *Woodstock Sentinel-Review*, 24 March 1887, 1.

46 See, for example, Craig Heron's examination of working-class Hamilton: "Boys Will Be Boys: Working-Class Masculinities in the Age of Mass Production," *International Labor and Working-Class History* 69 (Spring 2006): 12–15.

47 Stephen Thorning, "Bare Knuckles, Blazing Pistols, Lynching: Crime in Elora 125 Years Ago," *Elora Sentinel and Fergus Thistle*, 13 April 1993, 6.

48 In Connon's letter, the girl's surname is illegible. According to the 1891 census, the only girl with the name Alberta in Elora was Alberta Drury, age thirteen, whose father was a lime burner. See LAC, Census of Canada, 1891, Schedule No. 1, Ontario, Centre Wellington, Village of Elora, accessed 17 July 2023, https://recherche-collection-search.bac-lac.gc.ca/eng/home/record?app=census&IdNumber=26844435.

49 WCMA, A1977.67, Connon Family Correspondence, 1852–1930 (microfilm), Thomas Connon to John Connon, 27 February 1890.

50 *Elora Express*, 12 July 1899, 8.

51 Ruth M. Mann, "Struggles for Youth Justice and Justice for Youth: A Canadian Example," in *Juvenile Crime and Delinquency: A Turn of the Century Reader*, ed. Ruth M. Mann (Toronto: Canadian Scholars' Press, 2000), 7.

52 Sangster, *Girl Trouble*, 15. For consistency's sake, the same definition has been used when referring to juvenile delinquents in this discussion.

53 COA, RG2, Series 6 Treasurer, Box 1, Subseries A, Administration of Justice 1850–1887.

54 Sangster, *Girl Trouble*, 15.

55 Town of Tillsonburg, 1800–1909 By-Laws, By-Law 0665 Curfew—Children Under 14, Effective Date: 11/18/1912, accessed 27 July 2023, https://lfpp.oxfordcounty.ca/WebLink/DocView.aspx?id=37702&dbid=0&repo=Tillsonburg-Public. For a history of juvenile curfew laws in Canada, see Tamara Myers, "Nocturnal Disorder and the Curfew Solution: A History of Juvenile Sundown Regulations in Canada," in *Lost Kids: Vulnerable Children and Youth in Twentieth-Century Canada and the United States*, eds. Mona Gleason, Tamara Myers, Leslie Paris, and Veronica Strong-Boag (Vancouver: University of British Columbia Press, 2010), 95–113.

56 No evidence has been uncovered about where this children's shelter was, how long it existed, and who managed it.

57 Dubinsky, *Improper Advances*, 121.

58 See COA, Series 2, By-Laws (1850–1867), No. 59, By Law No. 2, By Law for the purpose of protecting and enforcing the observance of Public Morals within the County of Oxford and By Law No. 65 Of the Municipal Council of the County of Oxford for licensing and regulating bowling alleys kept for amusement profit or hire.

59 "Rules and Regulations For the orderly keeping of Inns, Taverns, and places of entertainment in the East Riding of Wellington, recently adopted by the Board of License Commissioners," *Elora Express*, 10 May 1899, 5.

60   AO, GS 111, Dresden, Kent Co., Council Minutes 1872–1899, By-Laws 1882–1899, By-Law No. 210.

61   See COA, RG2, Series 6 Treasurer, Box 1, Subseries A, Administration of Justice 1850–1887; Box 2, Subseries A, Administration of Justice, 1887–1907; Box 3, Subseries A, Administration of Justice, 1908–1925.

62   Miss Helen R.Y. Reid, "Compilation," in *Women of Canada: Their Life and Work*, compiled by the National Council of Women of Canada at the request of the Hon. Sydney Fisher Minister of Agriculture for distribution at the Paris International Exhibition, 1900, 331.

63   "OACAS: History of Children's Aid," Family Aid Society, accessed 25 January 2024, http://www.familyaid.org/html/0132.html.

64   Mrs. Tilton, "Compilation," in *Women of Canada: Their Life and Work*, 332.

65   *Tillsonburg Liberal*, 1 December 1910, 5.

66   Lynne Marks, "The 'Hallelujah Lasses': Working-Class Women in the Salvation Army in English Canada, 1882–92," in *Gender Conflicts: New Essays in Women's History*, ed. Franca Iacovetta and Mariana Valverde (Toronto: University of Toronto Press, 1992), 74.

67   Marks, "No Double Standard?" 52.

68   ANHS, Documentary Artifact Collection, Agnes McGregor File, "Memories" by Agnes Christine McGregor (an autobiography), written 20 April 1959.

69   *Elora Express*, 28 July 1892, 1.

70   "She Got the Money," *Tillsonburg Observer*, 14 September 1894, 5.

71   For more on the respectability of domestic servants, see Magda Fahrni, "'Ruffled' Mistresses and 'Discontented' Maids: Respectability and the Case of Domestic Service, 1880–1914," *Labour/Le Travail* 39 (Spring 1997): 74–75.

72   Dubinsky, *Improper Advances*, 117.

73   Ibid., 115.

74   Poutanen, "The Homeless, the Whore, the Drunkard, and the Disorderly," 46.

75   James Crankshaw, *The Criminal Code of Canada and the Canada Evidence Act, 1893 with an Extra Appendix Containing the Extradition Act, the Extradition Convention with the United States, The Fugitive Offenders' Act, and the House of Commons Debates on the Code and an Analytical Index* (Montreal: Whiteford and Theoret, Law Publishers, 1894), 126.

76   Glasbeek, *Feminized Justice*, 97.

77   Poutanen, "The Homeless, the Whore, the Drunkard, and the Disorderly," 33.

78   Joan Sangster, "'Pardon Tales' from Magistrate's Court: Women, Crime, and the Court in Peterborough County, 1920–50," *Canadian Historical Review* 74, no. 2 (1993): 165.

79   Arrests for vagrancy included walking the streets at night, prostitution and night walking, and prostitution and street walking.

80   Myers, *Caught*, 47.

81   Glasbeek, *Feminized Justice*, 96.

82 Susan Sessions Rugh, "Civilizing the Countryside: Class, Gender, and Crime in Nineteenth-Century Rural Illinois," *Agricultural History* 76, no. 1 (Winter 2002): 73.

83 "To Cope with Rural Crime," *Farmer's Advocate and Home Magazine* 43, no. 827 (30 July 1908): 1213.

84 "Increase of Crime," *Tillsonburg Observer*, 27 December 1900, 4.

85 See Rugh, "Civilizing the Countryside," 64.

86 Stephen Thorning, *The Model Village and the Struggle for Success: A History of Elora, Ontario* (Fergus, ON: Wellington County Historical Society, 2023), 343.

87 Susan Sessions Rugh, *Our Common Country: Family Farming, Culture, and Community in the Nineteenth-Century Midwest* (Bloomington: Indiana University Press, 2001), 99. Pauline Greenhill has completed extensive research on the history of charivaris/shivarees in Canada and how they served as ways to exact judgement in small communities over perceptibly inappropriate behaviours; see Greenhill, "Make the Night Hideous: Death at a Manitoba Charivari, 1909," *Manitoba History* 52 (June 2006): 3–17; and *Make the Night Hideous: Four English-Canadian Charivaris, 1881–1940* (Toronto: University of Toronto Press, 2010).

88 COA, RG2, Series 6 Treasurer, Box 1, Subseries A, Administration of Justice 1850–1887; Box 2, Subseries A, Administration of Justice, 1887–1907; Box 3, Subseries A, Administration of Justice, 1908–1925.

89 *Tillsonburg Observer*, 17 May 1895, 1.

90 Paul Voisey, *High River and the Times: An Alberta Community and Its Weekly Newspaper, 1905–1966* (Edmonton: University of Alberta Press, 2004), xxvii.

91 DPL, *North Kent Leader Souvenir Centennial Edition*, 23 June 1982.

92 *Tillsonburg Observer*, 23 July 1875, 3.

93 Dan Azoulay, *Hearts and Minds: Canadian Romance at the Dawn of the Modern Era, 1900–1930* (Calgary: University of Calgary Press, 2011), 108–9.

94 *Guelph Weekly Herald*, 29 January 1891, 1.

95 Wamsley, "State Formation and Institutionalized Racism," 80.

96 "Nuisances; Disorderly Houses Defined," in Crankshaw, *The Criminal Code of Canada and the Canada Evidence Act, 1893*, 117; 118.

97 Ibid., 120.

98 Francis Hoffman and Ryan Taylor, *Much to Be Done: Private Life in Ontario from Victorian Diaries* (Toronto: Natural Heritage /Natural History, 1996), 202.

99 UGASC, Marston-Archibald Collection, XR1 MS A371, Box 1, Olive Snyder diary, 1913.

100 "Games, Harmless, and Otherwise," *Tillsonburg Liberal*, 4 May 1905, 7.

101 Henry Reeve, "Amusing Parlor Games for Winter Evenings," *Farmer's Advocate and Home Magazine* 29, no. 350 (15 January 1894): 33.

102 *Tillsonburg Observer*, 29 January 1903, 1.

103 *Tillsonburg Observer*, 5 July 1895, 1.

104 Aitken, *Never a Day So Bright*, 25.

105 Robert Brandon, *The History of Dresden* (Dresden, ON: Dresden Centennial Committee, 1982), 33.

106 Occupations found on various pages in LAC, Census of Canada, 1901, Schedule No. 1, Ontario, Bothwell, Town Dresden, accessed 17 July 2023, https://recherche-collection-search.bac-lac.gc.ca/eng/Home/Search?DataSo urce=Genealogy%7CCensus&ApplicationCode=28&YearOfImmigration-slider=0&Age-slider=0&YearOfBirth-slider=0&ProvinceCode=ON&Place=D resden.

107 Kathy Peiss, *Cheap Amusements: Working Women and Leisure in Turn-of-the-Century New York* (Philadelphia: Temple University Press, 1986), 29.

108 Roger Munting, *An Economic and Social History of Gambling in Britain and the USA* (Manchester: Manchester University Press, 1996), 26.

109 "Games, Harmless, and Otherwise," *Tillsonburg Liberal*, 4 May 1905, 7.

110 "Aristocratic Lady Gamblers," *Elora Lightning Express*, 5 August 1880, 2.

111 "Women Who Play Poker," *Elora Express*, 14 May 1885, 7.

112 "Recreation," *Canada Farmer* 2, no. 1 (15 January 1870): 33.

113 "Games, Harmless, and Otherwise," *Tillsonburg Liberal*, 4 May 1905, 7.

114 Mark Clapson, *A Bit of a Flutter: Popular Gambling and English Society, c. 1823–1961* (Manchester: Manchester University Press, 1992), 97.

115 Wetherell and Kmet, *Town Life*, 233.

116 AO, GS 111, Dresden, Kent Co., Council Minutes 1872–1899, By-Laws 1882–1899, By Law No. 210.

117 COA, RG2, Series 6 Treasurer, Box 1, Subseries A, Administration of Justice 1850–1887. It is possible that Ignahus Balentin's first name was Ignatius.

118 Craig Heron, *Booze: A Distilled History* (Toronto: Between the Lines, 2003), 126.

119 Douglas McCalla, *Consumers in the Bush: Shopping in Rural Upper Canada* (Montreal and Kingston: McGill-Queen's University Press, 2015), 72–79.

120 Newman, *Reminiscences about Tillsonburg*, 13.

121 Glasbeek, *Feminized Justice*, 123.

122 *Elora Express*, 19 May 1892, 1.

123 WCMA, A1977.67, Connon family correspondence, 1852–1930 (microfilm), 25 May 1890.

124 Aitken, *Never a Day So Bright*, 56.

125 COA, Series 2, Box 2, File 7#11, By-Law No. 189, By-Law to enforce the observ-ance of Public Morals in the County of Oxford.

126 "Rules and Regulations For the orderly keeping of Inns, Taverns, and places of entertainment in the East Riding of Wellington, recently adopted by the Board of License Commissioners," *Elora Express*, 10 May 1899, 5.

127 Glasbeek, *Feminized Justice*, 119.

128 Ibid., 120.

129 Ibid., 119.

130 Dubinsky, *Improper Advances*, 134.

131 Stephen Thorning, "Temperance Workers Such as T.E. Bissell Finally Found Success in Early 1900s," *Elora Sentinel and Fergus Thistle*, 1 February 1994, 6.

132 Conversation between Patricia Phelps and the author, 13 June 2012. The information about the presence of a wine cellar was taken from an interview with former domestic servant Myrtle Dreyer in 1984. See ANHS, Documentary Artifact Collection, Annandale House maid, Myrtle Dreyer (née Morden), born 8 July 1894, interview conducted 24 July 1984.

133 Heron, *Booze*, 204–5.

134 ANHS, Documentary Artifact Collection, Annandale House maid, Myrtle Dreyer (née Morden), born 8 July 1894, interview conducted 24 July 1984.

135 Aitken, *Never a Day So Bright*, 130.

136 Sharon Anne Cook, *"Through Sunshine and Shadow": The Woman's Christian Temperance Union, Evangelicalism, and Reform in Ontario, 1874–1930* (Montreal and Kingston: McGill-Queen's University Press, 1995), 7.

137 Information taken from the *Tillsonburg Observer* between the years 1889 and 1910.

138 Cook, *"Through Sunshine and Shadow,"* 148.

139 AO, GS 111, Dresden, Kent Co., Council Minutes 1872–1899, By-Laws 1882–1899, Municipal Council Meeting 8 February 1877, By Law No. 72.

140 DA, 2021.88, Helen Burns Papers, Handwritten, "Dresden's Early Years."

141 Cheryl Krasnick Warsh, "'Oh, Lord, Pour a Cordial in Her Wounded Heart': The Drinking Woman in Victorian and Edwardian Canada," in *Drink in Canada: Historical Essays*, ed. Cheryl Krasnick Warsh (Montreal and Kingston: McGill-Queen's University Press, 1993), 76.

142 *Guelph Herald*, 1 September 1868, 2.

143 Lesley Erickson, "'A Very Garden of the Lord'? Hired Hands, Farm Women, and Sex Crime Prosecutions on the Prairies, 1914–1929," *Journal of the Canadian Historical Association* 12, no. 1 (2001): 134.

144 *Tillsonburg Observer*, 9 April 1880, 1.

145 Lynne Marks, "Religion, Leisure, and Working Class Identity," in *Labouring Lives: Work and Workers in Nineteenth-Century Ontario*, ed. Paul Craven (Toronto: University of Toronto Press, 1995), 288.

146 Constance Backhouse, *Petticoats and Prejudice: Women and Law in Nineteenth-Century Canada* (Toronto: Women's Press, 1991), 41.

147 AO, RG 22-2669-0-1, Kent County, County Court Judge's Criminal Court Minute Book 1907–1918.

148 Information taken from various issues of the *Woodstock Sentinel-Review*. For more, see Constance Backhouse, "Desperate Women and Compassionate Courts: Infanticide in Nineteenth-Century Canada," *University of Toronto Law Journal* 34, no. 4 (1984): 447–78.

149 Dubinsky, *Improper Advances*, 93.

150 Glasbeek, *Feminized Justice*, 22.

151   W. Peter Ward, "Unwed Motherhood in Nineteenth-Century English Canada," *Historical Papers/Communications historiques* 16, no. 1 (1981): 47.

152   "A Young Couple of Color," *Woodstock Sentinel-Review*, 10 January 1895, 8.

153   AO, MS 8496, RG 22-392, Supreme Court Criminal Indictment Files Oxford County, 1890–1907, Thomas Marshall Case.

154   "The Assize Court. The Seduction Case," *Woodstock Sentinel-Review*, 22 March 1895, 4.

155   For more on Black Canadian men and women in the criminal justice system, see Barrington Walker, *Race on Trial: Black Defendants in Ontario's Criminal Courts, 1858–1958* (Toronto: Osgoode Society for Canadian Legal History by University of Toronto Press, 2010). Pages 145–57 detail a seduction case in the small Ontario community of Raleigh that involved a White female and a Black man.

Conclusion

1   John MacDougall, *Rural Life in Canada: Its Trend and Tasks*, with introduction by Robert Craig Brown (Toronto: University of Toronto Press, 1973), 131.

2   Ruth Sandwell, *Canada's Rural Majority: Households, Environments, and Economies, 1870–1940* (Toronto: University of Toronto Press, 2016), 80.

3   *Tillsonburg Observer*, 26 November 1875, 2.

4   This information was taken from a variety of Dresden, Tillsonburg, and Elora newspaper articles.

5   Lynne Marks, *Revivals and Roller Rinks: Religion, Leisure, and Identity in Late-Nineteenth-Century Small-Town Ontario* (Toronto: University of Toronto Press, 1996), 208.

6   Adam Crerar, "Writing across the Rural-Urban Divide: The Case of Peter McArthur, 1909–24," *Journal of Canadian Studies* 41, no. 2 (Spring 2007): 112.

7   Donica Belisle, *Retail Nation: Department Stores and the Making of Modern Canada* (Vancouver: University of British Columbia Press, 2011), 64.

8   Beatrice Craig, *Backwoods Consumers and Homespun Capitalists: The Rise of a Market Culture in Eastern Canada* (Toronto: University of Toronto Press, 2009), 202. Concerning consumerism and modernity in the interwar period, see Cheryl Krasnick Warsh and Dan Malleck, eds., *Consuming Modernity: Gendered Behaviour and Consumerism before the Baby Boom* (Vancouver: University of British Columbia Press, 2013).

9   Nancy B. Bouchier, *For the Love of the Game: Amateur Sport in Small-Town Ontario, 1838–1895* (Montreal and Kingston: McGill-Queen's University Press, 2003), 132.

10 Ibid., 139.

11 "How Very Lady-Like," *Tillsonburg Observer*, 21 December 1871, 2.

BIBLIOGRAPHY

Archival Sources

ANHS—Annandale National Historic Site (Tillsonburg, ON)
Documentary Artifact Collection
    Agnes McGregor File
    Catherine Marilla Tillson File
    Laurel's Booklet *E.D. & Mary Ann* original drafts
    Lillie File
    Marguerite Sinclair Scrapbook
    Myrtle Dreyer Interview
    Overview of Tillsonburg Sports and Recreation Highlights, 1900 to Present
    Social History Files
    Thomson Family Files
    Tillson Family Scrapbook
    "A Tillsonburg Woman's Memory of a Party of the Days of Confederation"
    Travel Club
    "William Harcourt Popham Remembers"
Photograph Collection
Pollard Photos

AO—Archives of Ontario (Toronto, ON)
F 26, Charles Clarke Fonds
F 373, Tweedsmuir Histories Collection
GS 111, Dresden, Kent Co., Council Minutes
MS 8496, RG 22-392, Supreme Court Criminal Indictment Files, Oxford County
RG 22-2669-0-1, Kent County, County Court Judge's Criminal Court Minute Book

COA—County of Oxford Archives (Woodstock, ON)
Wadsworth, Unwin & Brown. *Topographical and Historical Atlas of the County of
    Oxford, Ontario.* Toronto: Walker & Miles, 1876.
RG2, Series 6 Treasurer, Administration of Justice Files
Series 2, By-Laws

DA—Dresden Archives (Dresden, ON)
2021.88, Helen Burns Papers, Handwritten, Dresden's Early Years
2021.90, Helen Burns Papers, Shipping History, "Launching of the 'Byron Trerice'...
    May 4th, 1882"
Dresden Area Schools
Jim Coyle Collection
Keith Wells Collection
Marie Carter, *100 Years of IODE, Catherine McVean Chapter originally Sydenham*
    Chapter 1914–2014 Dresden, Ontario
Photograph Collection

DPL—Dresden Public Library (Dresden, ON)
North Kent Leader Centennial Edition, Progress Issue
Saint Andrew's Presbyterian Church, Dresden, Ontario, One Hundredth Anniversary
    1872–1972

NDMA—Norwich and District Museum and Archives (Norwich, ON)
2002.62.1, Minnie Smith Collection
X79A-XX1-15, Francis Poole Diary

TPL—Tillsonburg Public Library (Tillsonburg, ON)
A Century of Travel 1900–2000 Tillsonburg Ladies' Travel Club Established 1900. N.p.,
    2000

UGASC—University of Guelph, Archival & Special Collections (Guelph, ON)
s0131b25, Olive Anderson Snyder, *Little Towns.* Elora, ON: Elora Express Printery,
    1900.
XR1 MS A114, Connon Collection
XR1 MS A192067, Regional History Collection, Elora Women's Institute Tweedsmuir
    History
XR1 MS A371, Marston-Archibald Collection
XRI MS A564, Federated Women's Institutes of Ontario Collection, F.W.I.O.
    Membership in Wellington

UWSCA—University of Waterloo, Special Collections & Archives (Waterloo, ON)
GA91, Schantz Russell Family Fonds

WCMA—Wellington County Museum and Archives (Fergus, ON)
A1952.225.1, Man 18, Mu 3, Diary of an unidentified student, likely in Elora, some
    local and family names references. 1898-1900, 1915.
A1977.67, Connon Family Correspondence

A1981.92, Ann Amelia Day/Sunley Diary, Eramosa Township, 1878–1879
A1982.13, Elora Women's Institute Tweedsmuir History
A1985.54, Series 2: By-Laws, 1858–1927
A1996.112, Diary of Annie Hill (née Drury) of Fergus, Ontario, 1912–1923
A1996.129, Margaret A. Templin Diary
A2002.51 MU 437, Emma Clarke Files
A2004.91, Muriel Clark Letters
Photographs
    A1952.311.96, ph 503
    A1978.223, ph 6299
    A1998.42, ph 13426
    A2005.33, ph 18789
    A2006.112, ph20829
    A2006.112, ph 20835
    A2008.122, ph 29601

WUASC—Western University, Archives and Special Collections (London, ON)
Christ Church Dresden Papers, 1859–1935
Women's Institute, Tweedsmuir History, Tillsonburg Branch (Oxford County, Ontario)

Historical Newspapers and Periodicals

Canada Farmer
Canadian Wheelman
Delineator
Dominion Medical Monthly and Ontario Medical Journal
Dresden Times
Elora Express
Elora Lightning Express
Elora News
Farmer's Advocate and Home Magazine
Guelph Herald
Guelph Weekly Herald
Harper's Bazaar
Ladies' Home Journal
Missionary Outlook
Rural Canadian
Tillsonburg Liberal
Tillsonburg Observer
Woodstock Sentinel-Review

Primary Sources

Aitken, Kate. *Never a Day So Bright*. New York: Longmans, 1957.

Austin, Benjamin Fish. *Woman; Her Character, Culture and Calling. A Full Discussion of Woman's Work in the Home, the School, the Church and the Social Circle; With an Account of her Successful Labors in Moral and Social Reform, her Heroic Work for God and Humanity in the Mission Field, her Success as a Wage-Earner and in Fighting Life's Battle Alone; With Chapters on all Departments of Woman's Training and Culture, her Claims to the Higher Education, and the Best Methods to be Pursued Therein*. Brantford, ON: Book and Bible House, 1890.

Benton, Carolyn French. *Fairs and Fetes*. Boston: Dana Estes & Company, 1912.

Canada's Greatest Store: Christmas Catalogue, 1897, the T. Eaton Co. Limited. Toronto: D.E. Scott, 1897.

Census of Canada, 1870–71. Vol. I. Ottawa: I.B. Taylor, 1873.

Census of Canada, 1880–81. Vol. I. Ottawa: Maclean, Roger, and Co., 1882.

Census of Canada, 1890–91. Vol. I. Ottawa: S.E. Dawson, 1893.

Co-Operating Organizations of the Presbyterian and Methodist Churches, County of Huron, Ontario. *Report on a Rural Survey of the Agricultural, Educational, Social, and Religious Life*. Prepared for the Huron Survey Committed by the Department of Temperance and Moral Reform of the Methodist Church, the Board of Social Service and Evangelism, and the Board of Sabbath Schools and Young People's Societies of the Presbyterian Church. December–January 1913–1914.

Crankshaw, James. *The Criminal Code of Canada and the Canada Evidence Act, 1893 with an Extra Appendix Containing the Extradition Act, the Extradition Convention with the United States, The Fugitive Offenders' Act, and the House of Commons Debates on the Code and an Analytical Index*. Montreal: Whiteford and Theoret, Law Publishers, 1894.

Fifth Census of Canada, 1911. Vol. I. Ottawa: C.H. Parmelee, 1913.

Fifth Census of Canada, 1911. Vol. II. Ottawa: C.H. Parmelee, 1913.

First Report of the Bureau of Labor of the Province of Ontario for the Year Ending December 31st 1900. Toronto: L.K. Cameron, 1901.

Fourth Census of Canada, 1901. Vol. I. Ottawa: S.E. Dawson, 1902.

Historic Canadian Maps Viewer. The Century Co. Ontario. Century Co., 1902. https://www.lib.uwo.ca/madgic/projects/canadianoriginals/007.jpg

Hoffman, Professor. *Parlor Amusements and Evening Party Entertainments*. London: G. Routledge and Sons, 18–?.

The Home Treasury of Useful and Entertaining Knowledge on the Art of Making Home Happy, and an Aid in Self-Education; the Laws of Etiquette and Good Society; Home Amusements; Out-Door Sports; And Other Interesting Matter of Social and Educational Value. Toronto, London, ON, Brockville, ON, and St. John, NB: J.S. Robertson and Bros., 1883.

Horsman, E.I. *Home Amusements Are the Magnets of the Family Circle*. New York: H.C. Stoothoff, 1871.

Illustrated Historical Atlas of the Counties of Essex and Kent. Toronto: H. Belden and Co., 1880–81.

"Instructions to Officers." 1901 Census of Canada. https://www.nappdata.org/napp/resources/enum_materials_pdf/enum_instruct_ca1901a.pdf.

LAC—Library and Archives Canada. Censuses, 1871–1911. https://recherche-collection-search.bac-lac.gc.ca/eng/census/index.

Leypoldt, Augusta H., and George Iles, eds. *List of Books for Girls and Women And Their Clubs With Descriptive and Critical Notes and a List of Periodicals and Hints for Girls' and Women's Clubs*. Boston: The Library Bureau, 1895.

Lloyd, Frank P. *Historical Atlas of the County of Wellington, Ontario*. Toronto: Historical Atlas Pub. Company, 1906.

Lovell's Province of Ontario Directory for 1871. Montreal: John Lovell, 1871.

McLachlan, Alexander. *Poems and Songs*. Toronto: Hunter, Rose and Company, 1874.

Ontario Gazetteer and Business Directory. 1884–5. Toronto: R.L. Polk and Co., 1884.

Ontario Gazetteer and Business Directory. 1888–9. Toronto: R.L. Polk and Co., 1888.

Province of Ontario Gazetteer and Directory, Including the City of Montreal, P.Q. 1895. Toronto: Might Directory, 1895.

Selections from Scottish Canadian Poets being a collection of the best poetry written by Scotsmen and their descendants in the Dominion of Canada. Toronto: Imrie, Graham and Company, 1900.

Stowe, Harriet Beecher. *Uncle Tom's Cabin; or, Life among the Lowly*. Boston: John P. Jewett; Cleveland: Jewett, Proctor, and Worthington, 1852.

Third Report of the Bureau of Labor for the Year Ending December 31st 1902. Toronto: L.K. Cameron, 1903.

Town of Tillsonburg. 1800–1909 By-Laws. https://lfpp.oxfordcounty.ca/WebLink/Browse.aspx?id=37409&dbid=0&repo=Tillsonburg-Public.

Town of Tillsonburg. 1910–1919 By-Laws. https://lfpp.oxfordcounty.ca/WebLink/Browse.aspx?id=37658&dbid=0&repo=Tillsonburg-Public.

White, Annie Randall. *Twentieth Century Etiquette: An Up-to-Date Book for Polite Society*. Chicago: Wabash Publishing House, 1900.

Women of Canada: Their Life and Work. Compiled by the National Council of Women of Canada at the request of the Hon. Sydney Fisher Minister of Agriculture, for distribution at the Paris International Exhibition, 1900.

Wright, Julia McNair. *The Complete Home: An Encyclopaedia of Domestic Life and Affairs. The Household, in its Foundation, Order, Economy, Beauty, Healthfulness, Emergencies, Methods, Children, Literature, Amusements, Religion, Friendships, Manners, Hospitality, Servants, Industry, Money, and History. A Volume of Practical Experiences Popularly Illustrated*. Philadelphia; Brantford, ON: Bradley, Garretson, 1879.

Secondary Sources

100 Years of IODE in Dresden 1914–2014. Accessed 22 August 2022. http://dresden.
  ca/wp-content/uploads/2015/02/IODEbooklet.pdf.
Abbott, Frank. "Cold Cash and Ice Palaces: The Quebec Winter Carnival of 1894."
  Canadian Historical Review 69, no. 2 (1988): 167–202.
Adams, Annmarie. "Female Regulation of the Healthy Home." In *Home, Work, and
  Play: Situating Canadian Social History, 1840–1980*, edited by James Opp and
  John C. Walsh, 3–17. Don Mills, ON: Oxford University Press, 2006.
Adams, Carly. "Supervised Places to Play: Social Reform, Citizenship, and Femininity at
  Municipal Playgrounds in London, Ontario, 1900–1942." *Ontario History* 103,
  no. 1 (Spring 2011): 60–80.
Adams, Carly, and Darren J. Aoki. "'Hey, Why Don't We Have a Bonspiel?' Narrating
  Postwar Japanese Canadian Experiences in Southern Alberta through Oral
  Histories of Curling." *International Journal of the History of Sport* 37, no. 16
  (2020): 1715–33.
Adams, Mary Louise. *Artistic Impressions: Figure Skating, Masculinity, and the Limits of
  Sport*. Toronto: University of Toronto Press, 2011.
———. "Freezing Social Relations: Ice, Rinks, and the Development of Figure
  Skating." In *Sites of Sport: Space, Place, Experience*, edited by Patricia Vertinsky
  and John Bale, 57–72. London: Routledge, 2004.
———. "From Mixed-Sex Sport to Sport for Girls: The Feminization of Figure
  Skating." *Sport in History* 30, no. 2 (June 2010): 218–41.
———. "The Manly History of a 'Girls' Sport: Gender, Class and the Development of
  Nineteenth-Century Figure Skating." *International Journal of the History of Sport*
  24, no. 7 (2007): 872–93.
Agger, Helen. *Dadibaajim: Returning Home through Narrative*. Winnipeg: University
  of Manitoba Press, 2021.
Alessio, Dominic David. "Domesticating the 'Heart of the Wild': Female
  Personifications of the Colonies, 1886–1940." *Women's History Review* 6, no. 2
  (1997): 239–70.
Alexander, Ruth. *The Girl Problem: Female Sexual Delinquency in New York, 1900–
  1930*. Ithaca, NY: Cornell University Press, 1995.
Allan, Roberta. *History of Elora*. Elora, ON: The Institute, 1982.
Ambrose, Linda M. *A Great Rural Sisterhood: Madge Robertson Watt and the ACWW*.
  Toronto: University of Toronto Press, 2015.
———. "Cartoons and Commissions: Advice to Junior Farmers in Postwar Ontario."
  In *People, Places, and Times: Readings in Canadian Social History*. Vol. 2, *Post-
  Confederation*, edited by Cynthia R. Comacchio and Elizabeth Jane Errington,
  278–93. Toronto: Thomson Nelson, 2006.
———. "'Forever Lunching': Food, Power, and Politics in Rural Ontario Women's
  Organizations." In *Women in Agriculture: Professionalizing Rural Life in North
  America and Europe, 1880–1965*, edited by Linda M. Ambrose and Joan M.
  Jensen, 174–85. Iowa City, IA: University of Iowa Press, 2017.

———. *For Home and Country: The Centennial History of the Women's Institutes in Ontario*. Erin, ON: Boston Mills Press, 1996.

———. "Ontario Women's Institutes and the Work of Local History." In *Creating Historical Memory: English-Canadian Women and the Work of History*, edited by Beverly Boutilier and Alison Prentice, 75–100. Vancouver: University of British Columbia Press, 1997.

———. "Our Last Frontier: Imperialism and Northern Canadian Rural Women's Institutes." *Canadian Historical Review* 86, no. 2 (June 2005): 257–84.

———. "The Women's Institutes in Northern Ontario." In *Changing Lives: Women in Northern Ontario*, edited by Margaret Kechnie and Marge Reitsma-Street, 263–74. Toronto: Dundurn Press, 1996.

———. "'What Are the Good of Those Meetings Anyway?': Early Popularity of the Ontario Women's Institutes." *Ontario History* 87, no. 1 (March 1995): 1–20.

Ambrose, Linda M., and Margaret Kechnie. "Social Control or Social Feminism?: Two Views of the Ontario Women's Institutes." *Agricultural History* 73, no. 2 (Spring 1999): 222–37.

Armstrong, Christopher, and H.V. Nelles. *The Revenge of the Methodist Bicycle Company: Sunday Streetcars and Municipal Reform in Toronto, 1888–1897*. Toronto: Peter Martin Associates, 1977.

Aron, Cindy S. *Working at Play: A History of Vacations in the United States*. New York; Oxford: Oxford University Press, 1999.

Azoulay, Dan. *Hearts and Minds: Canadian Romance at the Dawn of the Modern Era, 1900–1930*. Calgary: University of Calgary Press, 2011.

Backhouse, Constance. *Colour-Coded: A Legal History of Racism in Canada, 1900–1950*. Toronto: University of Toronto Press, 1999.

———. "Desperate Women and Compassionate Courts: Infanticide in Nineteenth-Century Canada." *University of Toronto Law Journal* 34, no. 4 (1984): 447–78.

———. "Nineteenth-Century Canadian Prostitution Law: Reflections of a Discriminatory Society." *Histoire sociale/Social History* 18, no. 36 (November 1985): 387–423.

———. *Petticoats and Prejudice: Women and Law in Nineteenth-Century Canada*. Toronto: Osgoode Society by Women's Press, 1991.

Badger, Reid. *The Great American Fair: The World's Columbian Exposition and American Culture*. Chicago: Nelson Hall, 1979.

Bailey, Peter. "'A Mingled Mass of Perfectly Legitimate Pleasures': The Victorian Middle Class and the Problem of Leisure." *Victorian Studies* 21, no. 1 (Autumn 1977): 7–28.

———. *Leisure and Class in Victorian England*. London: Methuen, 1987.

———. *Popular Culture and Performance in the Victorian City*. Cambridge: Cambridge University Press, 1998.

Baltessen, Jody, and Shelagh J. Squire. "Winnipeg Women Getting Together: Study Groups and Reading Clubs, 1900–1940." In *Framing Our Past: Canadian Women's History in the Twentieth Century*, edited by Sharon Anne Cook, Lorna

R. McLean, and Kate O'Rourke, 10–14. Montreal and Kingston: McGill-Queen's University Press, 2001.

Barbour, Dale. *Undressed Toronto: From the Swimming Hole to Sunnyside, How a City Learned to Love the Beach, 1850–1935.* Winnipeg: University of Manitoba Press, 2021.

———. *Winnipeg Beach: Leisure and Courtship in a Resort Town, 1900–1967.* Winnipeg: University of Manitoba Press, 2011.

Barstow, Susan Torrey. "'Hedda Is All of Us': Late-Victorian Women at the Matinee." *Victorian Studies* 43, no. 3 (Spring 2001): 387–411.

Baskerville, Peter. *Sites of Power: A Concise History of Ontario.* Don Mills, ON: Oxford University Press, 2005.

Baskerville, Peter, and Eric W. Sager. *Unwilling Idlers: The Urban Unemployed and Their Families in Late Victorian Canada.* Toronto: University of Toronto Press, 1998.

Beausaert, Rebecca. "'Foreigners in Town': Leisure, Consumption, and Cosmopolitanism in Late-Nineteenth and Early-Twentieth Century Tillsonburg, ON." *Journal of the Canadian Historical Association* 23, no. 1 (2012): 215–247.

———. "'The Parties These Ladies Used to Put On!': Class and the Formation of Women's Leisure Activities in Tillsonburg, Ontario, 1881–1911." MA thesis, Western University, 2006.

———. "'Young Rovers' and 'Dazzling Lady Meteors': Gender and Bicycle Club Culture in Turn-of-the-Century Small-Town Ontario." *Scientia Canadensis: Canadian Journal of the History of Science, Technology and Medicine* 36, no. 1 (2013): 33–61.

Beechey, Laurel A. *E.D. Tillson: His Children and Their Grandchildren.* Tillsonburg, ON, 1991.

———. *Edwin Delevan Tillson and Mary Ann Tillson.* Tillsonburg, ON, 2000.

———. "OLHD22: Laurel Beechey Tillsonburg's Town Hall." https://www.youtube.com/watch?v=HDR9wTDBuYk&list=PLe1ZIhAe6zxv_VlEyS7KmGhm3aIVurzt9&index=5.

———. *The Father of Tillsonburg, Edwin Delevan Tillson and Mary Ann Tillson.* Tillsonburg, ON, n.d.

———. *Tillsonburg's Town Hall.* Tillsonburg, ON: Tillsonburg Architectural Conservation Advisory Committee, 1997.

———. *Tillson Family Homes.* Tillsonburg, ON, n.d.

Belisle, Donica. *Retail Nation: Department Stores and the Making of Modern Canada.* Vancouver: University of British Columbia Press, 2011.

———. *Purchasing Power: Women and the Rise of Canadian Consumer Culture.* Toronto: University of Toronto Press, 2020.

Benedict, Burton. "Rituals of Representation: Ethnic Stereotypes and Colonized Peoples at World's Fairs." In *Fair Representations: World's Fairs and the Modern World,* edited by Robert W. Rydell and Nancy E. Gwinn, 28–61. Amsterdam: VU University Press, 1994.

Borish, Linda J. "Benevolent America: Rural Women, Physical Recreation, Sport and Health Reform in Ante-Bellum New England." *International Journal of the History of Sport* 22, no. 6 (2005): 946–73.

Bouchier, Nancy B. *For the Love of the Game: Amateur Sport in Small-Town Ontario, 1838–1895*. Montreal and Kingston: McGill-Queen's University Press, 2003.

———. "Idealized Middle-Class Sport for a Young Nation: Lacrosse in Nineteenth-Century Ontario Towns, 1871–1891." *Journal of Canadian Studies* 29, no. 2 (Summer 1994): 89–110.

Braden, Donna R. "'The Family That Plays Together Stays Together': Family Pastimes and Indoor Amusements, 1890–1930." In *American Home Life, 1880–1930: A Social History of Spaces and Services*, edited by Jessica H. Foy and Thomas J. Schlereth, 145–61. Knoxville: University of Tennessee Press, 1992.

Brandon, Robert. *The History of Dresden*. Dresden, ON: Dresden Centennial Committee, 1982.

Brandt, Gail Cuthbert. "Organizations in Canada: The English Protestant Tradition." In *Women's Paid and Unpaid Work: Historical and Contemporary Perspectives*, edited by Paula Bourne, 79–86. Toronto: New Hogtown Press, 1985.

Brown, Dave. "The Northern Character Theme and Sport in Nineteenth-Century Canada." *Canadian Journal of History of Sport* 20, no. 1 (1989): 47–56.

Brown, Mary M. "Entertainers of the Road." In *Early Stages: Theatre in Ontario, 1800–1914*, edited by Ann Saddlemyer, 123–65. Toronto: University of Toronto Press, 1990.

Bulger, Margery A. "American Sportswomen in the 19th Century." *Journal of Popular Culture* 16, no. 2 (Fall 1982): 1–16.

Campbell, Claire. *Shaped by the West Wind: Nature and History in Georgian Bay*. Vancouver: University of British Columbia Press, 2005.

Canning, Charlotte M. *The Most American Thing in America: Circuit Chautauqua as Performance*. Iowa City, IA: University of Iowa Press, 2005.

Careless, J.M.S. "The Cultural Setting: Ontario Society to 1914." In *Early Stages: Theatre in Ontario, 1800–1914*, edited by Ann Saddlemyer, 18–51. Toronto: University of Toronto Press, 1990.

Carrigan, D. Owen. *Juvenile Delinquency in Canada: A History*. Concord, ON: Irwin Publishing, 1998.

Carter, Marie. *Building Heritage: A Guide to the Historical Houses of Dresden, Ontario*. Chatham, ON: Chamberlain/Mercury Printing, 2004.

———. "William Whipper's *Lands along the Sydenham*." In *The Promised Land: History and Historiography of the Black Experience in Chatham-Kent's Settlements and Beyond*, edited by Boulou Ebanda de B'béri, Nina Reid-Maroney, and Handle Kashope Wright, 73–90. Toronto: University of Toronto Press, 2014.

Carter, Marie, and Jeffrey Carter. *Stepping Back in Time: Along the Trillium Trail in Dresden*. Dresden, ON: Catherine McVean Chapter IODE, 2003.

Casey, Janet Galligani. *A New Heartland: Women, Modernity, and the Agrarian Ideal in America*. Oxford: Oxford University Press, 2009.

Chapple, Nina Perkins. *A Heritage of Stone: Buildings of the Niagara Peninsula, Fergus and Elora, Guelph, Region of Waterloo, Cambridge, Paris, Ancaster-Dundas-Flamborough, Hamilton and St. Marys.* Toronto: J. Lorimer, 2006.

Chenier, Elise. "Class, Gender, and the Social Standard: The Montreal Junior League, 1912–1939." *Canadian Historical Review* 90, no. 4 (December 2009): 671–710.

Clapson, Mark. *A Bit of a Flutter: Popular Gambling and English Society, c. 1823–1961.* Manchester: Manchester University Press, 1992.

Comacchio, Cynthia. *The Dominion of Youth: Adolescence and the Making of Modern Canada, 1920–1950.* Waterloo, ON: Wilfrid Laurier University Press, 2008.

Condee, William F. "*Hamlet*, Sunday School, *Zarrow's Pig Revue*: Cultural Regulation in America's Opera Houses." *Journal of American Culture* 22, no. 2 (1999): 59–64.

Connelly, Mark. *Christmas: A Social History.* London: I.B. Tauris, 1999.

Connon, John Robert. *The Early History of Elora, Ontario and Vicinity.* 2nd rev. printing, reissued with introduction by Gerald Noonan. Waterloo, ON: Wilfrid Laurier University Press, 1975.

Connors, Stompin' Tom. "Tillsonburg," *My Stompin' Grounds.* © 1971, Boot Records, BOS 7103.

Cook, Sharon Anne. "*Through Sunshine and Shadow*": The Woman's Christian Temperance Union, Evangelicalism, and Reform in Ontario, 1874–1930.* Montreal and Kingston: McGill-Queen's University Press, 1995.

Cooper, Afua. *The Hanging of Angélique: The Untold Story of Canadian Slavery and the Burning of Old Montreal.* Toronto: HarperCollins, 2006.

Cooper, John Irwin. "George Tillson." *Dictionary of Canadian Biography Online, 1861–1870.* Vol. 9, *1861–1870.* Accessed 11 February 2009. http://www.biographi.ca/009004-119.01-e.php?&id_nbr=4746.

Cowan, Ruth Schwartz. *More Work for Mother: The Ironies of Household Technology from the Open Hearth to the Microwave.* New York: Basic Books, 1983.

Craig, Beatrice. *Backwoods Consumers and Homespun Capitalists: The Rise of a Market Culture in Eastern Canada.* Toronto: University of Toronto Press, 2009.

Crerar, Adam. "Writing across the Rural-Urban Divide: The Case of Peter McArthur, 1909–24." *Journal of Canadian Studies* 41, no. 2 (Spring 2007): 112–37.

Croly, J.C. *The History of the Woman's Club Movement in America.* New York: H.G. Allen, 1898.

Cross, Gary S. *A Social History of Leisure since 1600.* State College, PA: Venture Publishing, 1990.

Cross, Gary S., and John K. Walton. *The Playful Crowd: Pleasure Places in the Twentieth Century.* New York: Columbia University Press, 2005.

Cruikshank, Ken, and Nancy B. Bouchier. "Dirty Spaces: Environment, the State, and Recreational Swimming in Hamilton Harbour, 1870–1946." *Sport History Review* 29 (1998): 59–76.

———. "'The Heritage of the People Closed against Them': Class, Environment, and the Shaping of Burlington Beach, 1870s–1980s." *Urban History Review* 30, no. 1 (October 2001): 40–55.

————. *The People of the Bay: A Social and Environmental History of Hamilton Harbour*. Vancouver: University of British Columbia Press, 2016.

Cunningham, Hugh. *Leisure in the Industrial Revolution: 1780–1880*. London: Croom Helm, 1980.

Danbom, David B. *Born in the Country: A History of Rural America*. 2nd ed. Baltimore: Johns Hopkins University Press, 2006.

David, Alison Matthews. *Fashion Victims: The Dangers of Dress Past and Present*. London: Bloomsbury Visual Arts, 2015.

Davies, Robertson. "The Nineteenth-Century Repertoire." In *Early Stages: Theatre in Ontario, 1800–1914*, edited by Ann Saddlemyer, 90–122. Toronto: University of Toronto Press, 1990.

Davis, Angela E. "'Country Homemakers': The Daily Lives of Prairie Women as Seen through the Woman's Page of the Grain Growers' Guide 1908–1928." In *Canadian Papers in Rural History*, vol. 8, edited by Donald H. Akenson, 163–74. Gananoque, ON: Langdale Press, 1992.

Davis, Gayle R. "Women's Frontier Diaries: Writing for Good Reason." *Women's Studies: An Inter-Disciplinary Journal* 14, no. 1 (1987): 5–14.

Davis, Susan G. *Parades and Power: Street Theatre in Nineteenth-Century Philadelphia*. Philadelphia: Temple University Press, 1986.

Dawson, Michael. *Selling British Columbia: Tourism and Consumer Culture, 1890–1970*. Vancouver: University of British Columbia Press, 2004.

de Groot, Joanna. "Metropolitan Desires and Colonial Connections: Reflections on Consumption and Empire." In *At Home with the Empire: Metropolitan Culture and the Imperial World*, edited by Catherine Hall and Sonya O. Rose, 166–90. Cambridge: Cambridge University Press, 2006.

Delgado, Alan. *Victorian Entertainment*. Newton Abbot, UK: David and Charles, 1971.

Deloria, Philip. *Indians in Unexpected Places*. Lawrence, KS: University Press of Kansas, 2004.

Dewar, Kenneth C. *Charles Clarke, Pen and Ink Warrior*. Montreal and Kingston: McGill-Queen's University Press, 2002.

Downey, Allan. *The Creator's Game: Lacrosse, Identity, and Indigenous Nationhood*. Vancouver: University of British Columbia Press, 2018.

"Dresden and Racial Discrimination." Canada's Human Rights History. Accessed 25 January 2024. https://historyofrights.ca/encyclopaedia/main-events/dresden-racial-discrimination/.

Dubinsky, Karen. *Improper Advances: Rape and Heterosexual Conflict in Ontario, 1880–1929*. Chicago: University of Chicago Press, 1993.

————. "'Maidenly Girls' or 'Designing Women'?: The Crime of Seduction in Turn-of-the-Century Ontario." In *Gender Conflicts: New Essays in Women's History*, edited by Franca Iacovetta and Mariana Valverde, 27–66. Toronto: University of Toronto Press, 1992.

————. *The Second Greatest Disappointment: Honeymooning and Tourism at Niagara Falls*. New Brunswick, NJ: Rutgers University Press, 1999.

Dunae, Patrick A. "Sex, Charades, and Census Records: Locating Female Sex Trade Workers in a Victorian City." *Histoire sociale/Social History* 42, no. 84 (November 2009): 267–97.

Dunkin, Jessica. *Canoe and Canvas: Life at the Encampments of the American Canoe Association, 1880–1910*. Toronto: University of Toronto Press, 2019.

Dunson, Stephanie. "The Minstrel in the Parlor: Nineteenth-Century Sheet Music and the Domestication of Blackface Minstrelsy." *American Transcendental Quarterly* 16, no. 4 (December 2002): 241–56.

Dunsworth, Edward. *Harvesting Labour: Tobacco and the Global Making of Canada's Agricultural Workforce*. Montreal and Kingston: McGill-Queen's University Press, 2022.

Eff, Ellen H. *Hamlet on the Otter: A Historical Sketch of Tillsonburg, Its First Hundred Years, 1815–1915*. Tillsonburg, ON: News Printing, 1963.

Ehlers, D. Layne. "This Week at the Opera House: Popular Musical Entertainment at Great Plains Opera Houses, 1887–1917." *Great Plains Quarterly* 20 (Summer 2000): 183–95.

"Elora Walking Tour: North of the Grand River." *Wellington County History* 17 (2004): 36–45.

"Elora Walking Tour: South of the Grand River." *Wellington County History* 17 (2004): 46–52.

Enstad, Nan. *Ladies of Labor, Girls of Adventure: Working Women, Popular Culture, and Labor Politics at the Turn of the Twentieth Century*. New York: Columbia University Press, 1999.

Erickson, Bruce, and Sarah Wylie Krotz, eds. *The Politics of the Canoe*. Winnipeg: University of Manitoba Press, 2021.

Erickson, Lesley. "'A Very Garden of the Lord'? Hired Hands, Farm Women, and Sex Crime Prosecutions on the Prairies, 1914–1929." *Journal of the Canadian Historical Association* 12, no. 1 (2001): 115–36.

———. *Westward Bound: Sex, Violence, the Law, and the Making of a Settler Society*. Vancouver: University of British Columbia Press, 2011.

Errington, Elizabeth Jane. *Wives and Mothers, School Mistresses and Scullery Maids: Working Women in Upper Canada, 1790–1840*. Montreal and Kingston: McGill-Queen's University Press, 1995.

"Explore Dresden." Downtown Dresden Business Improvement Area (B.I.A) and Dresden Community Development Association. Accessed 25 January 2024. http://www.dresden.ca.

Fahrni, Magda. "'Ruffled' Mistresses and 'Discontented' Maids: Respectability and the Case of Domestic Service, 1880–1914." *Labour/Le Travail* 39 (Spring 1997): 69–97.

Fehr, Rick. "Who Has Traded Cash for Creation? Approaching an Anishinaabeg Informed Environmental History on Bkejwanong Territory." PhD diss., York University, 2010. https://central.bac-lac.gc.ca/.item?id=NR80527&op=pdf&app=Library&oclc_number=1019480965.

Filice, Michelle. "Haldimand Proclamation." *Canadian Encyclopedia*. Accessed 25 January 2024. https://www.thecanadianencyclopedia.ca/en/article/haldimand-proclamation.

Flanders, Judith. *Consuming Passions: Leisure and Pleasure in Victorian Britain*. London: Harper Press, 2006.

Francis, Daniel. *The Imaginary Indian: The Image of the Indian in Canadian Culture*. Vancouver: Arsenal Pulp Press, 1992.

Fuller, Kathryn H. *At the Picture Show: Small-Town Audiences and the Creation of Movie Fan Culture*. Washington, DC: Smithsonian Institution Press, 1996.

———. "'You Can Have the Strand in Your Own Town': The Marginalization of Small Town Film Exhibition in the Silent Film Era." *Film History* 6 (1994): 166–77.

Gagan, David. *Hopeful Travellers: Families, Land, and Social Change in Mid-Victorian Peel County, Canada West*. Toronto: University of Toronto Press, 1981.

Gagan, Rosemary R. *A Sensitive Independence: Canadian Methodist Missionaries in Canada and the Orient, 1881–1925*. Montreal and Kingston: McGill-Queen's University Press, 1992.

Garvey, Ellen Gruber. *The Adman in the Parlor: Magazines and the Gendering of Consumer Culture, 1880s to 1910s*. New York: Oxford University Press, 1996.

Gilles, Rogers. *Women on the Move: The Forgotten Era of Women's Bicycle Racing*. Lincoln, NE: University of Nebraska Press, 2018.

Gillis, John R. *A World of Their Own Making: Myth, Ritual, and the Quest for Family Values*. New York: Basic Books, 1996.

Ginzberg, Lori D. *Women and the Work of Benevolence: Morality, Politics, and Class in the Nineteenth-Century United States*. New Haven, CT: Yale University Press, 1990.

Glasbeek, Amanda. *Feminized Justice: The Toronto Women's Court, 1913–1934*. Vancouver: University of British Columbia Press, 2009.

Gordon, Beverly. *Bazaars and Fair Ladies: The History of the American Fundraising Fair*. Knoxville: University of Tennessee Press, 1998.

———. *The Saturated World: Aesthetic Meaning, Intimate Objects, Women's Lives, 1890–1940*. Knoxville: University of Tennessee Press, 2006.

Government of Ontario—First Nations, Inuit, and Métis. "Map of Ontario Treaties and Reserves." Accessed 25 January 2024. https://www.ontario.ca/page/map-ontario-treaties-and-reserves.

Graham, W.H. *Greenbank: Country Matters in 19th Century Ontario*. Peterborough, ON: Broadview Press, 1988.

Greenhill, Pauline. "Make the Night Hideous: Death at a Manitoba Charivari, 1909." *Manitoba History* 52 (June 2006): 3–17.

———. *Make the Night Hideous: Four English-Canadian Charivaris, 1881–1940*. Toronto: University of Toronto Press, 2010.

Grier, Katherine C. "The Decline of the Memory Palace: The Parlor after 1890." In *American Home Life, 1880–1930: A Social History of Spaces and Services*, edited by Jessica H. Foy and Thomas J. Schlereth, 49–74. Knoxville: University of Tennessee Press, 1992.

Gucciardo, Dorotea. "The Powered Generation: Canadians, Electricity, and Everyday Life." PhD diss., Western University, 2011. https://ir.lib.uwo.ca/cgi/viewcontent.cgi?article=1376&context=etd.

Hage, George S. "Games People Played: Sports in Minnesota Daily Newspapers 1860–1890." *Minnesota History* 47, no. 8 (Winter 1981): 321–28.

Haight, Canniff. *Country Life in Canada*. With a new introduction by Arthur R.M. Lower. Belleville, ON: Mika Publishing, 1971.

Hall, Catherine, and Sonya O. Rose, eds. *At Home with the Empire: Metropolitan Culture and the Imperial World*. Cambridge: Cambridge University Press, 2006.

Hall, M. Ann. *Muscle on Wheels: Louise Armaindo and the High-Wheel Racers of Nineteenth-Century America*. Montreal and Kingston: McGill-Queens University Press, 2018.

———. *The Girl and the Game: A History of Women's Sport in Canada*. Peterborough, ON: Broadview Press, 2002.

———. *The Girl and the Game: A History of Women's Sport in Canada*. 2nd ed. Toronto: University of Toronto Press, 2016.

Halpern, Monda. *And on That Farm He Had a Wife: Ontario Farm Women and Feminism, 1900–1970*. Montreal and Kingston: McGill-Queen's University Press, 2001.

Hamlett, Jane. "'The Dining Room Should Be the Man's Paradise, as the Drawing Room Is the Woman's': Gender and Middle-Class Domestic Space in England, 1850–1910." *Gender and History* 21, no. 3 (November 2009): 576–91.

Hammill, Faye, and Michelle Smith. *Magazines, Travel, and Middlebrow Culture: Canadian Periodicals in English and French, 1925–1960*. Liverpool: Liverpool University Press, 2017.

Hanlon, Sheila. "The Lady Cyclist: A Gender Analysis of Women's Cycling Culture in 1890s London." PhD diss., York University, 2009.

Hart, E.J. *The Selling of Canada: The CPR and the Beginnings of Canadian Tourism*. Banff, AB: Altitude Publishing, 1983.

Heaman, Elsbeth. *The Inglorious Arts of Peace: Exhibitions in Canadian Society during the Nineteenth Century*. Toronto: University of Toronto Press, 1999.

Heron, Craig. *Booze: A Distilled History*. Toronto: Between the Lines, 2003.

———. "Boys Will Be Boys: Working-Class Masculinities in the Age of Mass Production." *International Labor and Working-Class History* 69 (Spring 2006): 6–34.

———. *Lunch-Bucket Lives: Remaking the Workers' City*. Toronto: Between the Lines, 2015.

Heron, Craig, and Steve Penfold. *The Workers' Festival: A History of Labour Day in Canada*. Toronto: University of Toronto Press, 2005.

Hill, Susan M. *The Clay We Are Made Of: Haudenosaunee Land Tenure on the Grand River*. Winnipeg: University of Manitoba Press, 2017.

Hind, Andrew, and Maria Da Silva. *Muskoka Resorts: Then and Now*. Toronto: Dundurn Natural Heritage, 2011.

Historic Sites and Monuments Board of Canada. "Elora Drill Shed." Accessed 25 January 2024. https://www.pc.gc.ca/apps/dfhd/page_nhs_eng.aspx?id=369.

Hoe, Ban Seng. *Enduring Hardship: The Chinese Laundry in Canada*. Gatineau, PQ: Canadian Museum of Civilization, 2003.

Hoffenberg, Peter H. *An Empire on Display: English, Indian, and Australian Exhibitions from the Crystal Palace to the Great War*. Berkeley: University of California Press, 2001.

Hoffman, Francis, and Ryan Taylor. *Much to Be Done: Private Life in Ontario from Victorian Diaries*. Toronto: Natural Heritage/Natural History, 1996.

Hoganson, Kristin L. *Consumers' Imperium: The Global Production of American Domesticity, 1865–1920*. Chapel Hill: University of North Carolina Press, 2007.

———. "The Fashionable World: Imagined Communities of Dress." In *After the Imperial Turn: Thinking with and through the Nation*, edited by Antoinette Burton, 260–78. Durham, NC: Duke University Press, 2003.

Holman, Andrew C. *A Sense of Their Duty: Middle-Class Formation in Victorian Ontario Towns*. Montreal and Kingston: McGill-Queen's University Press, 2000.

Howell, Colin D. *Blood, Sweat, and Cheers: Sport and the Making of Modern Canada*. Toronto: University of Toronto Press, 2001.

Hunter, Jane H. "Inscribing the Self in the Heart of the Family: Diaries and Girlhood in Late-Victorian America." *American Quarterly* 44, no. 1 (March 1992): 51–81.

Huskins, Bonnie. "The Ceremonial Space of Women: Public Processions in Victorian Saint John and Halifax." In *Separate Spheres: Women's Worlds in the 19th-Century Maritimes*, edited by Janet Guildford and Suzanne Morton, 145–59. Fredericton, NB: Acadiensis Press, 1994.

Jackson, Ashley, and David Tomkins. *Illustrating Empire: A Visual History of British Imperialism*. Oxford: Bodleian Library, University of Oxford, 2011.

Jasen, Patricia. "Native People and the Tourist Industry in Nineteenth-Century Ontario." *Journal of Canadian Studies* 28, no. 4 (Winter 1993/1994): 5–27.

———. *Wild Things: Nature, Culture, and Tourism in Ontario, 1790–1914*. Toronto: University of Toronto Press, 1995.

Johnson, Leo. "The Political Economy of Ontario Women in the Nineteenth Century." In *Women at Work: Ontario, 1850–1930*, edited by Janice Acton, Penny Goldsmith, and Bonnie Shepard, 13–31. Toronto: Canadian Women's Educational Press, 1974.

Jones, David C. "'From Babies to Buttonholes': Women's Work at Agricultural Fairs." *Alberta History* 29, no. 4 (1981): 26–32.

Kechnie, Margaret C. *Organizing Rural Women: The Federated Women's Institutes of Ontario, 1897–1919*. Montreal and Kingston: McGill-Queen's University Press, 2003.

Kelcey, Barbara E. "Dress Reform in Nineteenth-Century Canada." In *Fashion: A Canadian Perspective*, edited by Alexandra Palmer, 229–48. Toronto: University of Toronto Press, 2004.

Kilde, Jeanne Halgren. "The 'Predominance of the Feminine' at Chautauqua: Rethinking the Gender-Space Relationship in Victorian America." *Signs* 24, no. 2 (Winter 1999): 449–86.

Kinsey, Fiona. "Reading Photographic Portraits of Australian Women Cyclists in the 1890s: From Costume and Cycle Choices to Constructions of Feminine Identity." *International Journal of the History of Sport* 28, nos. 8–9 (May–June 2011): 1121–37.

Kline, Ronald R. *Consumers in the Country: Technology and Social Change in Rural America*. Baltimore: Johns Hopkins University Press, 2000.

Knupfer, Anne Meis, and Christine Woyshner, eds. *The Educational Work of Women's Organizations, 1890–1960*. New York: Palgrave Macmillan, 2008.

Koltun, Lily, ed. *Private Realms of Light: Amateur Photography in Canada, 1839–1940*. Markham, ON: Fitzhenry and Whiteside, 1984.

Kossuth, Robert S. "Dangerous Waters: Victorian Decorum, Swimmer Safety, and the Establishment of Public Bathing Facilities in London (Canada)." *International Journal of the History of Sport* 22, no. 5 (2005): 796–815.

———. "Spaces and Places to Play: The Formation of a Municipal Parks System in London, Ontario, 1867–1914." *Ontario History* 97, no. 2 (Autumn 2005): 160–90.

Kossuth, Robert S., and Kevin B. Wamsley. "Cycles of Manhood: Pedaling Respectability in Ontario's Forest City." *Sport History Review* 34 (2003): 168–89.

Labode, Modupe. "A Carnival for a Cathedral: The 1906 Carnival of Nations in Denver." *Colorado Heritage* (Autumn 2008): 14–25.

Lake, Robert J. "Gender and Etiquette in British Lawn Tennis 1870–1939: A Case Study of 'Mixed Doubles.'" *International Journal of the History of Sport* 29, no. 5 (2012): 691–710.

———. "Social Class, Etiquette and Behavioural Restraint in British Lawn Tennis, 1870–1939." *International Journal of the History of Sport* 28, no. 6 (2011): 876–94.

Lane, Hannah M. "'Wife, Mother, Sister, Friend': Methodist Women in St. Stephen, New Brunswick, 1861–1881." In *Separate Spheres: Women's Worlds in the 19th-Century Maritimes*, edited by Janet Guildford and Suzanne Morton, 93–117. Fredericton, NB: Acadiensis Press, 1994.

Lang, Marjory. *Women Who Made the News: Female Journalists in Canada, 1880–1945*. Montreal and Kingston: McGill-Queen's University Press, 1999.

Laverdure, Paul. *Sunday in Canada: The Rise and Fall of the Lord's Day*. Yorkton, SK: Gravel Books, 2004.

Lenton-Young, Gerald. "Variety Theatre." In *Early Stages: Theatre in Ontario, 1800–1914*, edited by Ann Saddlemyer, 166–213. Toronto: University of Toronto Press, 1990.

Levine, Lawrence W. *Highbrow/Lowbrow: The Emergence of Cultural Hierarchy in America*. Cambridge, MA: Harvard University Press, 1988.

Little, J.I. *Reading the Diaries of Henry Trent: The Everyday Life of a Canadian Englishman, 1842–1898.* Montreal and Kingston: McGill-Queen's University Press, 2021.

Lott, Eric. *Love and Theft: Blackface Minstrelsy and the American Working Class.* New York: Oxford University Press, 1995.

Lynes, Russell. *The Lively Audience: A Social History of the Visual and Performing Arts in America, 1890–1950.* New York: Harper and and Row, 1985.

Lyon-Jenness, Cheryl. "Bergamot Balm and Verbenas: The Public and Private Meaning of Ornamental Plants in the Mid-Nineteenth-Century Midwest." *Agricultural History* 73, no. 2 (Spring 1999): 201–21.

MacDougall, John. *Rural Life in Canada: Its Trend and Tasks.* With introduction by Robert Craig Brown. Toronto: University of Toronto Press, 1973.

MacEachern, Alan, and Edward MacDonald. *The Summer Trade: A History of Tourism on Prince Edward Island.* Montreal and Kingston: McGill-Queen's University Press, 2022.

Mackintosh, Philip Gordon. "A Bourgeois Geography of Domestic Cycling: Using Public Space Responsibly in Toronto and Niagara-on-the-Lake, 1890–1900." *Journal of Historical Sociology* 20, nos. 1/2 (March/June 2007): 126–57.

MacLachlan, Joann. *The Dundas Travel Club: Documenting a Journey.* Hamilton, ON: Lavender Hill Publishers' Services, 2021.

Mann, Ruth M. "Struggles for Youth Justice and Justice for Youth: A Canadian Example." In *Juvenile Crime and Delinquency: A Turn of the Century Reader,* edited by Ruth M. Mann, 4–18. Toronto: Canadian Scholars' Press, 2000.

Marks, Lynne. "No Double Standard?: Leisure, Sex, and Sin in Upper Canadian Church Discipline Records, 1800–1860." In *Gendered Pasts: Historical Essays in Femininity and Masculinity in Canada,* edited by Kathryn McPherson, Cecilia Morgan, and Nancy M. Forestell, 48–64. Toronto: University of Toronto Press, 2003.

———. "Religion, Leisure, and Working Class Identity." In *Labouring Lives: Work and Workers in Nineteenth-Century Ontario,* edited by Paul Craven, 278–334. Toronto: University of Toronto Press, 1995.

———. *Revivals and Roller Rinks: Religion, Leisure, and Identity in Late-Nineteenth-Century Small-Town Ontario.* Toronto: University of Toronto Press, 1996.

———. "The 'Hallelujah Lasses': Working-Class Women in the Salvation Army in English Canada, 1882–92." In *Gender Conflicts: New Essays in Women's History,* edited by Franca Iacovetta and Mariana Valverde, 67–117. Toronto: University of Toronto Press, 1992.

Marr, Lucille. "Sunday School Teaching: A Women's Enterprise." *Histoire sociale/Social History* 26, no. 52 (November 1993): 329–44.

Martin, Theodora Penny. *The Sound of Our Own Voices: Women's Study Clubs 1860–1910.* Boston: Beacon Press, 1987.

Mason, Courtney W. "Rethinking the Revival of the Glengarry Highland Games: Modernity, Identity, and Tourism in Rural Canada." *Sport History Review* 36, no. 2 (2005): 130–53.

————. *Spirits of the Rockies: Reasserting an Indigenous Presence in Banff National Park.* Toronto: University of Toronto Press, 2014.

Maynard, Steven. "'Horrible Temptations': Sex, Men, and Working-Class Male Youth in Urban Ontario, 1890–1935." *Canadian Historical Review* 78, no. 2 (June 1997): 191–235.

McCalla, Douglas. *Consumers in the Bush: Shopping in Rural Upper Canada.* Montreal and Kingston: McGill-Queen's University Press, 2015.

————. "Seeing Pioneers as Modern: Rural Upper Canadians Go Shopping." In *Temps, espace, et modernités: Mélanges offerts à Serge Courville et Normand Séguin*, edited by Brigitte Caulier and Yvan Rousseau, 137–50. Quebec: Les Presses de l'Université Laval, 2009.

McCallum, John. *Unequal Beginnings: Agriculture and Economic Development in Quebec and Ontario until 1870.* Toronto: University of Toronto Press, 1980.

McCorkindale, Deirdre. "Black Education: The Complexity of Segregation in Kent County's Nineteenth-Century Schools." In *Unsettling the Great White North: Black Canadian History*, edited by Michele A. Johnson and Funké Aladejebi, 333–56. Toronto: University of Toronto Press, 2022.

McKay, Ian. *In the Province of History: The Making of the Public Past in Twentieth-Century Nova Scotia.* Montreal and Kingston: McGill-Queen's University Press, 2010.

McMurray, David. "Rivaling the Gentleman in the Gentle Art: The Authority of the Victorian Woman Angler." *Sport History Review* 39 (2008): 99–126.

McMurry, Sally. "City Parlor, Country Sitting Room: Rural Vernacular Design and the American Parlor, 1840–1900." *Winterthur Portfolio* 20, no. 4 (Winter 1985): 261–80.

————. *Families and Farmhouses in Nineteenth-Century America: Vernacular Design and Social Change.* New York: Oxford University Press, 1988.

McNenly, Linda Scarangella. "Foe, Friend, or Critic: Native Performers with Buffalo Bill's Wild West Show and Discourses of Conquest and Friendship in Newspaper Reports." *American Indian Quarterly* 38, no. 2 (Spring 2014): 143–76.

McTaggart, Kenneth D. *The Victoria Day Disaster.* London, ON: McTaggart, 1978.

Mechefske, Lindy. *Ontario Picnics: A Century of Dining Outdoors.* Lunenburg, NS: MacIntyre Purcell Publishing, 2021.

Metcalfe, Alan. *Canada Learns to Play: The Emergence of Organized Sport, 1807–1914.* Toronto: McClelland and Stewart, 1987.

Mitchinson, Wendy. "Aspects of Reform: Four Women's Organizations in Nineteenth-Century Canada." PhD diss., York University, 1976.

————. *The Nature of Their Bodies: Women and Their Doctors in Victorian Canada.* Toronto: University of Toronto Press, 1991.

Mizener, David. "Furrows and Fairgrounds: Agriculture, Identity, and Authority in Twentieth-Century Rural Ontario." PhD diss., York University, 2009.

Moir, John S. *Enduring Witness: A History of the Presbyterian Church in Canada.* Canada: Bryant Press, n.d.

Morgan, Cecilia. *Building Better Britains? Settler Societies in the British World, 1783–1920*. Toronto: University of Toronto Press and the Canadian Historical Association, 2017.

———. *Commemorating Canada: History, Heritage, and Memory, 1850s–1990s*. Toronto: University of Toronto Press, 2016.

———. *Creating Colonial Pasts: History, Memory, and Commemoration in Southern Ontario, 1860–1980*. Toronto: University of Toronto Press, 2015.

———. *"A Happy Holiday": English Canadians and Transatlantic Tourism, 1870–1930*. Toronto: University of Toronto Press, 2008.

Morrow, Don, and Kevin B. Wamsley. *Sport in Canada: A History*. 3rd ed. Don Mills, ON: Oxford University Press, 2013.

Morrow, Don, et al. *A Concise History of Sport in Canada*. Toronto: Oxford University Press, 1989.

Motz, Marilyn Ferris. "Folk Expression of Time and Place: 19th-Century Midwestern Rural Diaries." *Journal of American Folklore* 100, no. 396 (April–June 1987): 131–47.

Munting, Roger. *An Economic and Social History of Gambling in Britain and the USA*. Manchester; New York: Manchester University Press, 1996.

Murray, Heather. *Come, Bright Improvement!: The Literary Societies of Nineteenth-Century Ontario*. Toronto: University of Toronto Press, 2002.

Myers, Tamara. *Caught: Montreal's Modern Girls and the Law, 1869–1945*. Toronto: University of Toronto Press, 2006.

———. "Nocturnal Disorder and the Curfew Solution: A History of Juvenile Sundown Regulations in Canada." In *Lost Kids: Vulnerable Children and Youth in Twentieth-Century Canada and the United States*, edited by Mona Gleason, Tamara Myers, Leslie Paris, and Veronica Strong-Boag, 95–113. Vancouver: University of British Columbia Press, 2010.

Nance, Susan. *How the Arabian Nights Inspired the American Dream, 1790–1935*. Chapel Hill: University of North Carolina Press, 2009.

Nasaw, David. *Going Out: The Rise and Fall of Public Amusements*. Cambridge, MA: Harvard University Press, 1999.

Nelles, H.V. *The Art of Nation-Building: Pageantry and Spectacle at Quebec's Tercentenary*. Toronto: University of Toronto Press, 1999.

Nelson, Paula M. "'Do Everything'—Women in Small Prairie Towns, 1870–1920." *Journal of the West* 36 (October 1997): 52–60.

Neth, Mary. *Preserving the Family Farm: Women, Community, and the Foundations of Agribusiness in the Midwest, 1900–1940*. Baltimore: Johns Hopkins University Press, 1995.

Newman, Bert. *More Reminiscences about Tillsonburg*. Edited by Dave Stover. Tillsonburg, ON: Otter Printing, 1987.

———. *Once Upon a Time: Further Reminiscences about Tillsonburg*. Edited by Dave Stover. Tillsonburg, ON: Otter Printing, 1988.

———. *Reminiscences about Tillsonburg*. Edited by Dave Stover. Tillsonburg, ON, 1986.

Nicholas, Jane. *Canadian Carnival Freaks and the Extraordinary Body, 1900–1970s.* Toronto: University of Toronto Press, 2018.

Nicks, Joan, and Jeannette Sloniowski. "Entertaining Niagara Falls, Ontario: Minstrel Shows, Theatres, and Popular Pleasures." In *Covering Niagara: Studies in Local Popular Culture,* edited by Joan Nicks and Barry Keith, 285–310. Waterloo, ON: Wilfrid Laurier University Press, 2010.

Noel, Françoise. *Family and Community Life in Northeastern Ontario: The Interwar Years.* Montreal and Kingston: McGill-Queen's University Press, 2009.

Norcliffe, Glen. *The Ride to Modernity: The Bicycle in Canada, 1869–1900.* Toronto: University of Toronto Press, 2001.

Norman, Alison. "Race, Gender and Colonialism: Public Life among the Six Nations of Grand River, 1899–1939." PhD diss., Ontario Institute for Studies in Education, University of Toronto, 2010.

Nurse, Jodey. *Cultivating Community: Women and Agricultural Fairs in Ontario.* Montreal and Kingston: McGill-Queen's University Press, 2022.

"OACAS: History of Children's Aid." Family Aid Society. Accessed 25 January 2024. http://www.familyaid.org/html/0132.html.

Odem, Mary. *Delinquent Daughters: Protecting and Policing Adolescent Female Sexuality in the United States, 1885–1920.* Chapel Hill: University of North Carolina Press, 1995.

Ontario Heritage Trust Plaque. "The Founding of Dresden." Accessed 25 January 2024. https://www.heritagetrust.on.ca/plaques/founding-of-dresden.

Ontario Heritage Trust Plaque. "The 'Victoria' Boat Disaster 1881." Accessed 25 January 2024. https://www.heritagetrust.on.ca/plaques/victoria-boat-disaster-1881.

Opp, James, and John C. Walsh, eds. *Home, Work, and Play: Situating Canadian Social History, 1840–1980.* Don Mills, ON: Oxford University Press, 2006.

Osterud, Nancy Grey. *Bonds of Community: The Lives of Farm Women in Nineteenth-Century New York.* Ithaca, NY: Cornell University Press, 1991.

Palmer, Daniel. "The McKee Treaty of 1790: British-Aboriginal Diplomacy in the Great Lakes." PhD diss., University of Saskatchewan, 2017, https://harvest.usask.ca/server/api/core/bitstreams/0d8047b0-baa5-4baf-b4e8-5f4621b66488/content.

Parker, Amy. "'Making the Most of What We Have': The Women's Institutes of Huron County, Ontario during the Inter-War Period." MA thesis, University of Guelph, 2007.

Parr, Joy. *The Gender of Breadwinners: Women, Men, and Change in Two Industrial Towns, 1880–1950.* Toronto: University of Toronto Press, 1990.

Pedersen, Diana, and Martha Phemister. "Women and Photography in Ontario, 1839–1929: A Case Study of the Interaction of Gender and Technology." *Scientia Canadensis: Canadian Journal of the History of Science, Technology and Medicine* 9, no. 1 (28) (1985): 27–52.

Pederson, Jane Marie. *Between Memory and Reality: Family and Community in Rural Wisconsin, 1870–1970.* Madison: University of Wisconsin Press, 1992.

Peiss, Kathy. *Cheap Amusements: Working Women and Leisure in Turn-of-the-Century New York*. Philadelphia: Temple University Press, 1986.

Pettit, Sherri. *The Van Norman Genealogy: Descendants of Joseph and Elizabeth (Wybern) Van Norman, 1772–1996*. n.p., 1996.

Pickles, Katie. *Female Imperialism and National Identity: Imperial Order Daughters of the Empire*. Manchester: Manchester University Press, 2002; distributed exclusively in the USA by Palgrave.

———. "Forgotten Colonizers: The Imperial Order Daughters of the Empire (IODE) and the Canadian North." *Canadian Geographer* 42, no. 2 (1998): 193–204.

Plante, Ellen M. *Women at Home in Victorian America: A Social History*. New York: Facts on File, 1997.

Pocius, Gerald. *A Place to Belong: Community Order and Everyday Space in Calvert, Newfoundland*. Montreal and Kingston: McGill-Queen's University Press, 1991.

Poutanen, Mary Anne. "The Homeless, the Whore, the Drunkard, and the Disorderly: Contours of Female Vagrancy in the Montreal Courts, 1810–1842." In *Gendered Pasts: Historical Essays in Femininity and Masculinity in Canada*, edited by Kathryn McPherson, Cecilia Morgan, and Nancy M. Forestell, 29–47. Toronto: University of Toronto Press, 1999.

Prentice, Alison, et al. *Canadian Women: A History*. 2nd ed. Toronto: Harcourt Brace, 1996.

Radford, Peter F. "Women's Foot-Races in the 18th and 19th Centuries: A Popular and Widespread Practice." *Canadian Journal of History of Sport* 25 (1994): 50–61.

Radke, Andrea G. "Refining Rural Spaces: Women and Vernacular Gentility in the Great Plains, 1880–1920." *Great Plains Quarterly* 24 (Fall 2004): 227–48.

Raibmon, Paige. "Living on Display: Colonial Visions of Aboriginal Domestic Spaces." In *Home, Work, and Play: Situating Canadian Social History, 1840–1980*, edited by James Opp and John C. Walsh, 18–32. Don Mills, ON: Oxford University Press, 2006.

Reid-Maroney, Nina. *The Reverend Jennie Johnson and African Canadian History, 1868–1967*. Rochester, NY: University of Rochester Press, 2013.

Rich, Kyle Andrew, Larena Hoeber, and Anne Weisgerber. "The Battle of Little Big Puck: Narratives of Community, Sport, and Relationships in Rural Canada." *Journal of Rural and Community Development* 15, no. 3 (2020): 45–64.

Richard, Bruce. "Edwin Delavan Tillson." *Dictionary of Canadian Biography Online*, vol. 13, *1901–1910*. Accessed 11 February 2009. http://www.biographi.ca/009004-119.01-e.php?&id_nbr=7106.

Riley, Glenda. "Victorian Ladies Outdoors: Women in the Early Western Conservation Movement, 1870–1920." *Southern California Quarterly* 83, no. 1 (Spring 2001): 59–80.

Roberts, Julia. *In Mixed Company: Taverns and Public Life in Upper Canada*. Vancouver: University of British Columbia Press, 2009.

Roediger, David R. *The Wages of Whiteness: Race and the Making of the American Working Class*. London: Verso, 1991.

Rogers, Nicolas. *Halloween: From Pagan Ritual to Party Night*. Oxford: Oxford University Press, 2002.

———. "Halloween in Urban North America: Liminality and Hyperreality." *Histoire sociale/Social History* 29, no. 58 (November 1996): 461–77.

Rosenzweig, Roy. *Eight Hours for What We Will: Workers and Leisure in an Industrial City, 1870–1920*. Cambridge: Cambridge University Press, 1983.

Rugh, Susan Sessions. "Civilizing the Countryside: Class, Gender, and Crime in Nineteenth-Century Rural Illinois." *Agricultural History* 76, no. 1 (Winter 2002): 58–81.

———. *Our Common Country: Family Farming, Culture, and Community in the Nineteenth-Century Midwest*. Bloomington: Indiana University Press, 2001.

Rutherdale, Myra. *Women and the White Man's God: Gender and Race in the Canadian Mission Field*. Vancouver: University of British Columbia Press, 2002.

Rydell, Robert W. *All the World's a Fair: Visions of Empire at American International Expositions, 1876–1916*. Chicago: University of Chicago Press, 1984.

Rydell, Robert W., and Rob Kroes. *Buffalo Bill in Bologna: The Americanization of the World, 1869–1922*. Chicago and London: University of Chicago Press, 2005.

Sandwell, Ruth. *Canada's Rural Majority: Households, Environments, and Economies, 1870–1940*. Toronto: University of Toronto Press, 2016.

———. *Contesting Rural Space: Land Policies and the Practice of Resettlement on Salt Spring Island, 1859–1891*. Montreal and Kingston: McGill-Queen's University Press, 2005.

———. "Notes toward a History of Rural Canada, 1870–1940." In *Social Transformation in Rural Canada: Community, Cultures, and Collective Action*, edited by John R. Parkins and Maureen G. Reed, 21–42. Vancouver: University of British Columbia Press, 2013.

Sangster, Joan. *Girl Trouble: Female Delinquency in English Canada*. Toronto: Between the Lines, 2002.

———. "'Pardon Tales' from Magistrate's Court: Women, Crime, and the Court in Peterborough County, 1920–50." *Canadian Historical Review* 74, no. 2 (1993): 161–97.

Schlereth, Thomas J. "Country Stores, County Fairs, and Mail-Order Catalogues: Consumption in Rural America." In *Consuming Visions: Accumulation and Display of Goods in America, 1880–1920*, edited by Simon J. Bronner, 339–75. New York: W.W. Norton, 1989.

Schmidt, Leigh Eric. *Consumer Rites: The Buying and Selling of American Holidays*. Princeton, NJ: Princeton University Press, 1995.

———. "The Fashioning of a Modern Holiday: St. Valentine's Day, 1840–1870." *Winterthur Portfolio* 28, no. 4 (Winter 1993): 209–45.

Scholtz, Matthew G., and Anna M. Bailey. *Tillsonburg Diary: A Chronological History, 1824–1994*. Tillsonburg, ON: Tillsonburg District Chamber of Commerce, 1995.

Semple, Neil. *The Lord's Dominion: The History of Canadian Methodism*. Montreal and Kingston: McGill-Queen's University Press, 1996.

Shaffer, Marguerite S. *See America First: Tourism and National Identity, 1880–1940*. Washington, DC: Smithsonian Institution Press, 2001.

Shaw, Ron W. *London Ontario's Unrepentant Confederates, the Ku Klux Klan and a Rendition on Wellington Street*. Carleton Place, ON: Global Heritage Press, 2018.

Simpson, Clare S. "Capitalising on Curiosity: Women's Professional Cycling Racing in the Late-Nineteenth Century." In *Cycling and Society*, edited by Dave Horton, Paul Rosen, and Peter Cox, 47–65. Aldershot, UK: Ashgate Publishing, 2007.

Spelt, Jacob. *The Urban Development in South-Central Ontario*. Assen, Netherlands: Van Gorcum, 1955.

Stairs, Michele. "Matthews and Marillas: Bachelors and Spinsters in Prince Edward Island in 1881." In *Mapping the Margins: The Family and Social Discipline in Canada, 1700–1975*, edited by Nancy Christie and Michael Gauvreau, 247–70. Montreal and Kingston: McGill-Queen's University Press, 2004.

Statistics Canada. Census Profile. 2016 Census. Dresden, Ontario. Accessed 25 January 2024. https://www12.statcan.gc.ca/census-recensement/2016/dp-pd/prof/details/page.cfm?Lang=E&Geo1=POPC&Code1=0238&Geo2=PR&Code2=35&SearchText=Dresden&SearchType=Begins&SearchPR=01&B1=All&GeoLevel=PR&GeoCode=0238&TABID=1&type=0.

Statistics Canada. Census Profile. 2016 Census. Tillsonburg, Ontario. Accessed 25 January 2024. https://www12.statcan.gc.ca/census-recensement/2016/dp-pd/prof/details/page.cfm?Lang=E&Geo1=POPC&Code1=0939&Geo2=PR&Code2=35&SearchText=Tillsonburg&SearchType=Begins&Search-PR=01&B1=All&GeoLevel=PR&GeoCode=0939&TABID=1&type=0.

Stelter, Gilbert A. "Combining Town and Country Planning in Upper Canada: William Gilkison and the Founding of Elora." In *The Country Town in Rural Ontario's Past: Proceedings of the Sixth Annual Agricultural History of Ontario Seminar, October 31, 1981*, edited by A.A. Brookes, 1–25. Guelph, ON: University School of Part-time Studies and Continuing Education, University of Guelph, 1981.

Stevens, Peter A. "Getting Away from it All: Family Cottaging in Postwar Ontario." PhD diss., York University, 2010.

Strachan, Glenda, Ellen Jordan, and Hilary Carey. "Women's Work in a Rural Community: Dungog and the Upper Williams Valley, 1880–1900." *Labour History* 78 (May 2000): 33–52.

Strange, Carolyn. *Toronto's Girl Problem: The Perils and Pleasures of the City, 1880–1930*. Toronto: University of Toronto Press, 1995.

Strange, Carolyn, and Tina Loo. "Spectacular Justice: The Circus on Trial, and the Trial as Circus, Picton, 1903." *Canadian Historical Review* 77, no. 2 (June 1996): 159–84.

Strasser, Susan. *Never Done: A History of American Housework*. New York: Pantheon Books, 1982.

Swyripa, Frances. "Negotiating Sex and Gender in the Ukrainian Bloc Settlement: East-Central Alberta between the Wars." In *Home, Work, and Play: Situating*

Canadian Social History, 1840–1980, edited by James Opp and John C. Walsh, 47–62. Don Mills, ON: Oxford University Press, 2006.

Sylvester, Kenneth M. "Household Composition and Canada's Rural Capitalism: The Extent of Rural Labor Markets in 1901." *Journal of Family History* 26, no. 2 (April 2001): 289–309.

Thompson, Cheryl. "*Black* Minstrelsy on Canadian Stages: Nostalgia for Plantation Slavery in the Nineteenth and Twentieth Centuries." *Journal of the Canadian Historical Association* 31, no. 1 (2021): 67–94.

———. *Uncle: Race, Nostalgia, and the Politics of Loyalty*. Toronto: Coach House Books, 2021.

Thompson, E.P. *The Making of the English Working Class*. London: Gollancz, 1963.

Thorning, Stephen. "Bare Knuckles, Blazing Pistols, Lynching: Crime in Elora 125 Years Ago." *Elora Sentinel and Fergus Thistle*, 13 April 1993, 6.

———. "Competitive Speed Skating Became a Local Fad in 1899." *Wellington Advertiser*, 8 July 2011, 10.

———. "The Drill Shed Was Elora's Own 'Theatre on the Grand.'" *Elora Sentinel and Fergus Thistle*, 15 June 1993, 6–7.

———. "The Elora Armoury Hall: Some Historical Notes." *Wellington County History* 3 (1990): 66–69.

———. "Elora Gorge Was a Big Tourist Attraction Over 100 Years Ago." *Wellington Advertiser*, 28 June 1999, 10.

——— "Elora Once Had Four Newspapers Serving 1,600 People." *Elora Sentinel*, 13 November 1990, 6.

———. "Elora Promoted Tourism and Fishing to Support the Village—in the Early 1900s." *Elora Sentinel*, n.d, unpaginated.

———. "Elora Rifles Called to Fight Invasion That Never Happened." *Wellington Advertiser*, 8 March 2019. https://www.wellingtonadvertiser.com/elora-rifles-called-to-fight-invasion-that-never-happened/.

———. "Elora Woman Left Town after Two-Day Charivari." *Wellington Advertiser*, n.d., unpaginated.

———. "First Elora Ice Rink Was Constructed in 1879." *Elora Sentinel*, 22 October 1991, 6.

———. "River Cleanup and Tourism Went Hand in Hand in 19th Century." *Elora Sentinel*, 25 May 1993, unpaginated.

———. "Santa Claus First in Elora in 1870s." *Elora Sentinel*, 17 December 1991, 6.

———. "Temperance Workers Such as T.E. Bissell Finally Found Success in Early 1900s." *Elora Sentinel and Fergus Thistle*, 1 February 1994, 6.

———. *The Model Village and the Struggle for Success: A History of Elora, Ontario*. Fergus, ON: Wellington County Historical Society, 2023.

"Tillsonburg Ladies Travel Club Focuses on Alaska, Hawaii." *Norfolk and Tillsonburg News*, 11 November 2015. https://www.norfolkandtillsonburgnews.com/2015/11/11/tillsonburg-ladies-travel-club-focuses-on-alaska-hawaii/wcm/e344b5e5-2340-c9fb-286e-842afe089c6c.

Tobin, Jacqueline, with Hettie Jones. *From Midnight to Dawn: The Last Tracks of the Underground Railroad*. New York: Doubleday, 2007.

Towner, John. *An Historical Geography of Recreation and Tourism in the Western World, 1540–1940*. Chichester, UK: John Wiley and Sons, 1996.

Trigger, Bruce G. "The Original Iroquoians: Huron, Petun, and Neutral." In *Aboriginal Ontario: Historical Perspectives on the First Nations*, edited by Edward S. Rogers and Donald B. Smith, 41–63. Toronto: Dundurn Press, 1994.

University of Michigan. "Neat Old Pictures." Accessed 24 July 2012. http://www.personal.umich.edu/~ksands/pictures.html.

Valverde, Mariana. *The Age of Light, Soap, and Water: Moral Reform in English Canada, 1885–1925*, with a new introduction. Toronto: University of Toronto Press, 2008.

———. "The Love of Finery: Fashion and the Fallen Woman in Nineteenth-Century Social Discourse." *Victorian Studies* 32, no. 2 (Winter 1989): 169–88.

Van Die, Marguerite. *Religion, Family, and Community in Victorian Canada: The Colbys of Carrollcroft*. Montreal and Kingston: McGill-Queen's University Press, 2005.

———. "Revisiting 'Separate Spheres': Women, Religion, and the Family in Mid-Victorian Brantford, Ontario." In *Households of Faith: Family, Gender, and Community in Canada, 1760–1969*, edited by Nancy Christie, 234–63. Montreal and Kingston: McGill-Queen's University Press, 2002.

Varty, Carmen Nielson. "'A Career in Christian Charity': Women's Benevolence and the Public Sphere in a Mid-Nineteenth-Century Canadian City." *Women's History Review* 14, no. 2 (2005): 243–64.

———. "The City and the Ladies: Politics, Religion, and Female Benevolence in Mid-Nineteenth-Century Hamilton, Canada West." *Journal of Canadian Studies* 38, no. 2 (Spring 2004): 151–71.

Vickery, Amanda. "Historiographical Review: Golden Age to Separate Spheres? A Review of the Categories and Chronology of English Women's History." *Historical Journal* 36, no. 2 (June 1993): 383–414.

Voisey, Paul. *High River and the Times: An Alberta Community and Its Weekly Newspaper, 1905–1966*. Edmonton: University of Alberta Press, 2004.

———. *Vulcan: The Making of a Prairie Community*. Toronto: University of Toronto Press, 1988.

Walden, Keith. *Becoming Modern in Toronto: The Industrial Exhibition and the Shaping of a Late Victorian Culture*. Toronto: University of Toronto Press, 1997.

———. "Respectable Hooligans: Male Toronto College Students Celebrate Hallowe'en, 1884–1910." *Canadian Historical Review* 68, no. 1 (1987): 1–34.

———. "Tea in Toronto and the Liberal Order, 1880–1914." *Canadian Historical Review* 93, no. 1 (March 2012): 1–24.

Walker, Barrington, ed. *Race on Trial: Black Defendants in Ontario's Criminal Courts, 1858–1958*. Toronto: Osgoode Society for Canadian Legal History by University of Toronto Press, 2010.

———. *The History of Immigration and Racism in Canada: Essential Readings*. Toronto: Canadian Scholars' Press, 2008.

Wall, Sharon. *The Nurture of Nature: Childhood, Antimodernism, and Ontario Summer Camps, 1920–55*. Vancouver: University of British Columbia Press, 2009.

Walvin, James. *Leisure and Society, 1830–1950*. London: Longman, 1978.

Wamsley, Kevin B. "State Formation and Institutionalized Racism: Gambling Laws in Nineteenth and Early Twentieth Century Canada." *Sport History Review* 29 (1998): 77–85.

Ward, [W.] Peter. *A History of Domestic Space: Privacy and the Canadian Home*. Vancouver: University of British Columbia Press, 1999.

———. "Courtship and Social Space in Nineteenth-Century English Canada." *Canadian Historical Review* 68, no. 1 (1987): 35–62.

———. *Courtship, Love, and Marriage in Nineteenth-Century English Canada*. Montreal and Kingston: McGill-Queen's University Press, 1990.

———. "Unwed Motherhood in Nineteenth-Century English Canada." *Historical Papers/Communications historiques* 16, no. 1 (1981): 34–56.

Warsh, Cheryl Krasnick. "'Oh, Lord, Pour a Cordial in Her Wounded Heart': The Drinking Woman in Victorian and Edwardian Canada." In *Drink in Canada: Historical Essays*, edited by Cheryl Krasnick Warsh, 70–91. Montreal and Kingston: McGill-Queen's University Press, 1993.

———. *Prescribed Norms: Women and Health in Canada and the United States since 1800*. Toronto: University of Toronto Press, 2010.

Warsh, Cheryl Krasnick, and Dan Malleck, eds. *Consuming Modernity: Gendered Behaviour and Consumerism before the Baby Boom*. Vancouver: University of British Columbia Press, 2013.

Waterston, Elizabeth, and Douglas Hoffman, eds. *On Middle Ground: Landscape and Life in Wellington County, 1841–1891*. Guelph, ON: University of Guelph, 1974.

Watson, Andrew. *Making Muskoka: Tourism, Rural Identity, and Sustainability, 1870–1920*. Vancouver: University of British Columbia Press, 2022.

Wayne, Michael. "The Black Population of Canada West on the Eve of the American Civil War: A Reassessment Based on the Manuscript Census of 1861." *Histoire sociale/Social History* 28, no. 56 (1995): 465–85.

Wellington County. Wellington County 2016 Population Estimates. Accessed 25 January 2024. https://www.wellington.ca/en/resident-services/resources/Planning/Population-Housing-Employment/Mid-2016-Population-And-Households.pdf.

Westfall, William. *Two Worlds: The Protestant Culture of Nineteenth-Century Ontario*. Montreal and Kingston: McGill-Queen's University Press, 1989.

Westhues, Kenneth, and Peter R. Sinclair. *Village in Crisis*. Toronto: Holt, Rinehart and Winston of Canada, 1974.

Wetherell, Donald. "Making New Identities: Alberta Small Towns Confront the City, 1900–1950." *Journal of Canadian Studies* 39, no. 1 (Winter 2005): 175–97.

Wetherell, Donald G., and Irene R.A. Kmet. *Town Life: Main Street and the Evolution of Small Town Alberta, 1880–1947*. Edmonton: University of Alberta Press and Alberta Community Development, 1995.

————. *Useful Pleasures: The Shaping of Leisure in Alberta, 1896–1945*. Regina: Canadian Plains Research Center, 1990.

Whiteley, Marilyn Färdig. *Canadian Methodist Women, 1766–1925: Marys, Marthas, Mothers in Israel*. Waterloo, ON: published for Canadian Corporation for Studies in Religion by Wilfrid Laurier University Press, 2005.

————. "'Doing All the Rest': Church Women of the Ladies' Aid Society." In *Framing Our Past: Canadian Women's History in the Twentieth Century*, edited by Sharon Anne Cook, Lorna R. McLean, and Kate O'Rourke, 18–21. Montreal and Kingston: McGill-Queen's University Press, 2001.

————. "'Doing Just About What They Please': Ladies' Aids in Ontario Methodism." *Ontario History* 83, no. 4 (December 1990): 289–304.

Widdis, Randy William. "Belleville and Environs: Continuity, Change and the Integration of Town and Country during the 19th Century." *Urban History Review* 19, no. 3 (February 1991): 181–209.

Wilson, Catharine Anne. *Being Neighbours: Cooperative Work and Rural Culture, 1830–1960*. Montreal and Kingston: McGill-Queen's University Press, 2022.

————. "Reciprocal Work Bees and the Meaning of Neighbourhood." *Canadian Historical Review* 82, no. 3 (September 2001): 431–64.

Wolfe, Roy I. "The Summer Resorts of Ontario in the Nineteenth Century." *Ontario History* 54 (1962): 149–61.

Young, David. *The Golden Age of Canadian Figure Skating*. Toronto: Summerhill Press, 1984.

INDEX

Bold page numbers indicate photos